Economics
PRINCIPLES IN ACTION

About the cover: These gold ingots, each representing about $285,000, were reclaimed from electronics manufacturing processes. (Photo by Tom Tracy)

Economics

PRINCIPLES IN ACTION

Third Edition

Philip C. Starr
Chaffey College

WADSWORTH PUBLISHING COMPANY
Belmont, California
A Division of Wadsworth, Inc.

Economics editor: Marshall Aronson

Editing, design, and production supervision: Brian and
 Suzanne Pfeiffer Williams

Copyediting: Elaine Linden

Design: Michael Rogondino

Photo research: Roberta Spieckerman

Cartoons: Bob Haydock

Technical illustrations: Carl Brown

Composition: Graphic Typesetting Service

A study guide has been specially designed to help students
master the concepts presented in this textbook. It may be
ordered from your bookstore.

Printed in the United States of America

 3 4 5 6 7 8 9 10 — 85 84 83 82

Library of Congress Cataloging in Publication Data

Starr, Philip C
  Economics.

  Includes bibliographical references and index.
  1. Economics. 2. Economics — Examinations,
questions, etc. I. Title.
HB171.5.S78 1981   330   80-23404
ISBN 0-534-00588-9

For Paul

whose pursuit of a meaningful life
is an inspiration to all who know him.

Contents

Introduction for Instructors

First, a word for instructors unfamiliar with this text: *Economics: Principles in Action* is an outgrowth of a particular one-quarter course we created at Chaffey (community) College called Economics 110, "An Introduction to Economics." The course has become so popular that enrollment in it accounts for more than one-third of total enrollment in all economics courses.

Economics 110 precedes the regular "principles" sequence. It is a course for non-majors, for students who may never take another course in economics (although in fact about 15 percent of the students do go on to take the principles series). It is offered because we believe that every student, no matter what his or her background, should have some exposure to economics.

Special Features of the Book

The book is not technical. Students coming into Economics 110 may be intimidated by the language of economics and fearful that economics will be largely made up of charts, graphs, equations, statistics. In this book, I have used as nontechnical an approach as possible. There are no algebraic symbols, few abbreviations, scant use of formulas, and the charts and graphs are kept as simple as possible (for instance, there are no references to x and y axes—only "horizontal" and "vertical"). A short chapter, 3A, "Understanding Graphs," is designed to help those students who are normally "turned off" by graphs. Instead of using the conventional multiplier-arithmetic, I have substituted an anecdotal treatment of the multiplier, with the help of humorist Art Buchwald—a much quicker way to convey this idea than by the traditional explanation of $1 \div (1 - \text{MPC})$.

The book is easy and entertaining to read. I have tried to make the text pertinent, newsworthy, and simple to read. Many examples from daily newspapers and weekly news magazines are used (for instance, stories on energy problems and on air pollution). One of the greatest compliments students paid me after reading the first edition of this book was to say that "all that stuff in the newspaper is beginning to make sense."

There are frequent biographies and case studies. Four biographical sketches are included: Adam Smith, Karl Marx, John Maynard Keynes, and Mao Tse-tung. Case studies (true stories) include the Reserve Mining Company case (pollution), paint manufacturing (price discrimination), and the egg industry (cartels).

Economic terms and concepts are continually reinforced. If there is one thing I learned from the education course I once took, it is that we need constantly to explain *why* we're doing what we're doing. I have attempted such reinforcement throughout. Each of the five parts describes what is to come. Each chapter opens with an overview, the headings throughout the chapter elaborate that overview, and the summary gathers the principal ideas into one or more brief paragraphs. In addition, the text of each chapter is preceded by a boxed list of "key words," signalling the principal concepts the reader will encounter in the chapter. The terms themselves appear in **boldface** in the text. Each chapter ends with discussion questions covering the main ideas.

The "back matter" of the text contains several useful learning aids. "Key Words with Definitions," an alphabetical list of all of the key words, not only gives a short definition of each concept but also refers the reader to the chapter and page in the text where the term is explained in context.

Other back-matter items are an index that includes the key words in boldface type, a list of spelled-out abbreviations, and an appendix with four tables showing GNP, real GNP, real DPI, and population by age groups.

Why Teach Micro First?

For years, I had been persuaded by the most popular one-year books that "macro" should be presented first because it would interest students more than "micro." The premise was that macro was headline stuff whereas, by comparison, micro was abstract and dull. I have come to believe this premise is incorrect. Students are interested in individual and local matters appropriate for micro analysis, whereas the macro manipulations of the economy in Washington seem relatively far away.

I suspect that micro is usually put in second place because of the graphical abstractions of costs and revenue that accompany it. I have deliberately omitted these graphs. Free of such entanglements, beginning students can find countless personal connections with micro theory, from buying a car to thinking about pollution.

Micro theory, therefore, is presented first in order to show that economics is relevant to everyday events in life. I have attempted to correct the impression left by the first edition of this book that micro and macro are separate entities by trying to show the links between them. I have taken considerable pains to emphasize to students that micro and macro are really just two ways of looking at supply and demand.

Presenting the Material: Possible Sequences

The book is divided into five parts for maximum flexibility. Instructors who wish to emphasize macro could assign Chapters 1–2 in Part 1, Chapter 3 in Part 2, and then jump to Chapter 10, which opens Part IV. Instructors wishing to emphasize micro could assign Parts 1–3 (micro) and then a stripped-down version of macro by assigning Part 4 but omitting Chapters 12, 13A, and 17.

Sadly, most of us faced with the time constraints of the quarter system are obliged to omit or skim the international section in Part 5. I say "sadly" because so many of our economic problems are intertwined with those of other countries, and those that are not may well be in the future.

Changes in the Third Edition

It cannot be stressed enough that this edition is a major overhaul. Almost every page and certainly every topic has been revised in some way to clarify meanings, to look at ideas from a fresh angle, or drop unnecessary material, as well as to include new and pertinent material.

The rewriting process always involves listening to several voices. The one common and loudest plea was: "No matter what, keep the book short!" I have tried to do this, despite the temptation to rattle on about some new topic. Many chapters have been shortened to make them more clearly manageable in one class period. For example, (1) the discussions of pollution and energy, formerly parts of Chapter 6 and 7, are now an optional, separate chapter; (2) the discussion of fiscal policy, formerly one chapter, has been divided into two chapters; and (3) the discussion of monetary policy, formerly one chapter, has also been split into two chapters.

In several instances, particularly in the macro section, the order of presentation has been changed. In the micro section, new topics have been added, like rent controls and profit-maximization for firms (without cost curves). Volcker's move on 6 October 1979 to retarget monetary policy, the "tax revolt," wage-price controls, the rational-expectations theory, and "supply-side fiscalism" are new to the macro section. Military spending and the Doomsday model reappear in the international section. Despite these additions, the third edition is shorter in words than the previous edition (albeit longer in pages, the format having been redesigned for greater readability) and more appropriate for one-term courses.

The Study Guide

A student guide has been prepared by Dale Sievert and David Martin of Milwaukee Area Technical College. The study guide consists of 27 self-instructional units. Each unit covers a small number of related concepts, a brief list of behavioral objectives, exercises consisting of explanatory input, practice, and posttests—all with answers for instant feedback. The study guide also contains sample midterm and final exams (both objective-type) with answers. I suggest using these same questions occasionally to encourage the use of the study guide.

Instructor's Test Bank

A separate test bank of multiple-choice objective questions prepared by Martin and Sievert is provided in the instructor's manual. We have been careful to see that the questions agree in content with the questions in the study guide.

In addition to questions on each chapter, the instructor's manual includes sample midterm exams (which can be combined into a final exam) and chapter outlines to make lecture planning easier.

Acknowledgments

Somehow, each edition seems to involve greater effort than the previous ones—or is it that the author gets older? Whatever the answer, this edition involves numerous and massive changes with the help of many hard-working people.

Ann Mcleary has once again typed and retyped the manuscript many times. Bonny McLaughlin has again provided a fine index together with the list of key words. Ms. McLaughlin also had the touchy job of extracting permissions from the media for art, photos, and quotes.

The manuscript for the third edition went through a very rigorous process of review and consequent revision. Among the reviewers I especially want to thank for their multiple and intensive reviews are the following: Professors Bruce W. Kimzey, Pepperdine University; John D. Lafky, California State University at Fullerton; Dale Sievert, Milwaukee Area Technical College; Kristi Weir, Bellevue Community College; and Ralph E. Worthington, St. Petersburg Junior College.

In addition, several other reviews were extremely helpful, those from Professors Carolyn A. Fost, Western Kentucky University; Roger Goldberg, Ohio Northern University; Eugene Kimmet, W. R. Harper College (Illinois); William J. Moore, University of Houston; John Neal, Lake Sumter Community College (Florida); and Robert Payne, Portland Community College.

This third edition is the first to be produced by Wadsworth, the first two having been created by Dickenson Publishing Company, a subsidiary. Wadsworth gave unstintingly of its resources in producing this book. I am grateful to Marshall Aronson, economics editor, for his pursuit of excellence; to Brian and Suzanne Williams for their tactful and attentive coordination of the project; to Michael Rogondino for his beautiful design; to Bob Haydock for his light-hearted cartoons; to Roberta Spieckermann for her imaginative photo research; and to Carl Brown for his fine graphs and charts. I especially want to thank Elaine Linden for her conscientious, skillful, and good-humored copyediting of a complex project.

I want to thank the library staff at Chaffey College, who permitted much extracurricular bothering and again saved many hours of hunting.

And last but not least, I want to thank my wife, Emily, for her line-by-line, professional contribution to the editing process.

Economics
PRINCIPLES IN ACTION

1

Introduction:
What Economics Is About

This part consists of two chapters. Chapter 1 describes typical problems economists try to analyze, what economics means, and how the word "economics" is defined. Chapter 2 outlines how different types of economic systems try to overcome scarcity, with emphasis on the economic system of the United States.

1 What Is Economics? Trying to Improve Our Material Welfare

David Powers

Look at the front page of any large-city newspaper. Usually it will present you with a bewildering variety of economic issues—and the conflicts they give rise to: battles between environmentalists and industrialists, between unions and management; arguments among politicians over taxes, welfare, inflation, energy conservation, land use, unemployment, and on and on.

Behind the scenes there are usually economists helping to advise or influence one side or the other. A famous English economist, John Maynard Keynes, once said that we are, without realizing it, "usually the slaves of some defunct economist." Without realizing it, we are also often the slaves of living economists who occupy positions of great influence in universities, large corporations, and government. The main purpose of this book is to

Key Words

Inflation	Opportunity cost, trade-off
Thomas Robert Malthus	Secondary job market
Geometric increase	Primary job market
Rule of 72	Foregone income
Scarcity	Economics
Free good	Microeconomics
"Real" terms	Macroeconomics

help you think about personal, business, and public issues as economists do. The main purpose of this first chapter is to explain what economics is.

Most people have heard the word "economics" often enough—and certainly we are often told to "economize." Consequently, most of us have an intuitive grasp of one of the central meanings of economics: to be careful about spending. We are admonished to be careful about spending because by doing so we will (we hope) become better off. And this *is* what economics means. Economics is a social science that studies ways to improve human welfare in material terms. Nonmaterial aspects of human welfare like personal and social adjustment to one's own values or aspirations, to members of the opposite sex, or to one's contemporaries are left to other branches of the social sciences like anthropology, sociology, and psychology. However, it has been shown that, at least in the United States, income levels and degrees of happiness tend to rise or fall together.[1] It's easier to be happier with more material things than with less. Therefore, although economics is not directly connected with curing unhappiness, the chances are that economists can help make us happy if they can find ways to improve our material welfare.

This chapter is divided into three main parts—(1) why study economics? (2) can the earth support the human race? and (3) what is economics all about?—and a concluding note on how this book is organized.

Why Study Economics?

There are at least two ways of thinking about this question: (1) from the citizen's viewpoint, which looks at economics as a tool to improve welfare, locally, nationally, or internationally; and (2) from the viewpoint of a private individual, who asks, "How does this affect *me?*" Let's consider these two viewpoints.

What is my interest as a citizen?

Here are two important economic problems that affect us as citizens: a local problem and a national/international problem.

A local economic problem: housing

One of our severest problems is urban housing. For example, in the Bronx area of New York City there are acres of burned out and vandalized housing. Poor people still live there despite repeated muggings and burglaries because they can't afford to pay more than the low rents imposed by rent control. Yet rent controls discourage investors from building new housing units. Who wants to invest in a new building if the rent income from the building isn't profitable?

Moreover, as property values in the area decline, a city's revenues from property taxes decline, revenues that are used to support local schools, police forces, and fire departments. As these services decline, people have an incentive to leave the area, further hastening the increase in number of abandoned buildings—and so it goes.

This problem is by no means unique to New York City. In 1978, it was reported that there were 4,000 unoccupied housing units in South-Central Los Angeles.[2] The explanation: absentee owners—speculators—who bought and sold low-rent units for quick profits and were uninterested in maintaining the units in livable condition. Discouraged tenants either vacated voluntarily or were forced out by city authorities when the housing units failed to meet health standards.

Discouraged tenants vacated when housing units failed to meet health standards.

Note that in New York, the source of the problem was at least partly the result of government-regulated rent ceilings, whereas in Los Angeles the problem apparently resulted from lack of government regulation concerning maintenance of the buildings, providing arguments both for those economists who want to reduce government involvement and those who want to increase it. We'll discuss examples of this debate throughout the book.

Many other problems face local governments, among them public education, police and fire protection, street maintenance, trash collection, flood control, zoning for land use, public health and welfare—problems we cannot discuss in detail here. Let's turn now to a major national and international problem of concern to all citizens.

A national/international problem: inflation

Inflation simply means a rise in the general price level. (We discuss inflation in greater detail in Chapters 11 and 17.) Inflation is extremely important to understand because, within the United States, the presence of inflation means that a redistribution of income is taking place. When you have to pay a higher price for an item, the store that takes your money enjoys greater income. Of course, the store may have higher costs so that others (suppliers or employees) may enjoy higher incomes. The trick, when studying inflation, is to discover who wins and who loses.

Internationally, inflation is important because rising prices in the United States mean that foreigners will be reluctant to buy our products. In 1979, we exported more than $257 billion worth of goods and services to other countries. At stake are the jobs of approximately four million workers in export-related industries if foreigners take a dislike to our prices.

Moreover, if they take a dislike to our prices, their demand for our dollars (with which to buy U.S. products) will fall. (A full explanation of the financing of foreign trade and the exchange-rate mechanism is in Chapter 18.) When that happens the dollar will exchange for fewer Japanese yen, German marks, and so on, and products from these foreign countries or travel in them becomes more expensive. Finally, if it becomes more expensive to buy, say, a Datsun or Arabian oil, U.S. prices will tend to rise because U.S. auto producers don't have to compete as hard with the Japanese car manufacturers and because increased oil costs tend to raise the prices of almost everything.

Remember, the starting point of this saga was higher prices in the United States. Thus, higher prices beget a weakening dollar, and that begets higher prices—a vicious circle.

What has been happening to prices? The picture isn't very encouraging. Consumer prices have risen every year in the United States since 1954. From 1967 through 1980, consumer prices increased two and a half times, an average of about 11 percent per year. At that rate, prices would double every six and a half years. A savings account would have to earn more than 11 percent interest *after income taxes* to avoid a reduction in purchasing power every year the money is left in the bank.

Inflation usually hurts the people the most who can afford it the least: people living on savings or on fixed incomes in retirement and young people in nonunion jobs whose wages do not keep up with price increases.

There are many other national problems that concern us—the energy crisis, the "tax revolt," and pollution are among them. We'll discuss these topics in later chapters.

What's in it for me?

We'll turn now from our involvement in economics as citizens to our private concerns and ask, What is economics going to do for me? It can do mainly two things: (1) It can help you think more intelligently about personal economic decisions, such as buying, selling, saving, or investing. (2) It can help you function more successfully as an employee of a business firm. Chapter 9 deals with the problems of employees as union members. Chapter 8 discusses economic decision making by the managers of business firms.

You may also want to consider seeking a job as an economist. Over 120,000 persons worked as economists in 1978; about three out of every four of these were employed in private industry or research organizations. Of the remainder, about half were teachers and half worked for government agencies.

Business firms offer a wide range of activities for economists: planning the location of gas stations, supermarkets, telephone exchanges or banks; helping banks to invest depositors' money wisely; helping corporations plan long-term growth or helping them with price and output decisions to obtain desired profit; helping union executives bargain more effectively with management; helping stockbrokers advise their customers.*

In the preceding section we have reviewed some of the issues of interest to economists (and to our public and private selves). In the next section, we will examine one of the central questions that help define economics as a field of study.

Can the Earth Support the Human Race?

Economics exists because of the multitude of serious problems that affect our material welfare. A crucial question arises: Are the problems of unemployment, inflation, pollution, energy shortages, starvation in poor countries, and so on, short-term accidents, or are they symptomatic of long-term problems facing future generations? A number of circumstances occurring in the 1960s and 1970s made us realize that many of our most serious problems are of the long-term variety.

---

*For descriptions of several private sector jobs for economists, see Business Economics Careers, National Association of Business Economists, 28349 Chagrin Boulevard, Cleveland, Ohio 44122. Single copies of this twenty-one-page pamphlet are free. Additional copies are 30¢ each, as of this writing.

The post–World War II demand for natural resources

By the mid-1960s the industrial countries that had been involved in World War II demonstrated full recovery from the damage they had suffered, and in the early 1970s most of these countries enjoyed a business boom. This led to enormous increases in demand for resources (like oil) that were often not available in sufficient quantities. In addition, widespread drought and the two oil crises (1973 and 1979) helped to aggravate shortages and to accelerate price increases.

Total world production quadrupled between World War II and the mid-1970s—from $1 trillion to about $4 trillion in 1978. By the late 1960s signs of stress appeared: pollution became a front-page concern and food production capacity was strained as demand for food grew by 30 million tons per year.

In the fall of 1973, most nations became suddenly aware of the fact that there might not be enough oil to sustain current needs. The Arabs slapped an oil embargo on the countries that had been trading with Israel. In the United States there were long lines of cars at gas stations waiting to fill up. The people living in the northeastern United States had a cold winter as stocks of heating oil were exhausted. Many families used their fireplaces for warmth and for cooking. People used candles for light as oil-burning power stations were forced to reduce electrical output.

We began to realize that our planet might not be capable of giving us the essentials of life. Why? Mainly because the demands of an increasing population have begun to outrun the resources needed for production. As

The people living in the northeastern U.S. had a cold winter as stocks of heating oil were exhausted.

Thomas Malthus
The Bettmann Archive

far back as the late 1790s, a famous Englishman named **Thomas Robert Malthus** (1766–1834) worried about this problem.

The Malthusian
dilemma

Malthus theorized that human beings would increase their number at a rate of 3 percent per year, compounded every year, and that this increase in population would eventually outrun food production. To see what this rate of increase means, imagine you have put $100 in a savings bank at 3 percent interest. In 24 years the $100 will be $200. In 39 years it will be $300. In 48 years it will be $400. Thus, the time required to add another $100 becomes shorter and shorter. Mathematicians call this a **geometric increase,** and that is what Malthus was talking about.

The poor countries

Estimates are that by the year 2020, the earth's population will jump to 8 billion.* To appreciate this astounding increase, consider that it took *4 million years* to reach today's population, but it will take only *36 years* to double that!

Tragically, the growth rate is higher among the 93 poorest countries of the world, which contain about 75 percent of the globe's population. During the 1970s the population increase in these countries was 2.3 percent per year. In developed countries like the United States it was only 0.8 percent. The higher rate for the poorer countries means their populations will double in only 30 years, whereas in the United States it will take 90 years.

The problem is that the high rates of population increase in poor countries cut into any gains they make in food or industrial production. In one sense, aid from foreign countries (such as technical assistance, medical ex-

(Continued on page 10)

*According to the World Bank, world population will be 6.3 billion by the end of the century, 8 billion by 2020, and will peak and stablize around 11 billion by 2050.

The Handy "Rule of 72"

Within your lifetime the population of the world is expected to double.

Today we are in a period of rapid, geometric population increase, and within the next 36 years or so—within your lifetime—the population of the world is expected to double. During the 1960s and early 1970s, the world's population increased at the rate of 2 percent a year, reaching nearly 4 billion people in 1978. At this rate, it will double in 36 years, according to the **Rule of 72.***

The Rule of 72 is a convenient method of roughly determining how fast your money, or any number, will double at any rate of increase or any interest rate compounded annually.

The rule is as follows:

Divide any annual interest rate into 72; the answer gives you the number of years required to double the number.

Thus, if the world's population increases at a rate of 2 percent annually, the world's population will double in 72 ÷ 2 = 36 years. If the interest rate is 3 percent, the principal will double in 24 years (72 ÷ 3). If your money is in a savings and loan account paying 5 percent compounded annually, it will double in 14.4 years. The same formula can be used in studying inflation. If the rate of inflation is, say, 6 percent, in 12 years prices will double and the dollar will have lost half of its purchasing power. We used the Rule of 72 on page 5: an average annual rate of inflation of 11 percent means that prices will double in 6.5 years (72 ÷ 11 = 6.5).

*A note for instructors and math-minded students who might wonder why the Rule of 72 works. What is so magic about the number 72? Thanks to statistician Richard Penfield Ament, we have an answer: "The number 72 is an approximation (for convenient figuring) of a number that ranges from 69.3 to 74.3 for interest or growth rates ranging from near-zero to 15 percent, compounded *annually*. If interest is compounded daily or continuously, the number is exactly (to the nearest tenth) 69.3 for any rate of interest. This number is the natural logarithm of 2 multiplied by 100." Clear?

perts) aggravates the situation for it helps to assure that more people will live to reproductive age, meaning that in the absence of population control, there are more mouths to feed. Even with such aid there is widespread starvation: population experts estimate that as many as 20 million people in the poorer countries starved in 1975.

Malthus's scandalous book

Much of this had been predicted by Malthus, who theorized that food would not be produced fast enough to feed growing numbers of people because the amount of cultivatable land was fixed. Malthus believed that famine, wars, and disease might temporarily slow the rate of population increase, but the long-run trend was inevitably upward.

In 1798, Malthus's controversial book, *An Essay on the Principle of Population as It Affects the Future Improvement of Society*, was published anonymously. The book aroused a storm of criticism because Malthus held that "misery" from famine and disease and "vice"—prostitution rather than procreation—were the only limitations to population increase. The furor was so strong, in fact, that Malthus felt obliged to study the problem in depth for five more years. After that he published a revision of the book (this time not anonymously), confirming his previous theories. He also urged the postponement of marriage, "moral restraint," he called it, as the way to check the continuous rise in population, because he did not believe in birth control. Indeed, he followed his own advice and did not marry until he was thirty-eight years old.

Was Malthus right?

So far Malthus's predictions have not been fulfilled in the richer countries of the world—the United States, Canada, Japan, and those in Western Europe. They have managed with varying degrees of success to postpone the Malthusian day of judgment. Because of tremendous advances in agricultural technology—water systems, fertilizers, new seeds, farm machinery, farm methods, and food preparation—food production in those countries has increased so fast that it has far outstripped the rise of population. In the United States in 1929, a farm worker produced enough food to support 9 other people. However, by 1976—even though the number of people living on farms had dropped from 30.5 million to 8.3 million—a farm worker produced enough to support 48 other people. In other words, during that period, food production per farm worker increased more than five times. Humankind's ability to solve the food/population problem—so far—is in contradiction to Malthus, who did not believe technological change would be powerful enough to offset population growth.

What about the future?

Unfortunately, Malthus cannot be dismissed quite so easily. The Malthusian problem of population and food exists right now in many poor countries and may well afflict the rich countries in the future. Even with its low rate of population growth, the population of the United States is increasing at the rate of 1.5 million people per year, which means that by 1985 there may be 250 million—an increase of 45 million mouths to feed over 1970.

Food is only one of the worldwide shortages. As everyone knows, the energy crisis is another result of the pressures our apparently insatiable human demands are placing on the resources of our planet and on our ingenuity to supply those demands. Inevitably, all countries, including the United States, will have to face the Malthusian dilemma.

What Economics Is All About: Scarcity and Choice

The worldwide food and energy shortages that made headlines in the early 1970s help to illustrate what economics is all about. *Economics* exists as a field of study because the supplies of many things do not keep up with human wants. If, for example, the supply of oil is limited, economists ask, "Shall we use what oil there is for heating or for power, for plastics or for asphalt?" Because there is not enough oil to satisfy all these wants at once, the supply is called scarce. **Scarcity** exists whenever human wants exceed available supplies. Scarcity forces us to choose among alternatives. Economists try to estimate the effects *(costs)* such choices *(decisions)* will have on the material aspects of human welfare.

The costs of economic decision making

Does every decision necessarily involve a cost? Yes, almost every decision does involve a cost. One way to appreciate this fact of life is to consider what economists mean by a **free good.** A free good (or service) is one that exists in such abundance that people can take or use as much of it as they please without any effort or cost, and there will still be enough left to satisfy the wants of everyone else.

We used to call air and water free goods, but most of us who live in or near cities realize that *clean* air and water do not exist in unlimited quantities; there is usually a cost connected with obtaining sterilized, piped, purified, or bottled water and a cost connected with filtering air in our homes or, optionally, hiking to the nearest mountain peak. And so, sad but true, everything is to some extent *scarce.* When something is scarce, someone has to be paid to provide it; the price rewards the supplier for supplying the scarce good or service, and the price also helps to determine which buyers will be able to obtain it.

When goods and services are scarce, there is also a cost involved in choosing which ones we want to use. The cost of using more of our scarce oil supplies for heating is that car drivers won't have as much gasoline or diesel fuel, or that there won't be as much fuel for power stations and industry. The cost of the decision to refine more oil for heating is measured by the effects that less gasoline, diesel fuel, and so forth, will have on individuals and on the economy.

No matter how many goods we have—cars, stereos, whatever—there is always something else we want. Because our incomes are limited, when we buy one item, we give up the chance to buy anything else we could have bought. So the *cost* of that item is measured by the sacrifice we made in giving up all those other things. In short, any purchasing decision has a cost in **"real" terms**—that is the cost not in money but in the actual products or services given up when a choice is made.

We can also measure the cost of intangibles such as time. Because your time is limited, you cannot do all the things you would like to do. When you decide to spend your time doing one thing, you give up the opportunity to do all other things you could have done in that time.

Measuring the costs of our decisions

How should we measure the cost of anything—of a new motorcycle, a new freeway, or a rapid-transit system? Economists use a concept called **opportunity cost.**

To determine opportunity cost, we measure the value of the *next most desirable* opportunity we must sacrifice in order to take the course of action we have selected. When you go to class or decide to study in the library, you give up the opportunity to watch television at home. The opportunity cost of attending class or studying in the library is the value you place on the television program you miss.

What is the cost of the $1,000 motorcycle you want? It is not the price. The opportunity cost to you if you buy it is not $1,000 but the next most desirable product or service you might have bought with that $1,000. Notice that the money (price) is *not* the cost itself. The cost is your evaluation of the "real" things sacrificed.

So, money is a *means* of getting the things we want, price is a measure of how much money is required, and cost is the value of what we forego. The question economists ask is how much in actual products and services must be sacrificed to build whatever is being considered—a dam, hospital, school, rocket, weather satellite, and so on.

We can look at the opportunity costs of any decision, but one of the most important costs to consider is the cost of war. The obvious costs are lost lives and interrupted careers, wasted resources in the form of helicopters, guns, bullets, uniforms, trucks, and all the rest of the military paraphernalia. Less obvious costs are the slum clearance, antipollution, public health, and welfare projects that might otherwise have been undertaken. Consider also costs in hospitals, doctors, medicine, and equipment devoted to veterans' care long after the war is over as well as the costs of the benefits paid to dependents. For instance, in 1967, more than 1,300 dependents of veterans of the American Civil War—a war that ended 102 years before—received *annual* benefits totaling more than $1 million. Veterans' benefits for the Spanish-American War amounted to $5.3 billion, or twelve times the original cost of that war.*

World War I benefits did not begin to show a decrease until 1966. World War II benefits are not expected to decline until the year 2000. Benefits to dependents of Vietnam veterans are expected to continue beyond 2100. See James L. Clayton, "Vietnam: The 200-Year Mortgage," The Nation, 26 May 1969, p. 661.

Economists use one other term to refer to opportunity cost: **trade-off.** What do we trade off—or lose—if we decide to do this or that? In a later chapter we will consider one of the most famous trade-offs, inflation versus unemployment. Some economists believe that in order to get prices to fall—reduce inflation—the government must manipulate the economy to the extent that unemployment may increase.

Every personal decision involves many calculations, but you should consider, at least briefly, the idea of opportunity costs when you make a decision. These are your personal trade-offs. As a student, the opportunity cost of doing your homework may be the sacrifice of a tennis game, drinking beer with your friends, or just goofing off, while the opportunity cost of marriage, children, or social activities may be poor grades.

Costs of work, study, or play

The opportunity costs of choosing a job are especially important to college students. There is a kind of triangular relationship between (1) part-time work or work in a **"secondary" job market,** (2) work in a **primary job market,** and (3) a college education.

"Secondary" market jobs are those with low pay, high turnover, little required skill, and little training by employers, such as waiting on tables, pumping gas, clerking in stores. "Primary" market jobs are those involving skill, investment by employers in training, higher pay, avenues for promotion, career possibilities for employees, and low turnover.

Frequently, college students take jobs in secondary markets because primary market jobs require more time than commitment to a college education will permit. One college student we know (we'll call him Kirk) took a job at night as a security guard in a manufacturing plant so that he could spend some of the time studying. The job required little skill or training. The company's executives knew Kirk, realized that he was management material, and were ready to promote him to a "primary" job. Kirk preferred to stay where he was in order to finish college.

The opportunity cost of Kirk's going to college can therefore be estimated as the sum of his college expenses plus the extra income he lost by staying in his security guard job (rather than taking a better-paying job) plus the chances of promotion he may also have lost. Economists have estimated that half of the cost of going to college is in the form of lost earnings (often called **foregone income**). Or, to put it another way, the true cost of going to college is double the money costs to students, parents, or taxpayers. Most economists believe that the college degree *is* worth it, and that investing in one's education has a higher return than that earned by savings accounts or by financial investments like stocks and bonds.

Social costs of individual decisions

A personal decision may impose costs, not just on oneself, but also on others. Consequently, the total cost to society ("social cost") is measured by the opportunity costs of any individual decision *plus* additional costs that may be borne by others. Examples are the purchase of a car that pollutes the atmosphere, a powerful stereo that keeps the neighbors awake, the noise and smoke trails from jet planes, disease-producing wastes from industrial production. Economists try to uncover these additional costs that may not be part of a buyer-seller transaction in order to estimate the total social cost of decisions to produce, buy, sell, use, or discard products or services.

A definition of economics

We can never judge the costs or benefits of any decision with certainty because the consequences of our decisions lie in the future. Economists like to say, "We live in a world of risk and uncertainty." Consequently, economic studies lead to estimates about *expected* future costs or benefits.

Economics can therefore be defined as a social science that analyzes the expected effects of private and public decisions on human material welfare. Economists measure the effects of these decisions by comparing social benefits with social costs.

How This Book Is Organized

This text is organized into three major areas: microeconomics, macroeconomics, and international economics.

Microeconomics (discussed in Parts 2 and 3) refers to a microscopic view of the economy—to bits and pieces rather than to the economy as a whole. Microeconomic theory is concerned with how prices of individual products and services are determined. Prices in turn determine what is produced and who is able to buy.

Macroeconomics (the subject of Part 4) is concerned with the functioning of the whole economy—particularly the federal government's ability to manipulate the economy to provide jobs and stable prices.

International economics (Part 5) is concerned with the problems of international trade, the unequal distribution of income around the world, and the challenges of other economic systems, like those in China and the Soviet Union.

At the back of the book, beginning on page 440, there is a list of all the important abbreviations we use and an alphabetical list of key words with definitions. The list of key words is taken from those appearing at the beginning of each chapter. With each key word you will see numbers to show the chapter and pages on which the term first appears. For example, *demand* **3;** 42) means that *demand* is discussed in Chapter 3, page 42.

After the list of key words you will find four tables that show what has been happening to U.S. output, income, and population. Finally, there is an index with those items in **boldface** that also appear in the list of key words.

Summary

Economics is a discipline concerned with improving human material welfare. The world is currently faced with many attacks on welfare: inflation, unemployment, oil and food shortages, pollution, and urban blight are only a few. This book is written to help students understand these challenges.

Economics is a necessary and exciting field of study. But economics is full of controversy as is any discipline concerned with human behavior.

Malthus believed that population would increase geometrically while the supply of food would not increase nearly so fast. Unless people exercised moral restraint, he believed, the world was destined to be a place of misery, famine, and war.

Economics, as a social science, attempts to find solutions to problems like those Malthus raised. It is a study of the costs of decision making. Economists try to measure the expected costs of decisions compared with their expected benefits.

Economists insist that almost everything has a cost. Costs are measured by what must be sacrificed or foregone if a particular course of action is taken. The opportunity cost consists of whatever could have been done if a particular course of action had not been chosen. In every decision, we should consider the opportunity cost involved. These costs occur because of scarcity—we do not have unlimited time, goods, or services available to us. Economics is the study of choice and the costs of choosing.

Discussion Questions

1. So far Malthus's theories have not proved to be true in the Western countries. Why not? Is there a danger that the Western countries might some day suffer from an inadequate food supply? What methods could be used to reduce starvation and malnutrition in places like India and Pakistan?

2. Do you think everyone in the United States should have an equal supply of goods and services? What governmental programs are there that try to equalize everyone's share? What forces work against such equalizing?

3. What are the costs and benefits involved in buying a motorcycle? making or accepting a date? going to college? getting a job instead of going to college? working and going to college? living at home or in an apartment? Consider the costs and benefits to others as well as to yourself.

4. What are the costs and benefits of a welfare program? of not having a welfare program? of building highways? of fighting a war? of having a democratic system of government?

References

1. Norman M. Bradburn, *The Structure of Psychological Well-being* (Chicago: Aldine, 1969).

2. Henry Weinstein, "707 W. 82nd—Portrait of an L.A. Slum," *Los Angeles Times*, 3 August 1978.

2 How Different Economic Systems Deal with Scarcity

Daniel S. Brody/Stock, Boston

The message of Chapter 1 was that scarcity forces us to make choices in deciding how best to live. This chapter describes the different routes societies take in making these choices. The chapter is divided into three sections: (1) the three questions every economic system must answer, (2) three different ways of answering those questions, and (3) how a market-price system operates.

Key Words

Economic system	Socialism
Poverty	Communism
Traditional, planning, and market-price systems	Capitalism, mixed capitalism
Market	Factor payments: rent, wages, interest, profit
Factors of production: land, labor, capital, entre-	Consumer sovereignty
preneurship	Barriers to entry

The Three Questions Every Economic System Must Answer

First, what do we mean by **economic system?** An economic system is the particular body of laws, habits, ethics, customs (religious or otherwise) that a group of people observes to satisfy their material wants.

All systems, from primitive to advanced, face three fundamental questions: (1) What goods and services should be produced (and in what quantities)? (2) How should they be produced? (3) For whom should the goods and services be produced? Let's now examine each of these questions.

What goods and services should be produced?

Every economic system must decide, consciously or not, what goods (TV sets or stereos or bicycles) and services (doctors or lawyers or plumbers) are to be produced and in what quantities. These decisions require, of course, an evaluation of opportunity cost. If we decide to devote more of our resources to making cars, we will have fewer resources for building rapid transit systems. The opportunity cost of each new car is measured by the amount of rapid transit we could have provided but did not.

There are a couple of qualifications to this observation. For example, if people are unemployed, we might be able to use some of them to build cars without having to divert people already employed in rapid transit. Also, if new technology (new machines, tools, or new production methods) makes it easier to produce cars, that will release some people from automobile production to work on rapid transit. A surplus of workers and/or new technology enables us to have more of both.

How should the goods and services be produced?

Not only must every society decide what products and services it wants (and in what quantities), but also how it should produce them. The question of *how* involves choosing some mixture of technology and people. The opportunity cost is measured by what other purposes these resources (technology and people) could have been used for. But the problem is more complex than that.

As we all know, increased use of technology makes people more productive. But the time and effort it takes to produce the technology also have an opportunity cost—for example, the fish a tribe does not catch while it is busy making a fishnet.

In poor countries, this kind of trade-off is an excruciating problem. If the government in one of those countries decides to build a hydroelectric dam, many hundreds of people may have to be taken away from food-producing activities. The opportunity cost of the dam may be further starvation of the people. Thus, the question of *how* may involve some very difficult decisions.

For whom should the goods and services be produced?
Every society must decide who receives the products and services produced, which is another way of saying that a society must decide how income will be distributed among its people.

In the United States, income (one good measure of material welfare) is not equally divided. Table 2-1 shows the percentages of total income received by families in 1950 and again in 1977. The families (39 million in 1950 and 57 million in 1977) are divided into fifths in terms of income.

TABLE 2-1   Money Income of Families: Percentage of Total Income Received by Each Fifth

	1950	1977[a]
Lowest fifth	4.5	5.2
Second fifth	12.0	11.6
Middle fifth	17.4	17.5
Fourth fifth	23.4	24.2
Highest fifth	42.7	41.5
	100.0	100.0

[a]The upper limit of each fifth in 1977 was $7,903, $13,273, $18,800, and $26,000, respectively. (The last fifth was all families over $26,000.)
Source: *Statistical Abstract of the United States, 1979.*

Let's see what these figures mean. The 4.5 figure under 1950 means that in 1950 the lowest fifth (20 percent of families—about 11 million families) received only 4.5 percent of total income. Did their situation improve by 1977? Yes, but only a little. The highest fifth received more than 40 percent of total income in both years.

A look at poverty helps us view income distribution from a somewhat different angle. In the United States the definition of **poverty** is based on the cost of a nutritionally balanced diet as determined by the Department of Agriculture. This cost is then multiplied by 3 and, since 1969, has been adjusted upward each year to reflect changes in the cost of living. In 1977, the poverty-line figure for a nonfarm family of four was $6,191. Note that the definition assumes that food purchases account for one-third of a poor family's total budget. The number of people defined as below the poverty line is apparently going down, both in absolute numbers and as a percentage of total population. Table 2-2 compares poverty figures for 1959 with 1977.

TABLE 2-2   Persons Below Poverty Level, 1959 and 1977

Year	Poverty line[a]	Number (millions)	Percentage of total population
1959	$2,973	39.5	22.4
1977	$6,191	24.7	11.6

[a]Nonfarm family of four.
Source: *Statistical Abstract of the United States, 1978.*

Although Table 2-2 presents a hopeful sign that poverty is diminishing, the picture is still not clear. In 1973 there were fewer people in the poverty category (23 million) than in 1977. We'll have to wait a few more years to be sure of what is happening.

There is not only tremendous inequality in the distribution of income in the United States, there is also great inequality in the distribution of wealth.* The disparity in the ownership of wealth in the United States is shown most startlingly in the fact that the top *1 percent* of families own roughly *25 percent* of all personal and financial assets. Compare this with the 17 percent of families who own nothing (have no appreciable wealth at all) and another 8 percent of families who own *less than* nothing—they have negative net worth, their debts exceeding their assets.[1]

Part of the "for whom?" questions involves deciding which generation, present or future, should receive the goods and services produced. Often decisions to use resources for long-term projects like the Tennessee Valley Authority or cancer research mean a sacrifice for today's generation in favor of some expected benefit for tomorrow's. Much of the working population contributes to the social security fund for the benefit of older people. Research expenditures on power from hydrogen fusion are expected to be $1 billion per year for twenty years; commercial use of hydrogen fusion is not expected until the year 2015. Again, we must measure opportunity cost.

Three Ways to Answer the Three Questions

Economic systems through history fall into three broad categories depending on the method they employ to answer the three questions about goods and services: what? how? for whom? The three categories are traditional, planning, and market-price systems.

Traditional systems

Societies with **traditional systems** find the answers to the three questions by copying the decisions made by previous generations. The best examples of traditional systems are seen in primitive tribes. The decisions about what

---

*Wealth *refers not to one's income during the year from wages, dividends, rent, or interest, but to one's ownership of land, buildings, bank accounts, or stocks and bonds. Wealth produces income, and, of course, saving from one's income can be used to purchase additional wealth.*

crops will be produced (or what game will be hunted) and how this food will be produced and distributed are made by copying what the tribe has always done. Change is slow. Everyone's role in the tribe is understood. Tasks are assigned to members of the tribe in the same way the tasks were assigned in previous generations.

Although primitive tribes provide the best examples of traditional behavior, we often find such behavior in modern societies—particularly in the way we copy one another's dress and, despite having our consciousness raised by the women's movement, continue to train and hire female rather than male secretaries or male rather than female airline pilots.

Planning systems

Systems characterized by national economic plans like the five-year plans in the Soviet Union are called **planning systems.** (We will discuss the Soviet Union and the People's Republic of China in some detail in Chapter 19.) Often, planning systems involve a good deal of authoritarian control as in the Soviet Union, but national economic planning also appears in some of the western democracies like France. In France, business executives, government officials, and labor union leaders meet annually to discuss economic goals for industry for the next five-year period. Compliance is voluntary. For that reason, French planning is sometimes called "indicative planning" to convey the idea that goals are "indicated," not necessarily required.

Market-price systems

Economic systems based on prices and the bargaining that occurs between buyers and sellers are **market-price systems.** When the price is agreed upon and a sale is made, the three questions are answered. The buyer's agreement to pay determines what is produced, how it is produced, and, of course, for whom it is produced. Each buyer and seller represents an economic unit (individual, family, business firm, government agency, or foreign country) which is motivated by self-interest to make the best deal (or profit) it can for itself.

When buyers and sellers come together to agree on a purchase or sale, the transaction takes place in what economists call a **market.** The term "market" describes any method by which, or place at which, buyers can communicate with sellers. A good or service is purchased or sold for a price, and the price helps to determine what kinds of economic activity will take place in a market-price system.

The decisions made by buyers and sellers help to determine prices. And the prices in turn signal the ways our society decides what to produce, how to produce and for whom to produce. The quantity and quality of lettuce on hand in Los Angeles, for instance, is determined by hundreds of freely made producing and buying decisions. Each one of these decisions involves someone's conscious or unconscious assessment of opportunity cost. The farmer may wonder whether to grow lettuce or beets, the buyer may wonder whether to buy lettuce or spinach.

Many observers liken market-price systems to an *auction*, because somewhere behind the scene, buyers bid among themselves for the goods and services sellers want to sell. When you go to the supermarket, no bidding is apparent. The prices of everything are shown. You decide to buy or not to buy, or how much to buy, depending partly on price.

Where, then, is the auction? Your buying decisions cause changes in the store's inventory (often stored in a computer memory). When the inventory drops below desired levels, those who buy for the store must then *bid* (against other stores) for supplies offered by farmers (or brokers).

Your buying decisions will also influence farmers in their decisions about what crops to grow and how much land to devote to each crop, leading to decisions about what fertilizers, insecticides, delivery systems, and machinery they will need; those decisions will in turn influence the production decisions of firms that supply farmers.

While the United States is more nearly a market-price system than anything else, it is a mixture of systems just as it is a blend of capitalism and socialism. And while a market-price system is inevitably found in capitalistic countries, it is found also in traditional and in socialistic countries. Primitive tribes have primitive markets where exchange occurs. Often the method of exchange is barter, or trade, but money (shells, animals, skins) is also used to facilitate exchange. In socialist countries like the Soviet Union or China, private enterprise (small shops, private plots on farms) and private markets are still alive. (See the boxed essay on the next page.)

How a Market-Price System Operates

Our needs and desires are satisfied by the things we produce, but to produce these things we need resources. What is meant by *resources?* A resource is anything or anyone employed to produce the goods and services desired by society. In market-price systems, resources are divided into four categories called the **factors of production.** They are land, labor, capital, and entrepreneurship. Here is a description of each.

Land

The factors of production: resources to produce goods and services

Land is not only the soil used for growing agricultural products, it is also the source of all materials and food whether in liquid, solid, or gaseous form, in or above the earth. Perhaps we will soon include the moon in the land category.

Labor

Labor refers to human effort, when the effort is rewarded by some kind of pay, whether money, free room and board, or clothes (as in the military services).

The Isms: Socialism, Communism, Capitalism

In the last century, the world has been divided into two great economic and political camps.

While the division of societies into traditional, planning, and market-price economic systems spans the entire course of history, in the last century the world has become divided into two great economic and political camps representing socialism and capitalism.*

*In this discussion we are going to overlook the World War II versions of Nazism and fascism, which were capitalistic systems but under the control of the dictators Hitler and Mussolini.

As you read this discussion, you will find that the distinction between "socialism" and "capitalism" often becomes blurred, particularly when we try to pin a label on any one country. Nevertheless, there are important differences. In each case it is helpful to ask two questions: (1) Who owns the factories? (2) Who decides the answers to the three questions?

Under **socialism,** the government owns and operates the major industries of the country.

Capital

Capital is the hardest factor of production to explain. The word comes from Latin *caput,* meaning "head." It was sometimes used to refer to the headman. Somehow the word evolved to mean a stock of wealth. In economics, the term means a tangible, physical good (a *capital good*) that a person or society creates in the expectation that its use will improve or increase future pro-

Consequently, the government also decides—in those major industries—the answers to the three questions. There are almost as many variants of socialism as there are countries. In Britain, many of the major industries are nationalized. In the Soviet Union and China they *all* are. In the United States, there are municipally owned airports or utilities and federally owned projects like the Tennessee Valley Authority or Hoover Dam. Sweden is often called socialistic, but erroneously so because more property there is privately owned than in the United States. (We sometimes think of Sweden as socialistic because of its extensive welfare programs.)

Note that "socialism" does not imply dictatorship. Socialism can exist in democratic countries as well as authoritarian ones. The main reason for socialism's existence is that socialists hope that they can overcome capitalism's two major problems: (1) the unequal distribution of income and wealth, and (2) the uneven course of economic growth with periods of boom or bust. For that reason, socialist countries, whether democratic or not, tend to have a high (relative to capitalism) degree of economic planning and government regulation of the economy.

Communism is a form of socialism that is the dream of many socialists. Communist theory holds that the people themselves—not the government—own the means of production. In a communist state, everyone works at what he or she can do best. There is no system of wages or profits needed to spur people to work. Everyone simply takes from what is produced whatever he or she needs to live comfortably. No government or bureaucracy supervises what the people do.

Consequently, communism is considered an ideal, still to be realized, by those who believe in it. (We will discuss socialism, communism, the ideas of Karl Marx, and how his ideas apply to the Soviet Union and The People's Republic of China in Chapter 19.)

Capitalism has three aspects, as follows:

1. The institution of private ownership is generally accepted. Factories, land, goods, and services are privately owned by individuals or groups of individuals like stockholders.

2. Most people are free to pursue their own economic self-interest; that is, to work for personal gain. For this reason, capitalism is often called the *free enterprise* system; most people are free to choose their own occupations.

3. Because people are motivated by self-interest, they will compete with one another to get ahead, to make a better product, to control markets in order to obtain a bigger profit. The struggle for bigger profits leads (usually but by no means always) to a high degree of competition between business firms.

The description we have just given is of pure capitalism—capitalism without tax laws, licenses to buy, government ownership of some enterprises (city-owned airports), and myriads of government regulations. But that is clearly not the capitalism that exists in twentieth-century America. Economists frequently call our system **mixed capitalism.** That means our system is a mixture of free, privately owned enterprise on the one hand and government participation on the other.

duction. For example, before the Industrial Revolution, capital meant a tool—axe, hoe, bow and arrow—which was created to make future production easier. In modern society, we mean such things as machines, buildings, roads, harbors, trucks, and filing cabinets. Notice that in economics the word capital, or capital good, does *not* mean a sum of money (sometimes called "financial capital").

As the owner of the business he is an entrepreneur. As the manager, however, he is a laborer.

The process of creating a capital good is called *capital formation*. A common synonym for capital formation in economics is *investment*. Notice again that we are *not* talking about money. (Sometimes, outside of economics, the purchase of assets such as stocks and bonds is called "financial investment." These terms should be distinguished from investment as economists use that term.) When an Eskimo tribe takes time out to make a kayak, it is creating capital. It is investing in the hope that in the future it will increase the number of seals it catches—that is, obtain a return on its investment.

Economists also refer to *human capital.* When you invest in yourself by training or educating yourself to be more productive, you are creating a form of capital; you are investing. But unless we specifically refer to human capital in this book, we will mean some form of tangible, inanimate capital.

Economists also speak of *social overhead capital*, as contrasted with *private capital*. By social overhead capital we mean the kinds of capital we use together as members of the public—freeways, airports, harbors, dams. By private capital, we usually mean capital that belongs to some business concern in the form of buildings and equipment.

Entrepreneurship

The entrepreneur is the person who combines the other three factors of production to create some product or service to sell. He hopes for a profit, but he risks loss or bankruptcy.

What about the man who both owns and manages his hardware store? Is he an entrepreneur? An economist would say the man is wearing two hats. As the owner of the business, risking the chance of profit or loss, he is an entrepreneur. As the manager of the business, however, he is a laborer, just like the other store employees.

The distinction becomes more difficult when we think of a large corporation. Who is the entrepreneur? Technically, the stockholders are, because they bear the risk of loss, hoping for profit. Their money started the business; it purchased the necessary factors of production. Like the hardware store owner, the corporation president may be both a labor factor of production (earning a wage to manage the corporation) and an entrepreneurial factor of production (stockholder).

Money?

Is money a resource, a factor of production? (By money we mean any form of *financial* capital—cash, stocks and bonds, or bank accounts.) The question is a technical one. For the individual or individual firm possessing money, money might be said to be a factor of production because it enables that person or firm to buy or attract all four factors of production. Because it enables individuals or firms to increase their stock of resources, money is both a means of acquiring wealth and a way of measuring wealth.

For a nation as a whole, however, money represents only a claim on the resources owned by that nation—the real things like buildings, roads, dams, TV sets, automobiles, and raw materials. If we were to count a nation's supply of money plus its supply of real things, we would be guilty of what economists call double counting. Thus, although money is a *means* to acquire factors of production and is also a measure of wealth, it is not in itself a factor of production.

The factor payments: Income from producing goods and services

In market-price systems, entrepreneurs have to bid against one another for the use of the factors of production. The payments made by the entrepreneurs for each of the factors are called **factor payments.** The payments are made to the owners of the factors. The owners of land receive *rent.* Workers (the owners of their own labor) receive *wages.* The owners of capital receive *interest*, and entrepreneurs keep any *profits* their enterprises earn as a reward for their own risk taking. Economists divide all income into these four categories.

Rent

The theory of rent helps to explain why some land is used for hotels or department stores, while other land remains barren or is used for some poor crop like potatoes.

Rent is defined as the payment for the use of land—excluding payments made to all of the other factors of production.

Suppose you rent 100 acres of land from someone for $10,000 for one year and grow potatoes on it. In the first year you sell enough potatoes so that even after deducting the $10,000 and all other expenses you still earn $40,000. Knowing this, your landlord figures he can get away with raising the rent, and he does so every year until you find the rent so high that potato growing is no longer profitable. You give up the land. Now someone else may come along and rent the land for building a shopping center and find that that use will earn a profit. Of course, the landlord may raise the rent again, but eventually the rent charged the tenant will reflect and determine the most profitable use of the land, excluding each tenant's payments to other factors for working the land. Thus, we see that a market-price system prods entrepreneurs to use resources in such a way as to produce the greatest profit.

The pressure on entrepreneurs to earn the greatest possible profit helps to explain how market-price systems operate without the planning agencies one finds in socialist countries. Profit comes, of course, from an entrepreneur's ability to create something that consumers want. Thus, entrepreneurs' efforts to find profits are the mainspring that channels resources into uses most satisfying to consumers.

When a system operates in this manner to satisfy consumer wants, the system is said to be motivated by **consumer sovereignty.** The consumer is king. But there is considerable debate about this notion. Government agencies often interfere with production and pricing of goods and services. And large corporations are frequently able to manipulate consumer wants through advertising.

Wages

Like rent, a wage represents a bargain between a buyer (the employer) and a seller (the worker). If the bargain is freely made by both parties, the wage paid (say, $5 an hour) should cover the worker's opportunity cost in giving up all of the other jobs he or she might have had. On the other hand, the employer will want to be sure that the worker (just like the land) is being used in the most productive (profitable) way.

This theory of wages is useful in demonstrating the opportunity-cost concept, but it is not always accurate in describing wages in our society. Some people are paid more than is really necessary to keep them on a given job, and some are paid less. If we asked a successful entertainer making $4 million per year how much it would take to keep her doing what she is doing, she might reply that she would do it for only half a million dollars. Society nevertheless gives her the extra $3.5 million as a measure of its willingness to pay for her special talents. The extra $3.5 million is sometimes called "quasi-rent," which means any payment for a resource that is more than enough to bring it into production.

On the other hand, many people are stuck in jobs that do not reflect opportunity costs and their talents are poorly used. Why do they not change? There are many reasons. They may lack information about better jobs. They may be blocked by race, sex, or age discrimination. Other jobs may require expensive occupational licenses or expensive union dues. In short, there are what economists call **barriers to entry**—restrictions on the movement of labor and other resources. Thus, although opportunity cost (both to the individual and society) is an excellent measure of the correct use of a resource, even in a capitalistic society resources are not always free to move to the use that might be most desirable.

Interest

Capital, you'll recall, means tools, equipment, and buildings. How can such inanimate things earn interest?

As an example, consider 10 members of a primitive tribe who live by catching fish. Using fishing lines, they catch 5 fish per man per day. Now suppose someone gets the bright idea of making a fishnet. The 10 men take one day off and make the net. The opportunity cost of the net, then, is 10 men × 5 fish, or 50 fish—the fish they could have caught while making the net. But with the net suppose they catch 60 fish per day, or 6 fish per man per day.

The process of making the net is called capital formation or investment. The return on the investment is measured by the extra 10 fish per day. (We are pretending there are no extra costs in using the net such as repairing and drying, which might have to be deducted from the return.) The return, then, can be expressed this way:

$$\frac{10 \text{ fish (Extra fish)}}{50 \text{ fish (Cost of the net)}} = \frac{1}{5} = \begin{array}{l} 20\% \text{ return on} \\ \text{investment} \end{array}$$

The return on the investment in capital can be expressed in percentage terms as an interest rate. The interest rate also expresses how long it will take to make up for the cost of the net (five days). Like rent and wages, the interest rate helps us think about the return we are going to get compared with the sacrifice that the investment requires.

Two other matters need to be mentioned in connection with interest. First, unlike our fishnet example, interest is always measured by its return per year, not per day. Second, interest is compounded; that is, both the investment and the interest it earns, earn interest.

It is evident that because of the productivity of the net not as many men need to fish as before. Some can now be released for other capital formation (investment) such as kayak-making. Thus, the original investment permits growth in many directions.

Profit

Entrepreneurs earn profit to repay them for the risk of loss. Suppose you decide to invest in a snack bar serving hamburgers, fries, milkshakes, and the like. You plan to work in the snack bar at least forty hours a week. Assume you know you could earn $250 a week working for someone else. Will you be content if your snack bar earns only $250 per week? Obviously not. Remember, you have money tied up in the building, equipment, and unsold food—money that could have earned interest in a savings account. Also, you are taking the risk you may go bankrupt. Profit, then, represents the return over and above the money you could have earned doing something else with your time and money. This extra amount is viewed as the reward for risk taking.

How much profit is necessary to persuade you to risk starting the snack bar? There is no easy answer. It depends on you—how much you enjoy working for yourself, cooking hamburgers, cleaning up, and so on. But there is still a principle. Suppose you knew before you started that the maximum profit you could earn was $50 per week (over and above an allowance for your own wages and lost interest). Would you still start the enterprise?

Most economists would argue that any ceiling on profits will always discourage *someone* and therefore cut down on total investment in new enterprises. Some entrepreneurs will not take the risk unless there is some chance—even if it's only one in a hundred—of striking it rich, of having that snack bar turn into a successful national chain of snack bars. And if that one-in-a-hundred chance does not exist, the limit on profits will slow the growth of the economy.

The factor payments in the United States

Table 2-3 summarizes the factor payments (income) paid in the United States in 1979. One can see that employees (including business executives) receive the lion's share.

TABLE 2-3 U.S. Factor Payments in 1979

		Billions of dollars	Percentage of total
Employee compensation[a]		$1,459.1	75.8
Interest		129.7	6.7
Rent		26.9	1.4
Profit			
Unincorporated	130.0		
Corporate	178.5	308.5	16.1
Total factor payments		$1,924.2	100.0

[a]Includes employer contributions for social security and all fringe benefits.
Source: *Economic Report of the President, 1979.*

The circular-flow diagram: a picture of the market-price system

The operation of a market-price system can be described in a simplified way by Figure 2-1. The diagram is called a circular flow diagram because dollars move from households* to business firms, who pay them back to households, who use the dollars for more purchases. Around and around go the dollars.

The markets for goods and services are in the upper flow. The markets for resources (factors of production) are in the lower flow. Dollars (the dotted line) flow from households to business firms; this flow is called *dollar "votes"*

Defined as a single adult or group of persons occupying a housing unit; that is, a house, apartment, or any group of rooms that constitute separate living quarters. In 1978, there were 74 million households in the United States.

Figure 2-1. A circular-flow diagram of a market-price system.

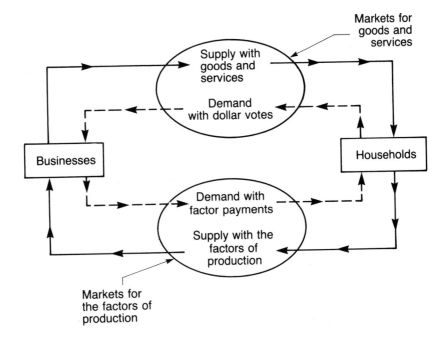

because the household's demands are, in effect, votes that express likes or dislikes for the goods and services that the firms supply. In response to the dollar votes, the business firms try to supply the goods and services the households want (the solid line).

In our society, we, the people living in households, are viewed as owning all resources (factors of production), because we own everything either privately or as taxpayers. As members of households we own unincorporated enterprises; as stockholders we own corporations; as citizens and taxpayers we own government-operated enterprises and national parks. Business firms must therefore buy the factors of production from households. These flows are in the lower loop where you can see the dollars (again the dotted line) flow from the business firms to the households as the firms bid for (demand) resources owned by the households. This dollar flow is in the form of the four *factor payments*—rent for land, wages for labor, interest for capital, and profits for entrepreneurs. The flow of dollars from enterprises to consumers determines the distribution of income. In return, the households sell the four factors of production to the firms (the solid line).

The upper-loop market for goods and services is closely related to the lower-loop market for resources. If consumers "vote" for more eight-track stereo tapes, enterprises will "vote" more strongly for the resources to make them. The prices of these resources will tend to rise and resources will be attracted away from other uses. Some people will find the opportunity cost of *not* working in the stereo tape industry too high and will move to the higher wages offered there.

The circular flow diagram is an oversimplification. For one thing, it leaves out the effect of the government. For another, it does not show the transactions made between business enterprises, so it does not show the flow of capital goods produced by one firm and sold to another. Nor does the diagram show the transactions between members of the public that occur in, say, garage sales and the private sale of used cars and houses. But, despite these shortcomings the circular-flow diagram is very useful in explaining the operation of our economic system. In Chapter 13 we will use it to examine several current problems.

Evaluating our system: how well does it work?

How well does the system operate in terms of human welfare?

Eighteenth-century economist Adam Smith (see box essay) believed that the market-price system would provide the most efficient possible allocation of resources and that all forms of land, labor, capital, and entrepreneurship would be employed to maximum advantage. He believed that the price system and the movement of resources to the most profitable use would lead to the highest possible total production and standard of living. If one occupation or product became more profitable than another, he stated, resources would instantly flow to it, bringing the price down and the quantity up so that consumers would always benefit and no entrepreneur could earn any unusual profit for long. These ideas were expressed in Smith's 1776 book, *An Inquiry into the Nature and Causes of the Wealth of Nations*, considered the beginning of modern economic theory. In one famous passage, he concluded that the market-price system would take care of itself if left alone. If each participant pursued his own self-interest, the system as a whole would produce the maximum quantity of goods, just as if an *"invisible hand"* were leading society to the best of all worlds. Smith's statement was therefore a basis for the laissez-faire political philosophy—noninterference by government in the workings of the economic system.

Here are his words:

> As every individual, therefore, endeavours as much as he can both to employ his capital in the support of domestic industry, and so to direct that industry that its produce may be of the greatest value; every individual necessarily labours to render the annual revenue of the society as great as he can. He generally, indeed, neither intends to promote the public interest, nor knows how much he is promoting it. By preferring the support of domestic to that of foreign industry, he intends only his own security; and by directing that industry in such a manner as its produce may be of the greatest value, he intends only his own gain, and he is in this, as in many other cases, *an invisible hand* to promote an end which was no part of his intention. Nor is it always the worse for the society that it was no part of it. By pursuing his own interest he frequently promotes that of the society more effectually than when he really intends to promote it.[2]

Smith's statement that a laissez-faire market-price system promotes the interest of society is at the center of some heated arguments among econo-

Adam Smith, 1723–1790: The Man with the "Invisible Hand"

The Bettmann Archive

(The university was at that time operating under a "do your own thing" system, with students literally teaching themselves whatever they wanted to know, a custom Smith thought was an exercise in futility.)

After Oxford he spent two years searching for a job and finally, in 1748, was appointed to a lectureship in English literature at Edinburgh University. He did so well that three years later, at the age of 28, he received the professorship of logic at Glasgow College and the next year ascended to the professorship of moral philosophy.

After thirteen years in Glasgow, Smith became a traveling private tutor to the Duke of Buccleuch, ward of Charles Townsend, the Chancellor of the Exchequer (and the man who was to help precipitate the American revolution). This position provided generous remuneration, as well as many side benefits in places visited and people met, and during this time, Smith began writing *The Wealth of Nations*. Unfortunately, the job unexpectedly terminated after two and a half years, and he returned to Scotland.

In Scotland he became Commissioner of Customs and settled down for the next ten years to purposefully writing his book. He also, unpurposefully, began perpetuating his reputation for absentmindedness. One morning, for instance, while strolling in his dressing gown in his garden, he became so engrossed in his thoughts that he walked fifteen miles from home before he became aware of his surroundings.

Adam Smith is especially noted for his theory of the "invisible hand" and his advocacy of free trade even though, in his position as Commissioner of Customs in Scotland, he dealt with import taxes.

The year 1776 marked the birth of a political revolution in America, and its birth certificate was the Declaration of Independence. In England it marked an intellectual revolution. Modern economic theory was born, and its birth certificate was Adam Smith's *The Wealth of Nations.*

Smith's beliefs are subject to controversy. Some people claimed he was a truly religious man. Others called him a cynical realist. Some said his sympathies lay with the laboring class. Others believed his way of life precluded any action that would harm the elite.

The son of a customs official who died before he was born, Smith was kidnapped by gypsies at the age of 4 and abandoned by the side of the road. He recovered, and by age 14 enrolled at Glasgow College. Three years later, he received a scholarship to Oxford, where he stayed for six years, even though he was miserable much of the time.

mists. Let us review six of the most important of them. The first two describe the system as Smith viewed them, the final four the system as it actually evolved.

Freedom and competition

Basic to Smith's contention are the advantages of freedom and competition. In a society where entrepreneurs and workers are free, he stated, competition among them will force them to produce the goods and services that consumers want most. Only in a free, competitive society where entrepreneurs and workers are free to pursue their special talents, and where consumers are free to choose products from a number of competitive firms, will the consumer know whether or not he or she is getting the best deal. If, as in a planned economy, you can buy only one type of coat, you have no way of comparing the coat offered (and its price) with another.

Free choice and competition not only give each consumer the best deal, they ensure the most efficient and most profitable use of each resource, as we saw in our example of rent (with land used for growing potatoes instead of for a shopping center). Furthermore, the fluctuation of prices (and profits) ensures the production and distribution of the quantities consumers will buy in each geographical location.

Thus, says Smith, freedom of choice, spurred on by self-interest, an absence of government interference, and competition, will provide the greatest benefits for consumers and society.

Interferences with market prices

In 1971, the Nixon Administration introduced wage and price controls in an attempt, unusual in peacetime, to reduce inflation. The costs of this kind of government interference with the market-price system became clearly evident. There were widespread shortages of meat and gasoline, as suppliers withheld products and services while waiting for higher prices. Prices of food items not subject to controls rose rapidly. When the controls were finally lifted in 1973, inflation resumed more rapidly than ever, as entrepreneurs and workers sought to make up for losses of profits and wages sustained during the period of controls.

Adam Smith argued that when prices are not controlled, the market price generally reaches a level where there is no shortage. If the product is scarce relative to human wants, *and if the price is free to change*, the price will rise high enough to exclude many poorer buyers. Only those who can afford to pay and those who want the product at that price will buy it, and the shortage will disappear. Today, many economists argue that the way to solve the energy crisis is to let the price rise until consumption drops enough to match our scarce supply. The market-price system is a rationing device based on the ability to pay. Interferences with it distort its ability to ration. Therefore, economists must weigh the costs of distorting the market with price controls against the costs of excluding poor people from buying.

Decline of competition

The motivation of self-interest causes a competitive economic system to become increasingly less competitive. No entrepreneur wants to be subjected to ruinous competition from a competitor. Instead, entrepreneurs want to insulate themselves from competition by becoming bigger (meaning that new firms will need to invest more if they are to compete), by participating in combinations, by advertising, by engaging in franchise agreements, by promoting licensing laws, by obtaining patent rights, and by otherwise erecting barriers to entry that prevent other firms from competing. Smith recognized these monopolistic tendencies and condemned them.

As competition lessens, the existing firms no longer need to worry so much about producing as efficiently, or producing as good a product, or charging the lowest possible price.

There is evidence that competition is lessening in the United States. More on this in Chapter 7.

Boom and bust

The very fact that a market-price system is operated by self-interested groups of entrepreneurs and workers in conflict with one another produces unstable levels of employment and prices. History has shown that the market-price system does not guarantee full employment. In 1933, when government participation in the private economy was negligible, the unemployment rate reached 24.9 percent. It was never below 14 percent in the years 1931 to 1940.

During the 1970s most segments of the economy suffered and are suffering from losses in real income caused by inflation. There is also evidence that inflation may result in unemployment because people may buy less when prices go up (with any given income), and less buying means fewer jobs. Supporters of the Adam Smith view argue that inflation is caused by government interference with free prices (price controls) and excessive government spending. Some of the critics, however, insist that inflation and unemployment are the inevitable consequences of conflict fueled by self-interest.

Income distribution

The market-price system guarantees no particular level of income distribution. As we pointed out, 20 percent of the people in the United States receive only about 5 percent of the total income. The market-price system is really an *auction* on the buyer's side. Suppose there are 30 students on an island and one six-pack of beer. Who gets it? In a primitive society, custom would decide. In a planned society, the planners would decide. In a market-price system, the beer would go to the people able and willing to pay the highest price. The market-price system is simply another way to ration scarce goods and services.

Social goods

Because the market-price system produces only what people are willing to pay for, it may not provide goods and services where profit is absent or is not apparent to potential entrepreneurs. Goods and services in this category are national defense, police forces, fire departments, roads, public schools, hospitals for poor people. These goods and services are **often called** *social goods* or public goods. Similarly, an entrepreneur is **often so motivated** by profit that he may use pollution-creating methods of production, which may involve a social cost to society in the form of bad air and water.

We have highlighted the major problems faced by market-price systems. The most important point to remember, however, is that every problem has a cost and the solution to every problem has a cost. Unemployment has a cost in human suffering. Reducing unemployment may involve the cost of additional taxes to finance programs for the unemployed. The job of the economist is to estimate the costs of problems, the costs of the solutions to those problems, and the chances of success of any proposed solution.

Summary

Every society must make three decisions: what goods and services to provide in what quantities, how they are to be produced, and for whom. The manner in which societies answer the what, how, and for whom questions determines the character of their economic systems, that is, whether the system is capitalistic or socialistic, whether it is traditional, planned, or market-price.

A capitalistic system is one in which the factors of production are privately owned and in which the answers to the three questions are determined by what goes on in the market. Socialism is defined as an economic system in which the government owns and operates the major industries.

Economic systems are also divided into three categories: traditional, planning, and market-price systems. The United States is a capitalistic example of the latter, although it has in it many elements of other systems. The United States is often called a mixed capitalist system. Human needs and desires are satisfied by goods (such as food, housing, and clothing) and services (such as health care and professional services). In order to provide these goods and services, a society must have resources: land and the raw materials in or above it; labor, or the human effort of extracting and processing these materials; capital, or the equipment and tools with which to process the materials; and entrepreneurship, or the willingness of persons to take the risk of acquiring the raw materials and equipment and hiring the laborers to produce goods or services for others. In economics, these four resources are called the factors of production.

The process of creating the equipment and tools used in production is called capital formation or investment. The equipment and tools that belong to the public and are in general use, such as freeways and airports, are called social overhead capital; this is in contrast to private capital, which is owned and used by private individuals or groups.

Each of the four factors of production receives payment for its use. Land receives rent, which reflects its desirability or productivity. Labor receives wages, reflecting the worker's value to the employer. Capital receives interest, reflecting the usefulness of equipment or tools in making labor more productive. Entrepreneurship receives profits or payment for the risks the entrepreneur takes when investing in equipment, hiring laborers, and so on. Ideally, each of the factors of production will be used in its most productive way. In the real world, however, barriers to entry frequently prevent this ideal from being realized.

The market-price system has two basic markets—the consumer market for goods and services, in which the people exchange "dollar votes" for what is produced, and the resources market, in which enterprises exchange wages, interest, rent, and profits for labor, capital, land, and entrepreneurship. In each market, the forces of demand and supply—the willingness and ability of buyers to buy, on the one hand, and ability of producers and sellers to produce and sell on the other—determine prices and the ultimate use or destination of all goods and services. What households pay to businesses for products comes back to them in the form of wages, interest, rent, and profits, creating a flow of dollars which can be shown by a circular-flow diagram.

Although Adam Smith believed that the market-price system would operate as if "by an invisible hand" to give an ideal solution to the questions of what, how, and for whom, in actuality the system creates many problems such as unemployment, poverty, pollution, and inflation.

Discussion Questions

1. Are you a resource? If you are, what is the opportunity cost of doing what you are doing? Does the benefit gained from what you are doing more than offset the loss of all the other opportunities you have given up?

2. Are there barriers to entry preventing you from doing something else you want to do? If so, what are they?

3. Does the system of wages operate the way land-rent does to ensure the best possible match between each worker and his job? Does our wage system allocate the labor resource in the best possible way? Explain.

4. If you have a job, ask yourself how your wages were determined. Explain fully. Consider the society or world in which you live.

5. If you were the dictator of a small country, how would you decide how to use each parcel of land? What job should each of your citizens be ordered to perform? How much effort should be put into capital formation at the expense of current consumption? (Assume your country is at peace, with no foreseeable threat of war.)

6. Does the "invisible hand" work? Why or why not? Would it work if there were no barriers to entry?

7. What decisions is the market-price system good at making? What decisions does it fail to make or make poorly?

References

1. See three provocative articles on the distribution of wealth and income by Peter Barnes in the *New Republic* (30 September 1972, 7 October 1972, and 21 October 1972). They are well worth classroom discussion.

2. Adam Smith, *An Inquiry into the Nature and Causes of the Wealth of Nations* (Chicago: Encyclopaedia Britannica, 1952), p. 194.

2

Prices and How They Work

In this part we will describe the basics of microeconomics (often called price theory). Microeconomics is concerned with economic decision making by consumers, business enterprises, and local agencies, as opposed to economic decisions made by national governments. And because the prices of everything are so important to these decisions, microeconomics asks how prices are determined and how prices answer the three questions—what? how? and for whom?—in a market-price system.

"Prices and How They Work" contains four chapters. The first (Chapter 3) shows how prices are determined. This is followed by a brief chapter, 3A, on understanding graphs. Chapter 4 discusses how prices change in response to changes in markets. Finally, Chapter 5 describes what happens when buyers react strongly to price changes or, conversely, when price changes have little effect on buying decisions.

3

Demand and Supply: The Contest Between Buyers and Sellers

Peter Southwick/Stock, Boston

This chapter continues our discussion of the market-price system. In it we will assume that prices are being determined in an Adam Smithian market-price system; that is, with a high degree of competition among self-interested buyers and sellers and a minimum of government regulation. Later on, in Part III, we will drop this assumption.

We have included several graphs or diagrams to explain how prices are determined. If you have trouble with graphs, now is the time to read Chapter 3A, beginning on page 66, which explains very simply what graphs mean.

This chapter describes first what models are and why economic models are useful, then discusses in turn the three functions of price, demand and supply, and how prices are determined.

Key Words	Substitution effect
Model	Substitute and complementary goods
Ceteris paribus	Inflation psychology
Exclusion principle	Self-fulfilling prophecy
Demand, demand schedule, demand curve	Supply, supply schedule, supply curve
Law of demand	Equilibrium price
Income effect	Market power

What Models Are and Why Economic Models Are Useful

The decisions of buyers and sellers help to determine prices, and prices often determine the behavior of buyers and sellers. The package of frozen peas in your supermarket appears there because farmers and food processors believe it can be sold at a price that is profitable. This belief on their part has been nurtured by the willingness and ability of consumers to buy sufficient quantities at prices that *are* profitable. The price on any given day, along with the prices of all the alternatives to frozen peas, will help to determine whether or not we buy frozen peas and whether or not sellers will continue to supply the supermarket with frozen peas.

Our decisions to buy or not to buy arise from a network of extremely complicated influences. Our willingness to buy involves (1) the level of our present and expected future income and wealth, (2) attitudes about whether or not the good or service is something we want, (3) beliefs about whether or not the purchase of any good like frozen peas is the best way (as compared with dozens of options) to spend our money, (4) expectations about future changes in the availability of frozen peas or changes in the effects frozen peas may be said to have on our health. (The Food and Drug Administration might announce that certain levels of frozen pea consumption are toxic to laboratory animals!) Also, changes in the cost of growing or freezing the peas will affect prices, and these effects will in turn influence our buying decisions.

Because these influences on prices (and our reactions to them) are so complicated, economists try to simplify thinking about them in order to discover how prices are determined. They do this by using what are called (in any of the social sciences) **models.**

A *model* is a simplified version of the world requiring a set of assumptions. Consider a recipe:

> Take 2¾ cups whole-wheat flour. Add 1½ cakes yeast dissolved in 3 tablespoons lukewarm water. Add 1 cup lukewarm water, 2 tablespoons brown sugar, 1½ teaspoons salt, 3 tablespoons melted shortening. Shape into ball. Bake 45 minutes at 385° F. Makes 5 ″ × 10″ loaf of whole-wheat bread.

This is a model because it has ignored many details present in the real world. The thermostat on the oven could be faulty. The oven could have a leak. Some person could come along and peek in and change the cook-

A model is a simplified version of the world.

ing time. The water used could be full of chlorine and change the taste. And so on.

Thus, the recipe is a model in that it is a simplified version of the real world, and—without saying so—the recipe or model assumes that none of these dangers exist. If we assume they do not exist, we can say that the recipe will produce bread.

This is what economists try to do. By building models they try to arrive at a conclusion. The danger, of course, is that the model will involve so many assumptions that it no longer speaks for the real world. Consequently, a model is a theory that the creator hopes will work. The usefulness of the model depends on how well it explains or predicts outcomes in the real world. Research economists spend much of their time developing models to reduce unemployment and inflation, for example, and then testing them, using current and past data to see if they work.

Sometimes social scientists use the Latin phrase, **ceteris paribus**—"all other things remain the same"—to remind readers that a model is being used. In our example, *ceteris paribus* would mean that everything that goes into the oven is exactly what the recipe calls for, that nothing else changes in the real world (in the oven or outside the oven) to disturb the model.

The circular flow diagram at the end of Chapter 2 is a model because we assumed that money kept flowing to business enterprises and that the enterprises kept paying it out in the form of rent, wages, interest, and profit. None of the real-world interruptions to spending like saving or taxes were mentioned.

In this chapter there are several models which are used to describe why people buy more at low prices than at high prices and why sellers supply more at high prices than at low prices. But each of these models involves the *ceteris paribus* assumption. Many real-world changes in incomes, tastes, and population and disasters like wars, floods, hurricanes, or earthquakes are assumed not to occur. The world outside the model remains, *ceteris paribus*, the same.

Now let's turn to a discussion of what prices do in a market-price system and see how they are determined.

Three Functions of Prices

Prices have three main functions in a market-price system: (1) directing the use of resources, (2) rationing goods and services and resources, and (3) establishing the relative values of all resources and goods and services. We will consider each of these.

Directing use of resources

Suppose an entrepreneur can buy a wallet-making machine for $10,000 and that the life of the machine is one year. The machine has to be operated by one man making $40 per day. The man works, on the average, 220 days per year and therefore earns $8,800. Excluding other costs of raw material, electricity, fuel, maintenance, and so on, the total cost of the man and the machine per year is $18,800 ($10,000 + $8,800). Together, the man and the machine produce 10,000 wallets per year at a cost of $18,800, or $1.88 per wallet.

Let's suppose that the entrepreneur has the alternative of hiring 9 workers at $10 per day to do the same job. Excluding the cost of hand tools, total costs are, we will assume, $10 × 9 workers × 220 days = $19,800. Assume that the 9 workers can make 12,000 wallets per year. By using the workers, the cost per wallet drops to $1.65 ($19,800 ÷ 12,000).

What will the entrepreneur do? He will hire the workers. The point is that the price system has determined how the wallets will be made, who receives income for the job, and who can afford to buy them. The price system has determined which resources will be used and in what quantities.

Is everyone happy? No. The manufacturer of the machine did not sell it and may have to lay off employees. The skilled operator of the machine did not get the job.

This anecdote illustrates a fact of life. The price system provides the measuring stick that enables the entrepreneur to make choices. These choices may make some people happy, others unhappy. However, if the system works perfectly—with no *barriers to entry*—it may make consumers happier by providing wallets at lower cost.

For a moment, let's consider a price system in which there are barriers to entry and which therefore does not work perfectly. Suppose the workers could make only 10,000 wallets instead of 12,000. Then the cost per wallet would be $1.98 ($19,800 ÷ 10,000) instead of $1.65. Suppose now that the workers are all related to the entrepreneur. To keep peace in the family, the entrepreneur hires the workers anyhow. Now, barriers to entry block the purchase of the machine and the hiring of the skilled operator. Consumers will probably have to pay a higher price for wallets.

Rationing goods and services and resources

Suppose that the price of top quality sirloin steak is about $5 per pound. Who gets the steak? Only those who want it and can afford it at that price. Is everyone happy? Of course not. At that price many of us are excluded from the market for steak and are obliged to buy less expensive cuts of meat. This is a reminder that any price *excludes* some people from buying. The higher the price, the more people are excluded. This idea is called the **exclusion principle.** The price system determines who can buy goods and services and who cannot. In this way, the price system again performs the "for whom" function by rationing goods and services.

Establishing values of resources and goods and services

Prices establish a relationship between all resources and all goods and services. If a sweater sells for $20 and a pair of socks for $2, our society values 10 pairs of socks as the equivalent of one sweater. In this way, prices measure the relative values of everything in our society. The price measure helps us consciously or unconsciously to figure the opportunity cost of every purchase.

We have noticed that the system does not necessarily make everyone happy. It is simply one way—an amoral, sometimes cold-blooded way—of making choices. Would you rather have the choices made by some planner? Or by voting? Because we live in a mixed system, our choices are made in many ways, but it is important to recognize the problems (or costs) of choosing one system over another.

Demand: How Much Consumers Buy Determines Prices

Prices are determined by the forces of demand and supply. Let us first consider a model of demand. **Demand** is defined as the number of units of a product you (or a group of people) will buy at various prices during some period of time.

The demand schedule

Many years ago, a man we will call Fred wandered alone in the Sahara Desert. He had been deserted by his faithless wife and his best friend, who had departed with the only means of transportation, their one and only camel, and with all the food and water. The temperature rose to 130° F. Fred was on the verge of collapse from thirst when suddenly a truck appeared. As it approached, Fred began to make out lettering on the side of the truck. Could it be? Was it a mirage? The lettering spelled out: BEER.

In a haze of semiconsciousness, Fred heard the driver ask, "Would you like an ice-cold beer?" Fred could hardly believe his ears. He answered, "Please, please, I'll give you *anything* for a beer."

How much is Fred willing to pay for beer?

The driver, Sinbad, replied, "Well, would you pay $100?"

Fred considered this. He had only $86 in his wallet, which certainly was not doing him any good in the desert. But he was reluctant to give up the whole $86 at once. He answered, "$30."

Sinbad said, "Okay, have one."

Fred clutched the beer can with shaking hands. It was cold—perfect. He opened it clumsily and gulped it down, spilling precious ounces on his sand-caked face and hair.

There was a pause. Sinbad said, "Perhaps you'd like another?" Fred gasped, "My God, would I!" Sinbad, stone-faced, inscrutable, answered, "It all depends. The price is $30."

Fred considered. He was less thirsty now. He finally answered, "I'll pay $25."

Sinbad handed over the second beer, which Fred immediately drained, spilling less with steadier hands.

Let us now assume that Fred consumes 6 beers, but as his thirst and cash diminish he persuades Sinbad to accept a lower price for each successive can. We can show this on a table (Table 3-1). This table is called a **demand schedule.** It tells us how many units of a product a buyer (Fred) will be willing and able to buy during some period of time at various prices.

You might think that the price of 2 beers should be shown as $30 + $25 ÷ 2, or $27.50 each, but the table represents the price Fred is willing to pay for each beer if he can purchase them one at a time.

TABLE 3-1 Fred's Demand Schedule

Number of beers	Price Fred is willing and able to pay for each additional beer
1	$30
2	25
3	18
4	10
5	2
6	1

The law of demand

Notice that, in the *demand schedule*, as price falls, the quantity bought increases. This is called the **law of demand.** Price and quantity are inversely related. Economists speak of *three reasons for the law of demand*—that is, why the quantity purchased increases as the price falls:

First, as the price falls, we can afford to buy larger quantities out of any income. This is called the **income effect.** Pretend for a moment that you spend your entire income on tennis balls and that you make $100 per week. If the price of a can of 3 tennis balls is $2.50, you can afford to buy 40 cans per week. If the price should fall to $2, you can afford to buy 50 cans per week.

Second, as the quantity purchased increases, we are not willing to pay as much for each additional unit. Why not? Because the satisfaction we receive from each additional unit is less than the satisfaction given by the one before. As our thirst is gradually quenched, each additional beer becomes less important—we will not offer as much for it.

Table 3-1 explains this point. How much is Fred willing to pay for 3 beers? Seventy-three dollars. This is a good measure of total satisfaction—to Fred. If we ask, "What is the third beer worth to Fred?" the answer is, of course, $18. This is a measure of the satisfaction provided by the third beer only.

Third, as the price of a product falls, we will use it for other purposes. This point is not evident in our beer example, but let's suppose we are talking about paint thinner or diamonds. If the price of paint thinner fell far enough, some people would use it for weed killer. If the price of diamonds were $1 per cubic yard, we would substitute diamonds for gravel in making concrete. This is called the **substitution effect.** As the price falls we increase our purchases because we find more and more uses for a product and substitute it for others.

These reasons for the law of demand should not be considered as if they were independent of one another. They all operate together in varying degrees of importance in each situation. If the price of phonograph records should fall, we will (1) buy more out of any given income, (2) tend to substitute

Figure 3-1. Fred's demand curve.

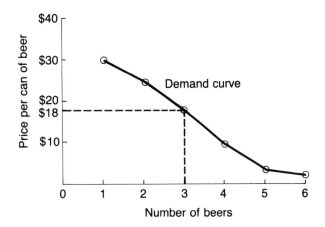

them for eight-track or cassette tapes, and (3) find that our satisfaction declines with each additional record, so that still lower prices are needed to motivate us to buy more.

The demand curve   Fred's schedule (Table 3-1) can also be presented in the form of a graph (Figure 3-1). The price that Fred is willing and able to pay during some period of time is shown on the vertical axis. The number of beers (quantity) he is willing to purchase at each price is shown on the horizontal axis. The line sloping down from left to right is called a **demand curve.** The dotted line at $18 shows that at that price he will buy 3 cans of beer.

Changes in demand   Suppose now that the price Fred is willing and able to pay for each quantity changes (Table 3-2). This new situation is what economists call a *change in demand.* Since Fred will pay more for each quantity and buy a larger quantity at each price, the change in Table 3-2 is called an *increase* in demand. Note that Fred is willing to pay $40 instead of $30 for the first beer

TABLE 3-2 Change in Demand

Number of beers	Old prices	New prices Fred is willing to pay
1	$30	$40
2	25	30
3	18	25
4	10	18
5	2	10
6	1	2

Figure 3-2. Example of
an increase in demand.

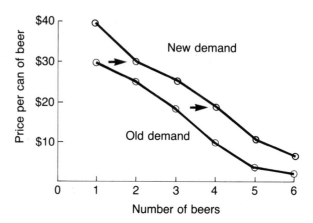

and higher prices for each of the other five. He is also willing now to buy
2 beers instead of 1 at $30, 3 beers instead of 2 at $25, 4 beers instead of
3 at $18, and so forth. In this case the demand curve shifts to the *right*.
Figure 3-2 shows these changes. If Fred decided to buy fewer beers at each
of the old prices, the demand curve would shift to the *left*. This change is
called a *decrease* in demand.

An important distinction must be made, and it requires a careful reading. If we look at the original demand curve (Figure 3-1), we see that as the
price falls from $30 to $25 to $18, and so on, the quantity Fred will buy
increases—we move *down* the demand curve. Moving along a given curve is
called a *change in the quantity demanded*; it is *not* called a change in demand.
Economists speak of a change in demand only when the line shifts to the left
or right—that is, when the buyer will buy larger or smaller quantities for
each and every price (Figure 3-3).

What causes changes in demand? There are five possible reasons, which
may occur all together or in any combination:

1. Changes in present or expected incomes

If your income (or wealth) increases, your demand curve will shift to the
right. You can afford to buy larger quantities at every price. Conversely, if your
income drops, your demand curve will shift to the left.

Figure 3-3. Figure at
left shows a *change in
the quantity demanded*
(movement along a given
demand curve, from A to
B). Figure at right shows
a *change in demand*
(movement or shift of the
demand curve itself).

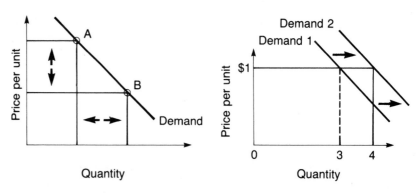

Figure 3-4. Competing substitute goods.

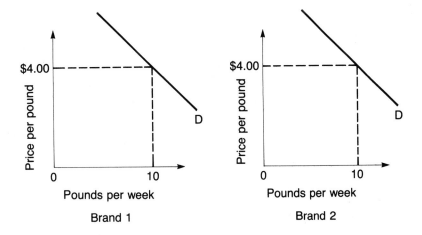

Brand 1   Brand 2

2. Changes in style

Buyers' tastes change constantly as fads and styles come and go. If a fad makes a product more popular, the demand curve for it will shift to the right. When something goes out of style, the demand curve will shift to the left.

3. Changes in the prices of substitute or complementary goods

Our demand for anything will change when prices of other products change. These products may be either substitute goods or complementary goods.

Substitute goods are goods that compete with one another—for example, two brands of essentially the same product, such as two brands of similar coffee. Suppose each brand sells 10 pounds per week in Pop's Grocery Store. Also suppose both sell at the same price, as in Figure 3-4. Now suppose that Brand 2 lowers its price to $3.75, as in Figure 3-5. The demand curve for Brand 2 indicates that there will be an increase in the quantity demanded

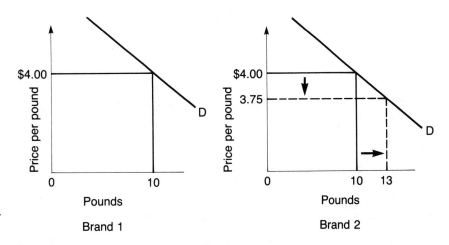

Figure 3-5. Brand 2 lowers its price.

Brand 1   Brand 2

Figure 3-6. Demand falls for Brand 1.

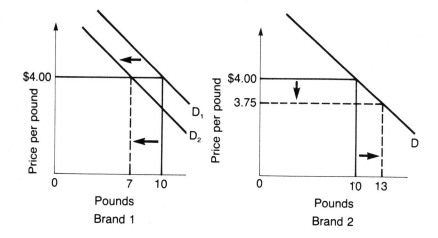

from 10 to 13 pounds. Where will this extra business come from? On the assumption that Brand 1 does not lower its price, Brand 2's gain will come from Brand 1's loss of business. This result is shown in Figure 3-6. If Brand 1 does not lower its price there will be a *decrease* in demand for its product. People will reduce their purchases of it from 10 to 7 pounds as they increase their purchases of Brand 2 from 10 to 13 pounds.

To summarize, a drop in the price of one substitute good, with no change in the price of the other, leads to a decrease in demand for the second product.

Complementary goods are goods that go together, like cars and tires. Consider the demand per month for cars and tires. A drop in the price of automobiles will *increase* (shift to the right) the demand for tires. Figure 3-7 illustrates the point. The two diagrams show that if the price of an automobile drops, people will demand more of them. (Has there been a change in demand? No, there has only been a change in the *quantity* demanded—the demand has not shifted.) But now consider the tires. With more cars on the street, people will demand more tires *at every price*. With the price of

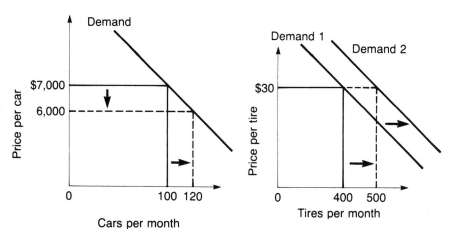

Figure 3-7. Effect of price change of one complementary good on demand for another.

tires unchanged at $30, people will increase their purchase of tires from 400 to 500 per month.

Substitute and complementary relationships may also work together. For instance, in August 1976 it was reported that gasoline had become so scarce in Saigon, Vietnam, that the price per gallon had risen to $12! Can you guess what happened? Gasoline and motorcycles are complementary goods. Motorcycles and bicycles are substitute goods. Thus, when the price of gasoline went up, the *quantity demanded* for gasoline decreased. And the decrease in the *quantity demanded* for gasoline caused a *decrease in demand* for any vehicle using gasoline, such as motorcycles and automobiles. On the other hand, the demand for people-powered bicycles skyrocketed. In fact, it was reported, the price of bicycles, went to *$600* apiece, whereas motorcycles, once in great demand, were selling for about a third of that.[1]

4. Changes in buyer expectations

Buyers also increase or decrease their demand with changes in expectations. If we expect prices to be lower next week, our demand will shift to the left this week; we will prefer to wait. If we worry about being laid off next week, our demand will also shift to the left; we will try to save to prepare for a period of unemployment. Conversely, if we expect to become more secure or prosperous in the future, we will "live it up"; our demand will increase this week.

These movements of demand with changes in expectations illustrate another fact of life. If we believe the future will be rosy, we will increase our purchases. Entrepreneurs will become more prosperous and hire more people. The belief will become reality. Unfortunately, there is a connection here with what economists call **inflation psychology.** If people believe prices are rising, they will increase current purchases—demand will shift to the right. This will further cause prices to rise as people try to buy before another round of price increases occurs. This again increases prices, and so on, so that there is an upward spiral of prices.

If we believe the future will be bleak, on the other hand, the spiral effect may plunge us downhill into depression or at least recession. (We use *recession* to mean a mild depression—see the list of key words beginning on page 440 for a more exact definition.) When buyers wait to buy at lower prices, entrepreneurs have to lay off employees. As people become unemployed, they and those still employed worry about the future and try to increase their savings (which may be difficult at lower incomes), further causing demand curves to shift to the left, which causes more people to be laid off. Social scientists call this tendency for a popular belief to become true a **self-fulfilling prophecy.**

5. Changes in number of buyers

Demand curves may change if the number of buyers changes. If a new factory is built and draws an influx of factory workers into a town, the increased number of people (buyers) will tend to cause prices to rise in the town

Figure 3-8. An increase in quantity at every price.

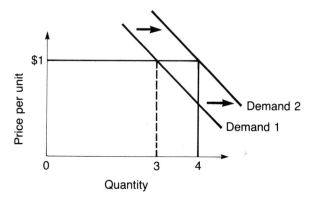

because larger quantities of foodstuffs, housing, and so on, may be demanded. This is true of the world in general. As the population of the world increases, our demands increase and prices tend to rise.

A quick review   Let us not forget the idea of a model and the *ceteris paribus* assumption. The law of demand states; "As the price falls, the quantity demanded increases (or vice versa)." We should add *"ceteris paribus"* to that statement. What we mean is that the quantity demanded will increase as the price falls *provided nothing else changes*—like incomes, tastes, prices of other products, expectations, or the number of other buyers. If any or all of these five variables change, we could have either an increase or a decrease in the quantity demanded *without* a change in price.

We can interpret an increase in demand in two ways: (1) It can be thought of as an increase in *quantity* at every price. See Figure 3-8. The specific numbers have been chosen arbitrarily, but the illustration shows that, at a price of $1, people will increase their purchases from 3 to 4 units. (2) An increase in demand can be thought of as the buyer's willingness to pay a higher *price* for every quantity. See Figure 3-9. Here the buyer is willing to pay $1.75 instead of $1 per unit when he or she buys 3 units.

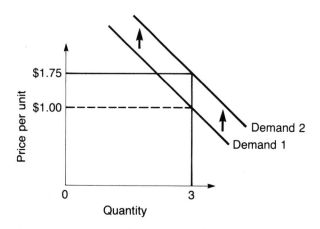

Figure 3-9. An increase in demand with no change in quantity.

Figure 3-10. A de-crease in demand.

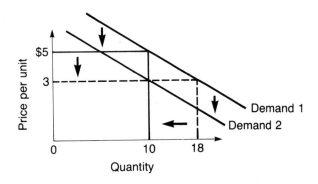

We can interpret decrease in demand the same way: (1) The decrease can be thought of as a reduction in the *quantities* demanded, with no change in price. (2) It can be thought of as a drop in *price* necessary to cause the buyer to demand the same quantity. Both cases are shown in Figure 3-10. If the price remains at $3, the quantity demanded will decrease from 18 to 10. The Demand 1 line shows that the buyer is willing to pay $5 apiece for 10 units. To persuade him or her to buy that same quantity, Demand 2 shows that the price must fall to $3.

Demand with multiple buyers

Fred and Sinbad were two individuals haggling. But the forces of demand (and supply) often represent the buying (or selling) decisions of many buyers and sellers. The example that follows helps to explain how a demand curve can be drawn to represent the buying decisions of several people.

Suppose there are 26 of you in your economics class. Imagine something that a lot of you want—say, an eight-track stereo tape deck with amplifier and a pair of speakers. Suppose each student wrote on a piece of paper what he or she would pay for one of these stereo combinations. When these "dollar votes" are all in, the results might look like Table 3-3.

TABLE 3-3 Prices 26 Students Would Pay for a Stereo

Student	Would pay	Student	Would pay	Student	Would pay
A	$300	J	$200	S	$100
B	50	K	100	T	500
C	150	L	300	U	0
D	450	M	50	V	0
E	600	N	40	W	5
F	75	O	400	X	1
G	0	P	10	Y	50
H	5	Q	0	Z	125
I	2.50	R	350		

TABLE 3-4   Demand Schedule for Stereos at Different Prices

If the price were	Number of students who would buy it	Student who would buy at each price
$600	1	Only E
500	2	E and T
450	3	E, T, and D
400	4	E, T, D, and O
350	5	E, T, D, O, and R
300	7	E, T, D, O, R, A, and L
200	8	E, T, D, O, R, A, L, and J
150	9	E, T, D, O, R, A, L, J, and C
125	10	All the above plus Z
100	12	All the above plus K and S
75	13	All the above plus F
50	16	All the above plus B, M, and Y
40	17	All the above plus N
10	18	All the above plus P
5	20	All the above plus H and W
2	21	All the above plus I
1	22	All the above plus X

Believe it or not, we can construct a demand schedule from this information (Table 3-4).

The demand curve would like Figure 3-11. For the sake of simplicity, we have shown only the beginning ($600) and end ($1) of the demand curve. Now the question is, what will happen if the stereo company announces a price of $400? How many sets will the class buy? Answer: four. Only four students are willing to pay that much or more. Once again, notice that the price system rations goods and services. There are 18 other students who

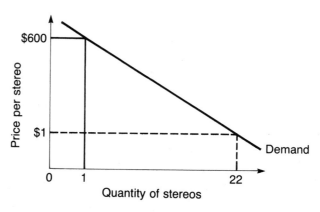

Figure 3-11. Demand curve for stereos at different prices.

would have purchased a stereo set for $350 or less. Some of them perhaps just did not want it badly enough, but others were probably excluded for financial reasons.

Is there really a demand curve?

The search for the demand curve in the real world is as elusive as searching for a pot of gold at the end of a rainbow. The entrepreneur can never be sure what the demand curve for his or her product looks like or whether or not it is shifting. People's attitudes, products, and other prices are changing constantly. But even if a demand curve for any particular product is hard to chart, it does exist. Knowing what controls the demand curve will help the intelligent entrepreneur study the market—the attitudes of people who buy the product—so that after experimentation and experience he or she can begin to forecast what will happen when prices are changed or when important buying habits of the customers change. Many entrepreneurs who may never have studied economics probably have an intuitive "feel" for their buyers' demand.

Supply: How Much Suppliers Offer at Various Prices

The other important force that determines price is supply. The supplier is anyone who produces or sells a good or service. **Supply** is defined as the maximum number of units a supplier of a product will offer for sale at various prices during some period of time.

Take as an example Hugh, a college freshman who lives at home and commutes to school in his 1968 car. The expenses of his car (repainting it, replacing the oil pump, buying new tires) have left him in great need of cash. Having washed windows at home, Hugh decided to try making some money at it and so he placed an ad in the local newspaper:

Windows washed. Exper'd. Professional equip. Call Hugh. 323-4772 eves.

Hugh received several phone calls, but when asked about rates he found he did not know what to charge.

Let us think of Hugh as the supplier of a service, window washing. How should he determine the price of his service? What will determine his supply decisions more than anything else?

Hugh's estimate about his *costs of production* will dictate the number of windows Hugh will wash at various prices. In Hugh's case, production costs consist of gasoline used to drive to the job, "professional equipment" (ladder, bucket, squeegee, soap, and chamois), and the opportunity costs of giving up driving around with his friends or doing homework. After Hugh estimates these costs, he must decide how many windows he will wash at each price people (demanders) are willing to pay. Thus, for Hugh as for any worker or firm, his supply decisions are *based on estimates of the cost of production.*

Assume now that Hugh is willing to wash 30 windows if the price is 50 cents per window and that, in fact, people do pay the 50 cents. (Here our model requires a large assumption: Hugh has in mind windows of only a

As the price per window that people were willing to pay went up, Hugh was willing to spend more time at window washing.

given size—unreal, but it won't hurt our conclusions.) At this rate Hugh is able to earn $15 per week. He does a good job, and his customers begin to tell others. The local newspaper helps by continuing to run his ad at very low cost.

As time goes by, Hugh's working hours begin to increase and the opportunity cost of sacrificing more leisure begins to increase—another way of saying that the cost of production increases. If Hugh had very little to do and lots of leisure time, one hour more or less of leisure time would have little importance. But if time in class, studying, and working, total say, 12 hours per day, one hour more or less for leisure would become more important.

He refuses to work more hours unless the price rises; however, he discovers, fortunately, that his customers will indeed pay more. He raises his price, first to 60 cents per window, then to 70 cents, and finally to 80 cents. As the price per window that people were willing to pay went up, he was willing to spend more time at window washing. The increased price per window offset the increased opportunity cost of lost leisure.

Like most suppliers of goods and services, Hugh will be motivated to increase the quantities he supplies as the price rises.

Supply schedule and supply curve

We can visualize a **supply schedule** for Hugh's service as shown in Table 3-5. When we graph these numbers in the usual way (Figure 3-12), putting price on the vertical axis and quantity (number of windows) on the horizontal axis, we have a **supply curve.**

TABLE 3-5   Hugh's Supply Schedule

Price per window	Windows Hugh will wash per week at each price
50¢	30
60	35
70	40
80	45

Compare Figure 3-12 (Hugh's supply curve) with Figure 3-13 (Fred's demand curve). Notice that the supply curve rises from left to right (a direct relationship), indicating that as the price rises the quantity supplied increases. The demand curve, on the other hand, falls from left to right. Price and quantity are inversely related on anyone's demand curve (or schedule).

The supply curve reveals again the operation of the price system. It determines the availability and use of resources—in this case Hugh's *labor*; his *capital*, in the form of the car, ladder, bucket, squeegee, and chamois; and his various materials from the *land*, such as soap and gasoline.

Just as demand does not change as we move along the demand curve, supply does not change as we along the supply curve. As the price rises, Hugh is willing to wash more windows, but there has been no change

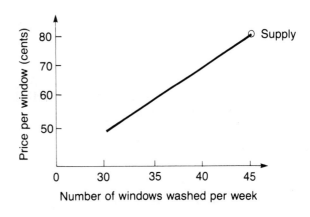

Figure   3-12.   Hugh's supply curve.

Figure 3-13. Fred's demand curve.

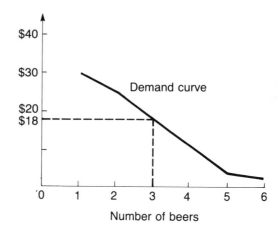

in supply. Hugh's supply curve—the number of windows he will wash at various prices in some period of time—changes *only* when he will wash fewer or more windows with *no* change in price.

The role of expectations   Let's leave Hugh for a moment and think of a business firm producing hundreds of units—say, tubes of Dazzle toothpaste—per week. If demand for the toothpaste increases, Dazzle executives will sense that they can raise the price, thereby increasing profit, and this expectation will motivate them to increase the quantity supplied. Thus, even the expectation that demand may increase (shift to the right) gives the green light to suppliers. The expectation that higher profits will come from higher prices helps to explain the direct relationship between price and the quantity supplied, and the fact that the supply curve is positively sloped upward from left to right.

Changes in supply   For supply to change we must have a whole new supply schedule and, correspondingly, a new supply curve. Suppose Hugh discovers a much easier way to wash windows—perhaps a better squeegee or better soap. The costs of production that determine Hugh's supply decisions now drop. Economists would call this a *technological change.* Hugh can now wash more windows in less time per window and make more money. Assume he will be willing to charge less per window.* His new supply schedule is shown in Table 3-6.

When we graph these two schedules, we see that the supply curve shifts to the right (Figure 3-14). S_1 is the old supply curve; S_2 is the new one. Figure 3-14 illustrates the same principles we observed in Figures 3-8 and 3-9. The change (increase) in supply can be thought of in either of two ways: (1) at a given price of, say 60 cents, the quantity offered for sale has increased from

---

*No seller in his or her right mind will offer the same quantities at the same price—regardless of improvements—unless forced to do so by competitors, *as we will see later in this chapter.*

TABLE 3-6 Supply Schedule and Technological Change

Windows Hugh will wash per week at each price	Old prices per window (in cents)	New prices per window (in cents)
30	50¢	40¢
35	60	50
40	70	60
45	80	70

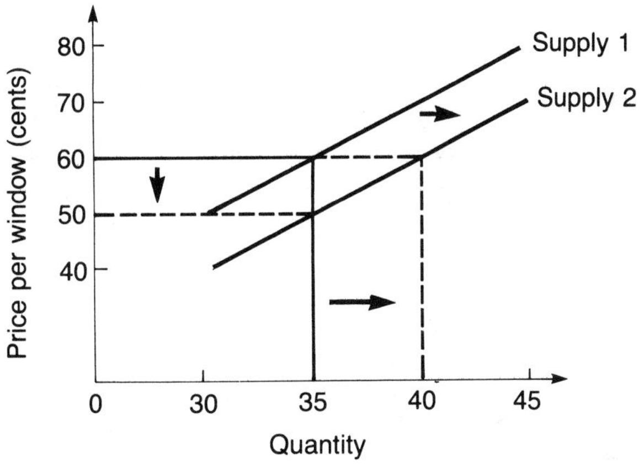

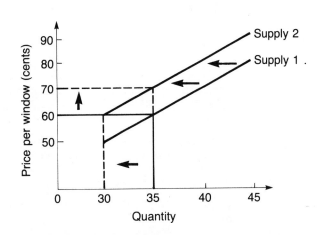

Figure 3-14. Increase in supply.

35 windows to 40 windows; or (2) at a given quantity of, say, 35 windows, Hugh's price for that quantity has dropped from 60 cents to 50 cents.

Let us visualize for a moment a shift to the left of the supply curve (Figure 3-15). The shift to the left indicates that Hugh will not wash 35 windows per week unless the price rises from 60 cents to 70 cents. The shift

Figure 3-15. Decrease in supply and a higher price.

to the left also indicates that, at a price of 60 cents, the number of windows he will wash drops from 35 to 30. The shift to the left represents a decrease in supply.

Why would these changes occur? The higher price for a given quantity could mean that Hugh's expenses have risen or that he places a higher value on lost leisure. It takes a higher price to persuade him to wash the same number of windows. The reduced quantity of windows at any price is simply another effect of these same causes.

There are three reasons for changes in supply, which may occur singly or in combination.

1. Changes in production costs

The supply curve will change if there are changes in the costs of production. If costs rise (owing to a tax increase, say, or a new union contract), the supply will generally shift to the left. Economists usually refer to this as a decrease or reduction in supply because less will be offered at each price. If costs fall because of a technological change or because of lower prices for resources or materials, the supply curve will shift to the right.

The shift to the right might also occur because a government subsidy offsets some of the entrepreneur's costs. The entrepreneur will be willing to increase the quantities offered at each price because his cost of production is lower.

We should also include in production cost changes any change in the entrepreneur's evaluation of the opportunity cost of sacrificed leisure—or any change in his preferences for money instead of leisure.

2. Change in number of suppliers

Generally, an increase in the number of suppliers (competitors) will cause the supply curve to shift to the right, driving the price down for any given quantity. A shift to the left will occur if there are fewer suppliers—less competition—enabling the remaining suppliers to raise prices for any given quantity.

3. Change in suppliers' expectations

Any change in the entrepreneur's expectations about the future will shift the supply curve. If he expects future misfortune (unemployment), he may be willing to work harder now to salt away some money, and the supply curve will shift to the right. Or, if the entrepreneur expects future sales to drop, he or she may reduce output. If the future looks bright and secure, he might say, "Great, I'll take it a little easier," and his supply curve will shift to the left.

It is often helpful for beginning economics students to think of demand and supply as separate forces, representing the desires of consumers on the one hand and producers on the other. It is also important to remember that the capability of a producer or a country to supply is often independent of what consumers may wish to buy. In the real world, however, particularly in a relatively free society like our own, demand and supply are usually interdependent. Supply may shift because suppliers expect future changes in demand, and demand may shift because buyers expect future changes in supply.

How Prices Are Determined

The two forces of demand and supply operate together to determine the prices and quantities of everything bought and sold—of all resources and all goods and services. In our society, they largely (but not completely) answer the question of *what* will be produced and sold (and in what quantities) and *how* and *for whom* they will be produced.

Prices are a measure of the value our society attaches to any good, service, or resource. The market price is determined by a compromise between the buyer's demand and the supplier's desire to supply. Market prices have a way of equalizing the quantities supplied with the quantities demanded. But when the forces of demand and supply are not free to determine prices, shortages and surpluses may develop.

Adjusting to shortages and surpluses

Table 3-7 presents some estimates of how many six-packs of Schmaltz Beer can be produced and sold at various price levels in a given week. We can see that at a price per six-pack of $1.60, 2,200 six-packs of Schmaltz will be produced and sold per week. At that price, the desires of demanders and supplier coincide.

If the price were $1.80, the supplier would produce 2,600 six-packs but only 1,000 would be purchased—there would be a *surplus* of 1,600 six-packs. If this happened, the supplier would gradually lower his price toward $1.60 until the unsold six-packs were gone.

TABLE 3-7 Price, Quantities Supplied, and Quantities Demanded for Schmaltz Beer

	Price per six-pack	Quantities supplied at each price per week	Quantities demanded at each price per week
Surplus	$2.20	3,400	0
	2.00	3,000	500
	1.80	2,600	1,000
Equilibrium	$1.60	2,200	2,200
Shortage	$1.40	1,800	3,000
	1.20	1,400	3,500
	1.00	1,000	4,000

If the price were $1.40, the supplier would produce 1,800 six-packs, but consumers would want to buy 3,000. There would be a *shortage* of 1,200 six-packs. If consumers were not getting all they wanted at some price, some of them might start offering higher prices. The price would start to creep up. Would the price start to creep up for some of the beer or all the beer the supplier had on hand? Answer: all of the beer. The supplier would have no reason to charge some people $1.40 when he can sell all the beer he has on hand for $1.60. Competition among buyers will force the price up to $1.60, where the quantity demanded is exactly equal to the quantity supplied.

To summarize this important point: If, at a given price, the quantity supplied exceeds the quantity demanded, the price will fall. If, at a given price, the quantity demanded exceeds the quantity supplied, the price will rise. If there is nothing to prevent these adjustments (price controls, for example), the price will reach a point where the quantity demanded equals the quantity supplied.

It is well to stress that surpluses and shortages are unlikely as long as the price is free to change; that is, there is always some price where the quantity demanded and the quantity supplied are equal.

Finding the equilibrium price

We call the price that makes the quantity demanded equal to the quantity supplied an **equilibrium price.** Economists use the word *equilibrium* to mean that automatic forces in the market will cause the price to move toward the price at which the quantity supplied will equal the quantity demanded. The equilibrium price sets the *value* of a product in our society. With our beer example, it determines the quantities of resources (land, labor, capital, and entrepreneurship) necessary to produce 2,200 units and the sacrifices consumers are prepared to make to buy those units.

Because at the equilibrium price the quantity demanded equals the quantity supplied, with no shortage or surplus, economists speak of the equilibrium price as the price that "clears the market" of any surplus. All goods produced are sold.

Notice also that at prices below $1.60 many more six-packs might be sold. Table 3-9 shows that if the price were $1, 4,000 six-packs would be demanded. If the price were less than $1.60, many who were unwilling to pay $1.60, or who could not afford to pay $1.60, would be willing to buy. When the price is $1.60, however, these people are excluded from the market. Remember the exclusion principle. Any price excludes some people, because the market-price system is a rationing device. The higher the price, the more people are excluded.

The equilibrium price of $1.60 can be shown on a graph (Figure 3-16) that combines the demand curve (D) and the supply curve (S). Figure 3-16 illustrates the point that the equilibrium price of $1.60 occurs at the intersection of the demand and supply curves. At that price—and only at that price—the quantity supplied and the quantity demanded will be equal, in this case at 2,200 six-packs. Will everyone be happy? No. At any price higher

Figure 3-16. Equilibrium price.

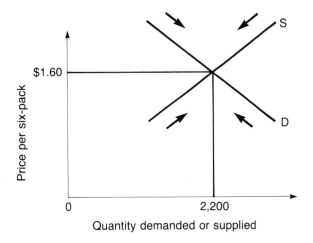

than $1.60, the supplier would have been eager to supply more beer—perhaps by hiring more people. But if the supplier tries to sell more than 2,200 six-packs at a price higher than $1.60 each, he will not succeed; consumers will not go along. The arrows indicate the automatic movements of price and quantity if the price is temporarily above or below the equilibrium price.

Let us go one step further. Figure 3-17 shows the surplus that occurs if the price at $1.80 is *above* equilibrium. The price line at $1.80 intersects the demand line at 1,000 units and the supply line at 2,600—the difference between demand and supply (1,600 units) is the surplus. Remember that if the price is above equilibrium, suppliers will get nervous about the unsold surplus and will tend to lower their price toward the equilibrium price. (The equilibrium price and quantity are shown in dotted lines.) Thus, when the price is above equilibrium, the price will tend to come down. As the price comes down, the quantity demanded will increase. The surplus will gradually evaporate as price and quantity approach equilibrium.

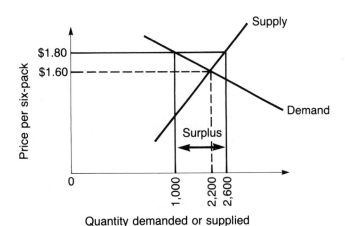

Figure 3-17. Picture of a surplus.

Figure 3-18. Picture of a shortage.

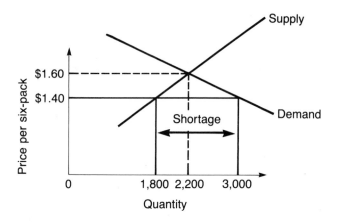

Now let us look at a picture of a shortage in Figure 3-18. At a price of $1.40, the price line intersects the supply curve at 1,800 six-packs and the demand curve at 3,000 six-packs. Thus, the horizontal distance between the two curves reveals the shortage of 1,200 six-packs. Because there is a shortage, the price will tend to rise as demanders bid the price up or as suppliers increase their prices. When price and quantity reach equilibrium, the shortage will disappear.

The Importance of Competition

Throughout this discussion we've omitted saying anything about *how fast* a market for any good or service will adjust to the equilibrium price.

Suppose for a moment that the price is below equilibrium and that there is only *one* buyer—you, for example. At the below-equilibrium price, suppliers aren't willing to supply the quantity you want to buy. From your point of view, there is a shortage at that price. If there were other buyers in the market, some of them might offer a higher price, and you would be forced to compete with them exactly as if you were participating in an auction. The price would surely rise. But if no other buyers are present, you can say to the supplier, "Either sell your products to me at the price I'm offering, or you won't sell any." The supplier can, of course, reply, "You're not going to get the quantities you want at this low price. My production costs won't permit it."

So, a period of haggling will ensue. The speed—and magnitude—of the price movement upward will depend on the power each one can exert on the other. The extent of this power—often called **"market power"**—will depend on whether or not you, the buyer, can find a reasonably close substitute at a price you are willing to pay and on whether or not the seller can locate any other, more willing, buyers.

By the same token, if the price is above equilibrium, a supplier might not worry about the resulting surplus if he or she is the only supplier. The supplier can say, "I'll wait and see if I can't force more buyers to meet my price." But if there are lots of suppliers and there is a general surplus in the market, then surely competition will force the price down. The magnitude of the price decrease will depend on the number of suppliers and how intensely they compete.

Consequently, we can see that price movements in the market are the result of competition among buyers and sellers. The speed and magnitude of price adjustments will depend on the intensity of this competition.

Competition in markets has a particularly important bearing on movements of the supply curve. Suppose, as on page 56, Hugh finds a cheaper way to wash windows, will his supply curve *necessarily* shift to the right? Will he *necessarily* agree to wash more windows at the same or lower prices? Why not keep his price the same and make more money in less time?

The answer is that he will have no reason to drop the price *unless* he has a competitor—someone else who offers Hugh's customers a better deal. Competition *is* important.

Suppose that in the "real world" an oil company, steel company, automobile manufacturer, or any enterprise that is likely to have considerable market power finds a way to produce more of its product at no increase in (or perhaps even lower) cost. Will that firm shift its supply curve to the right and lower its prices? Why not simply use the opportunity to increase profits and keep prices where they were? Or even raise them? Answer again: no reason unless the firm has competitors who are offering the same, or almost the same, goods or services at lower prices.

This question of competition is particularly acute in the oil business. Why should an oil company increase its production (even if prices are higher) if it is not forced to do so by competitive oil companies? We mention this point because the oil companies have been accused of cooperating with one another in determining price and output policies. More on this in Chapter 6.

Price competition may therefore encourage firms to move their supply curves to the right. Lack of price competition tends to keep supply curves where they are or even to cause them to shift to the left (for example, a decision by OPEC, the Organization of Petroleum Exporting Countries, to reduce oil production so oil prices can be further increased). The degree of competition may also determine the amount of price uniformity among different brands of the same product. If the market is highly competitive, the price of all brands will tend to be the same. If it is not, buyers will switch to the lower-priced brands. But we must be cautious here. Uniform and, usually higher, prices can also exist when there are a few very large producers, say, of automobiles, who tend to cooperate with one another in noncompetitive ways.

A final point. One very important element in price movements is the amount of *information* buyers and sellers have about the market. In very competitive markets, information about who is selling what for what price is easy to obtain. Sellers constantly bombard buyers with information (not always correct) about the price and quality of their products. In such a market, adjustments will be fast, and the price will tend toward uniformity. But, again, there are also markets where it is very difficult to get a clear picture about prices and qualities. Life insurance policies are one example. In this type of market, price adjustments will tend to be slow and price differences (even for essentially the same product) may exist. We will take up this important topic again in Chapter 7.

Summary

Prices serve three purposes in the market-price system: (1) they direct the use of resources; (2) they ration goods and services; and (3) they measure the relative values of everything in society.

Prices are determined by demand and supply. Economists define demand as the number of units of a product a buyer will be willing and able to buy during some period of time at various prices. The law of demand holds that, as the price falls, the quantity demanded increases. This occurs because (1) a consumer can afford to buy more if the price is lower (income effect); (2) the satisfaction he derives from each additional unit decreases with each additional unit he purchases; and (3) as the price of a product decreases, he will buy it instead of other products he might have bought (substitution effect).

On a graph, economists usually represent demand by a line sloping down from left to right, with prices on the vertical axis and quantity on the horizontal. When demand increases—when a buyer will pay more for every quantity—the line shifts to the right. When demand decreases, the line shifts to the left. Demand changes when (1) the buyer's income increases or decreases; (2) his or her tastes change; (3) the prices of other products change; (4) the buyer's expectations about the future change; or (5) the total number of buyers change.

There is an important distinction between movement along a demand or supply curve and a change in the curve. Changes in demand and supply occur only when the curve changes. The significance of this idea is that when the curve changes, more or less will be demanded or supplied without changes in price.

Supply is defined as the number of units a producer or seller of a product will offer for sale at various prices during some period of time. Economists represent supply graphically by a line sloping up from left to right. This direction of slope indicates that, as higher prices are paid for a product, more will be supplied.

A change in supply is represented by a shift in the supply curve. When the line shifts to the left, supply decreases because a smaller quantity will be offered at each price and a higher price is necessary for any given quantity. When the line shifts to the right, supply increases because a larger quantity will be offered at each price and because the same quantities will be offered at lower prices.

The two forces, supply and demand, operate together to determine all prices and quantities of everything bought and sold, thereby determining how much value our society attaches to any good, service, or resource. When shortages occur at a given price, the price tends to increase, causing the quantity supplied to increase until an equilibrium price is reached. When the equilibrium price is reached, the quantity demanded equals the quantity supplied. There is no shortage or surplus. The market is "cleared." Similarly, when a surplus occurs at a given price, the price tends to decrease, causing the quantity demanded to increase until an equilibrium is reached.

The degree of competition in a market will determine how fast price adjustments occur.

Discussion Questions

1. What is your demand curve for something you buy regularly (perhaps phonograph records or tapes)? Is it a straight line? Is the slope of the line steeper at lower prices than it is at higher prices? Why might this be? Jot down some prices and quantities of what you would buy over some period of time and try plotting a demand curve on some graph paper.

2. If the price of coffee rises from $4 to $4.50 per pound, will a change in demand occur? Why or why not?

3. If your employer offers you a raise and you decide to increase your working hours from 30 hours to 40 hours per week, what happens to your personal supply curve? What happens to your employer's demand for your services? See if you can diagram what happens and explain the diagram.

4. Why is competition important in analyzing shifts in supply?

5. Assume that the following table provides weekly demand and supply data for gasoline at your local gasoline station:

Quantities demanded (thousands of gallons)	Price per gallon	Quantities supplied (thousands of gallons)
40	$1.10	5
30	1.30	15
20	1.50	20
10	1.80	30
5	1.90	40

(a) First graph the data on graph paper.

(b) What will the equilibrium price be? Why?

(c) At what prices will there be lines of waiting cars with angry drivers? Why?

(d) What would you do to get rid of the lines? Would everyone be happy?

Reference   "City Moves on Leg Power," *Los Angeles Times*, 3 August 1976, pt. i, p. 1.

3A Time Out for Graphs

Clif Garboden/Stock, Boston

Economists often use graphs to illustrate their models. A *graph* is a picture of the relationship between two variables. A *variable* is simply a quantity whose numerical value is allowed to change. One variable is shown on the horizontal axis, and the other is shown on the vertical axis (see Figure 3A-1).

Figure 3A-1. How economists use graphs to picture relationship between two variables.

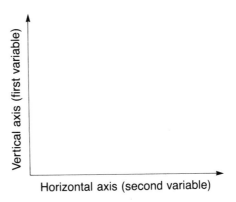

To take a simple example, suppose you have $10 in your pocket. With it you can buy 5 $2 movie tickets or 10 $1 six-packs of a soft drink. If you buy 5 movie tickets, you can buy zero six-packs. If you buy 4 movie tickets ($8), you will have $2 left and can buy 2 $1 six-packs. We can represent this relationship by a table. (Table 3A-1).

TABLE 3A-1 Movie Tickets or Six-Packs?

Number of $2 movie tickets	Number of $1 six-packs
5	0
4	2
3	4
2	6
1	8
0	10

Let us graph the relationship by putting the number of movie tickets on the horizontal axis and the number of six-packs on the vertical axis (Figure 3A-2). Note that in each case we start with 0 at the intersection of the horizontal and vertical axis (called the *origin*) and increase the numbers at equal intervals, moving right on the horizontal axis and up on the vertical axis.

Suppose we want to represent the option, 3 movie tickets and 4 six-packs. We read up from the horizontal axis at 3 to a point opposite 4 on the vertical axis, and we find a point that represents the combination of 4 six-packs and 3 movie tickets on the graph. If we find all of the points in the table and connect them by a line, we have a graph that slopes downward

Figure 3A-2. How to locate a point on a graph.

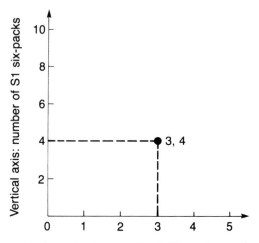

Horizontal axis: number of $2 movie tickets

from the left to the right, as shown in Figure 3A-3. This is called an *inverse relationship*, because the more movie tickets we buy the fewer six packs and vice versa—as one variable increases, the other decreases. (This example also illustrates opportunity cost: each additional movie ticket costs 2 six-packs; each additional six-pack costs one-half of a movie ticket.)

Now let us illustrate a *direct relationship*, one in which, as one variable increases, so does the other. Suppose you are earning $200 a week. You spend $180 and save $20. Now suppose you get a series of $5 raises—to $205, $210, $215, and so forth. With each $5 raise, you increase your spending $4—to $184, $188, $192 . . . This time we will cut out the part of the graph from 0 to $200 on the horizontal axis and from 0 to $180 on the vertical axis to

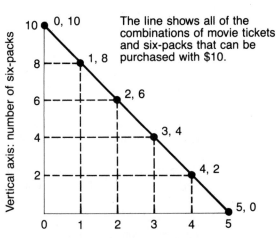

The line shows all of the combinations of movie tickets and six-packs that can be purchased with $10.

Figure 3A-3. Example of inverse relationship.

Horizontal axis: number of movie tickets

Figure 3A-4. Example of direct relationship.

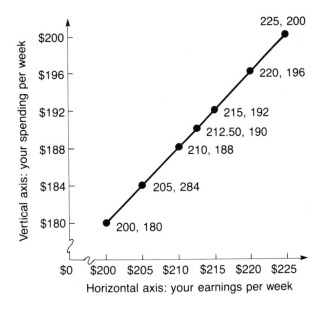

save space; the broken lines illustrate this omission. As Figure 3A-4 shows, the line connecting the points now slopes upward from left to right and represents a direct relationship. Graphs are handy to use because with one line we can represent many points—$200/$180, $205/$184, and so on—and even points in between, $212.50/$190.

Even when we don't know the exact numbers, a graph is a picture showing us instantly what the relationship is between two variables. What if the graph looked as shown in Figure 3A-5?

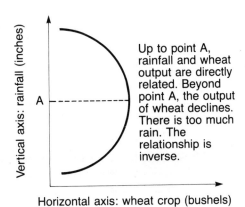

Up to point A, rainfall and wheat output are directly related. Beyond point A, the output of wheat declines. There is too much rain. The relationship is inverse.

Figure 3A-5. A changing relationship between two variables.

Graphs can also tell us if one variable has a large or small effect on the other. Let's consider the response of buyers to price changes for boxes of toothpicks:

Price per box (in cents)	Quantities an average family will buy every six months
10	2
15	2

The graph would look like Figure 3A-6.

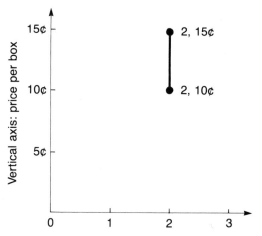

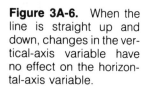

Figure 3A-6. When the line is straight up and down, changes in the vertical-axis variable have no effect on the horizontal-axis variable.

Suppose, however, we change the quantities as follows:

Price per box (in cents)	Quantities purchased
10	5
15	2

The graph would then look like Figure 3A-7. In other words, as the line becomes more horizontal, changes in the vertical-axis variable cause larger changes in the horizontal-axis variable. The slope of the line tells us as much as the direction of the line.

One more example: Malthus worried about population increasing faster and faster and food production lagging behind. We can visualize this predicament on a graph (Figure 3A-8). Food and population increases are both

Figure 3A-7. A small change on vertical axis produces a large change on horizontal axis.

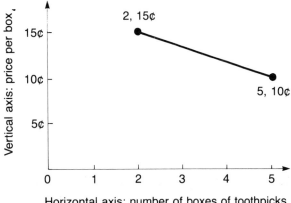

positively related with time, but the rising population curve shows an increasing rate of increase. In each 100 years the increase in population is greater than in the previous 100 years, as shown by the little triangles under the population line. Food production increases, but more slowly and the gap between population and food becomes larger and larger.

We hope this brief explanation has made you feel more comfortable with graphs. Remember that they are just pictures designed to show the effect of one variable on another—like the effect of caloric intake on weight, or, as in Chapter 3, the effect of prices on the quantities of things people will buy or sell. You will be looking at many more graphs throughout this book. We hope you will find them understandable, interesting, and useful.

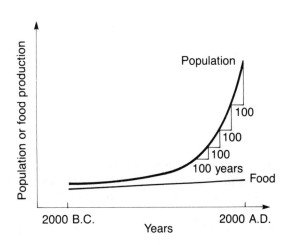

Figure 3A-8. Population increases faster than food.

4 Price Changes, Shortages, and Surpluses

© Janet Fries, 1979.

We have seen how buyers and sellers can arrive at an equilibrium price, so that the quantities supplied match the quantities demanded. In free markets, there is an automatic tendency for the price to achieve this equilibrium. Now let us discuss three variations on this theme: (1) price changes caused by shifts in demand and supply, (2) price changes when demand or supply is fixed, and (3) the effects of government price fixing.

Key Words

Qualitative changes   Variable prices

Variable supply   Fixed demand

Fixed supply   Price floor

Reservation price   Price ceiling

Price Changes Caused by Shifts in Demand and Supply

First we'll take a look at shifts in demand and shifts in supply, and see how all these changes affect prices.

Shifts in demand

The equilibrium price for everything is constantly changing. Consider the following example of demand and supply at your local gas station. Currently, the demand and supply schedules are about as shown in Table 4-1. Equilibrium price and quantity are clearly at $1.40 per gallon. At that price, the quantities demanded and supplied are equal.

TABLE 4-1. Demand and Supply of Argonaut Gasoline at Your Local Station (per week)

Price per gallon	Gallons supplied	Gallons demanded	
$1.20	4,000	8,000	
1.30	5,000	7,000	
1.40	6,000	6,000 ←	Equilibrium
1.50	7,000	5,000	
1.60	8,000	4,000	
1.70	9,000	3,000	

Now let's assume an increase in demand. Table 4-2 shows what happens. The new equilibrium price is now $1.50, where the quantities supplied and demanded (column 4) are equal at 7,000 gallons per week. Figure 4-1 shows the increase in demand graphically. Remember that there is *no change in supply*, because the supply curve has not shifted; there is only a *change in the quantity supplied.* (Review page 46 in Chapter 3 if you're not clear on this point.)

TABLE 4-2 Demand and Supply of Argonaut Gasoline at Your Local Station (per week)

(1) Price per gallon	(2) Gallons supplied	(3) Old gallons demanded	(4) New gallons demanded	
$1.20	4,000	8,000	10,000	
1.30	5,000	7,000	9,000	
1.40	6,000	6,000	8,000	
1.50	7,000	5,000	7,000	New equilibrium
1.60	8,000	4,000	6,000	
1.70	9,000	3,000	5,000	

What conclusions can we draw from this model of a gasoline market? When an increase in demand (shown by the horizontal arrows) occurs with no change in supply, there will be—*ceteris paribus*—an increase in the equilibrium price (shown by the vertical arrow) and an increase in the quantity bought and sold.

Now let's think about blue jeans. What would happen if dermatologists announced that wearing blue jeans causes skin disease? Assuming no change in supply, a decrease in demand will occur; the equilibrium price will fall and the quantities demanded and supplied will also fall. Figure 4-2 illustrates this effect.

In this figure we have adopted a common labeling practice: P_1 and P_2 mean first and second prices. (P_1 might represent $20 a pair; P_2 could mean $15 a pair.) Q_1 and Q_2 mean first and second quantities. D_1 and D_2 mean first and second (old and new) demand curves. The arrows help to show the changes in demand, price, and quantity.

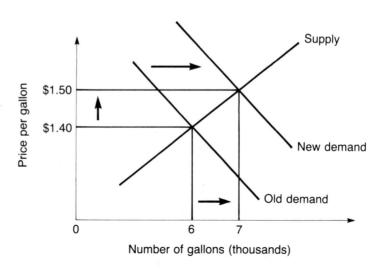

Figure 4-1. Effect of an increase in demand on prices and sales of Argonaut gasoline (per week).

Figure 4-2. Effect of a decrease in demand: price and quantity decrease.

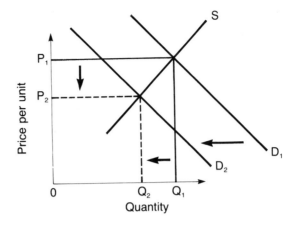

Shifts in supply   Shifts in supply will also have an effect on prices. Suppose roofing contractors face higher costs because of the higher prices they must pay for tar (a petroleum product). As Figure 4-3 shows, the supply curve shifts to the left because of increases in the cost of production. The equilibrium price of roofing rises from P_1 to P_2, assuming no change in demand, and the quantity falls.

If roofing contractors find it cheaper to install new roofs, visualize the supply curve shifting to the right, causing a drop in the price and an increase in the quantity demanded.

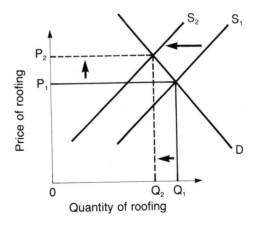

Figure 4-3. A decrease in supply.

Shifts in both supply and demand   If both supply and demand change, the result is difficult to forecast. It all depends on the direction of the shifts and whether or not supply shifts *more* or *less* than demand. (In the following figures, the two equilibriums are circled.) Let's assume that supply shifts more than demand and that both increase (Figure 4-4). The price falls as the quantity rises. What happens if supply and demand both increase, as in Figure 4-4, but demand rises more than supply, as in Figure 4-5? This time the increase in demand offsets the increase in supply and the price rises. In both cases, quantity rises.

Figure 4-4. Supply increases more than demand.

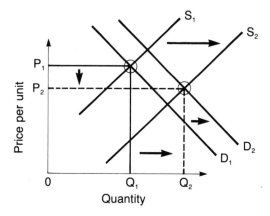

You should now be able to diagram what happens if supply and demand both decrease. If demand decreases more than supply, both price and quantity fall. If supply decreases more than demand, the price rises and quantity falls.

Figure 4-5 helps to explain what is currently happening in several markets where prices are rising probably because demand is increasing faster than supply: health care, housing, and oil products. However, there are difficulties in analyzing each situation. For example, health care expenditures are rising four times faster than average prices, but the increasing cost of health care may be partly because the *product* itself is changing; we now have sophisticated and very expensive machines for diagnosis and treatment that did not exist twenty years ago. Also, changes in the quality of a good or service **(qualitative changes)** are difficult to include in our demand-supply models; for example, changes in the quality of housing make price increases in that market hard to analyze.

The market for oil products is somewhat easier to understand. A barrel of crude oil is a barrel of crude oil. The product and its quality hasn't changed much over the years, but the price certainly has.

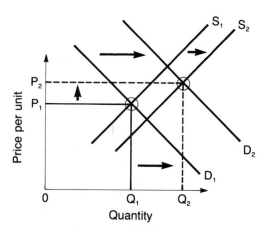

Figure 4-5. Demand increases more than supply.

The case of energy   The energy crisis (covered in more detail in Chapter 6), at least during 1960–1977, is an excellent example of what happens when demand increases more rapidly than supply.

The United States demand for energy increased at about 4 percent per year. Consumption of petroleum products rose from 3.6 billion barrels of oil in 1960 to 6.4 billion barrels in 1976, an 80 percent increase.

What about supply? In 1960, total *domestic* production of crude oil was 2.6 billion barrels. By 1977, this output had increased to about 3 billion barrels, an increase of only 15 percent.

In other words, demand increased 80 percent; supply increased 15 percent. Something had to give. Figure 4-5 tells the story. The price went up.

In this example we considered total consumption but only domestic production. The increased cost of *imported* oil would certainly cause prices to rise even further. These cost increases would be shown on a demand-supply diagram as a *decrease* (shift to the left) in supply because the quantities available at the old prices are now much less (or nonexistent). Figure 4-6 shows what happens to prices when there is an increase in demand and a *decrease* in supply.

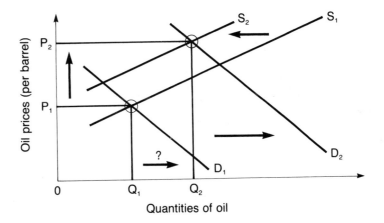

Figure 4-6. An increase in demand and a decrease in supply.

We can see our increase in demand for oil by the shift to the right from D_1 to D_2, which causes the price to rise. The decision by the OPEC countries to raise oil prices is shown by the shift in supply to the left from S_1 to S_2. Suppose the OPEC countries decide to curtail production, as they have on occasion. We would show such reductions in the same way—by a shift to the left of the supply curve. Either way, such changes will cause oil *prices* to rise.

What happens to quantity? (Note the question mark in Figure 4-6). If the decrease in supply is relatively greater than the increase in demand, the new quantity (Q_2) may actually be less than Q_1. The quantity change depends on whether or not supply decreases more than demand increases. Figure 4-6 shows that demand increases more than supply decreases; therefore, the quantity increases.

There is only one original Mona Lisa.

Price Changes When Supply or Demand Is Fixed

All of the supply curves presented so far involve the assumption that the quantity supplied increases as the price increases. The supply curve has been presented as rising from left to right. What does this mean? It means that entrepreneurs (1) are *able*, and (2) have the *time* to increase production when the price rises. The rising supply curve also indicates that higher and higher prices are necessary to persuade the entrepreneur to increase production. Consequently, the rising supply curve usually means that the per unit costs of production are increasing. (Can you visualize a supply curve that slopes *down* from left to right? What would that suggest about production costs? Costs per unit must be decreasing, perhaps because of automation—more efficient production at larger outputs.)

Fixed supply

When entrepreneurs can change the quantities they supply in response to changes in demand, we say that supply is **variable.** However, there are many examples in the real world of **fixed supply**—situations where the quantity supplied cannot change, particularly in a short period of time.

Examples of fixed supply are the number of parking spaces at your college or in your town, the number of hospital beds, theater seats, miles of roads, freeways, airport runways, TV repairmen, power lines, doctors, miles of sewer pipe, and so on. On any given day, the quantity of these things or people is fixed regardless of the price people are willing to pay for them. Another good example of fixed supply is a work of art. There is only one original Mona Lisa or Leaning Tower of Pisa. Finally, fixed supply frequently involves land. In your community there is a fixed amount of land available, whether it is used for industrial expansion, home building, or golf courses.

The question arises, when the supply is fixed, how is price determined? Pretend you own a sporty 1925 antique automobile with a 350-horsepower engine with 16 cylinders and 4 chrome exhausts coming out of the hood. The car is in magnificent condition and will reach 125 miles per hour in 20 seconds.

You decide to sell it. What should the price be? You first decide that you will not sell it unless the price is at least $50,000—it's worth that much to you. This **minimum price** you set is called your **reservation price.** Now, since you belong to a market-price economy, let us suppose you arrange for an auction. At the auction, several wealthy car collectors show up and bid the amounts shown in Table 4-3. The highest bidder, Mrs. Esterhazy, buys the automobile.

TABLE 4-3   Bids for Your 1925 Antique Automobile

Name	Amount bid	
Mr. Arbuthnot	$40,000	Bid rejected
Mr. Bumstead	50,000	
Mrs. Chanceller	60,000	
Mr. Deanville	70,000	
Mrs. Esterhazy	80,000	

What does the demand schedule look like? If the price were $40,000, all five would be willing to buy it; if five cars were available, all five would be sold. At $50,000, we would lose the lowest bidder, and so on. Table 4-4 shows the demand schedule. What does the supply schedule look like? Look at Table 4-5. Note that four of the five bidders are willing to pay the seller's reservation price or more. The two schedules are combined in Figure 4-7. Note that the equilibrium price makes the quantity demanded (1) equal to the quantity supplied.

TABLE 4-4   Demand for an Antique Automobile

Price	Quantity demanded
$40,000	5
50,000	4
60,000	3
70,000	2
80,000	1

TABLE 4-5   Supply Schedule with Reservation Price

Price	Quantity for sale	
$40,000	0	
50,000	1	Reservation price
60,000	1	
70,000	1	
80,000	1	

Figure 4-7. Demand, supply, and equilibrium price with fixed supply.

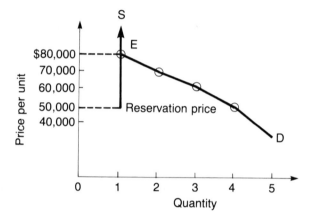

Let's suppose now that demand shifts—the buyers learn during the auction that Al Capone, the Chicago gangster, once owned the car. This makes it even more of a collector's item. Each bidder will now bid $20,000 more than his original bid. What happens to the selling price? It rises by $20,000. The highest bidder wins the car for $100,000.

The analysis of fixed supply has many applications. Suppose that there are 3,000 parking spaces at your college. The parking fee is $5 per semester. At peak hours, 5,000 students want to park. Figure 4-8 illustrates the problem: at $5 there is a shortage of 2,000 parking spaces. E stands for equilib-

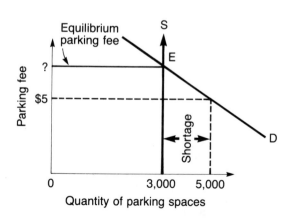

Figure 4-8. Fixed supply and equilibrium price for parking spaces.

rium price (parking fee). What can we do to eliminate the shortage? One solution is to raise the parking fee. There is some fee—at equilibrum—that will eliminate the shortage. Here again the exclusion principle plays a role. Poorer students will be forced into car-pooling or other means of transportation. This is a short-run solution. The college may eventually have to build more parking lots or garages (shifting supply to the right).

This kind of problem can often become more complicated. Suppose you live in a town with 3,000 parking spaces. The parking meters charge 10 cents per hour. Between the hours of 9:00 A.M. and 4:00 P.M. on weekdays, 5,000 people want to park. Between 4:00 P.M. and 9:00 P.M., 3,000 people want to park. Between 9:00 P.M. and 9:00 A.M., 500 people want to park. Figure 4-9 illustrates this situation. D_1 represents the 9:00 P.M.–9:00 A.M. demand, D_2 the 4:00 P.M.–9:00 P.M. demand, and D_3 the 9:00 A.M.–4:00 P.M. demand. E_1 represents the equilibrium price for D_1, E_2 the equilibrium price of D_2, and E_3 the equilibrium price of D_3.

At 10 cents per hour, D_1 shows us there will be a surplus of 2,000 parking spaces (the difference between the 1,000 demanded and the 3,000 available). During those hours, the parking fee could be lowered to 1 cent per hour without causing a shortage of space. The 10-cent charge is just right for D_2, but for D_3 there will be a shortage of 2,000 spaces at 10 cents. Raising the fee to perhaps 25 cents during the most popular shopping hours might solve the shortage. The diagram illustrates an important principle: **variable prices** will solve shortages and surpluses at different times or places.

The concept of fixed supply harks back to Malthus, who believed that the supply of the earth's resources was fixed. With a fixed supply of food or energy, what will happen with continued increases in demand? The price can only go up. If price controls (ceilings) are used to prevent price increases, shortages will result. The only possible solution to this dilemma is to make supply variable through technological advance—by finding more resources or learning how to use our present stock of resources more efficiently.

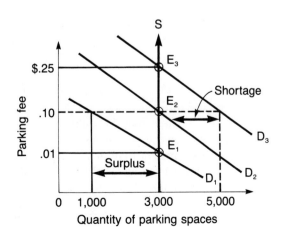

Figure 4-9. Fixed supply and changing demand.

Fixed demand   If demand were fixed, buyers would pay any price from zero to billions of dollars for the good or service in question. The demand curve would be vertical, exactly like the supply curve in Figures 4-8 and 4-9. Such a situation is hard to imagine, but there are probably some situations that approximate it. If the purchase of a good or service is a matter of life or death, we might be willing to give all of our resources and money to obtain it. In this case, we are entirely at the mercy of the supplier, just as Fred was at the mercy of Sinbad in the desert.

More commonplace situations involve the purchase of small quantities of minor items like matches or paper clips. We do not care whether the price is 10 or 15 cents a box. Our demand curve is fixed and vertical because, within that price range, the quantity we will purchase will not vary.

The Effects of Government Price Fixing

From time to time, the government may decide that the equilibrium price is too low and makes suppliers unhappy, or too high and makes consumers unhappy. Congress (or a state legislature) may then pass a law setting a minimum price, below which prices are not allowed to fall, or a maximum price, above which prices are not allowed to rise. Let us see what effects these two actions have.

Price floors and surpluses   When the government legislates a minimum price, that price is called **price floor.** The price is not permitted to fall below that minimum.

The price floor the government sets is independent of the forces of demand and supply. In fact, the price floor might be above, below, or equal to the equilibrium price that prevails at any particular time. However, the government officials' usual reason for setting a minimum price is that they believe the equilibrium price is too low. If, then, the price floor is set at some level above the equilibrium price, the quantity supplied will exceed the quantity demanded, and a *surplus* will result.

The government may then take the surplus (typically farm surpluses) off the market, probably by buying it at the price floor. The cost to taxpayers is the cost of buying the surplus, storing it, disposing of it (often overseas at below-market prices), *and*, as consumers, the higher prices they must pay for the smaller quantities farmers will sell to them.

Figure 4-10 is a picture of a surplus. P stands for the price floor per unit sold. Q_D represents the quantity demanded. Q_s is the quantity supplied. The difference between Q_D and Q_s is the surplus in number of units.

There may be political reasons behind the government's decision to assume the headaches of a surplus: members of a powerful interest group like farmers may demand protection from an equilibrium price that they consider too low. Lobbies and political pressure may lead to the passage of a price-floor law.

Figure 4-10. Picture of a surplus caused by a price floor.

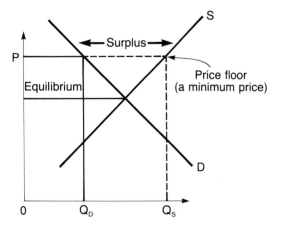

The government may also have an economic reason for a price floor. With a scarce resource such as oil, Congress might be persuaded that the equilibrium price is so low that people will buy too much of the resource. By setting a minimum price that is calculated to be above the market-determined equilibrium, Congress may hope to reduce the quantity demanded and to motivate suppliers to increase the quantity supplied. If the floor is set high enough, the quantity supplied will exceed the quantity demanded, and a surplus will result. In May 1980, President Carter proposed an import tax that would raise gas prices 10¢ a gallon to make the United States less dependent on Arab oil. Opponents argued that higher oil prices would make life more difficult for people with low incomes.

Price ceilings and shortages

When the government legislates a *maximum* price, the maximum legal price is called a **price ceiling.**

Keep in mind that the price ceiling may be above, below, or equal to the equilibrium price. Usually, however, the government believes the equilibrium price will reach a point that is too high.

Economic reasons (the need to control inflation, for example) may cause the government to set a price ceiling by freezing wages and prices if it believes the equilibrium price is too high for people with low incomes. Or the government may want to discourage the production of some item by reducing or eliminating profits for the producer (cars and gasoline for consumer use in wartime).

Even if the government has good reasons for setting price floors or ceiling prices, it faces enormous consequences when it interferes with equilibrium prices.

Assuming the government's maximum price, the price ceiling, is *below* the market-determined equilibrium, the quantity demanded will exceed the quantity supplied. A *shortage* will result.

(Continued on page 86)

Example of a Price Floor: What's a Fair Minimum Wage? (It Depends on Whether You're Employed.)

If the minimum wage is higher than equilibrium, the result may be unemployment.

Under the Fair Labor Standards Act, the government can set minimum hourly wages for all workers employed in interstate industries. The minimum wage is a price floor, because it is apparently above the equilibrium hourly wage for at least one age group—those between 16 and 19.

In 1978, when the federal minimum hourly wage was $2.65,* about 6 million people were unemployed and the unemployment rate for all workers was 6 percent. In that year, the unemployment rate among those between 16 and 19 years of age was about 17 percent—almost three times the national average.

Minimum wage laws are designed to help poorer workers by guaranteeing higher wages. But what if the minimum wage is higher than equilibrium? The result may be unemployment.[1]

The figure on the opposite page illustrates the problem. S represents the supply of teenagers who will work at various hourly wages. D represents the demand for teenage labor. Q_D stands for the person-hours of teenage labor demanded and Q_S for the number available.

*The minimum wage rose to $2.90 in 1979 and was scheduled to rise to $3.35 by January 1, 1981.

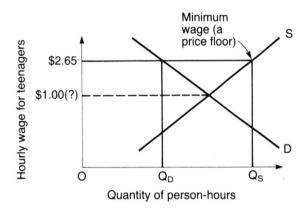

Impact of minimum wage law on teenage unemployment.

For Q_D workers—those hired—everything may be fine; the minimum wage may have raised their income. But the minimum wage, the price floor, has produced unemployment, a surplus of unemployed labor. Economic theory tells us we could have less unemployment and more employment if the wage fell. How far must the wage fall? There is no exact way of knowing (see the question mark at equilibrium).

Suppose the equilibrium wage is $1. At $1 there would be no teenage unemployment, a reminder that there is always an equilibrium price where the quantity demanded is equal to the quantity supplied. Would you favor that? The answer probably depends on whether or not you are unemployed. In any case, the cost of more unemployment may be increased welfare payments. This combination of rising unemployment and increased resort to welfare usually affects those people who are unskilled. The irony is that these are the people the minimum wage law is designed to protect.

The government can, however, take various measures to deal with the labor surplus created by the minimum wage. Just as it can clear the market by buying the surplus wheat produced by farmers when a minimum price for wheat is established, it can eliminate the newly created unemployment by hiring some of the unemployed to work on government projects. It can also lessen the economic loss to those put out of work by providing unemployment insurance, or it can increase the skills of those laid off by offering training programs. Or it can do nothing and allow the newly unemployed to fend for themselves. Recent amendments to the Fair Labor Standards Act have softened the unemployment effect for some groups of workers, by setting lower minimum wages for students and young people under 18 than for adult full-time workers. This change has led to accusations by some that "cheap" labor below age 18 is being substituted for more expensive adult labor, an effect that may be the cost of this particular decision.

Figure 4-11.   Picture of a shortage caused by a price ceiling.

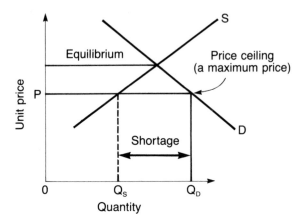

Figure 4-11 is a picture of a *shortage* caused by a price ceiling. This time, P stands for price ceiling per unit sold, and the quantity demanded (Q_D) exceeds the quantity supplied (Q_S). The difference is the shortage in number of units.

The case of rent controls

Rent controls are another example of price ceilings. The reason behind a community's desire for rent controls is that landlords have been raising rents to catch up with rising maintenance costs and taxes and to maximize their profits. But rent control laws in many major cities are serving to frustrate the attempts by landlords to raise the rent.

What happens? Figure 4-11 told the story. Any price below equilibrium like a ceiling on the maximum rents a landlord can charge creates a shortage (or perhaps worsens an already existing one). When landlords find they can't increase rents, they convert their apartment buildings to cooperatives or condominiums.* The National Association of Home Builders estimates that the number of rental units in the United States is declining at the rate of 1.5 percent—or *420,000 apartments*—a year.[2]

In the last eight years, for example, the supply of rental units in Washington, D.C., has dropped from 199,100 to 175,900; in New York City landlords abandon 30,000 units annually because they can't afford upkeep while only 2,000 new units are built.[3]

Rent controls show the shortage side of the fixed-price "coin," as minimum wages showed the surplus side. However, the effects may be similar. Minimum wages hurt the poor—those whom minimum wage laws are designed to protect—and rent controls may hurt those whom controls are designed to protect by reducing the supply of available apartments.

The buyer of a "cooperative" buys shares in a corporation that owns the building and land. He does not actually own the apartment and consequently cannot mortgage it. A condominium buyer owns his apartment outright and the land around the building jointly with other owners. A "condo" buyer can mortgage his property.

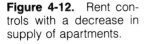

Figure 4-12. Rent controls with a decrease in supply of apartments.

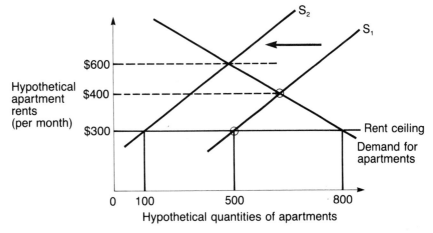

We can modify Figure 4-11 with Figure 4-12 to show not only the rent ceiling but also the decrease in supply.

S_1 represents the supply of apartments before landlords convert them to cooperatives or condominiums. The rent ceiling is set at $300 per month. The equilibrium rent is at $400. In that situation the (hypothetical) shortage is 300 apartments, because at the rent ceiling of $300, 800 units will be demanded but only 500 supplied.

S_2 shows what happens when landlords, frustrated by rent control laws, convert their buildings to cooperatives or condominiums. The decrease in supply of rental units now means that at the ceiling price of $300, only 100 units will be supplied, but 800 units are still demanded. The shortage is now (800 − 100) 700 units instead of 300.

Solving shortages

When there is a shortage, some form of rationing becomes necessary. One way to eliminate the shortage is by allowing the price to rise. If there is a shortage of parking spaces at your college, for instance, the administration may decide to raise student and faculty parking fees. Some people will be unhappy about the solution, of course, but the higher fees will force more car-pooling and bike-riding and the shortage will disappear.

One way an individual may overcome shortages caused by rent controls is to follow a practice common in New York City: Pay the landlord a "key charge"—a "bonus" for handing you the key. A similar, well-recognized way to get the bank to give you a Federal Housing Administration (FHA) mortgage that often carries a below-equilibrium rate of interest is to pay the bank "points"—each "point" being 1 percent of the mortgage. This kind of rationing excludes those without the financial means to engage in these activities.

Another way to overcome shortages is simply to overlook the problem and allow people to stand in long lines waiting to buy. Those seeking parking places, for example, might have to wait in line until an earlier arrival vacates a parking spot. This kind of rationing system (called queuing) excludes those at the end of the line when supplies run out.

The government may also devise an elaborate distribution system. It may issue food stamps or gasoline ration cards; it may ask buyers to fill out forms in quintuplicate; and it may set criteria for buying. During World War II, one had to establish proof of need to obtain a new car or telephone. The eventual result of rationing may be that some suppliers will engage in illegal black-market activities (selling at prices above those legally set by the government), which in turn entail costs to taxpayers in the form of policing, trying criminals, and so forth.

However, while ceilings cause shortages, they do function to control the higher market prices that exclude more people.

These illustrations help to show the usefulness of demand-supply analysis. We can predict that if the price is held above equilibrium, surpluses will result, and that if the price is kept below equilibrium, shortages will result.

Summary

The government may want to help entrepreneurs, farmers, or laborers by preventing prices or wages from falling. These minimum prices or wages are called price floors and tend to produce surpluses, or unemployment in the case of labor markets. Government-legislated maximum prices are called price ceilings. Price ceilings tend to produce shortages.

When supply is variable—that is, when the supply curve rises from left to right—and there are shifts in demand or supply, the price will change, but not by as much as when supply is fixed. When supply is fixed, changes in demand determine price changes. Fixed supply situations are frequently encountered in everyday life, from freeways to the Mona Lisa, from neurosurgeons to parking lots.

There may be some situations in which demand is fixed—situations involving life or death, and cases where price changes do not alter the quantity purchased, as in the purchase of small items.

Discussion Questions

1. If you owned a restaurant, would you charge the same price for a top sirloin steak meal every night of the week? Why or why not? Illustrate your answer with a diagram.

2. If more electric power is used in the summer than in the winter because of air conditioning, what would you suggest that the power companies do?

3. What will be the effects of requiring automobiles to be pollution-free? (What will happen to supply curves?)

4. If we wanted to help the poor by putting a price ceiling of 20 cents on a loaf of bread, what would happen?

5. If we raised the minimum wage to $5 to help unskilled workers stay off welfare, what might happen? Illustrate your answer with a diagram. Would you call such a minimum wage a price floor or a price ceiling?

6. If there were an interest ceiling of 4 percent to help the poor obtain low-cost loans, how would the banks react? Who would get the money? What might the government have to do?

References

1. See Milton Friedman, "Legislating Unemployment," *Newsweek*, 3 July 1972, p. 66.

2. "Apartments Wanted," *Newsweek*, 4 June 1979, p. 79.

3. Ibid.

5 Price Elasticity: How Price Changes Affect Us

Dick Alexander

In the last chapter we saw that price changes will occur with changes in demand and supply. In this chapter we will look at how strongly buyers or sellers respond to increases or decreases in price. The responsiveness of buyers or sellers to price changes is called "price elasticity."

Few topics in economics have so many and important applications in decision making. One example: Suppose we want Americans to reduce their consumption of gasoline by 25 percent. How much will the price have to rise, in percentage terms, for this to happen?

Our discussion of elasticity is divided into four major parts: (1) price elasticity defined, (2) price elasticity of demand, (3) price elasticity of supply, and (4) price elasticity of demand and supply together.

Key Words

Price-elastic   Absolute change

Price-inelastic   Relative change

Total revenue   Coefficient of elasticity

Price Elasticity Defined

Suppose a large department store drops the price of nylon jackets from $12 to $10. Sales thereupon increase from 100 jackets per month to 150. Revenue from sales increases from $1,200 ($12 × 100) to $1,500 ($10 × 150). Provided additional production costs or additional advertising and other selling expenses do not wipe out this gain, the sale is a success.

The demand for the product is thus described as being **price-elastic.** If the demand for something is price-elastic, entrepreneurs will take in more money if they lower the price because the increased volume of purchases will more than make up for lower unit prices. "Price-elastic" means the change in the *quantity* purchased is large relative to the *price* change, that the price change motivates consumers to increase their purchases by more than enough to offset price decreases.

Demand is also shown to be price-elastic when entrepreneurs raise the price and sales revenues fall. If, for instance, the department store raises its price on nylon jackets from $10 to $12, and consumers respond by reducing purchases from 150 per month to 100 and sales revenue falls from $1,500 to $1,200, that demonstrates that demand is price-elastic. Again, consumer response is large relative to the price change.

If, however, the store lowers its price from $12 to $10 and sales increase from 100 jackets per month to 110, demand is **price-inelastic.** The sale has laid an egg. **Total revenue**—which is defined as price times quantity—has dropped from $1,200 ($12 × 100) to $1,100 ($10 × 110). The drop in price was not offset by a sufficient increase in the quantity demanded. Consumers were relatively indifferent to the price change.

Revenues versus profits

A caution is necessary at this point. In the examples above we're thinking only about entrepreneur's *income* from sales—the money that goes into the cash register—not about the entrepreneur's *profit.* The price-elasticity of demand refers to the responsiveness of buyers (changes in the *quantity* demanded) to price changes. The concept says nothing about production costs. When the number of units the entrepreneur sells changes, so will the cost of production. If increased sales mean increased production costs, and the increase in cost is greater than the increase in revenue, profits will fall. Similarly, a reduction in sales volume could also be accompanied by lower production costs and profits could rise. Thus, we must take both costs and revenues into account in order to determine whether or not the price change was wise.

The drop in price was not offset by a sufficient increase in the quantity demanded.

Economists will often refer to the "demand side" or the "supply side" to help clarify whether they are talking about the responsiveness of buyers or changes in production costs. Both "sides" have to be looked at to determine profit.

Percentage changes in quantity and price

It is time now to define price elasticity more precisely. (In the discussion that follows, the word "price" will frequently be dropped. We will simply use "elasticity." Just remember we are talking about responses to *price* changes.)

Elasticity refers to the interplay between *percentage* changes in quantity and *percentage* changes in price. We must use percentages because we need to show the *relative* importance of price and quantity changes. A 10-cent price change is small if the price is $10. (Only 1 percent). But if the price is 20 cents, a 10-cent price change is *50* percent. The price change measured in money terms (10 cents) is called an **absolute change.** The price change measured in percentage terms in relationship to some starting point ($10 or 20 cents) is called a **relative change.**

Changes in the *quantity* demanded (or supplied) are measured in percentage rather than absolute terms for the same reason. If the percentage change in quantity exceeds the percentage change in price, demand or supply is price-elastic. If the percentage change in quantity is less than the percentage change in price, then demand or supply is price-inelastic.

Price Elasticity of Demand

Now, let us see how the price elasticity of demand works in practice. There are four possibilities, which we'll call Situations I, II, III, and IV.

Situation I: Increase in quantity exceeds decrease in price

Suppose you are the owner of the Dazzle Toothpaste Company, and you decide to sell more toothpaste by lowering your price. You have been selling 100 tubes of toothpaste per week to retail stores at a price of $1 each. You try reducing the price 10 percent, to 90 cents. Thereafter, sales increase 20 percent to 120 tubes per week. Demand is elastic because the percentage increase in quantity exceeded the percentage decrease in price; buyers (the stores) are relatively responsive to your price change.

Notice an important point. You are taking in more money than before. Before the price change, you were taking in $100 per week (100 tubes at $1 each). After the price decrease, you are taking in $108 (120 tubes at 90 cents)—$8 more than before. The price drop has been more than offset by an increase in sales.

Situation II: Decrease in quantity exceeds increase in price

We can also tell the story in reverse. Suppose you have been selling 120 tubes per week at a price of 90 cents each. You try increasing the price to $1. What happens? Sales drop from 120 to 100 tubes per week, and you take in less money. Demand is elastic.

Situation III: Increase in quantity is less than the decrease in price

Consider another possibility. Assume again that you are selling 100 tubes per week at $1 each. You decide to lower the price to 90 cents. This time sales increase but only to 105 tubes per week. Total revenue falls from $100 per week to $94.50 (105 tubes at 90 cents). In this case, the price was dropped 10 percent, but quantity increased only 5 percent. Demand is now *inelastic*; consumers were relatively indifferent to the price decrease. They did not jump to buy.

Situation IV: Decrease in quantity is less than the increase in price

There is one more possibility. Suppose you increase the price from $1 to $1.10. Sales drop. As long as we assume that the law of demand is operating—that price and quantity are inversely related (the demand curve slopes down from left to right)—people will buy less when the price goes up. How much less? Suppose sales drop from 100 per week to 95, a drop of 5 percent.

TABLE 5-1   Elasticity of Demand: Four Situations

Situation	Price per tube	Quantity (sales per week)	Total revenue	Type of demand
I and II	$1.00	100	$100.00	
	.90	120	108.00	Elastic
III	$1.00	100	$100.00	
	.90 .	105	94.50	Inelastic
IV	$1.00	100	$100.00	
	1.10	95	104.50	Inelastic

What happens to total revenue? Total revenue is now $104.50 (95 tubes at $1.10). Even though you sold fewer tubes, your total revenue went up. Why? Because this time, while price went up 10 percent, the number of units purchased went down only 5 percent. Consumers were relatively indifferent to the price increase—they wanted the toothpaste badly enough to go on buying almost the same quantity. Demand was inelastic.

Table 5-1 summarizes the four situations showing elasticity of demand.

What conclusions can we make?

Our first conclusion is: When demand is *elastic*, the entrepreneur takes in more revenue from sales when the price is lowered and less revenue when the price is raised. (Again, keep in mind we are thinking only about changes in revenue, not about profit. We do not know what's happening to production costs when the volume of sales changes.)

Our second conclusion is: When demand is *inelastic*, the entrepreneur takes in less revenue when the price is lowered and more revenue when the price is raised.

A third conclusion: If you are a good entrepreneur, you should lie awake nights asking yourself whether the demand for your product is elastic or inelastic and what price changes will cause your total revenue to increase or decrease. But you must also think about the changes in costs, and, therefore, profits that occur with changes in sales volume.

Changing elasticities along a demand curve

Let us now imagine that the demand schedule for Dazzle Toothpaste looks like Table 5-2. Notice that as the price falls, quantity constantly rises (the law of demand), but total revenue first rises and then falls. Why? At first, the percentage change in price is small compared to quantity changes. The price drop from $2 to $1.80 is 10 percent (the 20-cent change relative to $2), but the quantity doubles from 20 to 40—an increase of 100 percent. Because the percentage increase in quantity is larger than the percentage decrease in price, consumer demand is responsive to the price change— demand is elastic. Further, as the price falls, total revenue rises because the quantity increase *more than makes up for* the price decrease.

TABLE 5-2 Demand Schedule and Total Revenue for Dazzle Toothpaste

Price per tube	Quantity demanded per week	Total revenue per week (price times quantity)
$2.00	20	$ 40
1.80	40	72
1.60	60	96
1.40	80	112
1.20	100	120
1.00	120	120
.80	140	112
.60	160	96

At the bottom of the table, as the price falls from 80 cents to 60 cents, a drop of 25 percent (the 20-cent change relative to 80 cents), the increase in the quantity is about 14.3 percent (the 20-tube sales increase relative to 140 tubes).

Careful examination of Table 5-2 reveals an odd and perhaps confusing point. If we were to graph this demand schedule, we would find that the line is straight. It is straight because the relationship between the two variables, price and the quantity demanded, is constant. Every time the price changes by 20 cents, the quantity changes by 20 units. Yet the *elasticity* along the straight line *is constantly changing.* Why? Even though the absolute change in the numbers is the same, the relative (percentage) change may be different.

A quick example will help. While the absolute difference between 10 and 9 is 1, the relative percentage difference is 10 percent. What is the absolute difference between 1 and 2? Answer: again 1—but this time the relative percentage difference is 100 percent. Again we are reminded of the difference between relative and absolute changes.

The coefficient of elasticity

Economists have developed a formula to determine whether total revenue will rise or fall in response to a change in price. This formula produces a number called the **coefficient of elasticity.** To find a coefficient of elasticity, you divide the percentage change in quantity by the percentage change in price. If the coefficient is greater than one, demand is *price-elastic.* Price and total revenue move in opposite directions, one rising as the other falls. If the coefficient is less than one, demand is *price-inelastic.* Price and total revenue move in the same direction, both rising or both falling. If the percentage price change is exactly matched by the percentage quantity change, the elasticity of demand is called *unitary.* In this special case, total revenue does not change.

Here is how economists compute the coefficient. Let's take two prices and quantities from Table 5-2:

Price per tube	Quantity demanded per week
$1.60	60
1.40	80

What happens if the entrepreneur lowers the price from $1.60 to $1.40? Remember that we want to divide the *percentage* quantity change by the *percentage* price change. The quantity increase is 20 tubes—from 60 tubes to 80. This change of 20 tubes relative to 60 is one-third, or 33⅓ percent. The price decrease is 20 cents. This change of 20 cents relative to $1.60 is one-eighth, or 12.5 percent. Therefore, the coefficient of elasticity is 33⅓ percent divided by 12.5 percent = 2.666; call it 2.7

But see what happens when we reverse the situation. If our Dazzle entrepreneur wants to raise the price from $1.40 to $1.60, the coefficient will be somewhat different because the starting points are different. The quantity change will still be 20 tubes, but now the quantity starts at 80 and drops to 60—a drop of 25 percent. And the price still changes by 20 cents, but the starting point is $1.40. The price increase is therefore one-seventh (.20 ÷ 1.40), or about 14.3 percent. Now when we compute the coefficient, we have 25 percent divided by 14.3 percent—about 1.75, not 2.7.

To overcome this problem of getting two different answers, economists compute the percentage quantity change by comparing the *absolute* quantity change with an *average* of the two quantities, and by comparing the absolute price change with an *average* of the two prices. The percentage quantity change is therefore 20 ÷ average quantity (60 + 80 = 140 ÷ 2 = 70) = 20 ÷ 70 = about 28.6 percent. The percentage price change is 20 cents ÷ average price ($1.40 + $1.60 = $3.00 ÷ 2 = $1.50) = $.20 ÷ $1.50 = 13.3 percent.

The coefficient is therefore 28.6 ÷ 13.3 = about 2.1.* By using average quantities and average prices, we'll get the 2.1 answer whether we think about raising prices or lowering them.

What does the 2.1[†] coefficient mean? It tells us that demand is *price-elastic*, that total revenue will rise as the price falls, or that total revenue

---

*A somewhat easier way to get the same answer involves this formula: coefficient of elasticity = the absolute quantity difference/the two quantities added together ÷ the absolute price difference/the two prices added together.

$$\frac{20/140}{\$.20/\$3.00} = \frac{1}{7} \div \frac{1}{15} = \frac{15}{7} = 2.1$$

[†]Economists often put a minus sign in front of a coefficient of the elasticity of demand to remind readers that price and quantity are inversely related. In this discussion we shall ignore the minus sign.

will fall as the price rises. The number 2.1 means literally that, if the price rises 1 percent, quantity (sales) will fall 2.1 percent. The number also means that, if the price falls 1 percent, sales will increase 2.1 percent. The percentage change in quantity is about double the percentage change in price. Remember that price and quantity move in opposite directions because the demand curve slopes down from left to right and price and quantity are inversely related.

On the other hand, a 0.5 coefficient would tell us that demand is *price-inelastic* (because the coefficient is less than 1), and that total revenue will fall as the price falls and rise as the price rises. Can you translate the 0.5 coefficient? It tells us that the percentage quantity change will be only half of the percentage price change.

Finally, notice in Table 5-2 that as the price falls from $1.20 to $1, the quantity increases from 100 to 120 and total revenue does not change. At that point in the table the elasticity is unitary, and the coefficient is one.

One more observation. Remember that the coefficient changes all along a given demand schedule or curve, as Table 5-2 indicates. We cannot call any given demand curve all elastic or all inelastic. The general pattern is shown in Figure 5-1. Because the coefficients of elasticity vary all along the line, coefficients will be greater than one in the elastic portion, less than one in the inelastic portion, and equal to one in the unitary portion.

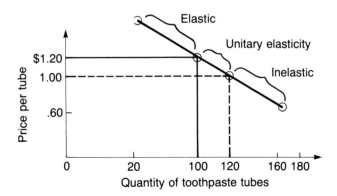

Figure 5-1. Changing elasticities along a demand curve.

The entrepreneur will not, of course, be thinking in terms of changing price from, say, $2 to 60 cents but in terms of small changes, perhaps $1.20 to $1.30. The point is, then, that a specific coefficient is relevant only to small changes in price and quantity at a particular time.

Four tests of price elasticity No one can accurately forecast why people want what they want, or why they want something badly enough to be unaffected by price increases (inelasticity) or strongly motivated to buy more because of price decreases (elasticity). Nevertheless, economists are generally agreed that there are four important tests of the price elasticity of demand. Every good entrepreneur should consider these tests and try to relate them to his or her product. As we proceed through the tests, think about Dazzle Toothpaste. Is it elastic or inelastic with respect to each test? What do the results of all four tests reveal?

Test 1: *Does the product have many substitutes?*

The availability of close substitutes is by far the most important test of elasticity. If many substitutes are available, people will switch from Dazzle to Dentobrite or Glisten if Dazzle raises its price (assuming *ceteris paribus*, nothing else changes). In such a case, the percentage drop in Dazzle's quantity demanded would exceed the percentage increase in Dazzle's price; Dazzle's total revenue would fall. The more close substitutes there are, the greater the elasticity.

Remember also that if Dazzle lowered its price relative to the prices of competing brands, sales might increase more than enough to offset the price decrease. Why? Because people would stop buying Dentobrite, Glisten, and the like, and buy Dazzle.

On the other hand, if there are no close substitutes, consumers will buy about the same quantity regardless of price changes. Demand is inelastic.

Keep in mind also that old models (like old cars) are substitutes for new ones. If we can repair the old one, our demand for the new one will be elastic.

Test 2: *How expensive is the product relative to the buyer's income?*

What percentage of the buyer's annual income does the price of the product represent? If the product is very *in*expensive, the chances are that the demand will be price-*in*elastic.

An example: There is a highly advertised brand of cupcakes, which are sold two to a package. A few years ago, a pair sold for 10 cents. In one jump, the price was raised to 13 cents—a 30 percent increase in price. Did anyone complain? Probably not. The point is that we tend to be indifferent to price changes of inexpensive items—paper clips, matches, bobby pins, and the like.

If, on the other hand, we are considering buying a car on a salary of $15,000 per year, a $5,000 car represents four months' work. A 10 percent change in the price of the car, $500, represents almost two weeks pay. The price change may affect us strongly. If the increase is $500, we may decide not to buy. Or, a $500 decrease may cause us to buy. We are strongly influenced by the price change either way.

Test 3: *Is the product a luxury or a necessity?*

If the product is a necessity, demand will tend to be price-inelastic. Buyers will be relatively indifferent to price changes.

The demand for luxury goods will tend to be price-elastic—the more luxurious, the more elastic. Since we can take a luxury or leave it, we will be strongly influenced by price changes.

Test 4: *To what extent are consumers habituated to the product?*

If one is hooked on heroin, heaven forbid, demand may be extremely price inelastic, almost vertical. (If the demand curve is absolutely straight up and down, it means that buyers will pay any price for a given quantity.) To a lesser extent, the same argument applies to people who insist on a certain brand of cigarettes, soap, deodorant, or toothpaste.

However, as time passes, a price difference may cause the habit to weaken. If a person is used to a particular brand of cigarettes, he or she may pay 5 cents more per pack for a while. But, as the time passes, the smoker may start wondering whether the brand is worth the extra 5 cents. Eventually, the person may drop the favorite brand and adopt another at a lower price. Thus, over time, demand becomes more price-elastic as the habit weakens.

Now what about Dazzle Toothpaste? What does each test tell us about it?

Test 1: Are there substitutes? Yes, many. Vote: elastic.

Test 2: Percent of buyer's income? The toothpaste price is a small percentage of income. Vote: inelastic.

Test 3: Luxury or necessity? To people who customarily brush their teeth, toothpaste is probably a necessity. But is any one brand like Dazzle a necessity? Probably not. Vote: elastic.

Test 4: Habit? Probably relevant. Unless the price change is large, toothpaste users probably stick to a brand they are used to. Vote: inelastic.

Now, what is the overall result? We have two votes for elastic and two for inelastic. Are the elastic votes more important than the inelastic? Probably not. Thus, the overall vote is inelastic. What does this mean? Touchy question. If Dazzle Toothpaste, a relatively inexpensive item, is well established, with a fair number of customers habituated to using it, a price change of perhaps 10 percent one way or the other probably will not affect sales much.

What should you, the entrepreneur, do then? You might experiment with slightly higher prices. Chances are that sales will *not* drop by as large a percentage as your percentage increase in price. With increased prices, total revenue should rise.

We have completed our discussion of the price elasticity of demand. The four main points to remember are as follows:

1. If demand is price-elastic, total revenue will rise if the price falls, and fall if the price rises.

2. If demand is price-inelastic, total revenue will rise if the price rises, and fall if the price falls.

3. Elasticity should only be associated with small changes in price and

quantity, since there will usually be different elasticities along any given demand curve or schedule.

4. If the coefficient is greater than one, demand is price-elastic; exactly one, elasticity is unitary; less than one, demand is price-inelastic.

Price Elasticity of Supply

So far, we have referred only to changes in the quantity *demanded* relative to price changes. Now we will consider changes in the quantity *supplied* when the price changes. For example, as laborers, we may be more or less anxious to work (supply our labor) when the wage rate goes up or down. If we respond readily to changes in wages (the price of labor), then supply is price-elastic.

How producers respond to price changes

The price elasticity of supply refers to the responsiveness of *producers* to price changes. If the producer increases the quantity for sale by more than 1 percent when the price rises by 1 percent, supply is *price-elastic*. If the producer increases the quantity for sale by anything *less* than 1 percent when the price rises by 1 percent, supply is *price-inelastic*.

What determines the price elasticity of supply? Unlike the price elasticity of demand with its four tests, there is only one main determinant of the elasticity of supply—namely, the rapidity with which an entrepreneur can change output. If the entrepreneur's operation is flexible enough so that he or she can adjust output to changes in price in a short period of time, then supply will be price-elastic.

Figure 5-2 is a picture of an elastic supply curve. If the price rises from P_1 to P_2, the quantity produced will rise by a larger percentage, from Q_1 to Q_2. Conversely, if the price should fall from P_2 to P_1, the quantity decrease from Q_2 to Q_1 would be relatively large.

Note that the total revenue test of elasticity does not work with the elasticity of supply. If the price goes up, causing an increase in the quantity supplied, total revenue (price times quantity) will always increase—whether

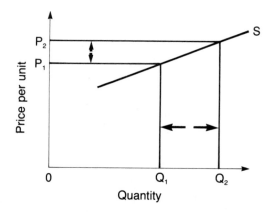

Figure 5-2. Elastic supply curve.

Figure 5-3. Elastic supply: reduced production in response to reduced demand.

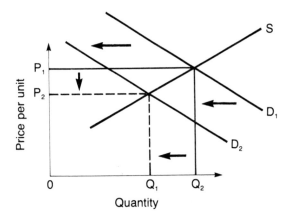

supply is elastic or inelastic. If the price falls, total revenue falls—regardless of elasticity. Can you see why? It is because, for suppliers, price and quantity decisions are directly related. (For demanders, price and quantity are inversely related.)

Elasticity and manufacturing

Typically, manufacturing firms such as Dazzle Toothpaste will have an elastic supply if the price falls because of a decrease in demand. They can quickly cut back production by laying off employees and reducing the operation of machines. This is shown in Figure 5-3. The decrease in demand causes the price to fall from P_1 to P_2. The producer reacts with a reduction in production from Q_1 to Q_2.

However, if a manufacturing plant is operating at or near capacity, it may obviously have difficulty in increasing production in the event of an increase in demand. Increasing the number or the size of buildings, for example, is a time-consuming, complicated business. Thus, as plant capacity is approached, supply tends to become less and less elastic (more and more inelastic). At Q_1 in Figure 5-4, the factory is operating close to capacity. Further increases in production are difficult regardless of price changes.

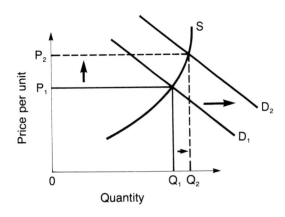

Figure 5-4. Inelastic supply: plant operating near capacity.

When this point is reached, the supply curve starts to curve up. When the factory is at full capacity, with no further increases possible (until sufficient time passes for completion of additions to the factory), the supply curve will be vertical.

Elasticity: Demand and Supply Together

Let us now take a look at a few common situations in which elasticity is involved with both demand and supply. This is particularly evident in agriculture.

Elasticity and agriculture

When we apply the concept of elasticity to farming, we find a picture that is somewhat different from that of manufacturing. Once a hen starts to lay eggs, it goes on laying eggs for about one year. Egg prices may change because of shifts in demand or supply, but for any one farmer the supply of eggs will be fixed—independent of price—as long as he or she has the same number of hens and they continue to lay eggs.

The almost vertical or almost completely inelastic supply curve is common in agriculture. During the growing season, deliberate changes in supply are difficult, yet there may be unplanned changes as the result of too much or too little rain, insect pests, and so forth. The inability of the farmer to change crops rapidly becomes particularly important if there is a decrease in demand or an increase in supply.

The United States' demand for agricultural products is also inelastic. We buy about the same amount of food regardless of change in food prices or our own incomes. The price elasticity of U.S. demand for all food is estimated to be only 0.25. That is, a 1 percent drop in food prices would increase food sales by only one quarter of 1 percent. To put it another way, food prices would have to drop 40 percent to increase food sales 10 percent.

What does all this mean for the farmer? When both demand and supply are inelastic, the farmer is subject to wide swings in price and income. In Figure 5-5, demand and supply are both inelastic. If supply increases (be-

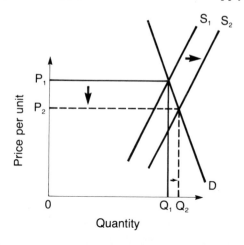

Figure 5-5. Inelastic demand and supply

cause good weather, say, or a new insecticide has resulted in the production of a bumper crop), prices fall sharply and the increase in quantity purchased is small, owing to the inelasticity of demand. Total revenue, or income for the farmer, drops with the fall in price.

Increases in supply have been typical in agriculture mainly because of technological breakthroughs. In the 1929–1979 period, farm production per farmworker person-hour increased more than five times.

Constant downward pressure on farm prices and incomes because of overproduction has led to increasing difficulties for small, less efficient farmers and the consolidation of small farms into large units often owned by large corporations. It has also led to considerable price and income support from government.

Elasticity and taxes   Branches of government will find it easier to raise money by taxing a product having an inelastic demand than one with an elastic demand. When a product is taxed (as in the case of sales tax), the price the consumer must pay rises, but if demand is inelastic consumers will continue to buy almost the same quantities as before the tax. Consequently, the government is relatively successful in collecting tax revenues from the sales of such products.

Kings in medieval times taxed salt because people and animals have to have salt to live. The demand for salt today (all brands combined) is still very inelastic. Other favorites today for heavy taxes are gasoline, cigarettes, and alcoholic beverages. In some states, state and federal taxes account for half of the price of cigarettes and alcoholic beverages. Many of us are so habituated to cigarettes and alcohol that when the price rises we continue to buy almost the same quantities.

Taxes may also be used where society judges the product to be unhealthy. However, although the tax may have a double motive—to raise money and to cause us to drink or smoke less—the motives are conflicting. If the tax *does* persuade us to smoke or drink less, the state will no longer find taxes on cigarettes or alcoholic beverages as good a source of revenue as before.

If governments impose a sales tax on commodities for which demand is price-elastic, entrepreneurs will find it difficult to shift the cost of the tax to consumers by raising prices. To some extent, consumers will simply stop buying the product and buy something else. A government's attempts to raise money from such products will be relatively unsuccessful.

Summary   When relatively small changes in the price of a product result in relatively large changes in the quantity demanded, demand is said to be price-elastic. When, on the other hand, relatively large changes in the price of a product have little effect on the quantity purchased, demand is said to be price-inelastic. An entrepreneur who manufactures a product for which the demand is price-elastic will take in more money if he or she lowers its price, because the increase in volume of sales will more than make up for the loss in revenue for each item sold. On the other hand, if the demand for the product is price-inelastic, the entrepreneur will take in more money by increasing the price, because the additional revenue from each item sold will make up for the decrease in the number of items purchased at the new price.

Price elasticity can be expressed by the coefficient of elasticity—the relative change in quantity divided by the relative change in price. If the coefficient is greater than 1, relative changes in quantity are larger than relative changes in price, and demand is price-elastic. If the coefficient is less than 1, relative changes in quantity are smaller than relative changes in price, and demand is price-inelastic.

The demand for a product tends to be price-elastic if (1) substitutes for the product are available; (2) its price represents a large percentage of the buyer's income; (3) it is a luxury product; (4) its purchase is not habitual with the buyer.

Supply may also be price-elastic or price-inelastic. One major factor determines the extent to which supply is price-elastic—namely, the time it takes a supplier to adjust the quantity supplied when the price changes. If it takes an entrepreneur a long time to increase the quantity supplied, as in the case of a farmer or a factory operating at capacity, supply is price-inelastic.

The concept of elasticity helps to explain why farmers often experience large changes in income and why governments prefer to tax products for which the demand is price-inelastic.

Discussion Questions

1. What is the price elasticity of demand of Crest toothpaste as compared with the elasticity for all toothpaste?

2. What is the price elasticity of demand for BMW motorcycles, Sony tape recorders, Zenith TVs? Explain, using the four tests.

3. If you are operating a hot-dog stand and you figure that the coefficient of elasticity of demand is greater than one for your hot dogs, should you experiment with higher or lower prices? Explain.

4. How may the elasticity of supply of apples in your supermarket today differ from the elasticity of supply of apples over the next year? Explain.

5. Explain the connection between changes in total revenue and elasticity. If you, a manufacturer of Kickapoo Joy Juice, believe the demand for your product is elastic, should you consider raising or lowering your price? Explain.

6. Assume that the coefficient of elasticity of demand for your Kickapoo Joy Juice is 1.2. Fill in the following blanks: For every _____percent change in price, there will be a _____percent change in the quantity demanded.

7. Assume that the coefficient of elasticity of demand for gasoline is 0.2. How much will the price have to rise to cause us to reduce our purchases of gasoline by 10 percent? (You will find the answer in the next chapter.)

3

Microeconomics
in the Real World

This part contains four chapters designed to show further how microeconomic theory helps to explain real-world problems. Chapter 6 deals with pollution and energy. The next three chapters take a close look at the struggle for market power by entrepreneurs and workers.

For instance, sellers (producers) erect hundreds of barriers to entry—patent rights, franchises, licensing agreements, occupational licenses, sheer size—to prevent other firms or individuals from competing. Employers, as buyers of labor, also try to exercise market power over the sellers of labor, their workers. And in return, the workers obtain power by forming unions.

Chapter 7 explains why sellers want power and where their attempts to gain power are taking us. Economic theory doesn't say much about how to get rich as an individual, but economic theory is very useful in showing how business firms can increase their profits; this is the task of Chapter 8. Chapter 9, the last microeconomic chapter, reviews the efforts of workers to increase their own incomes.

6

Pollution Control and Oil Shortages: Applying Price Theory

© Kent Reno/Jeroboam, Inc.

Chapters 3, 4, and 5 have shown that demand-supply models are extremely useful in helping us visualize many economic problems. The purpose of this chapter is to apply demand-supply analysis to two headline topics—pollution and energy.

Key Words	
Private costs	Effluent charges
External effects	Nonrenewable resource
External costs (or benefits)	Cartel
Social costs	White market
	Cogeneration

Economic Theory in Action: Pollution Control

In an Adam Smithian, self-interested world, entrepreneurs are expected to enlarge their profits as much as possible. The natural way to do this is to produce at the lowest possible cost. But at *whose* cost? It is obviously cheaper for entrepreneurs to dump waste into the nearest stream or into the atmosphere than to truck waste to some waste disposal facility or to filter it coming out of their chimneys. Therefore, what may be sensible for entrepreneurs may not be desirable for the community. Here is a classic trade-off: We can force entrepreneurs "to clean up their acts," but when we do, entrepreneurs have to adopt more expensive means of production or waste disposal. Inevitably they will charge higher prices, and, given no change in demand, the quantity demanded will drop and workers will be laid off. The trade-off is therefore cleaner air and water *or* more unemployment. Here is how economists think about this problem.

Private costs + external costs = social costs

The costs associated with the manufacturer's production or buyer's use of any product are called **private** *(internal)* **costs.** They are borne by the seller and the buyer and are included in the market price or in the costs of using the product after purchase.

Normally, transactions involve only a buyer and a seller. When a seller sells a pad of paper to a buyer, only two people are apparently involved in the transaction. But if the factory that makes the paper contributes to air or water pollution, economists say that people *outside the transaction* are affected or that the transaction has **external effects.** Because paper production in this instance is harmful to people unconnected with the production or purchases of paper, **external costs** are involved.

The term **social costs** refers to the total impact on society of the production, distribution, and use of whatever is produced. Thus, social costs are private or internal costs plus external costs.

The problem is that prices in a market-price system usually reflect only private (internal) costs and benefits.* If buyers and sellers don't have to

---

*External effects may involve benefits as well as costs. Two examples of external benefits: (1) the education of a biochemist helps to prevent disease in thousands of children; such education has a private benefit for the biochemist but also great benefit for others external to that transaction. (2) Person A receives a vaccination for some contagious disease. The vaccination gives A a private benefit but also an external benefit (protection) to others with whom A has contact.

consider environmental regulations, the equilibrium price will be below that necessary to cover external costs. The true costs to society are left out of price determination.

The Reserve Mining Company case

A famous and long-drawn-out case involving private versus social costs occurred during the late 1960s and most of the 1970s. It involved the Reserve Mining Company, located in a small town, Silver Bay, Minnesota, on the shores of Lake Superior. As *Time* magazine described it:

> Reserve Mining Company, which is owned jointly by Armco Steel and Republic Steel, produces 15% of the U.S.'s iron ore. It mines taconite around Babbitt, Minn., then ships the flintlike rock 50 miles to Silver Bay, on the shores of Lake Superior. There the iron content of the taconite is extracted, and the wastes, or "tailings," are dumped into the water at the rate of 67,000 tons per day. Any time that Reserve is attacked for polluting the lake—and the attacks have been continuous since 1967—it says that it might have to close the plant if ordered to stop. That would wreak economic havoc, since the company employs 3,200 workers in the area, or at least 90% of the local work force. But in February 1972, the U.S. Justice Department decided to sue for a cleanup anyway. The trial began in the summer of 1976.
>
> The key issue became public health. Asbestos fibers had been discovered in the drinking water that five communities, including Duluth, 60 miles down the shoreline, draw from Lake Superior. Federal scientists pinpoint Reserve's taconite tailings as the source of the asbestos. Company experts say that the material leaches naturally out of surrounding rock formations. Either way, the minute fibers are dangerous. If ingested or inhaled—and particles have been detected in the air over Reserve's Silver Bay plant—asbestos can cause cancer.
>
> The ideal solution would be for Reserve Mining to dispose of its wastes on land. But company officials testified that Reserve had no plan for land disposal, and would need time to prepare one. The executives also rejected a government proposal that Reserve move its entire Silver Bay operations to Babbitt. Such a move would cost $187 million, said federal officials. Reserve argued that the move would cost $575 million.[1]

The end of the story has finally been written. Following more court battles in 1977 and 1978, the Reserve Mining Company agreed on July 7, 1978, to build a $370 million facility to process taconite waste on land and to meet a federal court deadline of April 15, 1980, for ending the dumping of wastes into Lake Superior.

What happens to prices when pollution is controlled?

The Reserve Mining story describes the pollution problem solely in human terms. Now let's see how price theory deals with a similar dilemma.

If, say, a steel mill is forced to put in antipollution equipment, the company's product costs will rise. Its supply curve will shift to the left because a higher market price is necessary now to induce the mill to produce any given quantity. Assuming no change in demand, the shift in supply will cause the product price to rise and the quantity demanded to fall.

Figure 6-1. Example of demand and supply when antipollution equipment is installed in a steel mill.

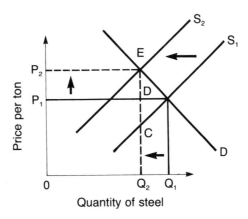

We can show what happens with a demand-supply diagram (Figure 6-1). Higher production costs are shown by the shift of the supply curve from S_1 to S_2. The price rises from P_1 to P_2, causing the quantity demanded to decrease from Q_1 to Q_2. As the quantity demanded falls, the steel mill will buy fewer resources, among them, labor. Employees will be laid off. Note also that the higher price that buyers must pay may or may not be socially desirable, depending on how different income groups are affected.

Ideally, the vertical distance between the two supply curves (the distance CE in Figure 6-1) reflects the external cost of producing the steel. We have to say "ideally" because the measurement of external costs may be extremely difficult. (We can never be sure, for example, if the lung cancer of people in the community hospital has been caused by emissions from the steel mill's stacks or by excessive smoking.)

Nevertheless, we shall assume that this estimate of external costs can be made and that we can force the steel company to absorb all external costs by installing, say, a filter in its chimneys at an average cost of CE per unit. The diagram now tells how this cost will be split between the mill and the buyer. At the new quantity, Q_2, the vertical distance between the supply curves, the additional cost of producing each unit at Q_2, is distance CE. We notice that the price rises from P_1 to P_2, the same as from point D to point E, or only about half the full distance, CE. It is apparent, therefore, that the additional costs of production are shared by the buyer (who absorbs part of the cost in the form of higher prices) and by the steel mill.

(Rather than forcing an enterprise to use some specific solution like chimney filters, many economists prefer to charge polluting firms so much a pound for the waste they spew into the air or water. Such charges are called **effluent charges.** They are based on the legal idea that the firms are trespassing on property rights all of us share—the rights to clean air and water—and should pay for doing so. The economist's preference for the effluent charge is that business firms are thereby given the freedom to find their own best solution to the problem—or pay the charge.)

The analysis of pollution highlights a typical economic problem. Measures to correct pollution will raise the prices of those products that, when produced, used, or disposed of, pollute the environment. The increased prices of these products will cause a decrease in the quantity demanded (assuming no change in demand), a move upward along the demand curve. At higher prices, more people will be excluded from buying and less of the product will be sold. The drop in sales will cause an increase in unemployment in that industry. The opportunity cost of protecting the environment is therefore increased unemployment and an increased burden for those in lower income groups.

We can hope that eventually all prices will reflect the total social cost of production, distribution, use, and disposal of all goods and services and that therefore consumer choice will be based on prices that include all of these costs. Eventually, too, but after difficult periods of adjustment, the unemployment effects of pollution control will diminish as those who become unemployed as a result of the controls find jobs in nonpolluting industries or perhaps with business firms that manufacture pollution-control devices.

The dollar benefits of pollution control

Although external costs are hard to measure, a fascinating study in a new field called environmental economics provides some answers to the problem.[2]

The economists involved in the study adopted two approaches: (1) By comparing clean-air areas with dirty-air areas, they estimated the increase in property values that would occur in the dirty-air areas if the air was cleaned up. Their conclusion: A 30 percent improvement in air quality would increase real estate values in Los Angeles by $950 million a year, or $500 per household. (2) They interviewed residents in twelve neighborhoods and asked them how much they would pay (in what the researchers described as a "bidding game") for improved air quality. The result: $650 million a year, or $350 per household—not greatly different from the $500 per household calculated independently. In this way, pollution control and external costs were given a market price. By extending their pricing estimates to the whole country, the researchers found that total, national benefits could amount to as much as $50 billion annually.

The question—not covered—is who should pay? If we all pay as consumers (higher prices for products produced by cleaner industries), the people who own property in a dirty-air area may receive a subsidy in the form of higher property values. And if we *all* pay, the cost may be disproportionately borne by people in lower income groups.

Price Elasticity and the "Energy Crisis"

Although the energy crisis does involve all forms of energy, we will confine our remarks almost entirely to the availability of oil. Certainly it was the shortage of oil in 1973 that put energy in the headlines. And in 1979, the laws of demand and supply and the principle of elasticity were clearly demonstrated by the requirement of alternate-day gasoline purchases and steadily increasing prices.

Our review of the energy crisis will cover (1) the background of the crisis, (2) our dependence on oil, (3) why the crisis occurred, (4) and what can be done.

Background of the crisis

During the November 1973 negotiations to halt the Arab-Israeli war, the Arabs announced an embargo on oil shipments to countries friendly to Israel. Because the United States had been supplying arms and dollars in support of Israel, it was the main target of the embargo. Suddenly the United States did not have enough oil to satisfy the demand for heating, transportation, and myriad industrial uses.

The Arab action forced Americans to respond to an energy shortage that had been developing over decades. In 1952, the Paley Commission appointed by President Eisenhower forecast the energy crisis by projecting increased energy use and diminishing supplies. In the mid-sixties, blackouts and brownouts occurred in the northeastern states. Thus, the Arab announcement merely precipitated a crisis that would probably have occurred at some time during the 1970s, given the country's unwillingness to act on its knowledge of coming energy shortages.

Another oil crisis shook the world during the winter of 1978–1979. The revolution in Iran suddenly deprived oil-consuming nations of about 6 million barrels per day, about 10 percent of total world consumption of 64 million barrels per day. For the United States it meant a loss of 900,000 barrels per day, roughly 5 percent of our daily consumption of 19,000,000 barrels.

Our dependence on oil

We depend more on oil than we used to. Table 6-1 shows how oil has grown in importance as a source of energy, how much more oil we buy now from other countries, and how the price and total cost of oil have increased.

TABLE 6-1 Facts About Our Increasing Oil Use

	1970	1979
Percentage of total energy from oil	44%	50%
Percentage of oil imported	15%	50%
Price per 42-gallon barrel	$2	$15–$40
Total cost of imported oil per year	$1 billion (483 million barrels)	$50 billion (2.4 billion barrels)

Sources: U.S. Departments of Energy and Commerce

A 42-gallon barrel of oil provides us with everything from gasoline to toilet seats (Figure 6-2). By far the most important use of oil is as gasoline: 19.6 gallons of the 42-gallon barrel. The next most important use is as heating oil and diesel fuel: 13.2 gallons of the 42.

Figure 6-2. Barrel boun-
tiful: oil's many uses.

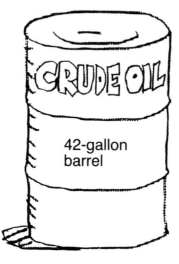

Gasoline
19.6 gallons
Heating oil and
diesel fuel
13.2 gallons
Jet fuel
2.6 gallons
Asphalt
1.3 gallons

42-gallon
barrel

Petrochemical
feedstocks
1.4 gallons
Liquefied gas
2.4 gallons
All others

Source: *Statistical Abstract of the United States, 1979.*

Oil is a basic raw material in many industries—chemicals, paints, plastics, drugs, and synthetic textiles. In fact, the 1.4 gallons of "petrochemical
feedstocks" in each barrel of crude oil provide raw materials that eventually
go into an estimated 3,000 items, including such diverse products as peni-
cillin, aspirin, bleach, perfume, ice cream, and toilet seats.

Figure 6-2 gives us another look at opportunity cost. To obtain more
heating oil, we have to give up something else like gasoline; there is a "trade-
off" of heating oil for gasoline. Unfortunately for heating oil users, however,
refineries cannot extract more than 12 gallons (30 percent) of heating oil
from the 42-gallon barrel of oil. In the 1973 crisis, which occurred in the
winter, heating-oil users often went without. Wood fires, candlelight, and
long underwear became very popular.

**Why did the crisis
occur?**

The simplest reason for the energy crisis is the old Malthusian problem: The
earth's resources are becoming scarcer relative to increases in demand. Resources are also becoming harder to find and develop. As population grows
and the demand for resources increases, shortages occur.

Let us consider this from the standpoint of both supply and demand.

Inelasticity of supply

The most important fact about the supply of oil is that it is a **nonrenewable
resource.** Unlike a forest of trees producing timber, once oil is gone, it's gone
forever. There are varying estimates (and arguments) about the amount of
oil left on the earth. One estimate is that there is a twenty-year worldwide
supply of usable oil left;[3] another is that the United States has a ten-year
supply left.[4] The trouble with any estimate is that there is no way of knowing
how much oil we can squeeze from oil shale or the tar sands of Canada (or

what the costs of extraction would be) or how much oil we can find in Alaska or by off-shore drilling.

What we do know is that production in the United States has remained unchanged for several years. We produced about as much oil in 1976 as we did in 1965, 3 billion barrels in 1976 versus 2.8 billion barrels in 1965, and a good bit less than the 3.5 billion we produced in 1970.[5]

The Malthusian argument is that as supplies run low, increases in supply become more and more difficult to obtain. Once the easily accessible sources of oil have been tapped, we have to look harder in more remote or difficult-to-exploit areas. The cost of finding and producing new sources will undoubtedly rise rapidly, and higher and higher prices will be necessary to give suppliers an incentive to expand production. In terms of elasticity, the percentage increase in price will probably have to be greater than the percentage increase in the quantity supplied; the supply of energy sources (presently in use) is becoming more and more inelastic. Figure 6-3 shows supply becoming more and more vertical (inelastic). A price increase from P_1 to P_2 is necessary to induce suppliers to achieve the relatively modest increase in quantity from Q_1 to Q_2. This model suggests that relatively large price increases and large expected profits will be necessary to persuade producers to increase production.

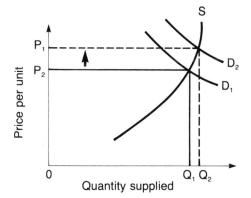

Figure 6-3. Inelastic supply, increases in demand, and rising prices of oil.

What about profits?

After the two crises of 1973 and 1979, the oil companies were frequently accused of conspiring to reduce supplies in order to force prices up and enlarge their profits. And following both crises, oil company profits did increase.

The billion dollar question we as consumers ask is: "Are these large profits being used to find more oil?" Or, are the large oil companies simply sitting on their oil waiting for the price to go up?

As it turns out, there is no clear-cut answer to these questions. Let's review the problem by looking at (1) how big the profits actually are and (2) what the profits are being used for.

How large are oil company profits? In dollar terms, the profits of large oil companies are huge. In 1979, Exxon became the first industrial company in American history to earn more than $4 billion. In that year, the eight* largest American oil companies reported combined profits of $15 billion—a jump of 67 percent over the year before.[6] But, are these profits excessive?

There are two ways of measuring the size of any company's profit: (1) profit as a percentage of income from sales and (2) profit as a percentage of the money stockholders have invested (called "stockholder's equity"). Economists usually prefer the latter measure because it represents the return to entrepreneurs for risk taking.

By either measure, oil company profits in 1979 were not excessive. The average profit as a percentage of sales for the eight large oil companies was 5.5 percent as compared with 5.8 percent for all manufacturing companies. The same relative profit picture occurred during the previous three years, 1976–1978.

After-tax profits as a percentage of stockholder's equity are also in line with other industries, averaging around 15 percent. Mobil, whose 1979 profit was $2.01 billion, tried to make this point in a 60-second TV commercial to be shown on ABC, CBS, and NBC.[7] The commercial was designed to show that profits as a percentage of stockholder's equity were actually higher for the stockholders of the three networks than for Mobil's stockholders. The networks refused to run the commercial, pleading that they could not sell time for the discussion of public issues.

What are the oil firms doing with the profits? Here the evidence is very mixed. The money has been spent in at least five ways: (1) exploration, (2) expansion of refining facilities, (3) reduction of long-term debt, (4) increased dividends for stockholders, and (5) purchase of other companies. We cannot give you a good picture of spending under the first four categories.

In connection with the last spending category, the oil firms have come under a good deal of criticism. For example, Atlantic Richfield spent $100 million of its $1.4 billion 1979 profit to expand its coal-mining and solar-energy facilities, an investment that may help provide alternate fuel sources when oil runs out but also promotes monopolization of these other industries. Atlantic Richfield also used some of its profit to buy a newsmagazine, the *London Observer*. Mobil bought Montgomery Ward. Gulf bid $30 million to buy Ringling Brothers Barnum and Bailey Circus. These latter adventures can hardly help to reduce oil shortages; still, they are miniscule in size when compared with the oil companies' total profit.

The economics of sitting on, rather than selling, oil. Economic theory (and common sense) suggests a way of determining whether to hold onto any asset (like oil) for a number of years in hopes that the price will rise.

Standard Oil (Ohio), Texaco, Mobil, Gulf, Standard Oil (California), Exxon, Atlantic Richfield, Standard Oil (Indiana).

Speculators do this all the time with commodities like gold, silver, stamps, old coins, paintings, diamonds, baseball cards—you name it. One example: On May 29, 1980, one 24-ounce bottle of Chateau Lafite red Bourdeaux wine made in 1822 sold for $31,000 ($1,291.67 per ounce). If you were an oil company (or the owner of fine old wine), how would you decide whether to "hang on" or to sell?

The answer is fairly simple. If you believe that the value of your asset is growing faster than the value of anything else you could put the money (from selling the asset) into, then you should hang on. The opportunity cost of hanging on isn't high enough to validate selling.

Therefore, you should try to estimate the annual increase in value of your asset and compare that increase with the rates of return from other possible uses of your money. Let's see what has actually happened to oil prices and then decide as oil entrepreneurs whether to hang on or to sell.

Back in 1970, the average price of a barrel of crude oil was about $2. By 1980, the price had increased thirteen times to about $26, an increase of about 27 percent per year. Not bad, you say. Could you have done as well by putting your money into something else? Doubtful. Consequently, it would seem perfectly rational for the oil companies to "hang on," rather than sell (but proving that they do so is very difficult).

OPEC's role

The Organization of Petroleum Exporting Countries has also had a great influence on the supply of oil and its price.* The thirteen OPEC countries are members of a **cartel,** an organization whose members agree on prices and outputs. The goal of the cartel is to prevent members from underselling one another so that buyers have to meet a minimum price set by all the members of the cartel. Cartels often collapse because one or more members undersells the others.

The apparent ability of the OPEC to maintain a united front is undoubtedly the result of increases in world demand for oil. The OPEC countries produced the same total quantity of oil in 1979 as in 1973. Yet during that period, their total annual revenues went from $31 billion to $275 billion, a twelvefold increase. When any entrepreneur can be assured of such increases in revenue with no drop in sales, there seems little reason not to continually push prices upward. The success of OPEC therefore results from (1) inelastic demand and (2) continuing increases in demand.

Increase in demand

The United States consumes about one-third of the world's energy, although it has only 6 percent of the world's population. Our energy consumption per

---

OPEC has thirteen members: Saudi Arabia, Iran, Iraq, Venezuela, Kuwait, United Arab Emirates, Qatar, Libya, Algeria, Ecuador, Nigeria, Gabon, and Indonesia. See U.S. News & World Report, 12 March 1979, for a summary of the oil production for each OPEC country.

capita has doubled since 1940, but consumption has been increasing even faster in recent years.

One can argue that the U.S. consumption of energy is acceptable because the United States also produces one-third of the world's goods and services and one-third of the world's income. It is tempting to excuse our use of energy for this reason, but the excuse does not work. The Swedes have a higher per-person income than Americans, but they consume just 60 percent of the energy (on a per-person basis) that Americans do. West Germans use only three-quarters as much energy as we do per dollar of output; France only half.

Many of our friendliest trading partners—Japan and the democracies in Western Europe—are unhappy about our low oil prices and excessive use of energy. Throughout both energy crises, their gasoline prices were at least double ours. They had no shortages, no gas lines.[8] They see the United States as contributing to high gasoline prices because of our demand for OPEC oil.

In 1979, it began to look as though the demand for petroleum was slowing. Estimated consumption of oil during 1979 was about 6.4 billion barrels, down from 7.0 billion in 1978. This drop in consumption did not mean Americans were *paying* less for oil. While imports of oil stabilized at around 9 million barrels per day during the four-year period, 1977–1980, the total annual *cost* of that oil increased during the same period from $45 billion to $80 billion owing to OPEC price increases.

Inelasticity of demand

The question of the price elasticity of the demand for gasoline is crucial. Let us assume we want to cut gasoline consumption by 10 percent. An estimate of the price elasticity of demand should tell us how much gasoline prices will have to rise so as to reduce the quantity demanded by 10 percent.

In late 1973, Data Resources Incorporated studied the reduction in gasoline consumption that might result from higher taxes on gasoline.[9] The study indicated that the demand for gasoline is extremely *in*elastic, that the coefficient of elasticity is about 0.2.

You will recall (page 97) that a coefficient of 0.2 means that a price increase of 1 percent will cause the quantity demanded to decrease by 0.2 percent (one-fifth of 1 percent). To put it another way, any given percentage change in price will be five times the percentage change in the quantity demanded. Thus, if we were to let the free-market equilibrium-price mechanism operate to reduce gasoline consumption by the desired 10 percent, the price of gasoline would have to rise by 50 percent (5 × 10).*

Demand and supply together: the problem of price ceilings

Many experts share the view that price ceilings are at least partly to blame for oil shortages; that oil prices have been kept so low by government regu-

---

This is the answer to Question 7 at the end of Chapter 5.

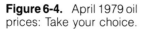

Figure 6-4. April 1979 oil prices: Take your choice.

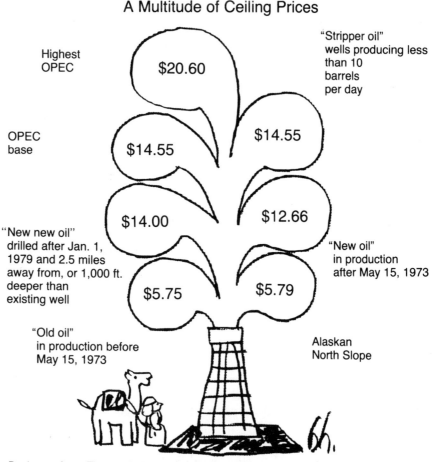

A Multitude of Ceiling Prices

Highest OPEC — $20.60

"Stripper oil" wells producing less than 10 barrels per day — $14.55

OPEC base — $14.55

"New new oil" drilled after Jan. 1, 1979 and 2.5 miles away from, or 1,000 ft. deeper than existing well — $14.00

$12.66 — "New oil" in production after May 15, 1973

"Old oil" in production before May 15, 1973 — $5.75

$5.79 — Alaskan North Slope

Redrawn from Time, *16 April 1979, p. 67. Reprinted by permission from* Time, The Weekly Newsmagazine; *copyright Time Inc., 1979.*

lation that the oil companies have had no incentive to look for oil and the public has had every reason to waste it. Both theory and practice tend to support this view.

The arithmetic of oil pricing has been, and is, confusing. Just prior to the Arab oil embargo, the federal government regulated oil prices under the Emergency Petroleum Act of 1973.

Since the embargo of 1973–1974, the regulations covering oil prices have become enormously complicated. Figure 6-4 summarizes the rules covering old and new oil in 1979. As you can see, there are price ceilings that regulate "old oil" and "new oil," "new new oil," and "stripper oil." OPEC prices are also shown.

When inelastic or large increases in demand are joined with an inelastic . or slowly increasing supply curve *and* price ceilings, the reasons for shortages become even more evident. Figure 6-5 shows a modest increase in supply from S_1 to S_2 but a large increase in demand from D_1 to D_2. The two equilib-

Figure 6-5. Inelastic supply, rising demand, and price ceilings.

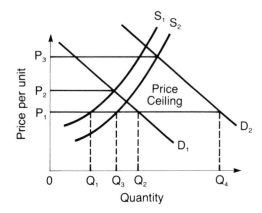

rium prices necessary to remove the shortages are shown at P_2 and P_3. P_1 represents a price ceiling imposed by the government. Before the increase in demand and supply, the shortage is the distance between Q_1 and Q_2. But after the changes in demand and supply, the shortage, caused by the ceiling, is much greater—the distance between Q_3 and Q_4.

What can be done?   There are five possibilities as to how the oil crisis might be resolved from the point of view of economic theory: (1) let the free market solve the problem (or a variant of this); (2) save energy; (3) ration available energy supplies; (4) develop renewable energy sources and new ways to use present ones; and (5) tax the devil out of gasoline.

1A. Let the free market solve the problem

This strategy advocates removing price controls and allowing energy prices to rise (assuming they are below equilibrium). The theory is that when the equilibrium price is reached, the shortage will be eliminated. What could be simpler? No government regulation or bureaucracy is involved.

The market-price system is an easy automatic rationing device. No one in Washington has to do a thing. The free market will take care of shortages and surpluses. Some professionals urge us to remember this point. Economist Milton Friedman at the University of Chicago argues that the Department of Energy is perpetuating the crisis by keeping the price of gasoline below equilibrium.* He points out that the 20,000-employee Department of Energy costs us $10.8 billion per year or about 9 cents per gallon and that we were "much better off . . . before we had the Department of Energy."[10]

But there are problems. The higher the price rises, the greater the burden upon low-income users. Furthermore, a price increase of *50 percent* would be necessary to reduce gasoline consumption by the desired 10 percent.

In December 1979, the price of imported oil approached $30 per barrel while some domestic oil—under price controls—sold for $6 per barrel.

1B. Let the free market solve it, but tax oil companies and share the money with the poor

In the spring of 1979, President Carter proposed the "deregulation" of oil; price ceilings would be gradually removed until, by October 1, 1981, they would no longer exist. It took the Carter Administration one year to sell Congress on the deregulation idea. Finally on April 2, 1980, President Carter signed into law the "Crude Oil Windfall Profit Tax Act of 1980."

The provisions of the Act are complicated, setting different tax rates on oil, depending on the type of oil, the method of production, and the size of the producing company. In addition to these complications, some oil was exempted from the law—Alaskan oil, oil owned by American Indians, and oil owned by state or local governments. But, in general, the law provided for taxes on oil in production before 1979 at 70 percent of the difference between its actual selling price and $12.81 per barrel. The tax rate (based on the same formula) for oil produced during and after 1979 is 30 percent—the lower rate is to encourage post-1979 exploration for oil.

The decontrol of oil prices is expected to give the oil companies "windfall" profits of $1 trillion during the decade of the eighties. Of this, current state and local taxes will subtract $552 billion. The new law subtracts another $227 billion, leaving the oil companies with the remaining $221 billion.

The $227 billion collected by the new law will be used in a variety of ways: $136 billion in tax credits for business firms and homeowners for finding new (nonoil) energy sources (like solar panels) and for efforts to conserve (like better insulation); $34 billion for energy development and mass transportation systems. The remaining $57 billion will be used to offset the impact of high oil prices on the poor. The plan is to distribute this money to the states for aid to families with "lower living standards" as defined by the Bureau of Labor Statistics (below $11,000 for a family of four in 1979).

One can see in this new law an attempt by the Carter Administration to please everyone. As of this writing (June 1980), many of the details of parceling out the money were still in the hands of Congress. Time will tell whether or not the law will (1) provide enough incentive for the oil companies to explore, (2) encourage the development of non-oil sources of energy, and (3) avoid catastrophic damage to the living standards of low-income families.

2. Save energy

Figure 6-6 indicates that about two-thirds of the energy we use is wasted (released into the environment in the form of nonproductive heat). Many experts believe our best energy source is the saved energy we can realize from conservation. Dow Chemical, one of the United States' three largest users of energy, has reduced its energy consumption by 40 percent per pound of product during the last decade. Gillette now uses 40 percent less energy to make a Paper Mate pen that it did five years ago. A study at Princeton University estimates that we can reduce our energy use in the home by 67 percent through relatively simple changes like better insulation around win-

Figure 6-6. Wasting away: The U.S. loses about two-thirds of the energy it consumes. Perhaps half of that is unavoidable but conservation could cut down the waste.

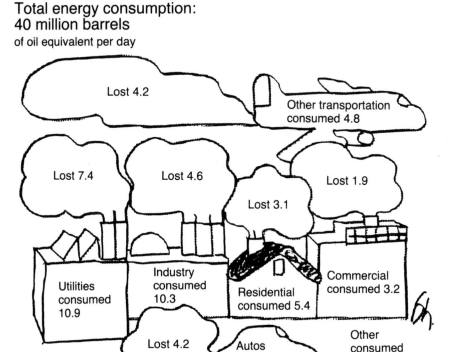

Total energy consumption: 40 million barrels
of oil equivalent per day

Lost 4.2

Other transportation consumed 4.8

Lost 7.4

Lost 4.6

Lost 1.9

Lost 3.1

Industry consumed 10.3

Utilities consumed 10.9

Residential consumed 5.4

Commercial consumed 3.2

Lost 4.2

Autos consumed 4.9

Other consumed .7

Source of data: Brookhaven National Laboratory, 1978 estimates. Figure redrawn from illustration in Newsweek, *26 February 1979, p. 63.*

dows, basements, and attics, and plugging of air leaks. Altogether, we could save as much as 30 to 40 percent of the energy we use without undercutting our standard of living.[11]

3. Ration available energy supplies

In 1977, there were more than 100 million cars (excluding trucks and buses) in the United States using an average of 14 gallons of gasoline each week. The government could force a reduction in demand by issuing ration tickets, as it did during World War II, to limit average use to, say, 8 gallons per week.

However, the difficulties of rationing are considerable. First, rationing requires a gigantic bureaucracy to apportion supplies fairly and to administer the program. Second, rationing encourages cheating such as forgery of ration tickets and black-market sales of gasoline. Third, the government must still find a way to motivate business firms to find and produce more energy.

But there are ways to avoid these largely administrative difficulties. One way is to allot a certain number of coupons per month to each licensed driver and allow those who use less gas to sell their coupons at whatever price they can get to those who use more gas. This would create a **white** (rather than black) **market** because it establishes a free market for the coupons. The coupons would soon be sold at an equilibrium price that would equalize the supply of unused coupons with demand for them; that is, the price system would ration the coupons.

The white market idea is appealing because once the problem of distributing the coupons to licensed drivers has been solved, further administration is minimal. The free market for the coupons will determine who finally receives them.

Unfortunately, there are still many objections. People who have to drive for a livelihood will need more coupons. Also, those who drive little and can sell their coupons will receive a gift of extra income from the sale of unused coupons.

4. Develop renewable energy sources and new ways to use present ones

This is hardly the place to examine the feasibility of energy from solar cells, windmills, methane gas or alcohol from waste or garbage, or from wave motion or the tides. These possibilities involve engineering studies too complex and too "iffy" for review here. But there are three points we would like to make:

1. The continued use of nonrenewable fuels like oil or uranium inevitably costs more each year as these fuels become harder to find. These cost increases hurt poorer people more than richer people; poorer countries more than richer countries, especially the less-developed countries that have no oil or uranium.

On the other hand, the cost of energy from new systems like solar panels will undoubtedly come down. Though the price of photovoltaic cells from which the panels are made has been cut in half since 1975, the cost is still $9 per watt, amounting to *$40,000* for a one-family home. The Department of Energy has set a goal to reduce the cost per watt to $2 in 1982 and 30 cents by 1990. Commitment to renewable types of fuel holds promise for everyone.

2. Continued reliance on nonrenewable fuels exhausts capital that could be used to finance other needed projects like rapid transit, public health, or housing. In 1972, energy production accounted for 13 percent of total U.S. business investment. By 1978, the figure had risen to 23 percent.[12]

3. Present-day power plants emit 60 percent of the energy they take in in the form of heat. One way to avoid this loss is through **cogeneration,** using the heat that would be lost when electricity is created to heat a nearby building, shopping center, apartment/condominium complex, or neighborhood of homes. Heat and electricity are cogenerated simultaneously.

Environmentalist Barry Commoner provides us with this example: "One recently designed cogenerator . . . is simply a four-cylinder gasoline engine of the sort ordinarily used to operate a Fiat automobile. The engine's drive shaft turns a generator that produces electricity; the engine's cooling system, which in the automobile gives off its heat into the environment by way of the radiator, is connected to a heat exchanger—a nest of interwoven pipes which transfers the heat produced by the engine to, say, a building's heating system."[13] Ninety percent of the engine's output is utilized; when used in an automobile, the engine's power output is at most 30 percent of the fuel's energy.

Some experts have suggested a mix of solutions to the problem of energy—a combination of energy conservation, exploiting (relatively abundant) coal as a fuel over the short term, and developing renewable energy resources (solar, thermal, and so on) over the long term.

5. Tax the devil out of gasoline

As the presidential election campaigns began to warm up in early 1980, an intriguing idea surfaced: tax gasoline up to 50 cents a gallon at the pump. The idea came from Congressman John B. Anderson (Rep., Illinois), one of the hopefuls.

What about the effect on people with low incomes who have to drive to work? Anderson had an answer: The money collected could be used to reduce Social Security taxes. His point was that we should be taxing something we want to conserve and reduce taxes that (1) hurt low-income people* and that (2) reduce their chances of employment.

According to present (February 1980) law, Social Security taxes will rise by 1982 to 6.7 percent of the first $31,800 you make; that is, $2,130 per year. One problem is that employers have to match that contribution. As we know from Chapter 3, the higher price employers have to pay for employees (on top of their wages) will reduce the quantity demanded for employees. Any payroll tax hurts employment. Mr. Anderson had a point. Nevertheless, President Carter's new budget for 1980–1981 contained no provision for additional gas taxes or changes in Social Security legislation.

The bright side Yes, there is a bright side. The energy crisis is more persuasive than any president's speech in making Americans examine the pluses and minuses of their market-price system and their way of living. For example, escalating oil prices (and, indirectly, other prices) remind us that continuing price increases exclude poorer people and that they need help to offset the impact of inflation.

We are becoming aware that price ceilings distort our values. Price ceilings on oil enable our market system to price cotton shirts and Perma-press shirts the same, say, at $15. But the price ignores the fact that cotton is a renewable resource, whereas the Perma-press shirt is made from synthetic fibers requiring considerable quantities of oil and natural gas.

Some physicians believe that our buildings and homes are overheated in winter and that we would be healthier if they were cooler. Also, if we drove less and walked or bicycled more, we might be healthier. If the airlines

---

*The Social Security tax hurts low-income people more than high-income people because the tax is imposed on only a portion of the high-income person's income. We'll discuss this point in more detail in Chapter 10.

fly fewer flights, they may become more efficient (and more profitable). If oil prices rise high enough, entrepreneurs will be motivated to find other sources of power in order to reduce fuel costs. As oil substitutes are developed, the elasticity of demand for oil will increase and a smaller increase in gasoline prices will be needed to equalize the quantities supplied and demanded. If people become more conscious of ways to conserve energy, they may be readier to form car pools and vote the funds necessary for rapid transit. When more efficient ways of moving people are found, pollution from transportation fuels will be reduced.

So, the energy crisis can be looked upon as an opportunity as well as a problem. It has made everyone realize, as Malthus did back in 1799, that the earth's resources are scarce and that we must devise new ways to cope with a world of scarcity.[14]

Summary

Supply and demand analysis can be used to help solve or clarify many contemporary problems. In the case of pollution, the market-price system has not resulted in an efficient use of resources because the external costs of transactions—the pollution of air, oceans or streams, or the disposal of used items by consumers—are not included in the price of products or services. If polluters had to pay effluent charges for the use of the air, water, or land they despoil, then the products they sell or use would include the cost of removing pollution, and more efficient, less polluting methods of production or distribution would probably be developed. The study of pollution indicates that the opportunity cost of cleaner air may be increased unemployment, but also that cleaner air increases property values and that people are willing to pay for such benefits.

One of the probable reasons for the energy crisis is that ceiling prices have encouraged consumption and discouraged production. Solving the problem involves a complicated set of trade-offs. We may hurt lower-income people with higher prices. A large government bureaucracy will become involved if rationing is used. Programs to save energy or develop new sources will take time to implement and bear fruit.

The energy crisis reminds us of the Malthusian problem—that human demands are increasing faster than increases in supply. We must plan now before the problem overtakes us.

Discussion Questions

1. Are there transactions with no external effects? What about the purchase of toothpaste or deodorant?

2. What are the external effects of education?

3. What is your definition of an efficient allocation of resources? How do you want everything divided among everyone? (Don't neglect external effects which may involve either social costs or benefits.)

4. How much would *you* be willing to pay to live in a cleaner environment?

5. Which of the five solutions to the energy crisis do you favor? Why?

References

1. Excerpted from *Time*, 6 May 1974, pp. 77–78. Reprinted by permission from *Time*, The Weekly Newsmagazine; copyright Time Inc., 1974.

2. This study, made by the Environmental Protection Agency, is described in "L.A. Smog: A Clean-up Could Save Millions," *Los Angeles Times*, 5 May 1979, pt. ii, p. 1.

3. D. L. Meadows et al., *Dynamics of Growth in a Finite World* (Cambridge, Mass.: Wright-Allen Press, 1974).

4. U.S. Geological Survey, 1974.

5. *Statistical Abstracts of the U.S.* (1978).

6. "Where Oil Firms Are Putting All Those Profits," *U.S. News & World Report*, 11 February 1980.

7. *Newsweek*, 11 February 1980, p. 75.

8. "Gasoline Abroad Plentiful but Costly, Survey Shows," *Los Angeles Times*, 22 May 1979, pt. iv, p. 1.

9. See John F. Lawrence, "Tax Could Cut Gas Thirst 15 Percent, Study Finds," *Los Angeles Times*, 21 December 1973, pt. i, pp. 1, 23.

10. Milton Friedman, "Blaming the Obstetrician," *Newsweek*, 4 June 1979, p. 70.

11. Daniel Yergin, "Energy Conservation: Success Stories Amid the Gloom," *Los Angeles Times*, 3 June 1979, pt. v, p. 1.

12. Barry Commoner, "Reflections," *The New Yorker*, 30 April 1979, p. 46 ff.

13. Commoner, "Reflections."

14. See Robert M. Solow, "Is the End of the World at Hand?" *Challenge*, March/April 1973, pp. 39–50; Donella H. Meadows, Dennis L. Meadows, Jorgen Randers, and William W. Behrens III, *The Limits to Growth* (New York: Universe Books, 1972); and Robert L. Heilbroner, "The Human Prospect," *New York Review of Books*, 24 January 1974, pp. 21–34.

7 Doing Business in the Real World: The Struggle for Market Power

Owen Franken/Stock, Boston

The real world is much more complicated than the simple models shown in Chapters 3, 4, and 5. Sellers compete against other sellers in their attempts to persuade buyers to buy (as we see in price competition among supermarkets). Buyers compete against other buyers (as we see in auctions). Buyers compete against sellers (as we see in the contest between employers as the buyers of labor and unions as the sellers of labor).

This chapter is about competition among sellers in their efforts to control markets. Sellers try to strengthen their own position, to weaken that of competing sellers, so that they, the winners, can charge higher prices. Their motive is to give buyers as few options as possible by reducing the number of suppliers. To whatever extent a buyer's options are reduced, a seller can control the market price. The seller's power to influence the price is called **market power.**

Key Words

Market power	Information costs
Explicit costs	Monopolistic competition
Implicit costs	Nonprice competition
Implicit wages	Oligopoly
Implicit rent	Monopoly
Implicit interest	Natural monopoly
Normal profit	Horizontal merger
Economic profit	Vertical merger
Pure competition	Conglomerate merger

This chapter is also about the kind of market activity that increasingly characterizes our economy, especially the development of giant sellers and the growing mix of public and private enterprise, and the government's response to market activity through regulation.

Adam Smith and the Blessings of Competition

Let us begin by reexamining Adam Smith's "invisible hand." You will recall that Smith believed that entrepreneurial self-interest, in a political environment of minimal government interference, would "promote the public interest." Smith meant that the free, unregulated search for profit by entrepreneurs and the unending competition among them for profit would result in the largest possible output of goods and services, produced in the most efficient manner possible, enabling consumers to buy the utmost abundance at the lowest possible prices.

How much profit is necessary to attract competitors?

Further, all resources—land, labor, capital, and entrepreneurship—would be channeled into their most efficient and best uses. If any resource could achieve any gain by moving from one occupation to another, it would do so until all resources were allocated in such a way as to give each one its highest return. If consumer wants then changed, causing prices and profits to change, the profitability of using resources in any given way would change. This process of change would again cause a shift in the use of resources, until the new desires of consumers were satisified.

The engine that was supposed to drive this system was the competitive battle among entrepreneurs for profit. The appearance of profit in any industry would attract other entrepreneurs to the fray like ants to honey. But when we say entrepreneurs will be drawn in by profits, what do we really mean? How much profit is necessary to attract competitors?

How do we calculate economic profit?

Assume that Jane Pennyworth has an egg ranch and that she sells 150,000 dozen eggs each year at 60 cents a dozen. For Jane, the profit question is this: How much profit must there be in the 60 cent price for her to be willing to buy and operate the factors of production (land, labor, capital, and her own entrepreneurship) in such a business? Jane's situation is shown in Figure 7-1.

Figure 7-1 tells us that Jane's total revenue will be 60 cents × 150,000 dozen eggs per year, or $90,000. Now let's assume that all Jane's money costs (every cost that requires paying someone some money), all expenses, even including taxes, are $70,000. These money costs are called **explicit costs.**

Apparently Jane has made $90,000 − $70,000 = $20,000 as profit. The $20,000 is called *accounting profit*, not economic profit.

To determine Jane's economic profit, economists first ask the question "What would Jane have made if she had done something else with her resources—labor, land, and capital?" The income from employing resources in some other way is foregone. This income is called the **implicit** (opportunity) **cost** of doing business.

First, what could Jane have earned if she had gone to work for someone else? The answer involves some thought and a good deal of guesswork. Assume she could have made $12,000 a year in a nice, safe 40-hour-a-week

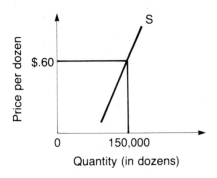

Figure 7-1. Jane's supply curve: The dozens of eggs she will want to sell at each price.

job. This is what she gave up to produce eggs, and egg raising involves perhaps far more of her time, nervous tension, and energy than would working for someone else. But if she values working for herself very highly, she might adjust the $12,000 figure downward to reflect the fact that the $12,000 sacrifice is not really that great after all. In any case, economists call the wages she *could* have earned in another employment **implicit wages.**

If the egg business includes a building or land she owns, she must also calculate the rental income she might have received if she had rented the land or building or both. Let us assume that she estimates the rental income she has sacrificed in this manner at $5,000 per year. As you might guess, this is called **implicit rent.**

Now assume that Jane has $30,000 tied up in her egg business in the form of buildings and equipment. Clearly Jane has lost the income her $30,000 might have earned.

Jane's purchase of $30,000 worth of capital for her egg business has two opportunity costs. One opportunity cost results from the interest she could have earned by putting her money in a savings account. The other opportunity cost results from the profit she could have earned by buying all or part of *another* business.

These two opportunity costs sound like the same thing but there is an important difference between them. Money put in a bank earns interest because the bank must pay Jane for her sacrifice in foregoing the use of it. When we become entrepreneurs like Jane, money used to purchase a business is expected to earn a "return" (profit) sufficient to reward us for the possibility of losing the money if the business fails. Thus interest is a return for foregoing consumption; profit is a reward for assuming the risk of loss.

Imagine that Jane's $30,000, now tied up in the egg business, is split into two parts, and that one part, $10,000, is put in a savings account earning 8 percent per year, or $800 per year. This sacrificed income that Jane could have earned is called **implicit interest.** And further imagine that the remaining $20,000 of her $30,000 could have been "invested" in *another* business and that this investment could have earned a profit of, say, $1,800 per year. This last opportunity cost is called **normal profit.** Normal profit is also an implicit cost because it is an opportunity cost like implicit wages, rent, and interest that does not entail any actual payment of money.

If we add up all of these implicit costs of using Jane's resources in the production of eggs, we have the following:

Implicit wages	$12,000
Implicit rent	5,000
Implicit interest	800
Normal profit	1,800
Total implicit costs	$19,600

Note that the implicit costs pair off with each of the four factor payments: wages, rent, interest, and profit. The sum of the implicit costs—the $19,600—is viewed as a *cost of production*, not as profit of any kind, because Jane's egg business must earn at least $19,600 to offset the opportunity cost (implicit cost) of using the resources she owns. If the egg business doesn't earn at least $19,600 after taxes, then Jane might well be better off doing something else with her time and capital.

Now where do we stand?

Income from sales	$90,000
Explicit (money) costs	− 70,000
Accounting profit	$20,000
Implicit costs	− 19,600
Remainder	$ 400

The remainder—$400—is called **economic profit.** Sometimes it is also called *pure profit.* It means that the enterprise is earning more than enough to offset the opportunity costs of using the entrepreneur's resources in a particular way.

What economic profit means in Adam Smith's world

In Adam Smith's world, what should happen now?

The existence of *economic* profit suggests that the resources employed in producing eggs are earning a surplus over and above what they could have earned in other forms of employment. This surplus (economic profit) suggests that some entrepreneurs not presently in the egg business will make the same calculations (because information is assumed to be immediately and freely available; see page 132) and conclude that entry into the egg business is worthwhile. As new entrepreneurs enter, the supply curve will shift to the right, driving the price down (assuming no change in demand). As the price falls, the economic profits will be squeezed out.

How far will the price fall? As it falls, some less efficient firms will find that their accounting profit does not cover the implicit costs. These firms will leave the egg industry. The firms that decide to remain will earn just enough to cover implicit costs and no more. All economic profit will be squeezed out because, as long as it exists, new entrepreneurs will continue to enter the industry and compete, forcing the price down to one that covers normal profit only.

This Adam Smithian view of a market-price system is beautiful from the point of view of consumers. They will always win by being able to buy goods and services at bargain prices. But what a bleak, cold world for enterpreneurs! Consequently, the first item of business on any intelligent entrepreneur's agenda is to discover how to prevent competing entrepreneurs from driving profits down.

The Four Markets

In order to analyze these movements away from intense competition, economists use four terms to describe the level or degree of competition among sellers: *pure competition, monopolistic competition, oligopoly*, and *monopoly*, the latter three representing movements to avoid competition. These are not separate categories but rather describe four areas on a spectrum, from lots of competition to none.

Pure competition

In the language of economics, there are four quite specific characteristics of a purely competitive industry.

1. Many small firms that cannot affect price.   In a purely competitive industry, there are thousands of small firms. However, each firm is so small that it has no influence over the market price. Regardless of how much or how little the firm supplies, it cannot, alone, change the market price. Examples of this are small farmers, who must accept the market price for their produce on any given day.

2. All firms make the same product.   All of the purely competitive firms in the industry make exactly the same product, so the only reason consumers have for choosing one firm's product over another is the product price, not its packaging, advertising, smell, or anything else.

The best example of this situation is that of a small grain farmer or egg rancher, whose product is the same as everyone else's. When this small entrepreneur comes to some large wholesale produce market, he or she is in no position to bargain but must accept the market price for his or her product that exists on any given day.

3. Mobile resources.   In the purely competitive world it is assumed that resources are instantly mobile. Thus, if profit suddenly appears in an industry, entrepreneurs will instantly rush into that industry. It is also assumed that there are no barriers to entry. As new entrepreneurs move in, supply shifts to the right. Given no change in demand, the price will fall.

At this point there may be some confusion. Whereas no *one* entrepreneur can influence the price, if substantial numbers of firms move into or out of an industry, the market price will fall or rise with changes in the total supply provided by all firms. The market price might also change because of a change in consumer demand.

4. Knowledge of other profitable opportunities.   The last requirement in the definition of pure competition is that knowledge of more profitable opportunities for any of the resources is immediately and freely available. For example, suppose that you earn $10 an hour as a worker in a television manufacturing plant in Boston. The rate for the same job in Miami suddenly hits $20 an hour because of an increase in demand for TV sets there and a local shortage of workers with your particular skill. In the world of pure competition, you would know of this opportunity immediately.

As others move to Miami, the labor shortage will ease.

Assuming that resources are perfectly mobile, you would be able to move to Miami with perfect ease and get the job with no difficulty (there would be no barriers in terms of difficulties in joining a local union, for example). As you and others move to Miami, the labor shortage will ease. Wages may very well come down as the supply of labor shifts to the right. As labor costs fall, TV entrepreneurs may be willing to sell more TV sets at lower prices. The end result is that, again, the change in consumer demand has been answered by a satisfying and immediate response.

Note the emphasis on the information being freely available. If the information is difficult or costly to obtain (if you had to make several long-distance telephone calls to Miami to inquire about the job), this difficulty constitutes another serious barrier to entry. Economists are becoming more and more interested in **information costs.** The federal government is establishing "job banks" in which all job vacancies are computerized and then matched with job applicants (like computer-dating bureaus).

Information costs exist in almost every transaction. Think of the time you spend shopping for a car, comparing the deals that various car dealers offer you. The time you spend driving around or phoning involves actual

The federal government is establishing job banks in which all job vacancies are computerized.

costs (gas expense and phone bills) and opportunity costs. These costs are not included in the car prices you consider and should be taken into account before you buy the car (or anything else). If you are planning to buy something inexpensive and the information costs about the quality (or the prices of other brands) are high, you might want to save yourself the cost of obtaining all the information and buy the first version of the product or service you see. The point to remember about information costs is that, when they are high, business firms can charge prices higher than those charged in markets where information costs are low. (Whenever you can easily compare prices, no one entrepreneur can "get away" with a price that is too far out of line.)

How efficient is pure competition?

Economists not only criticize the market-price system's failure to provide full employment, stable prices, social goods, an equitable distribution of income, and so forth, but also stress the failure of pure competition to improve the quality of products or to produce goods and services as efficiently as possible. (Of course, absolutely "pure" competition has never existed.)

If there are no barriers to entry, resources are instantly mobile, information is immediate and free, and economic profits are continuously wiped out, entrepreneurs will be unable to put resources aside for research and development to improve the quality of their products or their methods of production. This argument against pure competition is used by large firms to justify their size and their need for economic profit, although in fact many important inventions—air conditioning, automatic transmissions, power steering, the gyrocompass, the helicopter, the jet engine—have come from individuals or small companies rather than large corporations.

Another argument against pure competition is that it may be so easy for new entrepreneurs to compete because of low entry barriers that many of them will not be qualified to manage a business. Miscalculations of this sort mean wasted resources—empty stores, vacant offices, and factory buildings standing idle for months until other entrepreneurs find a way to make them pay. Finally, because the barriers to entry are low enough to let in unsophisticated or inexperienced entrepreneurs, the production methods used by many of them may not be very efficient. Because of this, a purely competitive price may be *higher* than it would be if less competition were present.

Why economists *usually* prefer competitive markets

The difficulty is that one can never be sure whether a price is "high" or "low" if there are no competitive substitutes available to the buyers. The noncompetitive markets in utilities (gas, power, telephone) are good examples of common situations in which buyers have no choice. In such situations, we have no way of knowing for sure if the service provided is priced as low as possible and is of the highest possible quality. There is no way we can compare the service we receive with that offered by other, competing companies. Consider also the marketplace of ideas. If there is only one newspaper to read or only one or two (government-controlled) television stations to watch (or only one economics instructor to listen to), how can we know for sure if we're getting the truth? We don't. The presence of alternative services or viewpoints for comparison is extremely important. For these reasons, most economists favor more competition rather than less.

Monopolistic competition

The world of pure competition is a cold, hard world for entrepreneurs. They are faced with a continuous life-or-death struggle for survival. If they succeed in making an economic profit, this brief moment of comfort evaporates as competing entrepreneurs force the market price down. Against all of these forces, they are powerless because they are too small to influence the price. They have no market power.

What do normal entrepreneurs do? As long as they remain entrepreneurs—as opposed to giving up and working for someone else—they must find a way to remove themselves from this daily struggle. The best way to do this is to try to convince consumers that their products are in some way different from, and superior to, all others in the industry. If they can sell the idea of this difference, they may be able to charge higher prices than those given to them by the impersonal forces of the market.

Such entrepreneurs, rather than being *price takers*, might succeed in becoming *price makers*. Their objective is to achieve sufficient power to earn and keep an economic profit. Thus, they will do everything they can do to remove themselves from the arena of pure competition by persuading buyers that their products are something special and that buyers should forget about what other sellers are selling.

Each firm tries to persuade the public that it has something special to offer.

The first step away from purely competitive markets is **monopolistic competition.*** Monopolistic competition is defined as a market in which there are many sellers—typically small stores, small farms, small manufacturing firms—and where the product of each seller is similar. This is the market we see every day in the older shopping areas of cities. Competition among large numbers of small clothing stores, drug stores, hardware stores, barber shops, grocery stores, dry cleaning establishments, and restaurants is often fierce. Each firm tries to persuade the public that it has something special to offer—perhaps easy credit, better service, or free delivery—that its competitors do not have.

The term *monopolistic competition*, therefore, describes a world where a great many small shops and factories operate and where the barriers to entry are low. The distinguishing characteristic of this form of competition is that the products produced by different firms in a particular industry are no longer exactly alike because *name brands* are attached to them.

As a toothpaste entrepreneur in a world of monopolistic competition, you might first attach a brand name like Dazzle to your product and then launch a sales campaign to convince buyers that Dazzle really is special and

---

All markets which are not purely competitive are called "imperfect" markets, meaning that some barriers to entry, some information costs, and some degree of market power are present.

Think of all the ways sellers differentiate their products.

worth its higher-than-market price. Your sales campaign might begin with a new label and local newspaper advertising extolling the qualities of Dazzle. The sales campaign would seek to convince consumers that Dazzle's special ingredients whiten and brighten the teeth and immediately and dramatically enhance personal attractiveness. With the help of an advertising agency, you might develop a sales slogan: *Dazzle Does It!*

Think of all the ways sellers differentiate their products. Brands of gasoline advertise special ingredients, as do nationally advertised soaps, detergents, shaving creams, razor blades, cigarette filters, and so on. The object, of course, is to remove oneself from the jungle of price competition. Competition among competing brands, not in terms of price, but in terms of special ingredients or services (such as free delivery) is called **nonprice competition.**

In the world of monopolistic competition, there is still plenty of price competition because entry barriers, such as capital requirements and franchises to buy, are still so low that if economic profit appears, other firms can enter and compete without too much difficulty. We are still not far away from Adam Smith's world of pure competition; entrepreneurs have little market power. But is this the real world in the United States?

Oligopoly   **Oligopoly** means that just a few producers or sellers supply a major portion of an industry's output. (The prefix *mono-* means one, and the prefix *oligo-* means few.) An oligopolistic industry is one in which there are three or four large firms, each one of which is large enough and has sufficient market power to influence the market price and total industry output.

In this situation, each firm must be extremely wary of the price and output decisions of the others. A price cut by one may cause the others to lower prices, resulting in lower revenues for all. If one firm raises its price and the others do not go along, it may lose customers to the firms with lower prices. However, some evidence, particularly in the automobile industry, indicates that when one firm raises its price, the others also raise theirs. When they act in concert, each of the firms maintains its share of the market.

Although deliberate collusion is illegal, economic theory suggests that oligopolistic firms cooperate by tacit agreement, so that no one of them interferes with the market and so that each firm's sales and profits remain relatively stable. Lack of cooperation by any one firm involves too many risks for all. For example, consider what happened in 1956 when Ford and General Motors raised their prices:

> The Ford Motor Company initially announced an average price increase on its 1957 models of 2.9 percent. Two weeks later, however, when GM increased its 1957 model prices by an average 6.1 percent, Ford promptly revised its prices upward to match the GM prices almost dollar for dollar (and Chrysler soon followed suit). . . . This kind of coordinated pricing occurs regularly in the highly concentrated industries. Official government reports reveal the receipt from supposed competitors of hundreds of sealed bids that are identical to the fourth decimal place in the purchase of steel, aluminum, electrical, and other products.[1]

Although this report appeared over twenty years ago, nothing has changed. On September 21, 1976, General Motors announced a 4.9 percent increase in the average base price of its new big-model cars for 1977. (GM earlier had announced an average 5.9 percent price boost for all its 1977 models.) One week later, Ford raised its average prices 5.6 percent. Chrysler then followed with a 5.9 percent increase and American Motors with a 4.8 percent increase.[2] Again in 1979, the four firms went through four rounds of increases that raised prices an average of 8.5 percent over 1978.

The well-known economist John Kenneth Galbraith believes that oligopoly is the "characteristic market of the industrial system."[3] Many economists also believe that the trend toward oligopoly has been irresistible and inevitable. Just as pure competitors struggle to free themselves from the bleak prospects of pure competition, so do the monopolistic competitors struggle to free themselves from the high degree of competition that exists in the world of monopolistic competition.

If you, the Dazzle Toothpaste entrepreneur, convince the public that your product is superior, you may be able to use the economic profit you earn thereby to further remove yourself from competition. You will be able to advertise and to purchase the capital goods necessary to produce your product more efficiently. The more successful you become, the more difficult it is for other firms to compete. Think of how tough it would be to compete with a nationally advertised soft drink, cereal, or cigarette. A new steel plant or automobile factory requires at least $250 million in capital equipment.

The best known oligopolies in the United States are the automobile industry, in which 3 firms control about 90 percent of the U.S. output of passenger cars; the gypsum industry, in which 4 firms provide 90 percent of the industry's output; and the aluminum industry, in which 4 firms provide almost all of the aluminum produced. In addition, in each of the following fields, 4 or fewer firms produce more than 50 percent of the products: breakfast cereals, chewing gum, cigarettes, computers, household washers and dryers, light bulbs, linoleum, matches, razors and razor blades, refrigerators, soap and detergents, steel, tin cans, tires and tubes, and typewriters.

Monopoly   The fourth type of market is **monopoly.**

The term means that there is only one seller of a product or service in the market and that there are no good substitutes available for its products or services. The firm need not be large. It might be the only drug store in a town so small and geographically isolated that consumers cannot afford to drive to a competing drug store in another town. Or the monopoly may be a giant. Until World War II, The Aluminum Company of America was the only producer of aluminum in the United States.

When an industry has a monopoly and there is no competition, its power may be great. ("May be" because being a monopoly does not guarantee success—it could be the only supplier of something no one wants.)

With some monopolies, other products may provide a form of competition. For example, with aluminum there is competition from other metals, plastics, and fiberglass.

Utilities are probably the purest form of monopoly because available substitutes for electricity, natural gas, piped water, and telephone service are not very satisfactory. There are two main reasons why we are not permitted to buy utility service from more than one firm: (1) It would be clearly inconvenient to have the streets in continuous disrepair from constant tearing up by competing water companies, gas companies, power and telephone companies. (2) Utilities are usually decreasing-cost industries.

A *decreasing-cost industry* is one in which unit costs go down as output increases. Utilities are usually in this category because, once the pole line or pipeline is built, it is relatively easy to add customers. These facts of life lend economic support to granting utilities dominance in a particular market. Utilities are often called **natural monopolies** because the conditions that justify their existence seem natural or attributable to nature.

In exchange for the privilege of being a natural monopoly for a given geographical area, the monopoly becomes subject to regulation by a utility commission, usually an agency of a state government. The commission's job is to see to it that the prices charged do not give utility owners (stockholders)

(Continued on page 141)

The Battle for Shelf Space

Today, besides chicken with rice soup, there is chicken gumbo, chicken noodle, curly noodle with chicken, cream of chicken, creamy . . .

Although price competition among oligopolists is often nonexistent or at least difficult to measure, the battle among large firms for the public's eye is often intense. Campbell Soup now makes 3 lines of soup with 80 varieties. Today, besides chicken with rice soup, there is chicken gumbo, chicken noodle, chicken noodle O's, curly noodle with chicken, cream of chicken, creamy chicken mushroom, chicken vegetable, chicken alphabet, chicken and stars, chicken 'n dumplings, and chicken broth.

Why? To hog shelf space and prevent competitors from reaching the public.

The Coca Cola foods division recently added 2 new lines of drip coffee, 2 new varieties of fruit juice, and 2 new lines of powdered drink mixes. The drink mixes come in 9 flavors and 2 sizes. The company has also added a tenth and eleventh flavor (punch and tangerine) to its existing Hi-C line of canned drinks.

Not to battle risks disaster. The Liggett & Myers Tobacco Company held 20 percent of the market thirty years ago. Now its market share has dropped to 3 percent. The company failed to match its rivals in introducing new brands to the public.

Before 1950, most smokers smoked Camels, Luckies, Old Gold, Chesterfields, all uniformly 2¾ inches long. Now retailers must stock 58 varieties taking up 33 feet of shelf space. They also would have to provide 176 feet of shelf for candy and chewing gum, 193 feet for soft drinks, 210 feet for dog and cat dinners (up 80 percent in seven years), 229 feet for refrigerated foods, and 290 feet for frozen foods in order to accommodate all brands of these items.

Some experts believe that consumers sometimes become so confused by the variety of "choices" that they leave the stores without buying or buying less than they had planned. But the chances are that no one firm can trust its rivals to give up the battle, and advertising agencies, whose total revenue was $43.7 billion in 1978, are unlikely to discourage their customers from continuing to add brand names to their offerings.[4]

more than a "fair return" on their investment. As you might imagine, there is considerable argument (with no firm answers) as to what constitutes a fair return. Furthermore, it takes great expertise on the part of the commission to determine whether or not the monopoly is being run in an efficient manner.

Summing up the four markets

Table 7-1 reviews the major characteristics of the four stopping places on the spectrum of markets.

Where Are We Headed?

We have seen that entrepreneurs have very good reasons to graduate from highly competitive markets to those where they can earn and keep economic profits over a long span of time. Now the question is, Where is our market-price system headed?

Toward the end of *The American Business System in Transition*, Morton Baratz concludes that there are two major differences between our market-price system now and what it was in 1900. First has been the growth of the large corporations, not merely in size, but in diversification. For these, Baratz uses the term "superoligopolies."

Second, in 1900 "the line of demarcation" between public and private ownership could be "confidently distinguished" but now there is a "blending" of the two sectors: "The dividing line between public and private enterprise, never too distinct, has all but vanished. The two sectors, to put it baldly, are becoming increasingly amalgamated."[5]

TABLE 7-1 Summing Up the Four Markets

Market characteristics	Pure competition	Monopolistic competition	Oligopoly	Monopoly
Product differentiation (brand names)	No	Yes	Yes	Yes
Price competition	Intense	Intense	Occasionally, but cooperative behavior often present	Occasionally with producers of substitute goods or services. Prices of "natural monopolies" subject to regulation
Advertising (nonprice competition)	None	Intense	Intense	Often, to promote public good will
Barriers to entry	None	Low	High	High
Information costs	None	Low	High	High
Opportunities to earn and keep economic profits	None	Few	Many	Many, though often regulated

This section will take up these two points and a third one: (1) the advent of the "superoligopolies," (2) the "blending" of public and private enterprise, and (3) the economic effects of government regulation.

The advent of the superoligopolies

There is no doubt that the American industrial scene is dominated by giants. Consider: There are about 12 million individual firms and farms in the United States. While 99.8 percent of them have fewer than 500 employees, *two-tenths of 1 percent*, with 1,000 or more employees each, account for 38.1 percent of total employment.

☐ Six firms take in more sales income than *any* state government takes in taxes.

☐ Ten percent of U.S. corporations account for 75 percent of all sales and employ 60 percent of all workers.

☐ Twelve hundred large farms produce as much as 1.6 million smaller farms.

☐ Eight percent of U.S. farms produce 50 percent of our agricultural products.

Even among the top 500 corporations, which own two-thirds of all manufacturing assets, there are tremendous differences in size—the very few giants at the top of the pyramid have by far the greatest share of sales and profit. Of the 500 largest firms, sales of the top 50 equal the combined sales of the other 450. The profits of the top 10 are about equal to the combined profits of the other 490.[6]

Is bigness necessarily badness? There are arguments pro and con. We may need large firms in order to compete more effectively with large foreign companies. On the other hand, industrial innovation and invention has typically come from small firms, not from the research laboratories of large corporations.

But what is perhaps more significant than the size of business firms is the fact that large firms are buying companies in many diversified industries. These acquisitions are called mergers.

Mergers: when firms get together

Mergers can be of three types: horizontal, vertical, and conglomerate. **Horizontal mergers** are those in which one company acquires another in the same type of business. Example: Jane Pennyworth buys another egg ranch. **Vertical mergers** are those in which one company buys another that supplies it or buys another that, in turn, sells its product to retail customers. Example: Jane Pennyworth buys a chicken feed company or a grocery store that retails her eggs.

These two types of mergers have been frowned on by antitrust agencies because they tend to reduce competition (see Box Essay). For example, if oil companies merge (horizontal merging), price competition lessens. If oil

(Continued on page 144)

Antitrust Legislation (or, Keep Your Eye on the Traffic Cop)

Laws, like a traffic cop, prevent the more flagrant attempts by firms to monopolize markets.

The U.S. government tries to keep markets competitive with antitrust legislation—and litigation. Three famous laws deserve mention: the Sherman Anti-Trust Act of 1890, which made it illegal for firms to combine "in restraint of trade"; the Clayton Act of 1914, which tried to plug loopholes in the Sherman Act "where the effect would substantially lessen competition"; and the Celler Anti-Merger Act of 1950, which tried to block the acquisition of one company by another—again where the effect would lessen competition.

The difficulty with prosecuting under the Celler Act is that it "frowned" on the merger of two large firms in the same market, but it did not discourage the takeover of small firms by big ones or conglomerate mergers involving different markets.

There is much debate about how successful these laws have been. The courts have had great difficulty in defining such phrases as "substantially lessen competition." Nevertheless, economists generally believe that the laws—like a traffic cop—prevent the more flagrant attempts by firms to monopolize markets.

companies control drilling, refining, and retailing (through vertical merging), they can control the price consumers have to pay, particularly if the vertically organized companies cooperate with one another about prices.

But the most prevalent type of merger since 1925 has been the **conglomerate merger** in which one company buys control of one or more, often several, unrelated companies. In 1977, 70 percent of all mergers were of this type.

The expansion of International Telephone and Telegraph Company (ITT) provides an excellent example of increasing power through mergers and diversification. In 1961, ITT decided to enlarge by acquiring other companies. Over the next seven years, it purchased a controlling share of the assets of 107 other companies with assets of $1.5 billion. By 1966, according to writer Richard Barber, ITT had "acquired an odd assortment of enterprises: . . . Hayes Furnace Co., Aetna Finance, Great International Life Insurance, Hamilton Management Co. (a $400 million mutual fund), Avis Rent-A-Car, ABC-Paramount (itself diversified, with broadcasting, theater, phonograph record, and publishing assets), and Airport Parking (with facilities at air terminals in 59 of the nation's largest cities)."[7]

More recently, ITT has acquired Continental Baking, Marquis Who's Who Inc., Sheraton Hotel Corporation, Levitt and Sons (housing), and Hartford Fire Insurance. With annual sales now of $6 billion and more than 350,000 employees, ITT is one of the largest companies in the world.

Why should we worry about mergers?

Senator Edward Kennedy, for one, believes that mergers not only are tending to reduce competition but are also reducing the number of "decision-makers [who] now determine matters tangibly affecting all Americans—the kind and quality of clothes we wear, the food we buy or the books we read."[8] Kennedy's latter reference was to the fact that 10 publishers control 90 percent of paperback sales, and that these "publishers" are such huge firms as RCA, Gulf & Western, and CBS, which now dominate the entire book market.

Mergers involving large corporations have recently increased both in number and magnitude. In 1975, there were 14 mergers of firms with more than $100 million in assets or sales. By 1978, there were 80 such mergers. The combined value of the merged companies was about $12 billion in 1975, $34 billion in 1978.

Now let's turn to the second characteristic of our economic life that Professor Baratz has noted—the increased blending of public and private enterprise.

The blending of public and private enterprise

"Blending" does not necessarily come from outright government ownership. Only about 2 percent of total income is generated by publicly owned enterprises, including municipally owned utilities and federally owned enterprises such as the Tennessee Valley Authority.

Much of the blending occurs in joint ventures by government and private industry. In many cases, federal installations such as the atomic energy plants are contracted out to private concerns like General Electric, Westinghouse, and the Union Carbide Corporation. In the Communications Satellite Corporation (COMSAT), the federal government shares ownership and control with American Telephone and Telegraph (AT&T) and International Telephone and Telegraph (ITT).

Another type of blending occurs when the government is the major customer of many large corporations and countless small ones, as in the field of defense. Defense Department purchases usually account for more than 75 percent of the sales of seven major aircraft manufacturers. Many observers believe that aircraft and missile firms are so closely connected to the Defense Department that they have roughly the same status as the Postal Service.

The dependence of these firms on military contracts gave rise to the famous caution in President Eisenhower's farewell address shortly before he left office in 1961:

> This conjunction of an immense military establishment and a large arms industry is new in the American experience. . . . In the councils of government we must guard against the acquisition of unwarranted influence, whether sought or unsought, by the military-industrial complex.

The federal government also supplies about 60 percent of the funds for all research and development (R&D) by industry, universities, and hospitals. These funds further increase the marriage between key government officials and business executives throughout the country.

Not only have corporations become increasingly dependent on the federal government to buy their goods and services and to supply R&D funds, on several occasions corporations have gone to federal agencies for financial assistance when sales and profits have lagged. In the box essay on the steel industry (pages 146 and 147), note journalist Samuelson's comment that big steel companies want a "more political breed of executive," and note also that government involvement often comes at a business firm's request.

Government regulation of private enterprise

Beyond outright government ownership, joint government-private operations, or the behind-the-scenes influence seekers and peddlers, there is a growing array of enterprises formally regulated by government agencies: railroads, bus lines, trucking companies, barge lines, taxicab companies, and, of course, the utilities.

Regulating agencies are of two types: (1) agencies identified with specific industries and (2) those representing a "public interest." In the first category are public utility commissions in each state and federal agencies such as the Federal Power Commission (FPC), the Federal Communications Commission (FCC), the Civil Aeronautics Board (CAB), the Interstate Commerce Commission (ICC), and the Food and Drug Administration (FDA).

Steel: A Free Enterprise That Really Isn't

When government makes, or approves, key decisions, it's as good as running the industry.

Unless you're a connoisseur of corporate minutiae, you probably missed the recent groundbreaking ceremony at Monessen, Pa., where

Wheeling-Pittsburgh Steel Corp. hopes to build a new rail mill with a $105 million government-guaranteed loan. It doesn't sound like much in

In the second category are a new set of agencies that do not represent any specific industry but instead represent various public interest groups. Examples in this category are the Equal Employment Opportunity Commission (EEOC), the Environmental Protection Agency (EPA), the Occupational Safety and Health Administration (OSHA), and the Consumer Product Safety Commission (CPSC).

What are the costs of regulation?

Economist Murray Weidenbaum, head of the Center for the Study of American Business at Washington University, divides regulatory costs into two categories: administrative costs and compliance costs.

Administrative costs are the total amounts spent by the federal government to operate regulatory agencies. These costs have "rocketed" from $74.5 million in 1970 to $4.8 billion in 1979.[9]

the way of news, but it constitutes a telling commentary on the steel industry—which, more and more, is becoming a ward of the state.

American steel executives think otherwise, and ridicule state-owned firms abroad that survive only with massive government help.

But the difference between the U.S. industry and many of its overseas counterparts is increasingly one of form, not substance. When government makes—or approves—key decisions about costs, prices and investment, it's as good as running the industry. And that's precisely what's happening today.

Item: The specialty-steel industry, which makes stainless and other high-grade steel products, has mounted an intensive lobbying and publicity campaign to have the Administration renew import quotas first adopted by President Ford. By holding down imports, the quotas have clearly boosted both profits and employment.

Item: At least six companies—including Wheeling-Pittsburgh—have applied for federal loan guarantees that could ultimately total nearly $500 million. The loans will support investments that wouldn't otherwise be made and, in a few cases, may prevent—or, at any rate, delay—firms from going bankrupt.

All this has subtly changed the industry's character. Having fought for years with the government—over prices and over environmental and safety rules—the steel companies now see regulation as inevitable, and have decided to twist it to their advantage. This tactical shift has made the industry's public relations increasingly aggressive, and may explain the rise of a more political breed of executive: men like Richard P. Schubert, a former undersecretary of labor, recently named president of Bethlehem Steel Corp., the nation's second-largest producer.

The drift is unmistakable. The government—through its loan-guarantee program—is acquiring an increasingly large steel investment that it will need to protect. Industry and labor are eager for the protection, and urge it through a variety of administrative and technical proposals. We will continue to have the mantle of free enterprise, and the reality of government control.

Robert J. Samuelson, "Steel: A Free Enterprise That Really Isn't," *Los Angeles Times*, 5 April 1979, pt. ii, p. 7. Reprinted with permission from National Journal.

Compliance costs are the costs to business firms and consumers for complying with regulations. These costs are much larger. For example, the Environmental Protection Agency's administrative costs were $416 million in 1976, whereas its rulings forced industry to spend $7.8 billion in compliance. Weidenbaum estimates that total administrative costs in 1976 were $3 billion while total compliance costs were $63 billion. Total regulatory costs for 1980 are estimated to be $100 billion. These costs are usually paid by consumers in the form of higher prices.

There are other than dollar costs. Sometimes the rulings of regulatory agencies conflict with one another and make rational decision making almost impossible for business executives: While in 1979, the Department of Energy was busy pushing business firms to use more coal and to save oil, the Environmental Protection Agency was penalizing firms for polluting the air with coal smoke.

Or, sometimes the rulings are wasteful and nonsensical: Interstate Commerce Commission rules prohibit trucks from two-way hauling. Trucks can deliver soup ingredients to a soup factory but are forbidden to haul the soup away. Some truckers can haul milk, but not butter; cream but not cheese; bananas but not pineapples. But bananas *and* pineapples are allowed if they are mixed. And some trucks are allowed to haul two-gallon cans of paint but not five-gallon ones.

And what are the benefits?

The proregulation lobby, consisting of consumerists like Ralph Nader and environmentalists like Barry Commoner, argue that Weidenbaum's estimates fail to take into account the costs to society of no regulation or the hidden costs of dirty or dangerous production. Nor, they argue, does Weidenbaum consider the benefits of saved lives or of better health. According to Labor Secretary Ray Marshall, "A relaxation [in regulation] will increase the real social costs that our traditional economic indexes don't measure."[10]

The problem is that public expenditures are usually easy to measure; public benefits aren't. We can measure the cost of a new sewage system, but measuring the long-term benefits of disease reduction which may follow is extremely difficult, partly because of the difficulty of tying a particular benefit to the cost. (Who can say whether a reduced incidence of dysentery comes from a new sewage system or from better food preparation—or from some other factor which improves our health?)

How does politics influence regulation?

Perhaps inevitably, there is a connection between regulatory agencies and politics. Consider air and water pollution. In 1970, for instance, one survey concluded that polluters sit on antipollution boards:

> The inquiry revealed that the membership of air and water pollution boards in 35 states is dotted with industrial, agricultural, municipal and county representatives whose own organizations or spheres of activity are in many cases in the forefront of pollution. The roster of big corporations with employes on such boards reads like an abbreviated blue book of American industry, particularly the most pollution-troubled segments of industry. . . . One Colorado state hearing on stream pollution by a brewery was *presided over by the pollution control director of the brewery* [emphasis added]. For years a board member dealing with pollution of Los Angeles Harbor has been an executive of an oil company that was a major harbor polluter. The Governor of Indiana recently had to dismiss a state pollution board member because both he, the board member, and his company were indicted as water polluters.[11]

The political influence problem is pervasive and bipartisan. In 1966, the Johnson Administration dropped an antitrust case against Anheuser-Busch three weeks after brewery chairman August A. Busch, Jr., his wife, and other executives and wives contributed $10,000 to the "President's Club," which had been created by President Kennedy with the implication that large contributors would have easy access to the President. Part of the furor of the

Watergate scandal of 1972–73 involved the allegation that the Nixon Administration had blocked (through import quotas) the importation of milk products and had raised price supports on milk as a result of a $2 million campaign contribution to the Republican Party by a trade association of milk producers.

The blending of government and business in the United States is a fact of life. What is less clear is how it happened. The following story about the egg industry will help to show why business firms sometimes seek government assistance and government regulation.

A Case of Eggs: Whatever Happened to Adam Smith?*

On a typical American family farm of the 1930s the husband worked in the fields and his wife tended a hen house and raised chickens. Perhaps a few dozen eggs a day were sold to neighbors, passersby, and sometimes to a retail store. Egg sales added a little to the farm's income.

This was a world of pure competition. The farmers were selling an undifferentiated product. Everybody's eggs were like everyone else's. There were virtually no barriers to entry since the purchase price of a laying hen was around $3. Each egg farmer (or his wife) provided such a small portion of the total supply that he had no control over the market price. On a few farms of the period, however, egg raising was a real business. A farm might have a flock of 2,000 hens laying approximately 100 dozen eggs per day.

Beginning in the early 1940s, this almost purely competitive industry went through a period of extremely rapid change. Since then, the egg business has become an industry of mammoth farms each owning more than 1 million laying hens and often as many as 5 or 6 million hens. The birds are kept in completely automated, climate-controlled hen houses where machines feed them, clean their cages, and collect, sort, grade, and package their eggs. Two men, whose main job is to keep the machinery running, can now take care of 200,000 hens. These gigantic firms are oligopolies, in many cases regulated and protected by government agencies.

How did these changes come about? Our story starts in 1940 in Southern California, where grocery stores began growing into chains of supermarkets. The big stores were not interested in dealing directly with the ranchers unless the ranchers would deliver at least 500 cases[†] of eggs a week (180,000 eggs). In those days, 500 cases of eggs constituted the entire weekly production of 32 egg ranches, and the largest ranch could supply only 50 cases. Because local associations of egg ranchers could not meet this requirement, they joined together and formed the Council of Poultry Cooperatives, which functioned successfully for several years.

The author is extremely grateful to two Southern California egg ranchers, Ronald S. Rossitter and Walter Zentler, for the details of this story. The author is, of course, fully responsible for any errors.

†*One case of eggs contains 30 dozen eggs: 30 × 12 = 360 eggs.*

Big stores were not interested in dealing with the ranchers unless the ranchers would deliver at least 500 cases of eggs a week.

With the formation of the council, the purely competitive scene began to disappear, and the egg ranches began to grow. Southern California, with its temperate climate, was a perfect place for poultry. The high profits and high rates of return attracted entrepreneurs. High profits also encouraged technological change. The key innovation—a cage—sounds terribly simple, but up to this time, chickens had typically been kept in a house with a floor. They were fed and watered by hand, eggs were gathered by hand, and the floor was cleaned by hand. The cage, where four hens were crammed into a space 12 inches by 18 inches, permitted the beginning of automated feeding, cleaning, and egg gathering. The cage also made it much easier to check each hen's egg production and health.

As the ranches adopted the cage and grew larger and more efficient, Southern California gradually ceased being an importer of eggs from other parts of the country and became self-sufficient and then an egg exporter. The supply curve was rapidly shifting to the right. As it shifted to the right, the egg ranchers tried to increase their production, causing the price to fall. As the price fell, they tried to increase production still more, causing the price to fall still further. As prices fell, each producer had to sell more to maintain a given level of income. This was especially true where fixed costs were large (as, for example, when a farm had borrowed heavily to expand its physical plant and had to continue to pay interest on its bank loan and other plant expenses regardless of production).

At the same time, producers found that the demand for eggs, as for many other agricultural products, was extremely inelastic. As egg prices fell because of shifts in supply, consumers did not proportionately increase their purchases. If demand was inelastic and the price fell, what happened to the

Figure 7-2. A case of eggs: the increase in supply drops the price.

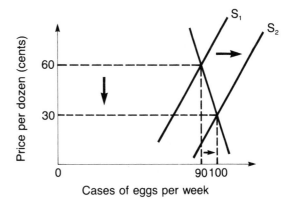

producer's revenue? It also fell. (See the discussion of elasticity and agriculture in Chapter 5.)

Figure 7-2 summarizes the predicament facing the egg ranchers. The prices and quantities are hypothetical, but they illustrate what happens to the egg rancher's income when supply increases and demand is inelastic. When the equilibrium price falls from 60 cents a dozen to 30 cents, consumers increase their purchases from 90 cases per week to 100. Keep in mind here that a case of eggs is *30 dozen* eggs. At 60 cents a dozen, the egg rancher's revenue is

$$60 \text{ cents} \times 90 \text{ cases} \times 30 \text{ dozen} = \$1620$$

When the price falls to 30 cents, the rancher's revenue is

$$30 \text{ cents} \times 100 \text{ cases} \times 30 \text{ dozen} = \$900$$

The rancher's income has dropped drastically because demand is inelastic. The 50 percent drop in price outweighs the 11 percent (the increase from 90 to 100) increase in sales. The rancher is in trouble.

It took about five years for the egg surplus in California to become a real problem because the ranchers were able to export the surplus to eastern markets. This solution to the oversupply problem soon disappeared, however, as the technology of producing eggs spread eastward and particularly when climate-controlled hen houses made it just as easy to produce eggs in the Middle West and East as in Southern California.

The egg cartel   In 1965, to meet the challenge of falling prices and the surplus of eggs, the Southern California ranchers formed another voluntary association, the Southwest Egg Producers (SWEP).

With SWEP, each rancher was given an equitable production base—a kind of weekly quota expressed in numbers of cases. SWEP agreed to buy this quota at prices it fixed and then sell the eggs to retail grocery stores. Prices on quota quantities were called "Pool 1" prices. If the market became glutted—say, oversupplied by 20 percent—it was agreed that Pool 1 prices would apply only to 80 percent of each rancher's base. The other 20 percent of this production would be sold at substantially lower prices—called "Pool 2" prices—with the understanding that Pool 2 eggs would not appear in California grocery stores.

The ranchers called this process a *surplus disposal* program. The objective, of course, was to limit the supply of eggs sold in California and thereby keep prices at profitable levels.

For a while the SWEP plan worked. Retail prices climbed to a high of $1 per dozen in some stores in late 1969. But then rising profits and improved technology caused the supply to continue its rapid increase. Even at its zenith, SWEP members controlled only 70 percent of all the eggs produced in Southern California, and the surplus eggs produced by nonmembers could often be sold at prices higher than Pool 2 prices. Dissension grew in SWEP ranks. The largest and most influential producers who had grown the fastest resented the quota system.

After trying a variety of plans, SWEP finally dissolved because the ranchers were unable to agree to limit production and to stick together.

SWEP, we must remember, was a *cartel*, like the OPEC countries. It was an association of companies that existed for the purpose of preventing competition among its members and for the purpose of controlling the overall quantity supplied and therefore the market price. Cartels are usually illegal, but many agricultural products are exempted from antitrust laws, and cartels in agriculture are often legal.

Being in a cartel requires discipline. Members must agree not to undersell one another no matter how tempting price cutting might be. The temptation is enormous because one member could steal large amounts of business from other members by offering to sell at a lower price, let's say, to a large supermarket chain. Because each rancher's eggs are excellent substitutes for every other rancher's eggs, the demand for any one rancher's eggs becomes extremely elastic if he or she cuts the agreed-upon price. "Cheating" becomes irresistible.

Price-cutting and lack of cooperation caused the break-up of SWEP. The individual ranchers went back to an "every-man-for-himself" philosophy. As a result, the oversupply grew, and prices went down and down.

Egg producers and government assistance

By 1971–1972 the oversupply was so huge and egg prices so low (they fell to Depression levels) that farmers, instead of earning $3 or $4 per year per hen, lost money. Many ranchers went bankrupt, and low prices forced others to merge into all kinds of associations and combinations in desperate attempts to control the market. But the ranchers could still not get together on price, and the surplus of eggs kept growing.

California ranchers solved their problem by invoking a 1937 state law permitting producers of many agricultural products to band together and vote to subject themselves to state control in the form of marketing boards.

The egg ranchers voted in June 1972 to give control over egg production and pricing to a state marketing board, which in turn issued a "marketing order" aimed at removing nearly 10 percent of California eggs from the market. The order permitted each producer to sell 200 cases per week at any price he or she pleased. Then the producer had to reduce production by 10 percent or turn the surplus over to the marketing board, which could dump it or sell it for animal feed or new uses and give the producer a low price. The immediate effect of the program was to increase egg prices by 3 to 4 cents a dozen[12] and to yield the typical egg rancher additional revenue of $600,000 per year. Thus, in accepting compulsory regulation, the California egg ranchers found a way to control prices.

Who is on the marketing board? Answer: egg ranchers. (Who else understands the business?) The result is, of course, controlled supply and higher prices. Private enterprise died in the California egg industry.

Conclusion

The egg case helps to show why entrepreneurs move along the spectrum of markets from pure competition to oligopoly. Part of the urge comes from a natural desire to escape the zero-economic-profit world of pure competition. Part of the movement comes from the success of a technological breakthrough like the cage for egg-laying hens.

But the bigger the firms become, the more they find reason to cooperate, perhaps to form cartels. If these attempts fail, then large firms often seek the protection of a government agency.* Ironically, as economist Robert Heilbroner observes, though both socialistic and capitalistic views of society assumed that economic systems control their politics, now capitalism is "continuously subject to political direction."[13] In fact, many economists believe that our economics courses and textbooks should now be called "political economics" instead of, simply, economics.

Summary

Until 1930, Adam Smith's view of free enterprise as the ideal economic system was accepted by democratic countries in Western Europe and the United States. It was believed that, of all economic systems, pure competition provided the best allocation of resources, the most efficient production, and the largest possible output of goods and services at the lowest prices. Pure competition exists only when (1) there are enough entrepreneurs in an industry so that no single firm can influence the price of the product; (2) the product each firm sells is exactly the same; (3) resources needed in production are instantly mobile; and (4) knowledge of more profitable opportunities for any of the resources is instantly available. No entrepreneur would receive economic profit above and beyond her or his implicit costs because, whenever

---

In December 1979, the federal government gave the Chrysler Corporation loan guarantees of $1.5 billion to save the corporation from bankruptcy. The fear was that, if the firm "went under," 600,000 workers might lose their jobs (those directly employed plus those working for suppliers). Moral: If you're big enough, you get help.

a person developed a profitable business, others would rush into the business until it became no more profitable than any other business.

Despite the appeal of pure competition, economists sometimes argue that, if no one receives economic profit, there will be no money to put aside for research or expansion. Also, pure competition may be an inefficient system for allocating resources if many unqualified people enter into business (in the absence of entry barriers) and then fail.

Because of the lack of market power they have in competitive industries, entrepreneurs try to escape into other market situations that economists classify as monopolistic competition, oligopoly, and monopoly. Under monopolistic competition, each firm attempts to differentiate its product from other similar products by labeling it and advertising it. Because few barriers to entry exist, however, there is still a high degree of competition and little market power. An oligopoly is said to exist where a few companies become so big and powerful that they control most of the market, where any one of the companies can influence the market price, and where outside firms have difficulty entering the industry because of barriers, such as the large amount of capital required. In the least competitive system of all, monopoly, there is only one seller, and no close substitutes for that seller's product are available. Utilities are called natural monopolies because they are decreasing-cost industries—each additional unit costs less than the previous one to produce—and because the inconvenience and inefficiency of allowing competing firms to supply services in a given area is considered too great to permit.

The tendency has been for the government to become more and more involved in business, either through outright ownership, joint public and private operation, attempts to influence government decision making, or government regulation. While governmental controls have seemed a logical means of overseeing industry when competition is no longer in effect, regulatory agencies have their limitations. Board members often operate so as to protect the industries they regulate by influencing the government to establish price supports, quotas, and the like.

The egg industry provides a case study of what has been happening in most sectors of the economy for the last 100 years. Adam Smith's world no longer exists (if it ever did). Instead, giant companies, intimately related to government, control large sectors of the economy.

Discussion Questions

1. Would a purely competitive system be ideal? Why or why not?

2. Under what circumstances would a purely competitive industry exist for a long time (say, 100 years)?

3. Would the products produced under this system be as high quality and/or as low-priced as those produced under conditions of oligopoly? That is, would consumers be better or worse off?

4. If you were a pure competitor, would you be willing to remain one? If not, then what is wrong with permitting conglomerates like ITT to form? Further, if the conglomerates do form, would you subject them to government regulation?

5. Suppose you buy a home worth $100,000. The remaining balance of your mortgage is $60,000. Other than taxes, insurance, and maintenance, what are the *implicit* costs of living in your home?

6. Estimate the implicit costs of owning a business in which you have invested $50,000. Assume you work in the business full time.

7. If you had been an egg rancher in "Case of Eggs," what would you have done?

8. Name as many entry barriers as you can. Are they all bad? What about the barrier of sheer size?

9. How would you decide whether or not to regulate an industry? How would you go about it?

10. What will our economic system be like in 100 years? Will we have private property? Will one be able to start one's own business?

References

1. Richard J. Barber, "The New Partnership—Big Government and Big Business," *The New Republic*, 13 August 1966, p. 19.

2. *Facts on File*, 1976.

3. John Kenneth Galbraith, *The New Industrial State* (Boston: Houghton Mifflin, 1967), pp. 179–180.

4. See A. Kent MacDougall, "Market-Shelf Proliferation—Public Pays," *Los Angeles Times*, 27 May 1979, pt. i, p. 1, and "Madison Avenue Takes on Washington," *U.S. News & World Report*, 18 June 1979.

5. Morton S. Baratz, *The American Business System in Transition* (New York: Thomas Y. Crowell, 1970), p. 5.

6. Ibid., p. 6.

7. Barber, "The New Partnership," p. 18.

8. William J. Eaton, "Kennedy Sees Mergers as Threat but Industry Sees Them as Necessity," *Los Angeles Times*, 6 May 1979, pt. vii, p. 1.

9. Jay Palmer, "The Rising Risks of Regulation," *Time*, 27 November 1979.

10. *Time*, 27 November 1978, p. 87.

11. "Polluters Sit on Antipollution Boards," *New York Times*, 7 December 1970, p. 1.

12. Robert Fairbanks, "New Program May Boost Egg Prices 3-4 cents a Dozen," *Los Angeles Times*, 1 September 1972.

13. Robert L. Heilbroner, "The Future of Capitalism," *World*, 12 September 1972.

8 How Business Firms Try to Increase Their Profits

James R. Holland/Stock, Boston

The previous chapter described the activities of groups of firms seeking market power through mergers or cartels and guarantees of continuing power through alliance with government. In this chapter we will discuss the pricing policies of individual firms in their search for profits. The chapter is divided into two parts. In the first part we extend our example of Jane Pennyworth's egg farm to explain the basic economic theory behind decisions that business firms make to increase their profits. (It is an important part to study if you ever start your own business.) The second part describes why business firms sometimes charge two different prices for the same product. "Unethical!" you say. Maybe, but it's done every day.

Key Words

Fixed costs	Imperfect markets
Variable costs	Price discrimination
Market period	Variable pricing
Short run	Consumer surplus
Long run	Marginal-cost pricing
Marginal revenue	Monopsony
Marginal cost	Private labeling

Making Profits in Jane's Egg Market (and Other Markets)

Although economic theory has very little to say about how we as individuals should try to get rich, it has a good deal to say about how business firms should try to increase their profits. The economic theory of business operation is often called "profit-maximizing" theory. Profit-maximizing theory can be applied to many different kinds of firms. In this discussion we will confine ourselves to a study of the decisions Jane Pennyworth should make in her egg business to maximize her profits (or minimize her losses).

Jane's situation as a price taker: no influence on price

Assume that Jane operates in a purely competitive market; that she is a *price taker* because she has no control over the market price. No matter how many eggs she supplies, her contribution to total supply is too small to shift the market supply any measurable distance.

No matter how many eggs Jane supplies, her contribution to total supply is too small to shift the market supply any measurable distance.

Under these conditions, what does the demand curve for her eggs look like? (Remember that she can sell all the eggs she has to sell at the market price.) Economic theory's answer is that her demand curve is perfectly horizontal—perfectly *elastic*—at the market price. ("Perfectly elastic" because all of the other small egg ranches supply perfect substitutes for Jane's eggs.) Figure 8-1 shows the demand curve for Jane's eggs compared with the total demand and total supply curves for all eggs in a large market like Chicago's or New York City's.

The equilibrium market price is 60 cents. No matter whether Jane supplies Q_1, Q_2, or Q_3, her selling price will always be 60 cents. She has no reason to sell for less because she can sell all she has at 60 cents. If she tried to sell at a higher price, say, 61 cents, she wouldn't sell *any*. Why not? Because the purely competitive market price tells us that there are large numbers of small firms whose selling price is 60 cents. People will prefer to buy from these other firms at 60 cents than from Jane at 61 cents. If total market demand or supply change, the equilibrium price will change, and Jane's demand curve will shift to the right or left, along with the demand curves of all the other small firms.

Consequently, because Jane cannot control her selling price, her only chance to control her profits or losses comes from her *supply* decisions. And her supply decisions are based, as we saw in Chapter 3, primarily on her costs of production. As we shall now see, some costs are more important than others in determining how many dozens of eggs Jane should produce in order to make maximum profit.

Jane's situation as a supplier: deciding the important costs

In Chapter 7 we described costs as "explicit" or "implicit." From this point on, we'll assume that Jane includes implicit costs in her supply decisions (the opportunity costs of foregoing alternate uses of land, labor, and capital, and her own entrepreneurial skills).

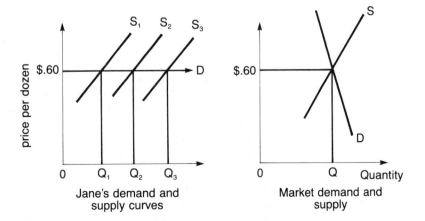

Figure 8-1. Jane's demand and supply curves compared with total market demand and supply.

Costs are also divided into **fixed costs** (sometimes called "sunk costs") and **variable costs.** Fixed costs are those costs that do not vary with changes in output (the number of eggs Jane decides to produce). Variable costs are those costs that change with output—with each additional egg she decides to produce.

There is no way to tell whether or not a particular item like chicken feed is a fixed or variable cost. It depends on whether or not Jane has made a *legal commitment* to pay the cost. If she has a contract with a feed company to buy so many pounds a week, then the feed is a fixed cost because it doesn't matter whether she produces one egg or 100,000; she still has to pay the bill.

Therefore, it is more accurate to say that fixed costs are those involving a past commitment; variable costs are those about which entrepreneurs can change their minds. Because past or future decisions are involved, economists like to divide time into three periods: the **market period,** the **short run,** and the **long run.**

In the market period all costs are in the past; the eggs have been put in cartons, trucked to the market, and are ready for sale. Because all costs have been incurred in the past, all costs are fixed. At this point, Jane has no more decisions to make; she takes what she can get.

The short run is defined as a period that includes both fixed and variable costs. We usually assume here that Jane's buildings and equipment (capital) have fixed costs (taxes, insurance, mortgage payments), but she can vary other costs like the amount of feed she decides to buy and the number of workers she decides to hire.

In the long run, she can vary any of the factors of production including capital. She can sell her business, reduce its size, or add to it. She can make any decision she wishes to about any of her costs. Thus in the long run all costs are variable.

To simplify this discussion, let's consider only the profit-maximizing decisions Jane should make in the *short run.*

Rule 1 for making money

We're going to play a game involving a model. Assume for the time being that Jane is operating in the short run; that she is faced with both fixed and variable costs and that she can make only two decisions: either to produce no eggs at all or to produce 100 dozen per day.

Now suppose she realizes one morning that whereas her selling price is 60 cents per dozen, her total production cost (including implicit costs) is 70 cents per dozen. Remember that Jane is making decisions in the short run. What should she do?

Her total revenue is 100 dozen $\times$ 60 cents per day = $60. Her total cost is 100 dozen $\times$ 70 cents = $70, a loss of $10 per day.

Jane reaches for her handy hand calculator and determines that her variable costs (feed, workers, electricity) are $50 per day and that her fixed costs (taxes, insurance, mortgage payments) average $20 per day. Should Jane produce zero eggs or continue producing the 100 dozen per day?

Notice that while she produces, her loss is $10 per day, but that if she stops, her fixed costs of $20 per day will continue. She is clearly better off to continue producing the 100 dozen eggs as long as we assume the *short run*.

(Obviously she can't go on losing $10 per day forever, but a decision to sell out is a long-run decision and our game is limited to the short run.)

Here is another example. Assume that Jane's total costs are $120 per day, that her variable costs are still $50 per day, but that her fixed costs are now $70 a day. What should she do?

If she doesn't operate at all, she will lose the $70 per day in fixed costs. If she does operate, her total revenue will still be $60. Her loss will be $60 − $120 = −$60. She will lose $60 if she operates and $70 if she does not. She is $10 better off to operate than not to operate.

Notice that in the first example Jane's fixed costs were $20. In the second example her fixed costs were $70. Yet in both instances her operating loss (if she produced and sold the 100 dozen eggs) was the same, −$10.

Where does the $10 come from? The total revenue of $60 is, in both cases, $10 more than the variable costs. Thus Jane's revenue from sales more than covers the variable costs of producing the eggs. Jane can use the extra $10 to reduce her fixed costs by that much.

Our first conclusion is called *Rule 1: When total revenue is greater than variable costs in the short run, a business firm should continue to operate, even if it is losing money.*

This analysis leads us to Rule 2. Rule 2 explains *how many* units of a product a firm should produce in the short run in order to maximize profit or minimize loss. (We can drop the assumption that Jane must either produce zero or 100 dozen eggs.)

Rule 2 for making money

We have determined by Rule 1 that Jane should continue to operate in the short run. Now Jane wonders if she should increase output. Should she increase her production to, say, 120 dozen eggs per day? Let's assume the numbers of the first example: Total revenue was $60, total costs were $70, divided into $50 of variable costs and $20 of fixed. She knows that fixed costs aren't going to change but what about variable costs? More chickens and more feed will be needed and perhaps more electricity and labor. She estimates that her variable costs will increase from $50 to $63. The situation is shown in Table 8-1.

TABLE 8-1 Should Jane Increase Production?

Case	Output (dozens)	Price	Total revenue	Variable cost	Fixed cost	Total cost
I	100	$.60	$60	$50.00	$20	$70.00
II	120	.60	72	63.00	20	83.00
II-A	120	.60	72	61.80	20	81.80

In Cases I and II, Rule 1 is satisfied (total revenue being greater than variable costs), but should she increase production to 120 dozen? Clearly not. Her revenue increases by $12 but her costs increase by $13. In Case I, total revenue exceeds variable costs by $10; in Case II by only $9.

Economists have a special way of analyzing this situation. Every time Jane sells one more dozen, total revenue changes by 60 cents. (Remember that Jane is operating in a purely competitive market. She has to accept the 60-cent market price.) Economists call the change in total revenue when one more unit (of anything) is sold **marginal revenue.** Marginal revenue for Jane is, therefore, 60 cents.

The change in variable costs (or total costs since fixed costs don't change) when *one* more unit is produced is called **marginal cost.** The change in variable costs from Case I to Case II is $13. The change in output from 100 to 120 dozen is 20. Therefore, the marginal cost of each of these additional 20 dozen is $13 ÷ 20 dozen = 65 cents.

Now let's compare marginal revenue with marginal cost. Marginal revenue is 60 cents; marginal cost is 65 cents. Each of the additional 20 dozen eggs adds 5 cents more to cost than to revenue. If Jane increases production from 100 to 120 dozen, she will be 20 dozen × 5 cents = $1.00 worse off. In Case I, she lost $60 − $70 (total costs) = −$10. In Case II, Jane would lose $72 − $83 = −$11.

Before we spell out Rule 2, let's try one more example (see Case II-A, Table 8-1.) We'll change the variable costs in Case II to $61.80 instead of $63.00.

Marginal revenue is still 60 cents, but now marginal cost equals

$$\frac{\text{change in variable cost}}{\text{change in output}} = \frac{\$11.80}{20} = 59 \text{ cents}$$

Marginal revenue is now one cent more than marginal cost. Each time Jane sells one more dozen she receives 60 cents; she adds one more penny to revenue than to cost. She will be 20 dozen × one cent better off. Her loss in Case I was −$10. Now it's $72 − $81.80* = −$9.80.

Clearly, a firm should continue to increase production as long as marginal revenue (MR) is greater than marginal cost (MC), even if the difference is only one cent per unit or only one mill for that matter. There you have Rule 2: *Provided Rule 1 is satisfied, expand production as long as MR exceeds MC.*

Although we have used the example of Jane's purely competitive egg farm to derive Rule 1 and Rule 2, the two rules work in any kind of market to guide entrepreneurs to minimum loss or maximum profit policies. (When markets are not purely competitive, the arithmetic used to calculate marginal revenue is somewhat different. Otherwise, the analysis applies to all markets.)

---

*Variable costs of $61.80 plus fixed costs of $20.

Our discussion was also limited to the short run. If in the long run, total revenue doesn't cover both variable *and* fixed costs, then the entrepreneur ought to sell out.

But the problem many entrepreneurs with losing businesses have is that they can't sell out as fast as they would like. Then the question arises: Should they try to keep going even if the business is losing money? Rule 1 says *yes* as long as the total revenue each day covers the variable costs of staying open. If total revenue doesn't cover variable costs, then board up the place and sell out as fast as possible.

How others and you can apply rule 2

Once upon a time, Continental Airlines asked itself whether it should continue flying from city X to city Y even though it was losing money. To answer the question, it first determined what costs were marginal—the extra costs solely connected with flying from city X to city Y and the fixed costs associated with airport expenses, salaries, insurance, and depreciation—costs that would be incurred whether the flight went or not.

This is what Continental found:[1]

Total cost of one flight, city X to city Y	$4,500
Marginal costs only	2,000
Revenue from the flight	3,100

Decision: Go, continue flying the route. Although the flight would lose $1,400 ($4,500 − $3,100), Continental would lose $2,500 if the flight *did not* go. Why? If total costs were $4,500 and marginal costs were $2,000, fixed costs that would be incurred, go or no-go, would be the difference—$2,500. By continuing the flight, Continental would earn $3,100—an excess of $1,100 over the marginal costs of $2,000. This extra $1,100 could be used to reduce the loss from $2,500 to $1,400.

So far, we have described a golden rule—Rule 2—which all entrepreneurs should follow, whether they are in highly competitive markets or markets having some degree of monopoly. But the golden rule works just as well in everyday life. All it says is, "If the extra benefit of doing something is greater than the extra cost, then do it."

Suppose you are driving east from Los Angeles to Flagstaff, Arizona. Your eventual destination lies beyond: the Grand Canyon, Bryce Canyon, and Zion National Park. Should you take a twenty-mile detour north of Flagstaff to see the Sunset Crater National Monument? Should you consider the costs of getting to Flagstaff? These are fixed costs because they will not change whether you visit the Sunset craters or not. They have already been incurred. You should consider only the extra or marginal cost of the detour (gas and oil plus opportunity cost of time spent) and compare that extra cost with the extra satisfaction of seeing the craters.

What's your vote? *You* decide. This question brings up a problem we mentioned before. We often have difficulty measuring the extra costs and benefits because they're unknown. Entrepreneurs are in the same boat. They have to estimate as best they can.

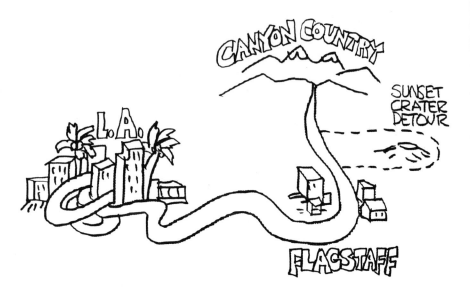

What does a detour cost?

The importance of thinking "marginal"

The idea of "marginality"—of looking at the costs and benefits of any decision to do something extra or additional—is one of the most important ideas in economics—right up there with demand, supply, and elasticity. "Marginal" usually refers to the last or extra unit of something. We look at this extra unit and then wonder if it is going to be the ultimate measure of satisfaction or if it will be the "straw that breaks the camel's back."

When economists analyze a public issue like the energy crisis or pollution, the bottom-line question is "Will the additional (marginal) social benefit that results from XYZ policy justify the additional (marginal) cost of doing it?"

Economists also refer to "marginal" people. For example, if your college decides to raise parking fees (or any fee), there will be some students for whom that last expense is the "last straw" that causes them to change their behavior in some important way—perhaps even to drop out. Another usage: If gas prices go up and rapid transit becomes more available, some people "at the margin" will switch from cars to rapid transit. Economists will try to estimate how many people there are at the margin in determining whether or not taxpayers should subsidize rapid transit, and, if so, how large the subsidy should be.

Selling the Same Product at Different Prices

Jane's egg business was in a purely competitive market because she was a "price taker." Markets that are not purely competitive are called **"imperfect."** In imperfect markets, entrepreneurs can sometimes sell the same product at different prices in more than one market at the same time. Rule 2 still applies, but because such entrepreneurs have the market power to select their own prices, Rule 2 will involve more than one marginal revenue. Rule 2 will then help the entrepreneur to decide how much to sell at each price.

All markets in the real world are to some extent imperfect because resources are not instantly mobile, there are some barriers to entry, and some information costs are always present.

When information costs exist, it may be possible for entrepreneurs to sell to different people at different prices, because the people buying at the high price lack information about the low price. As we will see, the entrepreneur has every reason to hope that information costs are sufficiently large to prevent the two groups of buyers from getting together and comparing notes.

The practice by which entrepreneurs charge different prices for the same product is called **price discrimination.** The entrepreneur is discriminating *against* the buyer who had to pay the high price and *in favor* of the buyer who is charged the low price.

Our discussion of price discrimination is divided into six parts: (1) the definition of price discrimination, (2) why entrepreneurs discriminate, (3) a case study of the Velvetex Paint Company, (4) marginal-cost pricing, (5) private labeling, and (6) the question of legality.

Price discrimination: what it is

Price discrimination is the sale of essentially the same product or service to different buyers, or even the same buyer, *by the same seller* at different prices. Typically, price discrimination occurs when a manufacturer sells a given product (say, a brand of lipstick) to different stores at different prices.

In the strictest economic sense, price discrimination is defined as charging different prices for exactly the same good or service. We will expand this definition to include the sale of *essentially similar* products that may vary somewhat in costs of production, delivery, or sales.

For example, consider a two-door, six-cylinder, stick-shift, 100-horse-power, compact car with radio and heater that sells for $7,000. This is the economy version. Now assume the manufacturer adds some chrome, racing stripes, and more expensive seat covers. These added features cost the manufacturer perhaps $150, but this deluxe version sells for $8,000. The two cars are *almost the same*, but they are styled and priced to appeal to two different kinds of buyers.

This form of price discrimination is used widely on deluxe and economy versions of appliances of all types. It is also used in marketing many household products.

We define price discrimination, therefore, as the sale of the same, or almost the same, products or services by the same seller at different prices, where the price differences cannot be accounted for by cost differences.

Why does the entrepreneur discriminate?

What would you say if you paid $1 for toothpaste and then learned from a friend that, on the same day, from the same store, he had bought the same toothpaste for 60 cents? You might be angry enough to complain to the store owner. If the incident involved a large amount of money, you might take the

TABLE 8-2 Price Students Would Pay for Stereo[a]

If the price were . . .	Number of students who would pay this price or a higher price
$600	1
500	2
450	3
400	4

[a]Excludes all those who would not pay more than $400.

store owner to court and sue him for unfair treatment. Yet entrepreneurs do adopt practices similar to this.

Why do entrepreneurs try to do this, at the risk of making customers angry? The answer is simple: they will make more money.

Once again, consider Table 3-3, our hypothetical example of the prices college students would pay for the eight-track stereo tape deck with amplifier and two speakers. Our assumption was that the company's price is $400, and that at that price four students would buy it. An abbreviated version of that table is given in Table 8-2.

Notice the difference between the demand curve for Jane's eggs, shown in Figure 8-1, and the demand schedule for stereos in Table 8-2. The demand curve in Figure 8-1 was horizontal; it was perfectly elastic. If we were to graph the demand schedule for stereos in Table 8-2, it would slope downward from left to right. More stereos can be sold at low prices than at high prices. A sloping demand curve means that the market is "imperfect" and that entrepreneurs have sufficient market power to select their own price. (A necessary condition for price discrimination).

Let's look at Table 8-2. If the stereo company has announced a price of $400, only four students will buy the stereo combination. The company's total revenue will be 4 × $400 = $1,600. *But*, why shouldn't the company consider what its total revenue could be if it sold the stereos one at a time? To put it another way, what if the entrepreneur could extract from each purchaser a price that matched the amount each purchaser was willing to pay? If the entrepreneur could find variable prices that would accomplish this noble objective, he or she would take in the amounts shown in Table

TABLE 8-3 Variable Prices for Stereo

	Price	Number of students who would pay each price
	$600	1
	500	1
	450	1
	400	1
Totals	$1,950	4

TABLE 8-4 Price, Quantities Supplied, and Quantities Demanded for Schmaltz Beer

Price per six-pack	Quantity supplied	Quantity demanded
$2.20	3,400	0
2.00	3,000	500
1.80	2,600	1,000
1.60	2,200	2,200
1.40	1,800	3,000
1.20	1,400	3,500
1.00	1,000	4,000

8-3. In this way, the entrepreneur's total revenue would rise from $1,600 with uniform pricing to $1,950 with **variable pricing.** Variable pricing is obviously the only way to fly if consumers can be approached one at a time.

We can use the example of the Schmaltz Brewery given in Chapter 3 to further illustrate this point. You will recall that the demand and supply schedule looked like that given in Table 8-4. When the demand and supply schedules were graphed, they looked like Figure 8-2.

Notice that some of the Schmaltz consumers are willing to pay a higher price than the equilibrium price of $1.60. Some of them would have paid $2. These people have it made—they find the price they have to pay is lower than the price they would have been willing to pay. This difference is called the **consumer surplus.** The people who are willing to pay a higher than equilibrium price are receiving a *surplus* of satisfaction per dollar over the consumer who can just afford the equilibrium price of $1.60.

The area under the demand curve but above the equilibrium price line in Figure 8-2 represents the consumer surplus. Another version of the figure will help you visualize it; see Figure 8-3.

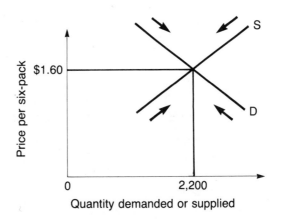

Figure 8-2. Equilibrium price of Schmaltz Beer.

Figure 8-3. Picture of a consumer surplus.

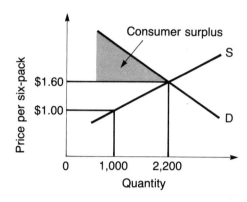

The important point to remember is that consumers would have paid higher prices for all quantities less than 2,200. When there is a uniform price of $1.60 for all 2,200 six-packs, the brewery will take in $1.60 × 2,200 = $3,520 per week. Now look back at Table 8-4. It tells us (look at demand) that the brewery can sell the first 500 for $2 each. Let us suppose it does. The brewery can sell the next 500 for $1.80 each because the demand schedule tells us that a total of 1,000 would be sold at $1.80. It can sell the other 1,200 (this makes our total of 2,200 = 500 + 500 + 1,200) for the equilibrium price of $1.60.

If the brewery acts in this manner it will take in the amounts shown in Table 8-5.

Remember that if the brewery sells all 2,200 for $1.60, it takes in only $3,520. The $200 difference ($3,720 − $3,520) is the dollar measure of the consumer surplus. All good entrepreneurs should plan how they can wipe out the consumer surplus by selling their products at *variable* rather than *uniform* prices! In fact, entrepreneurs do just that.

Price discrimination: what it means to you

The significance of price discrimination is that if one seller (like Schmaltz Brewery) decides to *discriminate* among buyers, it will offer its product or service to different buyers for different prices. In some cases, the seller may offer the product or service to the *same* buyer for different prices.

"Quantity discounts" are given by sellers to the same buyers when the price per beer in a case of beer is less than that in a six-pack or of a single

TABLE 8-5 Amounts Schmaltz Brewery Takes In

Quantity		Price per six-pack		Income
500	×	$2.00	=	$1,000
500	×	$1.80	=	$ 900
1,200	×	$1.60	=	$1,820
			Total	$3,720

can. Cartons of cigarettes cost less per pack than single packs. The price per ounce of *anything* is usually less, the larger the container. And if you find that a size 8 dress sells for the same price as a size 18, the cost per yard is much less in the large-size dress.

Other examples of price discrimination are lower prices for movie and theater matinees than for evening performances. The theory here is that the demand for theater seats is not as high in the daytime as at night. Differences in demand may also account for differences in movie ticket prices for adults and children. If the entrepreneur tried to charge a uniform price for everyone or at all times, he or she would take in less money.

We need to be careful about one point. If *different stores* sell a given brand of, say, frozen orange juice at different prices, no price discrimination is involved because there are many sellers. The stores are simply competing with one another. But, if the *manufacturer* of a given brand sells at different prices to different stores, then the manufacturer is practicing price discrimination. By selling the same product at different prices, the manufacturer is discriminating in favor of some buyers and against others.

Now we're going to examine a case of price discrimination in the real world that met with disaster.

The perils of price discrimination: the case of Velvetex paint

Once upon a time (in the 1940s) there was a paint manufacturing company called Velvetex.* The Velvetex company was one of the early discoverers of water-base paint—no fuss, no muss, the paint dries in thirty minutes, etc. etc. The company introduced its line of water-base paint with extensive advertising. The label on the paint can was colorful and expensive.

At first, competition was minimal and the name and the paint soon caught on. Three hundred paint stores bought the line. But soon other companies began to compete because water-base paint is easy to make (the entry barriers are low). Dozens of competitors entered the fray. The supply curve shifted to the right, driving the price down. Gradually Velvetex began to lose sales because it no longer had something special to offer.

At about this time, Velvetex paint was retailing at $6.95 per gallon. Paint stores purchased the paint from the factory for $4.50 a gallon. In order to increase sales, Velvetex decided to price discriminate, to sell some of the paint in plain cans at lower prices as a new line for paint contractors. The "new" line of paint was called Commercial Formula. The black and white label was austere, businesslike. The paint received almost no advertising and was attractively priced for volume sales; paint stores bought Commercial Formula for $3.50 and sold it for $4.95 to paint contractors.

Can you guess what happened? Probably. Since the same stores were buying Velvetex and Commercial Formula, they eventually realized that the two lines of paint were the same. (Information costs were not high enough.)

The company and brand names are fictitious; the story is sad but true.

They stopped buying Velvetex, bought only Commercial Formula, and sold it to retail customers for $5.95 while continuing to price it at $4.95 for contractors.

Velvetex's paint-store clients gradually substituted Commercial Formula for Velvetex, and the company found that it was selling no more paint than before and was making less money doing it. Furthermore, the paint stores became steadily angrier as more and more reports circulated that Velvetex could be purchased at retail at a variety of prices below $6.95. Velvetex's formerly loyal customers began to drop the line and pick up others with more uniform sales policies.

What was the colossal mistake? It was that Velvetex did not sell at different prices in *different markets*. The same paint stores bought both lines and merely substituted the cheaper line for the more expensive one.

Sales of both lines began to plunge, and so Velvetex made one last attempt at price discrimination. This time Velvetex decided to sell some of the paint to Premier Paint Stores, a large chain of discount paint dealers, at a much lower price. The agreement was that Premier would bring truck-loads of its own cans with its own "Vinyl Finish" label to the Velvetex factory. Velvetex would fill the cans at a price of $1.50 per gallon. Premier would retail the paint through its chain of stores for $2.95, with an excellent profit margin of 49 percent of the retail price (excluding the cost of the can, transportation, and handling).

One would think that Velvetex's regular customers would hear of this and threaten to discontinue the line. Curiously, that did not happen. Velvetex had found a separate market. (Information costs about Premier's operations were high.) Few complaints were heard at the factory. The business with Premier almost doubled Velvetex's sales, reaching 40,000 gallons of paint per month to Premier alone.

But after six months, a Premier executive phoned Velvetex and said, "Awfully sorry, we've decided to make our own line of Vinyl Finish. It's been nice doing business with you." One year later, after continuing loss of sales, Velvetex gave up and went out of business.

Rule 2 again

Was the Premier agreement a good idea? From the standpoint of price discrimination, it was. Judging from the very few complaints received, the Premier stores constituted a separate market. Sales to Premier, while they lasted, were *extra* sales; they did not subtract from regular sales.

But how profitable was the arrangement? Counting everything, executive salaries, taxes, insurance, and other expenses, it cost Velvetex about $2.50 to manufacture a gallon of paint. Why would it want to sell paint for $1.50?

It happened that the *extra* (marginal) variable costs of producing the paint—mainly materials—were $1.40 per gallon. (The additional paint could be produced with the same number of workers.) When Premier agreed to pay $1.50 per gallon, Rule 2 was satisfied. Marginal revenue of $1.50 exceeded marginal cost of $1.40 by 10 cents. By selling 40,000 gallons of paint per month to Premier, Velvetex made an extra $4,000 (40,000 × 10 cents) that could be used to pay some of its fixed costs. Even though it was a losing proposition, Velvetex's loss was $4,000 less than it would have been. Of course, Velvetex could not continue this practice indefinitely (beyond the short run) because it was losing money. But for a while, obedience to Rule 2 made a lot of sense.

Economists sometimes call Velvetex's price policy for Premier **marginal-cost pricing.** The theory is that, for the long run, it may be worthwhile to price discriminate by selling at one price high enough to cover *all* costs (both fixed and variable) and at another price to cover marginal costs only.

Premier's power over Velvetex

One other point needs to be made. Velvetex allowed itself to become heavily involved with one buyer, Premier, which bought half of its output.

This was a risky arrangement. At any time, Premier could have asked for extras like special packaging or free delivery and Velvetex would have been stuck with higher costs. Velvetex depended too strongly on Premier and unwisely refrained from developing other markets.

When buyers of a product are powerful enough to exercise control over a seller, economists say there is an element of **monopsony** present. Whereas monopoly means one seller, monopsony means one buyer. Monopsony also exists in labor markets if employers (buyers of labor) are large enough to influence the wage rate. Velvetex should have been wary of the monopsonistic relationship with Premier.

Another kind of price discrimination: private labeling

The Velvetex story, however disastrous, provides an example of another business practice, one that is extremely common. When the Premier Paint Store chain sold Velvetex under its own "Vinyl Finish" label, it was using **private labeling.** There are probably very few large manufacturers who do not engage in a private labeling arrangement with firms that can provide large retail sales and retailing firms that constitute apparently separate markets.

When a store puts its name on a package rather than the manufacturer's brand name (that is, when it is engaging in private labeling), there is no way of telling who made the product. The store's reputation, rather than that of the manufacturer, is behind the product. At another store or even in the same store (as in the Velvetex case) the identical product may be on display under a different label. This is a common example of price discrimination.

Private labeling may seem vaguely dishonest to you, but, remember, if entrepreneurs can price their products so as to cover the marginal costs of the extra production involved in private-label sales, there is a sound economic reason for engaging in this extra business.

The most visible examples of private labeling occur at large chain supermarkets and drugstores. Why do manufacturers prefer to deal with large chain stores? If manufacturers engage in too much private labeling with too many small accounts, their production lines would be constantly interrupted to permit label switching. A manufacturer needs long production runs with a few large accounts to make private labeling pay.

Unfortunately, there is no way of determining that the private-label item is exactly the same as the national brand. Even if a careful comparison of the appearance, listed ingredients, and any other visible clues suggests that the two versions of the product are identical, one never knows for sure. Information costs are present.

It is precisely because of this lingering doubt that the manufacturer can often successfully sell the same product under different labels and different prices. Some buyers will be motivated more by the national advertising that pushes the national brand than they will by the lower price on the private label. They will be willing to pay a higher price for the security they feel in buying a brand name. Other buyers will be willing to take a chance on the lower-priced, private-label brand. The two kinds of buyers support the "separateness" of the two markets—even in the same store.

Any manufacturer who engages in extensive private labeling must be aware of the possibility that consumers will stop buying the more expensive, nationally advertised version and buy only the cheaper, private-label version. On a national scale, manufacturers can undoubtedly get away with this practice because they sell to thousands of small accounts that carry only the national-brand version. Only a few very large accounts will be given the opportunity to buy at lower prices for private labeling purposes. In this way, the separateness of the low-priced and high-priced markets is preserved.

The question of legality

After reading the Velvetex story, you must be wondering if there is not something unethical, illegal, or at least unsavory about price discrimination.

Ever since John D. Rockefeller, Sr., founded Standard Oil, price discrimination has been, for many, a dirty word. In 1867, Rockefeller had gained control of a large oil refinery in Cleveland and was using railroads as his main method of transporting refined oil to other states. To lower the freight costs, he went to certain railroad companies and proposed to each one that he would ship all of his company's oil on that railroad in return for a special discount on freight rates. Since there were several competing rail lines anxious for his business, Rockefeller got his way and soon was receiving a rebate of 15 cents a barrel on the oil that he shipped. (In fact, he even received a similar rebate for every barrel his competitors shipped!)

Having thus persuaded certain railroads to price-discriminate in his favor, Rockefeller then went to competing oil refineries and offered to get the same shipping rebates for them in return for being allowed to buy controlling interest in their refineries (usually at a very low price). If they refused to sell, he said he would make sure that the railroads continued to charge them higher freight rates. Because freight charges were such a large portion of oil refining costs, one refinery after another gave in and sold control to Rockefeller. By 1904, Rockefeller's Standard Oil Company was refining more than 84 percent of the crude oil in the United States.[2]

One of the most famous muckrakers, Ida M. Tarbell, wrote an account of Rockefeller's practices, which was serialized in *McClure's* magazine in 1902–1903 and later published as a *History of the Standard Oil Company*. It and other exposés ultimately led to the Clayton Act of 1914, briefly mentioned in the previous chapter. The Clayton Act made several business practices illegal, such as price discrimination, rebates, exclusive sales contracts, and interlocking directorates. The difficulty was that Congress qualified their illegality by adding a "weasel" phrase: the acts were illegal only "where the effect will be substantially to lessen competition or tend to create a monopoly." Because the courts have had an impossible job in trying to decide what "lessen competition" really means, the Clayton Act has been largely ineffective. And so, many forms of price discrimination continue to be common.

Summary

According to economic theory, all entrepreneurs should adopt two rules to maximize profit or minimize loss: Rule 1 says that entrepreneurs should continue to operate in the short-run even though they are losing money, as long as total revenue equals or exceeds their variable costs. Rule 2 says that if they decide to operate—having satisfied Rule 1—they should continue to increase production as long as marginal revenue exceeds marginal cost.

If an entrepreneur's market is sufficiently imperfect, the practice of price discrimination can further be used to increase profits or to cut losses. Price discrimination is defined as the sale of the same, or almost the same, products or services by the same seller at different prices, where the price differences cannot be accounted for by cost differences.

Enterprises use price discrimination to increase total revenue. If enterprises can find some buyers for their product at higher prices and other buyers at lower prices, they stand to take in more money than if they charge the same price to all customers.

Price discrimination may be accomplished in several ways—by charging different amounts for the same product at different times, in different places, for different quantities, or for different groups of customers or by selling deluxe and standard versions of essentially the same item. When different groups are charged different rates, the producer needs to keep these groups separate so that those who pay the higher rate do not become hostile or start buying at the lower rate. Information costs must exist. Many producers keep their buyers separate by selling their product under different brand names or labels—selling the product with a well-advertised brand name at a higher price than a similar item that is distributed by a chain store under the chain store's label. When a chain store or other distributor puts its own label on a product, the practice is called private labeling.

A producer may be willing to sell a product at less than its total cost so long as the price is above the marginal cost of production. This practice is called marginal-cost pricing. The producer has to pay fixed costs anyway, and sales at prices above the marginal cost reduce fixed costs by the amount the price exceeds marginal costs. A marginal-cost pricing policy leads to price discrimination in that a manufacturer sells the bulk of his production at a high price, covering his total costs, and an additional portion at a lower price that still exceeds his marginal costs.

Laws like the Clayton Act have been passed to limit price discrimination, but they have not been very effective.

Discussion Questions

1. Are there types of price discrimination that may help the poor? Suppose your doctor charges the rich more than the poor. Ask him if he does and why.

2. If you were a small manufacturer producing Immortality, a skin cream for women over forty, would you engage in price discrimination? Why or why not? How would you go about it? Assume your production is 100 three-ounce jars per hour.

3. Again, as the manufacturer of Immortality, what should you think about if a chain of local health food stores asks you to sell the product to them under a private label?

4. Do you think it is fair for manufacturers to sell their products to big stores at lower prices than they charge small stores? Explain.

References

1. *Business Week*, 20 April 1963.

2. Arthur S. Link, *American Epoch*, 3rd ed., vol. 1 (New York: Alfred A. Knopf, 1963), p. 6.

9 How Workers Try to Control the Conditions of Their Employment

Jeanne Rasmussen/DPI

In the last two chapters we focused on the efforts of business firms to escape from Adam Smith's world of pure competition by gaining market power. Now we will shift our attention to problems faced by workers. Like the business firms that hire them, workers also want to escape the conditions imposed on them by impersonal market forces. Workers, however, do this by seeking bargaining power or legislation to force employers to pay wages and to provide working conditions they consider satisfactory.

This chapter is divided into two major sections: (1) labor unions and their impact on the economy; and (2) the economic status of women, teenagers, and minorities in the labor force.

Key Words	Exploitation
Wagner Act	Discrimination
Taft-Hartley Act	Job discrimination
Landrum-Griffin Act	Wage discrimination
Marginal revenue product (MRP)	Job participation rate
Derived demand	Role differentiation

Unions and Their Impact on the Economy

First, let's consider the goals and legal status of unions and their traditional and newer membership. Then, we'll discuss how wages are determined and the effects of unions on wages, prices, and employment.

The goals of unions

A labor union is an association of workers who join together for the purpose of negotiating a labor-management contract with an employer. Individual workers can easily be fired over, say, a wage demand, but when the employees form a group, firing them is much more difficult. The employer is faced with a power that is capable of interrupting his or her business through a strike if the group's demands are not met or negotiated.

Originally, union negotiations leading to a contract emphasized pay and hours of work. While bargaining still covers these issues, as unions have gained power they have become concerned with fringe benefits involving medical, dental, and optical care; pension funds (in addition to Social Security); and many job-related issues such as *job descriptions*, which tightly describe exactly who does exactly what and with what tools; *seniority rules*, which state who is laid off first or promoted first; and the *check-off*, the company's agreement to deduct union dues from the workers' paychecks and to turn the money over to the union.

All these areas for negotiation were usually interpreted by employers as interferences with management, and, until 1935, employers did everything they could to prevent the formation of unions. During the 1920s, employers banded together in associations under what they called the American Plan. The purpose of the plan was to crush the unions by getting their employer-members to support the *open shop*—that is, a workplace where an employer could assert the right to hire anyone, whether union member or not. Because none of the employers wanted a union, "open shop" really meant no union. In addition to the open shop, employers often asked newly hired workers to sign *yellow-dog contracts*, whereby the worker agreed not to join a union or engage in union activities. Workers who signed these contracts were called "yellow dogs" by union supporters.

During the 1920s, both sides fought—literally. There was much violence and people were killed. In the West Virginia coal mines, for instance, miners formed an army of 4,000 men, which was crushed by another army of federal troops. In Illinois, two miners were killed during a battle between striking mine workers and strikebreakers brought in by the Southern Illinois Coal Company, and miners retaliated by killing nineteen of the strikebreakers. Violence also occurred in many other industries.

The legal status of unions

Finally, in 1935, the National Labor Relations Act **(Wagner Act)** was passed which gave workers the right to form unions and to bargain collectively if they voted to do so. Voting was supervised by the National Labor Relations Board, which is still in operation today.

The Wagner Act gave unions tremendous power by permitting the *closed shop*. A closed-shop agreement requires the employer to hire only those who are already members of the union. The act also spelled out many restrictions on what were called *unfair labor practices*. If employers pressured employees in any way to stay away from unions, they were guilty of "unfair labor practices."

Although the Wagner Act spelled out all kinds of restrictions on employers, it imposed virtually none on labor. In 1947, the passage of the Labor-Management Relations Act of 1947 **(Taft-Hartley Act)** signaled a shift in public sentiment away from labor by outlawing the closed shop. The Taft-Hartley Act did, however, permit *union shop* agreements, in which labor and management could agree that newly hired workers did not have to be union members *before* employment but had to join the union some specified time *after* employment (usually thirty days). Even so, the Taft-Hartley Act gave individual states the right to pass so-called *right-to-work laws* which prohibited union shops, and about half the states have passed such laws. Although the phrase "right to work" was intended to signify that workers should have the right to work whether they joined a union or not, the effect was to seriously damage union power.

The Taft-Hartley Act also spelled out "unfair labor practices," but these were restrictions on union activities. Some of these are *featherbedding*, in which an employer is forced to pay for work not performed; coercing workers during organizing drives; refusing to bargain with the employer, and charging excessive initiation fees.

In addition, Taft-Hartley prohibited secondary boycotts. A *primary boycott* (which the law allows) occurs when union members refuse to buy or handle the products of an employer they are striking. A *secondary boycott*, on the other hand, occurs when unions pressure a third party not to deal with the employer—as when farm workers striking a grape grower persuade stores to stop selling the grower's grapes.

The act also included a no-strike clause for certain industries (such as aircraft and others connected with national defense) deemed by the President of the United States to be involved with the national "safety and well-being." This clause provides an 80-day cooling-off period, during which a union cannot strike even after a contract with its employer has expired. (The best-known instance of the cooling-off provision occurred in 1959 when President

Eisenhower initiated steps to halt a steel strike which had been in progress for 116 days. After the President's order, the workers went back to work. The conflict was then settled, in favor of the union, in slightly under two months.)

In 1958, Congress took another "swipe" at unions with the passage of the **Landrum-Griffin Act** (officially, the Labor-Management Reporting and Disclosure Act). With this Act, Congress tried to prevent union bosses from assuming dictatorial control of their unions and from misappropriating union funds. The Act limited borrowing from union funds by union officials to $2,000, made embezzlement a federal offense, and provided several regulations related to voting and the use of the secret ballot to protect the rights of rank-and-file members. The Act helped Attorney General Robert F. Kennedy to convict Teamster boss Jimmy Hoffa in 1964 of misuse of union funds, among other crimes.

Membership in unions

By far the largest organization of unions is the AFL-CIO. Until the 1930s, the AFL, the American Federation of Labor, consisted of craft unions of workers such as carpenters, electricians, plumbers, and others involved with specific trades. Oftentimes workers in a given factory were fragmented into many of these craft unions, and there were times when they could not agree with one another during negotiations with the employer. For instance, in 1919 the unions tried to coordinate a steel strike with a committee representing more than twenty crafts. Even today the carpenters and machinists are still unable to settle some of their differences as a result of this experience.

To overcome this splitting of union power, in 1935 John L. Lewis of the United Mine Workers and Sidney Hillman of the Amalgamated Clothing Workers formed the Congress of Industrial Organizations (CIO). The CIO aimed at unionizing entire factories with one union and became so successful that the AFL felt obliged to copy it with some industrial organizations of its own.

After considerable fighting among themselves involving *jurisdictional strikes*—strikes to force workers to join one union or another—the two giant organizations merged into one federation in 1955. In 1976, 16.5 million workers belonged to the AFL-CIO, out of a total of 21 million Americans in all unions. There are still two large unions that do not belong to the federation, however—the Teamsters Union (1.9 million members) and the United Automobile Workers (1.4 million).

The AFL-CIO, with its offices in Washington, D.C., exists mainly to exert political influence on the President and the Congress. However, the real power of the federation is with the locals, organizations of workers in specific towns and factories. The locals collect the dues and conduct negotiations with employers. The locals belong to national organizations and sometimes international ones (Canadian locals belong, too), both of which belong to the AFL-CIO.

Since 1968, union membership in the United States (excluding union members in Canada) has been growing slowly in numbers but declining slowly as a percentage of the total labor force. This is shown in Table 9-1.

TABLE 9-1   Membership in National and International Unions, 1940-1972

Year	Union membership (in millions)	Union members as percentage of total labor force
1940	8.7	15.5%
1950	14.3	22.0
1955	16.8	24.4
1960	17.0	23.6
1965	17.3	22.4
1970	19.4	22.6
1976	21.0	20.1

Source: *Statistical Abstract of the U.S., 1979.*

New directions for unions

The Wagner and Taft-Hartley Acts did not include agricultural workers. Farm workers, particularly the migrant workers who move from crop to crop, have suffered from low wages, substandard housing, and lack of medical care. One dramatic example of an effort to bring these workers into the mainstream of American labor began in 1962 with the work of Cesar Chavez and the United Farm Workers of America (UFWA). In 1975, after much pressure from Chavez and the UFWA, California passed the first collective bargaining law for agricultural workers. The law established an Agricultural Labor Relations Board to oversee elections. One of the significant aspects of the law is that it does *not* prohibit secondary boycotts. Therefore, the UFWA can legally urge the public and employees in stores (third parties) not to handle the products of companies with whom the union is having a dispute.

Agriculture is only one example of a new trend toward unionization of low-income workers in areas not previously unionized or where the unions lacked market power.[1] Other examples are the Laborers and Service Employees, Retail Clerks, and District 1199, National Union of Hospital and Health Care Workers. The International Ladies' Garment Workers' Union has started working among illegal aliens on the West Coast. White collar workers have also organized in recent years. Government employees now have the American Federation of State, County, and Municipal Employees (AFSCME). Teachers' unions—the American Federation of Teachers (AFT) and the National Education Association (NEA)—are growing* and are insisting on passage by the states of collective bargaining laws for teachers.

Now we want to see how unions affect wages, prices, and the level of employment. But first we have to find out how wages are determined in the absence of unions.

---

*AFT membership rose from 165,000 in 1968 to 446,000 in 1976, and AFSCME from 364,000 to 750,000 during the same period (Statistical Abstract of the United States, 1979). These are both gigantic increases compared with other unions; total union membership grew only about 400,000 during that time.

What sorts of things will run through your mind when you attempt to forecast a prospective employee's contribution to revenue?

What determines wages?

Wages are the price employers pay for human effort. Like any price, wages are determined by the forces of demand and supply. Let us take up demand first.

The demand for labor

Assume you are an employer making Dazzle Toothpaste. What will determine your demand for workers? The answer is fairly simple. Your demand, the number of workers you will hire at any given wage, will be determined by how much you expect each additional worker will add to your revenue. You will go on adding workers as long as the *additional revenue* each one brings in is *greater* than the *additional wages* you have to pay.

An employee's contribution to revenue is often called the **marginal revenue product,** abbreviated MRP. Here is what it means. Let's assume that you have an employee named Elaine Bright. Elaine's marginal revenue product is defined as the change in Dazzle's revenue that occurs when her contribution to output is sold, *holding all other resources constant.* If Elaine's contribution is an extra 24 tubes of Dazzle per day that sell for $1.25 each, then her MRP is 24 tubes × $1.25 = $30 per day.

Thus, Elaine is *theoretically* worth $30 per day to the Dazzle Company, and Dazzle's profit will increase as long as her wage is below $30. Consequently, Dazzle's demand for Elaine's services is based on Dazzle's estimate of her marginal revenue product.

Figure 9-1. Your demand curve for labor.

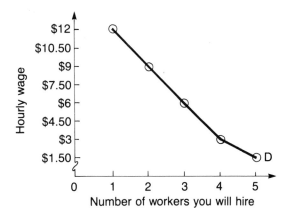

We say "theoretically" because the phrase "holding all other resources constant" describes a situation that doesn't occur in the real world. The phrase means that, in figuring Elaine's contribution, we assume no factors of production other than Elaine's own labor are involved. But Elaine's work will necessarily incur additional variable costs like materials and power provided by you, the entrepreneur. In fact, you can also argue that Elaine is *not* worth $30, because in addition to variable costs, her production is partly the result of capital (the factory with its tools and equipment) she uses and partly the result of selling efforts provided by you, the owner of Dazzle. Thus, the determination of an employee's MRP is a troublesome issue, and that is why many large unions hire economists to help in the bargaining process.

What sorts of things will run through your mind when you attempt to forecast a prospective employee's contribution to revenue? You will consider her or his intelligence, strength, looks (effect on other employees or the public), previous training, receptivity to further training in your plant, personality (ability to get along with people), education, previous employment, emotional stability, loyalty (will she or he argue convincingly that your product is best?), and so forth. You might also have certain prejudices. You might prefer whites to blacks, males to females, thirty-year-olds to teenagers. These preferences (illegal, but difficult to prove) will influence your demand despite the estimates you make about future employees' contributions to revenue.

Because the wage an employer is willing to pay depends on the employer's ability to sell the employee's production, the employer's demand for labor (or for any resource) is called **derived demand.** The demand for the resource (labor) depends partly on the demand for the product (the price consumers are willing to pay) and partly on the employee's ability to produce it.

As Figure 9-1 shows, your demand curve for labor will slope downward from left to right like any demand curve. You will be willing to hire more workers as the wage falls.

Figure 9-2. Example of the labor market for steel-workers before unionization.

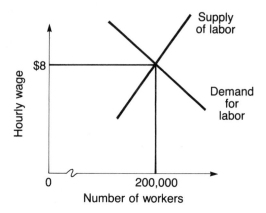

The supply of labor

What determines the supply of labor? There are no pat answers to this question. The number of people willing to work at different wages is determined by a host of complex economic and human factors: the total number of people who want to work, attitudes about education (alternatives to work), attitudes about different occupations (social status), attitudes about the opportunity costs of lost leisure time, and the worker's evaluation of the wages offered versus the cost of living.

Despite these complications we'll make an assumption about the supply of labor. We will assume that, as the wage rises, more people will offer themselves for work. Consequently, the supply curve for labor will rise from left to right. (We are ignoring the fact that, when the wage rises above some point, some people will work less, since the higher wages give them the income they want to pursue their leisure-time activities.)

The wage for any type of job or type of worker will be determined at the point where the number of workers willing to work is equal to the number of workers demanded. The wage is determined exactly like an equilibrium price, provided that the price is free to adjust to the forces of demand and supply.

In the following section, we will use the tools of demand and supply to analyze the impact of unions on labor markets.

Effects of unions on wages, prices, and employment

Let us begin by visualizing a large industry such as the steel industry *before* unions appeared on the scene. The employer's demand curve for labor is downward sloping. The employer will hire fewer people at higher wages, more people at lower wages. The supply curve for steelworkers slopes upward. Consequently, the labor market for steelworkers looks like Figure 9-2. The figure shows that there will be an equilibrium wage at $8 per hour, with 200,000 workers hired at that wage. Given our model, there is no unemployment because everyone who wants to work for $8 an hour gets a job.

Figure 9-3. Example of decreased demand for steel-workers when there is no unionization.

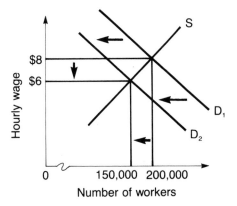

What happens if the country goes into a recession and the demand for steel falls? The demand for workers would certainly fall, too. Figure 9-3 shows what would happen. We can see that the drop in demand—*ceteris paribus*, assuming no change in supply—has caused the hourly wage to fall to $6 and the number hired to fall to 150,000. But notice: The number of people who *want* to work for $6 per hour is 150,000, and they will keep their jobs; 50,000 workers are laid off.

Do unions increase unemployment?

Now let us put a steelworkers' union into the picture. The union has a contract that states that the steelworkers must be paid at least $8 per hour. Figure 9-4 shows what happens when the decrease in demand occurs. We can draw three conclusions from this.

First, and most important, the number of workers hired drops from 200,000 to 100,000.

Second, the 100,000 laid off are involuntarily unemployed because all 200,000 *do* want to work at the $8 wage.

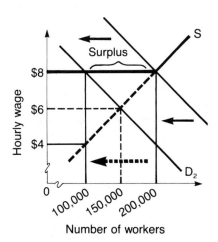

Figure 9-4. Example of decreased demand for steelworkers when wage cannot change as a result of a union-management contract.

Third, the union has weakened the buying power of the employer to hire labor at the wage the *employer* is willing to pay. Figure 9-4 shows that 100,000 people will be willing to work for $4, but the union has forced the employer to pay them $8 an hour—and the employer's demand curve shows that the steel company *can afford to pay $8.* The supply curve for labor is shown by the heavy line. The supply curve below $8 no longer exists, as indicated by the dotted line.

Notice that Figure 9-4 is very much like the picture of a minimum wage in Figure 4-11. The union says to the employer, "You can't pay less than $8." The union wage is therefore a minimum wage. If it is above equilibrium—as it is here after the decrease in demand—a surplus of labor (unemployment) results.

Do unions create price inflexibility?

When the wage is prevented from falling, the employer's labor costs, per unit produced, may remain the same. If per-unit labor costs remain the same, the employer will be reluctant to lower prices of the product (in this case, steel). When an important industry like steel refuses to drop its prices during a recession, companies manufacturing the thousands of products made from it will see no decrease in the cost of a basic material, and so these companies, too, will be reluctant to lower their prices.

What we have here is a picture of *price inflexibility.* No one wants to lower prices. With prices kept high, the quantities demanded will tend to decrease. When this tendency occurs, the recession will get worse. People will be laid off, and their incomes will fall. They will try to spend less and save more. Demand for many products will fall. People will buy fewer products—just as the steel industry "buys" fewer laborers—than the quantities they would buy if the price fell. The picture in the product market is apt to duplicate the picture of the resource (labor) market shown in Figure 9-4.

This discussion may seem to blame unions for the evils of price inflexibility. Economists recognize that in some situations unions are the ones who start the trouble but that, in other situations, large oligopolistic or monopolistic firms are responsible for keeping prices up.

Regardless of whether unions or large firms are at fault for inflexible prices, economists are convinced that price inflexibility makes recessions worse and contributes to inflation even in times of recession.

Have unions raised wages?

This is a tough question. *All* wages have been going up, and nonunion wages have been rising faster than union wages. Unions, of course, argue that they help to raise everyone's wages, that nonunion workers (or workers belonging to weak unions) can use union wages as a standard of comparison when they ask their employers for a raise.

The real difficulty in answering the question is that workers possessing considerable know-how (human capital), like electrical workers, tool and die makers, and commercial airline pilots, do earn much higher than average wages. But are their wages high because of union bargaining or because they possess skills vitally necessary to their employers? Nevertheless, despite these complications, studies have shown that wages of union workers exceed those of nonunion workers with similar skills by more than 25 percent.[2] Thus it would seem that belonging to a union does pay off.

Why unions want to restrict the supply of labor

The matter of *how* unions have raised wages is an interesting one. Certainly wages are raised by collective bargaining, backed by the threat of a strike. But that is only part of the story.

Unions have usually done what they could to restrict the supply of labor to increase wages for *all* workers and also to increase wages for workers in particular occupations. Unions promote wage increases for all by efforts to raise the school-leaving age, to lower the retirement age, to increase paid sick leave, to limit the income retirees can earn when receiving Social Security benefits, to reduce the weekly hours of work, and to increase the number of paid holidays and length of paid vacations. One example: average weekly hours worked in nonagricultural establishments declined from 38.6 hours per week in 1960 to 35.9 hours in 1978.

Unions try to increase the wages for particular groups of workers by creating barriers to entry into many occupations. If you want a job as a carpenter, you will find that first you need a union card but then that it is very difficult to join the union. Getting in requires (1) a hefty initiation fee, often of several hundred dollars, and (2) knowing the "right" person, perhaps a relative who is also a union official. And, once in the union, an apprentice period of two to three years must be served at lower wages.

But this scenario exists for dozens of other occupations. Think of the licenses one has to obtain to be a schoolteacher, a barber, a real estate salesperson, and so on, all of which involve hurdles—training periods, examinations, and money. And invariably the licensing procedure is in the hands of senior members of the occupation whose interest is in keeping newcomers out to protect the incomes of those who are already in.

Restricting the labor supply to increase wages is a form of worker self-protection. In the next section we want to review what happens to workers who lack the power to fight back.

Monopsony: the power of buyers of labor over sellers

When workers have no power to influence their wages and employers have all the power, this often creates a *monopsonistic* situation. Remember the Velvetex paint story in Chapter 8 in which the chain of Premier paint stores bought so much of Velvetex's paint that Premier was in a position to force Velvetex to do whatever Premier wished. This power of buyers over sellers is called *monopsony*. Literally, monopsony means *one* buyer. If you are a seller and there is only one buyer for your product, that one buyer has a great power over your selling price. Occasionally, in labor markets, we find employers who are monopsonists because they, as buyers of labor, have sufficient market power to control the wages they pay.

Monopsony power exists wherever employers do not have to bid against one another for an employee's services as, for example, in small towns with few employers who often have unwritten understandings with one another to keep wages low or in areas where there is only one large employer like the Reserve Mining Company mentioned in Chapter 6.

Professional athletes were also the victims of monopsonistic hiring practices until late 1976. For example, baseball team owners kept salaries down with what is called the *reserve clause* in their contracts with players. The gist of the reserve clause was that even after a player's contract expired, the team owner reserved the right to negotiate a new contract with him without any competitive bidding from other teams. The owner was a *monopsonist*.

The owner, of course, hoped that in the absence of competitive bidding he or she could negotiate a wage that was well below the player's actual contribution to revenue (his marginal revenue product). The greater the difference between the wage and the player's marginal revenue product, the greater the owner's profit. The player was prevented from dickering with other teams until he was released by the owner. Consequently, the players, who then formed their own unions, called the reserve clause "slavery."*

This discussion of monopsony power has a bearing on our next topic: the economic status of women, teenagers, and minorities in the labor force. As you will see, the income of these three groups of workers is less than that received by white males. The reasons for these income differences are complex. Undoubtedly, women, teenagers, and minority workers receive less because they are not well represented by unions. While women made up 40 percent of the civilian labor force in 1978, only 20 percent of union members were women. And while black union membership is on a par with white membership, among craftsmen and operatives in the construction industry, the ratio of whites to blacks is 2 to 1.[3]

So there is evidence to indicate that women and minority workers receive less help in combating the monopsony power of employers, and, as we shall see, there is considerable circumstantial evidence that employers prefer (demand) white adult (age 24 and up) males over all other groups of workers.

The Economic Status of Women, Teenagers, and Minorities

When we say that some employers may "prefer" white adult males over other groups of workers, what we mean is that some employers "exploit" their workers or "discriminate" against some workers in favor of others.

Exploitation exists when workers are paid less than their MRPs. Thus, if basketball player Kareem Abdul-Jabbar's MRP is $1 million per year (see footnote, below) and he receives only $900,000, he is exploited.

The owners' monopsony power was broken in late 1976. Immediately, the salaries of baseball players exploded—usually by more than 300 percent in one year (see Sports Illustrated, *9 December 1976). In early 1980, Kareem Abdul-Jabbar signed a contract with the Los Angeles Lakers for $1 million per year. Can anyone be worth that much? Certainly, as long as his MRP exceeds the wage.*

Exploitation in labor markets exists because (1) employees don't have sufficient information about what other employers might offer them; (2) employees may be prevented from considering employment elsewhere because of barriers to entry like the cost of moving, licenses to buy, or unions to join (high initiation fees); or (3) other employers fail to compete or have agreed not to compete (the baseball example) for an employee's services. When these elements exist in labor markets, employees may be trapped, knowingly or unknowingly, in exploitative jobs.

Discrimination exists when workers with the same MRPs are treated differently by employers. Employers may discriminate against workers in hiring or promotion on the basis of sex, race, or age **(job discrimination)** or by paying workers differently for doing the same job **(wage discrimination).**

There is enormous difficulty in defining discrimination. The employer can always argue, "I'm not turning Mary down because she's a female and Bob's a male. It's just that Bob will fit into my organization better, stay longer, and do a better job." The employer can make the same argument about different wages paid for the same job. The employer's arguments may be legitimate—Bob *may* in fact be a better risk. To prove discrimination, we would have to show that the employer is treating people of equal ability, personality, motivation, and intelligence differently, solely because of sex, race, or age.

What the numbers tell us about exploitation and discrimination

What is the evidence for exploitation and discrimination? We can divide it into three categories: income differences, differences in unemployment rates, and differences in education.

Income differences

Table 9-2 has a double purpose: (1) to compare women's incomes with men's and whites' incomes with blacks' and (2) to show whether or not these income differences have narrowed over time. Although the dollar differences are important, the ratios shown on lines (3) and (6) tell the story. Women's incomes are about 60 percent of men's. In fact, between 1970 and 1977, the ratio has gotten slightly worse [line (3)]. Black family incomes have worsened relative to white family incomes [line (6)].

Unemployment differences

The recent history of unemployment rates follows the income pattern, less income for women and blacks, higher unemployment rates for women and blacks. Table 9-3 shows this picture, including category for teenagers.

Note that the unemployment rates for teenagers are about three times the "All" or total figure for each category. Unemployment rates for blacks in every instance are more than double those of their white counterparts, and women, with the exception of female teenagers, have considerably higher unemployment rates than do men.

TABLE 9-2 Median[a] Money Income of Full-Time Male and Female Workers, All Black Families, and All White Families, 1970 and 1977

	1970	1977
(1) Women (full-time workers)	$5,440	$8,814
(2) Men (full-time workers)	9,184	15,070
(3) Ratio of women's incomes to men's [(1)/(2)]	.59	.58
(4) All black families	6,279	9,485
(5) All white families	10,236	16,782
(6) Ratio of blacks' income to whites' [(4)/(5)]	.61	.57

[a]The median is the middle figure of a series of figures when they are arranged in order of size. In the series 2, 3, 5, 7, 8 and the series 2, 3, 5, 7, 28, the median is 5 even though the mean (the sum of the figures divided by the number of figures) changes from 5 to 9 in the first to second series. Thus, the median is less influenced by extremes than is the mean. If the median dollar income of male wage earners in 1977 was $15,070; one-half of the male wage earners received more than $15,070 and one-half received less.

Source: *Statistical Abstract of the U.S., 1978.*

Don't let small numbers fool you. The 5.1 percent unemployment rate for white women over 20 is *46* percent higher than the 3.5 percent rate for white men over 20! (The difference, 5.1 − 3.5 = 1.6 is 46 percent of 3.5.)

Again, we can't say that these differences *prove* exploitation or discrimination, but the circumstantial evidence is strong.

TABLE 9-3 Unemployment Rates in Percentage of Civilian Labor Force by Age, Sex, and Race, December 1978

	White	Black and other minorities
Males		
16–19 years	14.6%	34.6%
20 years and over	3.5	8.4
All	4.5	10.6
Females		
16–19 years	13.8	35.3
20 years and over	5.1	10.2
All	6.1	12.5

Source: *Economic Report of the President, 1979.*

TABLE 9-4 Educational Attainment and Median Money Income, 1970 and 1977

	Income		Income ratios
	Women	Men	Women/Men
1970			
(1) Eighth grade graduates	$4,181	$7,535	.55
(2) High school graduates	5,580	9,567	.58
(3) College graduates	8,719	13,871	.63
1977			
(4) Eighth grade graduates	$6,564	$12,083	.54
(5) High school graduates	8,894	16,235	.58
(6) College graduates	12,656	20,625	.61

Source: *Statistical Abstract of the U.S., 1978*, table 752.

Education differences

What is the relationship of education to income and to possible exploitation or discrimination? Table 9-4 compares male and female incomes with education for the years 1970 and 1977.

First of all, Table 9-4 verifies the idea that income and education rise together, but higher education appears to help women more than men. Note that in 1970, and again in 1977, the ratio of women's to men's incomes improves very slightly with education. However, the income ratios are very slightly better for women in 1970 than in 1977, again an indication that women are falling behind. The income earned by a female *college* graduate is only $573 ($12,656-$12,083) per year larger (1977) than that earned by a male *eighth* grade graduate.

This brings us to Table 9-5, which considers educational attainment by sex and race. The first entry shows that 32.7 percent of white males (not of

TABLE 9-5 Educational Attainment by Age and Sex, 1977[a]

	White	Black
High school		
Male	32.7%	27.6%
Female	40.9	29.1
College		
Male	20.2	7.0
Female	12.4	7.4

[a]Percentage of each group completing high school and college.
Source: *Statistical Abstract of the U.S., 1978*, table 226.

the total population) completed high school in 1977. We can see that, in fact, proportionately more white women than white men completed high school, but proportionately more white men than women finished college. The blacks' percentages were considerably less than the whites', but, interestingly, a higher percentage of black women than of black men graduated from college.

What is the significance of this data? Education undoubtedly affects the demand for labor. However, if for any reason our society excludes some people from getting an education, some of the observed income differences come from *discrimination in education.* Although most educational institutions try hard not to discriminate, it takes money to go to school, and so we run into a circular problem. Low incomes deprive people of education, and people with less education have lower incomes.

Moreover, education becomes more costly as people continue their education, because (1) fees und tuition costs increase with each year of education, and (2) the opportunity cost of staying in school increases. When one goes through college, the income sacrificed (usually called *foregone income*) while one is in school is estimated to be 50 percent of the cost of college education. Consequently, education, particularly higher education, tends to exclude (exclusion principle) those with lower incomes. Unfortunately, this pattern can be repeated through generations. Attitudes of uneducated parents may also contribute to lower incomes by discouraging their offspring from getting an education.

Let's turn now to a discussion of how well women are doing in their efforts to overcome exploitation and discrimination.

The status of women: has there been any improvement?

A complete discussion of attempts by each minority to reduce exploitation and discrimination would require more space than we can provide. Suffice it to say that all minorities are actively involved on all levels of public life to do away with these conditions. Minorities have traditionally worked through such organizations as the NAACP (National Association for the Advancement of Colored People) and the Urban League and more recently through NOW (National Organization for Women) and AIM (American Indian Movement). Much has been accomplished in the area of legislation in the past twenty years—the Civil Rights Act of 1964, the Equal Pay Act of 1963, the Equal Employment Opportunity Commission set up to enforce the law, and, perhaps by the time this book appears, the Equal Rights Amendment to the Constitution.

All of these laws and organizations are trying to help minority groups get better jobs and better educations. In the case of women, what has happened?

Job participation rates

The total labor force of the United States is defined as the sum of (1) the Armed Forces plus (2) all those employed, plus (3) all those unemployed who are over 16, who are seeking employment, and who are not in a mental institution or prison. In 1978, there were 102.5 million people in the total

TABLE 9-6   Labor Force Participation Rates by Sex, 1960–1977

Year	Women	Men	Combined
1960	37.1%	82.4%	59.2%
1965	38.8	80.1	58.8
1970	42.8	79.2	60.3
1975	43.7	77.3	60.9
1977	47.8	77.0	61.8
1978	49.3	77.2	62.7

Source: *Statistical Abstract of the U.S., 1979,* table 645.

labor force, of whom 42.0 million were women and 60.5 million were men. The 42.0 million women represented 49.3 percent of the 85 million women old enough to work. The 49.3 percent is called a **job participation rate.** (The job participation rate for men was 77.2 percent.)

What is interesting is that the job participation rate for women has been growing. More and more of the women able to work are entering the labor force, whereas the job participation rate for men is declining. Table 9-6 tells the story.

Note that Table 9-6 also shows that the increase in women's job participation rates is more than enough to offset the decrease in men's rates so that the combined rates show a slight increase. (Obviously, an increase in the percentage of people who want to work, along with *absolute* increases in population, puts increasing pressure on the economy to create more jobs.)

So more women are entering the labor force. What kind of jobs are they finding? The income differences presented in Tables 9-2 and 9-4 suggest that women's jobs must pay less than men's. Jane Bryant Quinn's comments in the accompanying box essay confirm this conclusion. Women are not breaking into better-paying jobs despite the individual success stories we often see and read about in the news media.

Role differentiation

Frequently we hear comments like "Women don't really need as much money as men because they don't want to make the kinds of commitment [like the training and dedication necessary to become a physician] that higher paying jobs require." In other words, income differences between men and women can be explained away by saying that women are content as is.

We are thinking here of what is called **role differentiation.** This term is used to describe the gradual process of sex identity from babyhood during which boys traditionally have been conditioned to be masculine, aggressive, and competitive and girls to be pretty and passive. By adolescence, children frequently find that they are forced by society to play the roles they have learned, and so girls are more likely to become secretaries instead of executives, hygienists instead of dentists. (How many male secretaries are there on your campus?) Role differentiation may play a part in preventing women from obtaining all the education they might find helpful in increasing their

(Continued on page 193)

A Woman's Place

Some 75 percent of working women are still in low-level clerical and service occupations.

For all the careless talk about how you have to be a woman today to get a good job, the facts are otherwise. Women starting careers still have to prepare for a long, uphill struggle. It's true that more women now attend professional schools and take up entry-level management jobs. Government pressure has modestly increased their presence in the construction trades and desegregated the job classifications of certain major employers. There are more women bakers and bus drivers, and growing numbers of management women are getting ahead. But Ralph Smith, of the National Commission for Employment Pol-

icy, says that if you're the average woman now entering the labor market, you'll probably wind up in the same kind of job you'd have had fifteen years ago.

Some 75 percent of working women are still in low-level clerical and service occupations, or doing "women's work" in factories. Of the 16 percent classified as professionals, nearly two-thirds are teachers and nurses. Women are often paid less than men who do similar work, and have fewer chances for training or advancement. Some more facts you should know:

☐ Women account for 63 percent of the workers earning between $3,000 and $5,000 a year, but only 5 percent of those making more than $15,000. Women with college degrees earn, on the average, almost 40 percent less than college-educated men and 14 percent less than those with high-school diplomas.

☐ The forced compression of the huge and growing female labor force into a small number of occupations is perhaps the chief deterrent to their earning a better wage. Of 440 jobs in the Census Occupation Classification System, the majority of women are found in only twenty. Occupations that are more than 90 percent female include bank teller, typist, secretary, telephone operator, bookkeeper, and nurse.

Marcia Greenberger, of the Center for Law and Social Policy, points out that the segregation of most women into "female jobs"—with negligible prestige, few learning opportunities and little upward mobility—is today's sturdiest barrier to equal opportunity. Women entering the work force will find their best shot at good pay and advancement in "men's jobs" that, despite all the noise made about female preference, are still hard for a woman to get.

Condensed from Jane Bryant Quinn, "A Woman's Place," *Newsweek*, 26 February 1979, p. 73. Copyright 1979, by Newsweek, Inc. All rights reserved. Reprinted by permission.

incomes. Role differentiation thus leads to income differences between the sexes. (This same problem also exists when young blacks are conditioned by parents, teachers, and the larger society to accept lower paying jobs.)

Despite the role differentiation argument, however, professional observers are convinced that role differentiation does *not* satisfactorily explain income differences and that discrimination in hiring and paying people does in fact exist.[4]

Summary

Workers, like entrepreneurs, seek to control market conditions. One way they do this is by organizing into unions—associations of workers who join together for the purpose of negotiating a contract with an employer that sets out the conditions of employment.

The history of labor unions was a stormy one until the 1930s. Employers, particularly in the 1920s, fought hard to keep an open shop, using strike breaking and "yellow-dog contracts."

In 1935, the union movement was given powerful encouragement with the passage of the National Labor Relations Act (Wagner Act), which legalized collective bargaining, allowed the closed shop, and spelled out a number of unfair labor practices, thereby preventing employers from engaging in certain types of antiunion activity. In 1947, another Labor-Management Relations Act was passed (Taft-Hartley Act) which swung the pendulum the other way. It prohibited the closed shop and permitted states to pass right-to-work laws banning the union shop. The act also spelled out unfair labor practices by unions. A third important piece of labor legislation was the Landrum-Griffin Act, which Congress passed in 1958. The purposes of the Act were to restrain union bosses from illegally milking union treasuries and to guarantee to workers democratic participation in union affairs.

Traditional union membership has come from the crafts and from industries like steel and autos, but in recent years many nonindustrial workers—migrant farm workers, school teachers, and public employees—have been organized into unions. Most unions belong to the AFL-CIO Federation; two major exceptions are the Teamsters and the United Automobile Workers. About 20 million Americans belong to unions. This number has been growing slightly each year, but the union percentage of the labor force has been dropping, also slightly, since 1968.

Unions affect wages, prices, and the level of employment. Like any price, wages are determined by the forces of demand and supply. An employer's demand for labor is determined by each worker's contribution to revenue (marginal revenue product). The demand for labor is downward sloping because employers will increase the number of workers they will hire as the price of labor (the wage) falls. The supply of labor is determined by a host of factors, but we can assume that as the wage rises more people offer themselves for work and that the wage for any job will be determined at the point where the number of workers willing to work is equal to the number of workers demanded.

In the real world, a worker's contribution to revenue is only a partial predictor of his or her wage. Pure competition does not exist. Employers and unions exercise market power to control demand and supply. Barriers to entry exist in many occupations.

Unions may contribute to unemployment by maintaining wages above equilibrium. The policies of unions and of large companies may combine to make prices inflexible, and inflexible prices tend to aggravate unemployment in periods of recession and contribute to inflation. Unions also increase wages by restricting the supply of labor.

Labor exploitation exists when employees are paid less than the changes in an employer's revenue that occur after they are hired (their MRPs). Exploitation can be reduced or prevented if employers have to compete for an employee's services. Discrimination exists when workers with the same MRPs are treated differently in terms of promotion or pay.

Although exploitation and discrimination are difficult to prove, existing data provide strong circumstantial evidence that women, teenagers, and minorities suffer from both practices.

Discussion Questions

1. Does a right-to-work law give you the "right" to have a job? What does such a law actually give you?

2. How does the Taft-Hartley Act differ from the Wagner Act?

3. How do union policies affect the level of employment? Of prices?

4. What examples are there in your town of union/nonunion wage differentials? Compare the beginning wages in a nonunion department store with the wages in union-shop supermarket.

5. What entry barriers are there in the career you want to follow after college?

6. How can exploitation be reduced?

7. What overall policies do unions follow to reduce the supply of labor?

References

1. Jack Barbash, "Unionizing Low-Paid Workers," *Challenge*, July/August 1975, p. 39.

2. P. M. Ryscavage, "Measuring Union-Nonunion Earnings Differences," *Monthly Labor Review*, December 1974.

3. Orley Ashenfelter, "Discrimination and Trade Unions," in Orley Ashenfelter and Albert Rees, eds., *Discrimination and Labor Markets* (Princeton, N.J.: Princeton University Press, 1973).

4. This point is discussed in some detail in *Economic Report of the President, 1973*, Chapter 4.

4

The Macro View
and the Role of Government

We turn now from our study of individuals like Fred and Jane, from individual companies like Velvetex, from industries like the egg industry, and from problems affecting particular groups of workers to a discussion of how the national economy operates as a whole. Consequently, we leave the world of microeconomics and enter that of macroeconomics.

Two of the nation's main economic concerns are inflation and unemployment. The goal of this part is to help you understand the government's role in trying to solve these two difficult problems. We will begin with an overview in Chapter 10 of the government's role as a tax collector and as a provider of goods and services. The purpose of Chapter 11 is to show how the nation's total output is measured, because the nation's total output determines the level of employment and, to some extent, the price level. In Chapters 12 and 13 we will explain the economic theory behind the government's efforts to influence the level of employment and the rate of inflation. Chapter 14 deals with the public debt, while Chapters 15 and 16 show how the Federal Reserve System tries to control the economy by manipulating the supply of money. Chapter 17 ends the "macro" discussion with a trillion dollar question: *Can* the government effectively "fine-tune" the macroeconomic engine to smooth out the effects of unemployment and inflation?

10 Government Spending and Taxation

Steve Hansen/Stock, Boston

Nine times out of ten when someone mentions "the government," we think, perhaps vaguely, of the complex of government agencies in Washington, D.C. But of course the government exists at all levels, represented by the President of the United States on down to the sanitation workers employed by your city or town. In 1977, there were 79,913 units of government in the United States—one federal government, 50 states, and 79,862 local governments (counties, cities, school districts, and special districts for sewage, water, flood, and fire control). Therefore, unless we say otherwise, the "government" refers to all agencies of government at all levels.

The *purpose* of all of these agencies is (1) to protect the public against monopolistic or unhealthy business practices, (2) to provide goods and services the private economy is unlikely to provide, (3) to redistribute incomes

---

Key Words

Private good	Proportional taxes
Social good	Regressive taxes
Quasi-social goods	No-tax threshold
Transfer payments	Marginal tax rate
Federal revenue sharing	Average tax rate
Benefits principle	Tax loopholes
Ability-to-pay principle	Tax shifting
Progressive taxes	Tax incidence

---

in order to secure an adequate level of goods and services for all people in society, and (4) to provide stable prices, enough jobs, and sufficient economic growth to satisfy an increasing number of people who want continual improvements in their standards of living. Quite a job!

In Chapter 7, we discussed several aspects of government protection of the public against the excesses of private enterprise. In this chapter we will discuss government provision of goods and services and income redistribution through taxation, and in Chapters 11-13 we will study that most difficult purpose, the provision of stable prices, jobs, and economic growth.

This chapter is divided into four main sections: (1) what goods and services should the government provide? (2) the dollar growth of government, (3) how government spends and taxes, and (4) the economic impact of taxes.

What Goods and Services Should the Government Provide?

The answer to the question is deceptively easy. We need a government to perform those tasks that entrepreneurs in a market-price system fail to perform. Getting voters to agree on what those tasks are, or how a government agency should perform them, is infinitely more difficult.

Despite this difficulty, economic theory is helpful in identifying those areas where government interference with the system may be necessary. We will discuss these areas under four headings: external costs and benefits, private goods, social goods, and quasi-social goods.

External costs and benefits

Economists try to determine whether or not market prices cover all the costs and benefits of production to society. If the price does not cover all costs to society, market failure exists and government intervention becomes necessary.

Remember, in our discussion of pollution in Chapter 6 we said that *external costs* plus *private costs* together constitute *social costs*. Because external costs and benefits (external effects) are often not taken into account in demand and supply pricing or in the allocation of resources, some force outside the private economy, such as the government, must make sure that external effects are included in prices and, therefore, in buying and selling decisions. If buying and selling decisions include external effects, then we can come close to an allocation of resources that will be the most desirable for all of the people, inside or outside of the buying and selling transaction.

Private goods   A product like a ballpoint pen, you will recall, is called a **private good.** It is produced by a producer with private costs and private benefits (profits) and is sold to a buyer, the user, who also has a private cost (the price he or she has to pay) and the private benefit gained from using it.

If we can leave aside the possible external costs of producing the pen and disposing of it for a moment, we can say that the transaction affects no one else. There are two noteworthy aspects to the transaction: (1) the product is *divisible*; it can be produced and sold unit by unit to buyers; and (2) people who cannot afford to buy it are excluded from the transaction. The last effect is another reference to the exclusion principle.

The market-price system will allocate resources so as to produce the number of pens people are willing to buy at a certain price. Producers will compare production costs with potential profit, while buyers will compare the benefits of using the pen with the cost of buying it. In the absence of government intervention, external costs or benefits are usually ignored.

Social goods   A **social good** (often called a *public good*), on the other hand, is neither divisible nor can the purchase of it include some people and exclude others. An example of a social good often used by economists is a lighthouse. There is no way the light from the lighthouse can be divided up and sold unit by unit to individual buyers. And there is no way ships passing by the light can be excluded from seeing it.

If, therefore, the good is *indivisible* and there is no price that will exclude nonpayers who want to use the light from using it, there is *an absence of any possible profit* in the enterprise that might motivate entrepreneurs to produce it. If, then, groups of people such as shipowners want a lighthouse, they will have to persuade their local, state, or federal government (by voting) to provide it. The government will then tax shipowners (and probably others) to provide the lighthouse.

Government control through taxation of a situation like this has another purpose as well. What if all the shipowners *but one* decide to contribute $1,000 each to build the lighthouse without government help? If the lighthouse is built, our one rebel will get a *free ride.* In contrast, where the government does the job, all who use the light (and probably others) are compelled to contribute by paying taxes.

Thus, where goods or services are indivisible and where people cannot be excluded from the transaction, voters may decide that the government should step in and do the job.

What are some social goods? National defense is one. Although many people may disagree with particular military strategies, the maintenance of an armed force must be presumed to be a social good. There is no way the defense provided by an army can be said to give you any more defense than it gives another person. The good is indivisible; none are excluded.

Law and order are also social goods. Police forces, fire departments, forest rangers, and courts of law are institutions that involve people who are paid for defending the country internally. Again, like the external defense provided by the military services, internal defense is a social good.

Pollution is probably a social "bad." Although pollution is often caused by the production, use, or disposal of a private good (for example, beer cans) some kinds of pollution may also be caused by social goods (the smoke from a jet fighter, the exhaust from a police car). Resulting external costs are indivisible and include everyone (subject to the possible geographical limits of individual instances of pollution).

Quasi-social goods Some goods and services share the characteristics of social *and* of private goods. Typically, these goods or services impart divisible benefits to buyers, and nonbuyers can be excluded, but there still remain indivisible benefits or costs for nonbuyers outside the immediate transaction. These goods or services might be called **quasi-social goods.**[1] Three examples will illustrate.

Education is a divisible good. It can be sold unit by unit to buyers; nonbuyers can be excluded. It has the important characteristics of a private good. Yet, a literate citizenry is important to everyone. Presumably, being literate helps people to vote intelligently (at least in a democracy). Literacy may reduce crime, and educated people may help uneducated people to become more productive. The contribution to society by educated people in the form of technological improvements may also make possible a better life for the uneducated. Education has indivisible benefits for those outside the transaction.

National, state, and municipal parks provide another example. Again, the services of parks are divisible, and we could exclude people by charging for admission. But the existence of the park also confers benefits on non-buyers—for example, people in future generations whose interests should be protected by some branch of government.

Health care is another example. For instance, in some states, school teachers have to obtain a doctor's certificate every two years stating that they do not have tuberculosis. Failure to obtain the certificate means no pay. To obtain the certificate, an X-ray is necessary. A chest X-ray normally costs $20 to $25. The product is divisible and private, but a school teacher's freedom from tuberculosis also benefits his or her students. Consequently, chest X-rays are also available (for school teachers and anyone else who wants one) at county health departments for nothing or perhaps $1. The real cost of the publicly provided X-ray comes from taxpayers who share in the indivisible benefits of the teacher's health (and the health of others who obtain an X-ray).

TABLE 10-1 Total Government Receipts and Expenditures, 1929–1979 (in billions)[a]

Year	Receipts	Spending
1929	$11.3	$10.3
1940[b]	17.7	18.4
1950	69.0	61.0
1960	139.5	136.4
1970[b]	302.6	311.9
1979	771.9	757.9

[a]Unadjusted for inflation.

[b]Notice that in 1940 and 1970, all levels of government spent more than they received. This excess of spending over receipts is called "deficit spending," a topic we'll discuss in later chapters.

Source: *Economic Report of the President, 1980.*

Now let's examine the magnitude of government spending and taxing and then we'll see what we get for our money.

The Dollar Growth of Government

First, let's look at spending and taxing by all levels of government and note the reasons for the rapid growth; then we'll examine the budgets of federal and state and local governments in more detail.

Receipts and spending

Table 10-1 summarizes the growth of total government spending and taxing from 1929 to 1979.

As you can see, the dollar growth of government has been staggering. But there's another way of looking at it. The country has grown too. A common method of analysis is to show government spending or taxing as a

TABLE 10-2 Government Spending, 1940–1979 (in billions)[a]

Year	GNP Total output	Government spending[b]	Government spending as a percentage of GNP total output
1940	$100.0	$18.4	18.4%
1950	286.2	61.0	21.3
1970	506.0	136.4	26.9
1960	982.4	311.9	31.7
1979	2,368.5	771.9	32.6

[a]Unadjusted for inflation.

[b]From Table 10-1.

Source: *Economic Report of the President, 1980.*

The Meaning of One Billion

The rate of government spending every hour is about $91 million.

Now that we're involved with the macro, big picture, let's try to visualize the meaning of large numbers. One million is, of course, one thousand thousand. And one billion is one thousand million (Our total output of over $2,300 billion in 1979 is equal to more than $2 trillion.)

Here are some ways to think about the size of one billion. Take a ping pong ball of about 1½ inches. One billion of those equals almost 24,000 miles, roughly the circumference of the earth. A trip of one billion miles is equal to 4,000 trips to the moon. One billion hours equals 144,155 years. One billion *hours* ago was 142,155 years before the birth of Christ. When all agencies of government annually spend almost $800 billion, the rate of spending every hour is about $91 million.

percentage of the nation's total output of goods and services. In this way we can see the *relative* change in government spending. Table 10-2 does this.

We can see that spending has increased both absolutely and in relation to the nation's output. While the nation's output has grown roughly 24 times ($100 billion up to $2,386.5 billion), government spending has increased 42 times ($18.4 billion up to $771.9 billion).

Figure 10-1. Taxes as a percentage of total output.

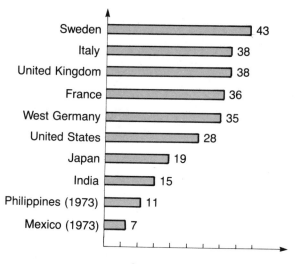

Sources: *IMF, OECD, and United Nations.*

The U.S. tax burden compared with that of other countries

By now you must be wondering how the size of the U.S. government compares with the size of government in other countries. It's difficult to compare spending because of statistical problems in determining what is, and what isn't, included. However, comparing tax burdens, rather than spending, gives us the picture of Figure 10-1.

One can see that, with the exception of Japan, higher tax burdens seem to go with industrialization; that low tax burdens go with nonindustrial, poorer countries. The reasoning behind this conclusion, along with other causes for the growth of governments, is examined in the next section.

What has caused government growth?

1. Urbanization
As countries become more industrialized, the need for social goods in the form of streets, sewage and water systems, utilities, harbors, and airports increases. Industries—and their workers—require efficient networks of power, transportation, and communication.

2. Population Increase
Between 1940 and 1978, the U.S. population grew from 132 million people to 219 million, adding about 1.5 million people each year. More people also means more demand for social goods.

3. Inflation
When prices rise, so do costs for social and quasi-social goods, necessitating ever larger government budgets.

4. Demand for Regulation
We have already seen in Chapter 7 that businesses often demand protection from competition, while the public demands regulation to provide environ-

mental quality, safe products, and safe working conditions. The extent and cost of government regulation is increasing rapidly.

5. Transfer Payments

One reason for the growth in government spending is the growth of what are called **transfer payments.** These are payments in such categories as welfare, unemployment insurance, social security, food stamps, and health. In 1940, such payments amounted to $3.1 billion. By 1978, they had jumped to $242 billion, a 78-fold increase!

Government welfare programs to help the poor have increased both absolutely and relatively, particularly since 1960. In that year public assistance programs amounted to 3 percent ($4.5 billion ÷ $151.3 billion) of all government spending. In 1976, public assistance had grown to 7 percent ($45.1 billion ÷ $626.1) of all government spending.

How Government Spends and Taxes

The budgets of the federal government and the other 79,912 units of government set the pattern of the taxes we pay and determine how our money is spent. First we will look at federal budgets and then at a combined budget for all state and local governments.

Federal budgets

Each January, the President sends to the Congress his budget recommendations for the fiscal year beginning the following October 1. Then the Congress has the freedom to change or eliminate programs in the President's budget or add programs not requested by the President.

The freedom of either Congress or the President to change the budget in any given year is severely limited. When all of past commitments are added up, about three-fourths of each federal budget is found to be uncontrollable, or fixed.* The passage of each budget commits the federal government to continue payments for such important items as veterans' benefits, unemployment insurance and social security payments, food stamps, and so forth. The federal government is also committed to pay interest on the public debt and to provide funds for construction projects for which contracts have been previously issued.

If you look at Table 10-3, you'll notice that the federal government spent a lot more—$29 billion—than it took in in receipts. How does the government cover this deficit? By selling government securities—Treasury Bills, Treasury notes, and U.S. Savings Bonds. As you are probably aware, the federal government frequently runs a deficit in its annual budget, and there are constant outcries that it should "balance the budget." We will discuss this subject in more detail in Chapter 14.

---

*See Statistical Abstract of the U.S., 1978, table 421, p. 259. This table divides the federal budget into "relatively uncontrollable outlays" and "relatively controllable outlays."

Figure 10-2. Federal budget receipts and spending, 1941–1978.

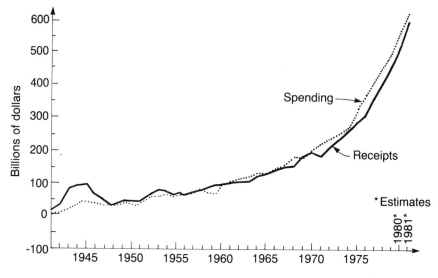

Source: *Data from U.S. Office of Management and Budget.*

More spending than receipts equals deficits

Since 1960, the federal budget has grown steadily. Every year since then, except in 1969, we have had a deficit, an excess of spending over monies received ("receipts"). In that year the federal government received $3.2 billion more than it spent, a consequence of the Nixon Administration's efforts to reduce government spending to control inflation (more on this point in Chapter 17). Figure 10-2 tells the story.

Figure 10-1 illustrates three points: First, we can see the excess of spending over receipts during World War II from 1941 to 1945. When the government spends more than it receives ("deficit spending"), where does the extra money come from? Answer: from selling government securities to individuals and business firms. Thus World War II was heavily financed by sales of government securities; that is, by deficit financing. Second, we can see the growth in federal spending from $10 billion in 1940 to $461 billion in 1978. (Remember that this figure does not include state and local spending.) Third, we can see that, since 1970, federal deficits have become more frequent and larger than in the past. From 1975 through 1978, the deficits totalled $201.9 billion, an average of over $50 billion per year.

While the federal government has run relatively large deficits, particularly in recent years, we need to remember that the federal government not only pays for its own operations, but supplies about 18 percent of all state and lcoal revenues (see page 210). When viewed in this light, federal deficits don't seem as "fiscally irresponsible" as many critics claim. Consequently, we get a more accurate picture of government finance when we compare total government spending—federal, state, and local—with total

TABLE 10-3 The 1980 Federal Budget: Where It Came From, Where It Went

	Billions of dollars	Percentage of total
Receipts		
Personal income taxes	$227	45.1%
Social security taxes	161	32.0
Corporate profits taxes	71	14.1
Excise taxes	18	3.6
Customs duties, estate taxes, and miscellaneous	26	5.2
	$503	100.0%
Spending		
National defense	$126	23.7%
Income security	179	33.6
Interest on the national debt	57	10.7
Health	53	10.0
Education and training	30	5.6
Veterans' benefits	20	3.8
All other	67	12.6
	$532	100.0%

Source: *Economic Report of the President, 1979.*

government tax revenues. By this measure, all levels of government actually ran a surplus in 1979, as Table 10-1 shows. The surplus was $14 billion ($771.9 billion minus $757.9 billion).

Where the money comes from, where it goes

Now let us look at where the federal government's money came from and where it went in 1980. In that year, the federal government received $503 billion, but it spent $532 billion, resulting in a deficit of $29 billion.* The deficit was financed by selling $29 billion worth of government securities to people who voluntarily bought them. Table 10-3 shows where the money came from and how it was spent—in actual dollars and as a percentage of total spending.

    Under "receipts" we see the kinds of taxes the federal government collects. Taxes can be classified in a variety of ways, many of which will be discussed later in this chapter. For the moment, note that taxes are compul-

*All of these federal budget figures are estimates made by the President's Council of Economic Advisors in 1978.

sory payments we make either (1) on our incomes or (2) on the things we buy or have bought in the past.

In the federal budget most of the government's revenues come from taxes on income: the personal income tax, social security taxes, and income earned by corporations. Together, these three taxes accounted for 91.2 percent of the federal government's income. Excise taxes,* customs duties, estate taxes, and miscellaneous are taxes on the things we buy (cars from Japan) or have bought (houses passed on to the next generation).

The two most important categories of spending are national defense and income security. The 23.7 percent earmarked for national defense probably understates the true story. If we want to know the portion of the federal budget earmarked in 1980 for all wars—past, present, and future—we should add the 3.8 percent for veterans' benefits and services, some of the interest on the debt, and some of the items buried in "other" (such as space research). Altogether, war-connected expenditures for the 1980 budget were probably in the range of 35 to 40 percent, down from an estimated 50 to 60 percent during the Vietnam war years.

The category of "income security" is listed second because it always *used* to be the second largest expenditure; it is now the first. It includes social security, unemployment and retirement benefits, food stamps, grants for social services, and vocational rehabilitation. Actually, the 33.6 percent figure *understates* the emphasis the federal budget now places on helping people. When we add the 10 percent for health and the 5.6 percent for education and training, we reach a total of 49.2 percent of the budget. Back in 1974, this total was 29 percent.

It would appear that war-connected spending is diminishing and that spending on human welfare is growing. Both measures are relative, because we used percentages. As the total budget grows, the *dollars* spent on any one category could grow absolutely, even when the percentage falls. This is what has been happening to spending for national defense. At the height of the Vietnam war (1969), military spending specifically labeled "national defense" amounted to $80.2 billion. In 1980, according to the Council of Economic Advisors, the national defense budget is an estimated $126 billion. Nevertheless, as you have seen, the percentage is falling.

State and local government budgets

Details about state and local government budgets take longer to collect. The numbers in Figure 10-3 are combined data for all 50 states plus all local governments for 1976.

Getting and spending in 1976

In that year state and local governments spent $304 billion but they received $305 billion. The pie charts in Figure 10-3 show how each dollar of revenue

---

*The term "excise taxes" refers to sales taxes on particular commodities like tires, alcoholic beverages, tobacco, and gasoline. Frequently, on such items, we pay a federal excise tax plus a state sales tax.

Figure 10-3. State and local government budgets, 1976.

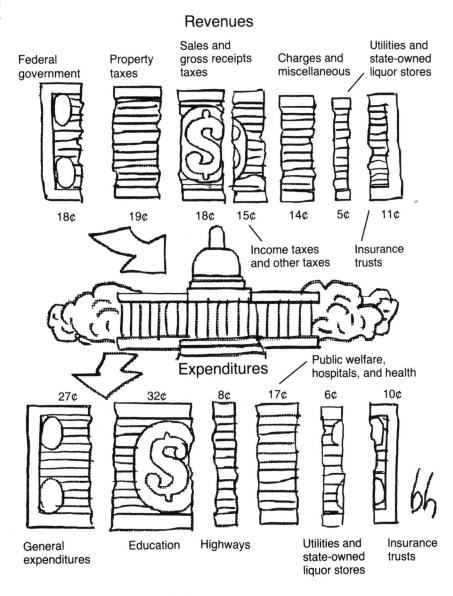

Source: *Statistical Abstract of the United States, 1978.*

and expenditure was divided—just as if we had divided up the budget by percentages. The left-hand pie shows that most of the money came from three sources: federal grants, property taxes, and sales taxes. The right-hand pie shows that by far the largest single category of expenditure was education.

When we delve further into the matter by using older data where more details are visible, we find that sales and property taxes are much more important than they appear to be. At the *state* level, excluding federal grants, sales taxes accounted for *42 percent* of the money raised within the states.[2] At the *local* level, property taxes accounted for *84.5 percent* of local taxes, when federal grants and income from municipally owned operations such as utilities and liquor stores are excluded.[3]

Revenue sharing: the flow of money from Washington

Figure 10-3 shows that in 1976 the federal government gave state and local governments 18 cents of each dollar they received, almost *one-fifth* of their income. This fact should be of considerable interest to those who are concerned about the federal deficits of the kind we saw back in Table 10-3. It is clear that if the federal government stopped providing state and local governments with any money, that would go a long way toward reducing the deficit spending. (But what politicians would be willing to give up federal money handed over to *their* states and local governments?)

Because so much federal money goes to state and local governments, some economists argue that the way to get a clear picture of government spending is to compare total federal, state, and local tax receipts with total federal, state, and local government expenditures. In 1979, for example, all federal, state, and local governments took in $771.9 billion in tax receipts but spent only $757.9 billion. In other words, all levels of government spent $14 billion *less* than they collected.

Federal contributions to state and local governments are called **federal revenue sharing.** In 1976, federal revenue sharing amounted to $56 billion out of total state and lcoal government receipts of $305 billion. By 1978, federal revenue sharing had risen to $77 billion.

The reason for this flow of money from Washington, D.C., to state and local governments is as follows. As you saw in Table 10-3, most (45.1 percent) of the federal government's receipts comes from the personal income tax. Moreover, the federal government's tax receipts may rise faster than the increase in everyone's income, because income tax rates increase faster than increases in income.

On the other hand, state and local governments obtain most of their income from sales and property taxes (37 percent). The problem is that, as incomes rise, revenues from these two sources rise *but not as fast as income.* When our paychecks go up, less of our income becomes subject to these two kinds of taxes. There are two reasons for this: (1) As our incomes rise, we tend to save a larger fraction of our incomes. The saving itself isn't taxed; the interest (or dividends or capital gains) is taxed as part of our income. (2) As our incomes rise, we tend to spend a larger fraction of our incomes on services like plumbers, tax accountants, lawyers, or dry cleaners. Our expenditures on these items are not subject to sales taxes. And property taxes don't rise as fast as income increases. If we get a 20 percent salary raise, do we spend 20 percent more on housing? Obviously not.

And so the federal government's receipts tend to rise faster than increases in income, while receipts for the states and local governments tend to increase sluggishly by comparison. Thus the rationale for federal revenue sharing.

When we pay taxes to the government, we give up all the "dollar votes" the money represents, and, in effect, give that voting power to the government. When the government provides us with goods and services with this money, it becomes a powerful force in determining the answers to the what, how, and for whom questions. For many students, government decision making influences their decision to go—or not to go—to college, and in some cases where programs are federally subsidized, a government agency may even influence the choice of one's career. (We have in mind the decision by taxpayers to provide public education and the decisions by government agencies to subsidize various programs or to give financial support to eligible students.) The following section shows how economists think about the effects of taxes on individuals' incomes.

The Economic Impact of Taxes

There are several issues that engage economists when they think about taxes: (1) who should benefit, (2) the relative burden of taxes on people with different incomes, and (3) taxpayers' efforts to shift the cost of taxes to others. This section is divided accordingly.

Two principles of taxation: deciding who should benefit

There are two broad principles of taxation: the benefits principle and the ability-to-pay principle. According to the **benefits principle,** the one who receives the benefit of a particular government service is the one who should pay (be taxed) for it. The gasoline tax is probably the best example of this If you drive a car, the 10 to 15 cents per gallon you pay in gasoline taxes is intended for highway construction. This principle seems very fair. It is just like buying a product in the free market for personal benefit.

Unfortunately, the benefits principle will not provide all the things we need, for two reasons: (1) benefits are hard to measure and are often geographically distant from individual taxpayers; and (2) if all taxes were designed along benefits-principle lines, low-income people would be unable to obtain social goods such as education. (Costs per year per student in our public schools average around $1,500.)

Consequently, other taxes are designed to obtain more money from the rich than the poor—the **ability-to-pay principle.** The income tax is the best example of this kind of tax. As income rises, the average tax rate also rises, so that the rich not only pay more dollars but also a greater percentage of their income (assuming no tax loopholes—an important assumption).

The relative burden of taxes: deciding who should pay

Taxes do not affect everyone equally. Some people are hit harder than others. Economists are interested in the *relative* burden of taxes on people of different income groups, and so they look at the taxes we pay as a percentage of the incomes we receive.

Three types of taxes: progressive, proportional, and regressive

When taxes are described with respect to our incomes, they are classified as progressive, proportional, or regressive. A **progressive tax** is one in which the tax as a percentage of income rises as income rises. The most common types of progressive taxes are inheritance taxes and income taxes.

Take two people, Mary Lovelace and Tom Strongheart. Tom's income is $10,000, while Mary's is $20,000. Tom's income tax will be approximately $1,200, while Mary's tax will be approximately $4,000. The tax is progressive, not only because Mary's tax is higher in dollars, but because her tax is a higher *percentage* of her income, 20 percent ($4,000 ÷ $20,000), while Tom's tax is only 12 percent ($1,200 ÷ $10,000) of his income. To be progressive, a tax must not only take a bigger bite in dollars as income rises, but also a bigger share (percentage) as income rises. Now suppose that Tom's tax had been $2,000 with Mary's at the same $4,000. What kind of tax would that be? Not progressive, because the tax as a percentage of income hasn't changed. In both cases the tax is 20 percent. When the tax as a percentage of income stays the same, the tax is called **proportional.**

It was once estimated that a proportional 13 percent income tax on all taxpayers—*without any loopholes*—would be enough to support the federal government. The voluminous income-tax code could be tossed in the trash. (Think of all those unemployed tax accountants and tax lawyers!) But it's not likely that a proportional federal income tax would be accepted by most people. "Why should I, a hard-working spouse with ten children, have to pay the same income tax as that live-it-up single person?" we can hear someone ask. Nevertheless, some states like Massachusetts and Nebraska do have proportional income taxes.

Taxes do not affect everyone equally.

The corporate income tax is a hybrid—to some extent proportional, to some extent progressive. All corporations pay a 20 percent tax on the first $25,000 of taxable profit. The next $25,000 of taxable profit is taxed at a 22 percent rate. Thereafter, the rate is 48 percent. When we consider loopholes available to corporations (tax credits for new machinery or depletion allowances) plus tax-shifting to consumers through higher prices, it is difficult indeed to determine whether a corporation's income tax is progressive or proportional.

A **regressive tax** is one in which the tax as a percentage of income rises as income falls. The best example is a sales tax or an excise tax, but property taxes and payroll taxes can also be regressive.

Because there are so few examples of proportional taxes, the following discussion will be limited to progressive and regressive taxes. The best known example of a progressive tax is, of course, the personal income tax.

The personal income tax schedule

As Table 10-3 showed us, the personal income tax is by far the most important source of revenue for the federal government, accounting for about 45 percent of its receipts. The income tax is based on one's total income, from which many deductions can be made, the principal ones being medical expenses, state and local taxes, charitable gifts, and interest payments on mortgages and loans. The federal government also allows an exemption ($1,000 in 1979) for yourself and for each dependent. After all exemptions have been deducted from your total income from all sources, the remainder is called *taxable income.* When taxable income has been determined, a table is used to determine the amount you owe the government.

How the tax schedule works.   Table 10-4 is a copy of a portion of the federal personal income tax schedule that single taxpayers filled out in the spring of 1979 for income received in 1978. The reference to "Schedule TC, Part 1, line 3" is to the taxable income that is left after all exemptions and allowable deductions are subtracted from the income single taxpayers received *before* the taxes that were withheld from their paychecks.

TABLE 10-4 Federal Tax Rate Schedule for Single Taxpayers, 1978 (selected tax brackets)

If the amount on Schedule TC Part 1, line 3 ("taxable income") is over	but not over	the tax is	amount over
$ 2,200	$ 2,700	14%	$ 2,200
$ 6,200	$ 8,200	$690 + 21%	$ 6,200
$20,200	$22,200	$4,510 + 36%	$20,200
$22,200	$24,200	$5,230 + 38%	$22,200
$82,200	$92,200	$39,390 + 68%	$82,200

TABLE 10-5 Tax Payments on Three Incomes

	Taxable income	Tax	Marginal tax rate	Average tax rate	Net income after tax
Joe	$ 7,200	$ 900	21%	12.5%	$ 6,300
Peg	21,200	4,870	36	23.0	16,330
Jackie	83,200	40,070	68	48.2	43,130

Note first that the table starts with a taxable income of $2,200 (sometimes called the **"no-tax threshold"**). Individuals below that pay nothing.

Now let us see how the table works. Take three single people: Joe Allen, whose taxable income is $7,200; Peg Jones, whose taxable income is $21,200; and Jackie Vanderbilt, whose taxable income is $83,200. We'll use Peg's income to show how the tax is calculated. Table 10-4 says that Peg must pay $4,510 plus 36 percent of the amount over $20,200. Therefore, she must pay $4,510 + 36 percent of $1,000 ($21,200 − $20,200). Peg's tax is shown below:

		$4,510
+ 36% of $1,000		+ 360
Peg's total tax	=	$4,870

Note there are actually *two* tax rates involved here. The 36 percent of Peg's last $1,000 of income is called the **marginal tax rate.** People often refer to the 36 percent as Peg's "tax bracket," but observe that this tax rate refers only to the dollars over $20,200, not to Peg's entire income.

But there is also an **average tax rate;** that is, Peg's total tax expressed as a percentage of her taxable income. In this case her average tax rate is $4,870 ÷ $21,200 = 23 percent.

Table 10-5 shows the tax rates on Joe's, Peg's, and Jackie's taxable incomes.

Progressive income taxes are always supposed to hurt the rich more than the poor. Sometimes they do, sometimes they don't. Those famous "loopholes" help many, usually higher-income people, to avoid income taxes.

Income tax loopholes.   The federal income tax schedule in Table 10-5 suggests that the income tax is extremely progressive, with marginal tax rates rising from 14 percent to 70 percent.* Most experts agree that these rates rarely apply in the real world, owing to a number of **tax loopholes.** (A

The highest marginal tax on earned income is 50 percent. The higher rates up to 70 percent apply to additional "unearned" kinds of income like capital gains, interest, dividends, and rent. Taxes based on these maximum rates are rarely paid. Owing to loopholes, Nelson Rockefeller's federal income taxes averaged only 24 percent of his average annual taxable income of $4.7 million during the years 1964–1973 (New York Times, September 1974, p. 34).

Marriages and Taxes*

Singles are apt to find that the penalty for marriage is severe.

What would happen if Peg and Joe decided to marry? Their combined taxable income would be $21,200 plus $7,200 equals $28,400. On the schedule for married couples filing joint returns (not shown) we find that their tax will be $6,092. Their present combined tax is $4,870 plus $900 = $5,770. They will lose $322 ($6,092 − $5,770) by marrying.

But if two single people have roughly the *same* taxable incomes, they are apt to find that the penalty for marriage is even more severe.

Assume that Peg and Joe each have taxable incomes of $21,200. Their combined income tax would be double Peg's, or $9,740 if they remain single. If they marry, their joint return will show a tax of $11,876—a $2,136 penalty for giving up singlehood!

---

*Based on the 1978 Federal Income Tax Schedule

How do the more affluent manage to avoid taxes?

loophole may be defined as a provision in the law which permits the taxpayer to reduce his or her taxable income or to receive income that is not taxed at all or that is taxed at a lower rate.) Edwin S. Cohen, former Assistant Secretary of the Treasury, once admitted that 112 Americans with incomes of more than $200,000 in 1970 paid no taxes for that year.[4] The Brookings Institution, a well-known economic research organization in Washington, D.C., has estimated that the highest *real* marginal tax rate is 32 percent, not 70 percent.

How do the more affluent manage to avoid taxes? There are several loopholes, which we shall discuss: tax-exempt bonds, capital gains, and business-expense deductions.

Many municipalities and school districts issue *tax-exempt bonds* to finance new buildings, sewage-disposal plants, and so forth. These bonds earn an annual interest income for the bond-holder that is often not subject to taxation. Tax-exempt bonds provide local governments with an important method of raising money. A person owning, say, $1 million worth of municipal or other tax-exempt bonds at 5 percent would receive $50,000 a year in income, and that income would be exempt from taxation by the federal government (though not by state governments). The interest on U.S. government bonds is, however, subject to the federal income tax.

Capital gains are realized when a person sells stocks, buildings, land, or other assets for more than he or she paid for them. Sixty percent of the capital gain (the profit) from selling it is tax exempt. The other 40 percent is taxed as ordinary income. Because only 40 percent of the capital gain is taxable, the maximum marginal tax rate on capital gains is really 28 percent (40 percent of the highest marginal tax rate of 70 percent).

TABLE 10-6 Impact of $350 Car Sales Tax on Peg's and Jackie's Incomes

	Peg	Jackie
Taxable income	$21,200	$83,200
Price of car	7,000	7,000
5% sales tax on car	350	350
Tax as a percentage of taxable income	1.7%	0.4%

Tax laws also provide important loopholes or subsidies in the form of *business-expense deductions.* While the deductions are legitimate, the use of them may not be. People who own or manage a business are able to charge off to the business many of their everyday living expenses such as lunches, entertainment, the use of an automobile, and in some cases even the expenses of maintaining all or a portion of their homes.

All loopholes or deductions taken together cost the federal government $77 *billion* each year, according to the Brookings Institution.[5] The problem is that almost all taxpayers enjoy some of the loopholes, such as deducting interest on home mortgages and on installment contracts. The debate about loopholes will undoubtedly continue.

Now we'll turn to three well-known kinds of regressive taxes: sales taxes, property taxes, and payroll taxes.

Sales taxes

Let us assume that Peg Jones and Jackie Vanderbilt each buy a $7,000 automobile. The 5 percent sales tax appears to be proportional because the percentage does not change, but note that the percentage applies to the *automobile,* not to the *purchaser's income.* The three terms "progressive," "proportional," and "regressive" involve the *relationship between the tax and the buyer's income,* not between the tax and the price of the item purchased.

What is the sales tax as a percentage of the buyer's income? The sales tax is 1.7 percent of Peg's income but only four-tenths of 1 percent of Jackie's. Because the percentage falls as income rises, the sales tax is a regressive tax. Table 10-6 shows the impact of this sales tax.

But, you may say, Jackie wouldn't buy a $7,000 car; she'd buy a $15,000 Cadillac (see Table 10-7). Oddly enough, it doesn't matter. Why? Because higher-income people will tend to save more, play the stock market more, and buy fewer things subject to sales (or property) taxes—*as a proportion of their incomes*—than will poorer people. Consequently, a smaller proportion of their income is subject to the sales tax. As long as Peg spends a larger percentage of her income on a car than Jackie does, the tax is still regressive. Table 10-7 shows that Peg's tax is still 1.7 percent of her income, while Jackie's tax as a percentage of her income is only nine-tenths of one percent.

TABLE 10-7 Impact of $350 and $750 Car Sales Tax on Peg's and Jackie's Incomes

	Peg	Jackie
Taxable income	$21,000	$83,200
Price of car	7,000	15,000
5% sales tax on car	350	750
Tax as a percentage of taxable income	1.7%	0.9%

One caution about any general conclusion that sales and excise taxes are necessarily regressive: Regressive effects can be lessened considerably if (1) food and other necessities are exempted and/or (2) the sales tax is made progressive by using higher rates for more expensive items—say, 15 percent on cars over $15,000, 10 percent on cars between $10,000 and $15,000, 7 percent on cars between $5,000 and $10,000, and so forth. Some economists believe that such progressive sales taxes, plus appropriate exemptions, may be preferable to income taxes as an efficient and fair way of collecting money because sales taxes are inescapable—there are no loopholes. The tax money is collected when the money is spent.

Property taxes and the "tax revolt"

Property taxes are usually levied by counties to finance the affairs of all governmental units within their boundaries. Funds collected are used to pay each town's bills like administration, police and fire protection, and educa-

Higher-income people will tend to save more.

tion, while county offices pay for themselves and such countywide costs as community colleges, streets, flood control, welfare, and county libraries. The states generally determine the formulas used by the counties in levying property taxes, but property taxes are approved by local voters in each county. Control by local voters creates differences among the states in their property-tax methods as well as some differences even among the counties of the same state.

Property taxes are regressive because, like food, clothing, or transportation, a high-income person like Jackie will spend a smaller amount on housing—relative to her income—than will a lower-income person like Peg. An $80,000-income person like Jackie may spend *twice* her income ($160,000) for a house, while a $20,000-income person like Peg may have to spend 3½ times her income ($70,000) for a house.

Given the variety in the form and magnitude of property taxes, we will limit the discussion to property taxes in California, before and after passage of the famous Proposition 13.

Before Proposition 13.   Property taxes are based on a county assessor's appraisal of the market value of one's house and lot. Again, let's use Peg Jones and Jackie Vanderbilt as our example characters.

Peg bought her house in 1970, for, we'll assume, $50,000. Like housing all over the United States, it had appreciated so much that by 1977 it had increased in market value to $80,000 according to the county tax assessor.

Before "13," the property tax was based on one-quarter of the market value, called the "assessed value," of the house and lot. Consequently, the assessed value was one-quarter of $80,000 = $20,000. Peg's property tax was computed by multiplying a tax rate by the number of $100s in her assessed value. In Peg's county, the voters had decided that the tax rate was $15 per $100 of assessed value. Because there are 200 $100s in $20,000, Peg's property tax was therefore 200 × $15 = $3,000.

That was the situation until November 1978. As housing increased in value in each year, often by as much as 20 percent per year, property taxes went up and up. Older people on fixed incomes had a difficult time paying increased property taxes and often were forced to sell their lifelong homes. And all people were paying more taxes on property whose increased valuation they had yet to realize.

Behind the leadership of real estate entrepreneur Howard Jarvis, the voters in 1978 passed a measure to reduce property taxes. The measure was called Proposition 13.

After "13."   Proposition 13 was an amendment to the California State Constitution. It changed the tax formula drastically. First, Proposition 13 changed the calculation to *one* percent of the *market* value rather than a tax rate times the $100s in the assessed value. Second, it prevented the rapid increase in property taxes by selecting a base year market value (fiscal 1975–1976) and limiting the increases in that value to 2 percent per year. And third, Proposition 13 made it almost impossible for local authorities or the state

TABLE 10-8 Sources of School Funding in Claremont, California

	1977–1978[a]	1978–1979	1979–1980
State	49.9%	71.2%	77.7%
Local	45.4	21.4	14.0
Federal	2.4	3.7	3.8
All others	3.2	3.7	4.5

[a]Pre-Proposition 13.
Source: "Sources of School Funding," *Claremont Courier*, 8 August 1979. Reprinted with permission from *The Claremont Courier*.

legislature to replace the tax receipts that Proposition 13 would lose, by requiring that new state tax measures must be approved by two-thirds of the legislature and new local tax measures must be approved by two-thirds of all local registered voters.

Now let's see what Peg's 1977 property tax would look like if calculated after "13." We'll have to assume a market value for the base year, 1975–1976, of, say, $70,000. Proposition 13 limits the increase in market value to 2 percent per year, so that in 1977 the market value of Peg's house was $71,400. Her post-"13" tax was one percent of $71,400 = $714—not $3,000 as it was pre-"13"!

Repercussions.   The passage of Proposition 13 had results probably unforeseen by its supporters. Local agencies, heretofore dependent on the property tax for revenue, were immediately hit hard. During 1979, however, disaster did not arrive because the state was able to help with an ample surplus of over $5 billion, the result of reduced state spending coupled with inflation-induced increases in tax receipts. Local bureaucracies—one of the targets of "13" supporters—continued almost intact. What was perhaps unforeseen was that local control of budgets was replaced by state control. Table 10-8 shows what happened to the school budget in the author's hometown.

We can see that state financing of local schools increased dramatically after "13." Before "13," the state paid about 50 percent of local school bills. By 1980, the state's share increased to almost 80 percent. Local school boards are still elected to approve personnel and curricula changes, but control of the school's income went to the state.

Another, much less visible, change in the pattern of local government finance gradually took place. Remember that Proposition 13 made the 1975–1976 (fiscal) year the base year. Thereafter, the market value of one's property could rise by only 2 percent per year. But Proposition 13 included a provision stating that when a property was sold, the market value for property tax purposes immediately became the same as the sales price of the property. This produced two interesting (to put it mildly) effects:

First, houses in the same neighborhood could have vastly different property taxes depending on whether or not their market values had been updated

TABLE 10-9 Property Taxes as a Percentage of Peg's and Jackie's Incomes

	Peg	Jackie
Income	$21,200	$83,200
Value of house	71,400	160,000
Property tax (1% of house value)	714	1,600
Property tax as a percentage of income	3.4%	1.9%

by a resale. Second, because homes are sold and resold much more often than business firms, property taxes on the former tended to reflect relatively more current market values; taxes on the latter tended more to reflect original base-year values. As a consequence, property tax revenues from homes increased faster than from business firms. Homeowners began to bear a larger and larger share of the property tax burden. In Los Angeles County, pre-"13," property taxes from commercial property accounted for 36 percent of total property tax revenue, with homeowners shouldering the 64 percent remainder. After "13," in 1979, the commercial share had dropped to 28 percent; the homeowners' share rose to 72 percent. An expert estimate at the time was that the mix would be 20–80 percent by 1984.[6]

National reverberations, often called the "tax revolt," followed the passage of Proposition 13. Thirty states (as of June 1979) called for a constitutional convention to prevent deficit spending by the federal government. Forty states outside California passed tax cuts amounting to $3.5 billion. In addition, twenty states (including California) are looking at new limitations on future state and local spending and taxes.[7] There is no doubt that voters are eager to control the size of government.

The desire to reduce taxes is understandable. But, as always, there are costs. Tax reductions may lead to poorer schools, less fire and police protection, unrepaired streets, and decreased garbage collection and more litter on sidewalks, parks, and beaches. Again, the problem is that it's easier for us to measure the benefits of private spending, perhaps for a new stereo, than for a public good like a better street. And so we usually opt for a policy that increases our private welfare at the expense of the public goods we enjoy together.*

But what about other forms of regressivity? Property taxes, however figured, are regressive because lower-income people like Peg will pay a larger proportion of their incomes for housing than will higher-income people like Jackie. This is apparent in Table 10-9.

---

*This problem of private versus public spending is described in some detail in John Kenneth Galbraith's The Affluent Society (Boston: Houghton Mifflin, 1958).

TABLE 10-10 Payroll Taxes as a Percentage of Peg's and Jackie's Incomes

	Peg	Jackie
Income	$21,200	$83,200
Taxable income under social security	22,900	22,900
Tax rate	6.13%	6.13%
Social security tax	$1,299.56	$1,403.77
Tax as a percentage of income	2.5%	1.7%

Payroll taxes

Payroll taxes (social security and unemployment insurance taxes) are also regressive. For example, the 1979 tax rate for social security was 6.13 percent of the first $22,900 earned. Consider the impact this has on Peg's and Jackie's incomes (Table 10-10). The burden on Jackie is relatively less than on Peg. The payroll tax is regressive.

Shifting the tax burden to others

One of the most interesting questions about taxes is, Who pays them? The transfer of the burden from one enterprise to another or to the retail customer is called **tax shifting.** The final resting place of the tax burden is called **tax incidence.**

Suppose you buy a tube of Dazzle toothpaste for $1. The salesperson adds 5 percent to the price because of a sales tax. You pay $1.05. Apparently, you are the taxpayer. You are, but only indirectly. The store is the taxpayer because it must now send the money to some government agency. Economists call the sales tax an *indirect business tax* because the business (enterprise) is being taxed but passes the burden of the tax on to the consumer.

Now put yourself in the place of the retail store. The entrepreneur, having had a course in economics, realizes that the demand curve slopes down from left to right and that she will sell fewer tubes of toothpaste at $1.05 than at $1. She may say to herself: "If the demand for toothpaste is elastic, I'll not only sell less toothpaste, but my total revenue will fall if the price goes up." To the extent that the entrepreneur believes this to be true, she may decide to absorb some of the tax herself. She might decide to charge 98 cents instead of $1.00. Then the consumer would pay $1.03. The entrepreneur absorbs 2 cents, the consumer 3 cents.

As a general rule, sales taxes are the most easily shifted. The ability of an enterprise to pass the cost of any tax along to buyers depends primarily on the elasticity of demand for the product. If demand is inelastic, the tax can be shifted; if it is elastic, the seller may have to absorb the tax. The final shares of the tax absorbed by sellers and buyers may involve an infinite variety of compromises.

Property taxes are usually shifted also, passing from landowners to tenants, from business enterprises to consumers. These taxes can be shifted where rental property or business property is involved.

Personal income taxes are the most difficult to shift except in cases where the taxpayer is a member of a strong union. In this situation, the union may succeed in shifting some of the burden of income-tax increases to the employer by demanding and getting wage increases when income taxes go up. Then, depending on the employer's market power, he may be able to shift some or all of those income-tax increases to consumers (some of whom will be members of the union) in the form of higher prices. When consumer prices rise, the union may again demand higher wages—and so it goes. The nonunion employee may be left behind because he lacks the power to increase his wages when losses in his take-home pay occur.

Redistributing income: does it work?

Another way to ask this question is, What is the *combined* effect of taxes on people with different incomes? The best answer is, No one knows for sure.

Two economists, Joseph A. Pechman and Benjamin A. Okner, have estimated that only the wealthiest 3 to 5 percent of American families and the poorest 10 percent pay *more* than 25 percent of their incomes in taxes (all taxes, all levels). The families in between all pay about the same percentage (25 percent) of their income in taxes.[8]

But taxes themselves are only part of the picture. Taxes can be shifted; the poor may receive transfer payments and the poor may also receive government services like subsidized public transportation that are not in the transfer payment category. Furthermore, we have to remember that *any* form of government spending probably favors people of different incomes differently. Who receives more benefit from freeways, schools, public hospitals, parks, police forces, fire departments—the rich or the poor? In some cases (public hospitals) the poor receive a larger share. But in others (police and fire protection of a large hilltop estate, for example), the rich receive a larger share. When all of these factors are taken into account, the combined impact of all government spending and taxes becomes much less clear.[9]

Summary

Most economists today believe that the government should be involved somehow in the provision, distribution, or regulation of social goods and those private goods that involve external costs or benefits. Social goods such as lighthouses cannot be divided up among consumers, and their use or purchase affects others outside the transaction. Quasi-social goods, such as education, park facilities, health care, and antipoverty programs, have both divisible benefits (to the recipients) and indivisible benefits (to society at large). Where social or quasi-social goods are involved, economists usually recognize the need for government intervention.

Government spending has increased from 18.4 percent of the nation's total output in 1940 to 32.5 percent in 1978. About one-half of this is federal spending, which goes primarily for income security and national defense.

State and local spending is mainly for education, highways, and public welfare. The principal source of government income at all levels is taxes—individual income, payroll, and corporate taxes for the federal government; sales taxes, federal grants, and property taxes for state and local governments.

Of all the types of taxes, income taxes are the most progressive, while sales taxes, property taxes, and payroll taxes all tend to be regressive—that is, they take up a smaller proportion of the rich man's income than of the poor man's income. State and local government taxes are mostly regressive, and the income from them has become increasingly inadequate. Federal revenue sharing has been adopted to help these governments meet rising needs.

Since the passage of Proposition 13 in California in 1978, which sharply limited (at least in the short run) the amount of tax one paid on one's house and lot, many states have acted to limit state and local spending and taxes as well as to try to prevent deficit spending by the federal government.

Determining who bears the burden of a tax is difficult because the cost of taxes can be shifted to people other than the legal taxpayer. The final resting place of the burden of a tax is called tax incidence; to ask what is the incidence of a tax is to ask who really pays the tax. Sales taxes can be most easily shifted. Property taxes can be shifted where rental or business property is involved. Personal income taxes are the most difficult to shift.

Discussion Questions

1. What is the difference between a social good and a quasi-social good? What kind of good or service is the U.S. Postal Service? What are the arguments pro and con for making it a government enterprise? In what sense is housing a quasi-social good? If it is, should some agency of government provide it or regulate it?

2. What are the important distinctions between a social good and a private good?

3. Comment on this quote: "All goods have some external effects attached to their production, use, or disposal. If, therefore, the government controls economic activities involving external effects, there are no theoretical limits to the enlargement of government power."

4. Has defense spending been declining? Discuss.

5. Examine the following income-tax schedule. Is it progressive, proportional, or regressive? Why?

Income	Tax
$ 5,000	$ 500
10,000	800
15,000	1,050
20,000	1,200

6. How might sales taxes be made less regressive?

7. Is the property tax an example of the ability-to-pay principle or of the benefits principle? Discuss.

8. Can income taxes be shifted? (Hint: Would membership in a strong union affect your answer?)

References

1. See James M. Buchanan, *The Public Finances*, 3rd ed. (Homewood, Ill.: Richard D. Irwin, 1970), ch. 4.

2. *Statistical Abstract of the U.S., 1975.*

3. Ibid.

4. Robert J. Samuelson, "Wealthy Tax-Nonpayers Widely Diverse Group," *Los Angeles Times*, 6 March 1972.

5. Robert E. Wood, "Loophole, Subsidy or Incentive? A Piece of the Action for All," *Los Angeles Times*, 2 April 1972.

6. Leo T. McCarthy [Speaker, California Assembly], Letter to the *Los Angeles Times*, 8 September 1979, pt. ii, p. 4.

7. "The Tax Revolt—A Year Later," *U.S. News & World Report*, 11 June 1979.

8. See also *Los Angeles Times*, 14 April 1974, p. 2.

9. Richard A. Musgrave and Peggy B. Musgrave, *Public Finance in Theory and Practice*, 2nd ed. (New York: McGraw-Hill Book Company, 1976), ch. 16.

11 The National Economy: Measuring Its Performance

Tom Tracy

"Fine-tuning" the economy to reduce unemployment and inflation is, as we have noted, one of the government's principal goals. To accomplish this objective, the government tries to control total output and total spending. These totals will determine the number of jobs available and, to some extent, the price level. In Chapter 10 we found that the government is a powerful force in the economy because all levels of government spend about one-third of total income in order to buy about one-third of total output. In this chapter we will describe how total output is measured. The chapter is divided into three sections: (1) the link between microeconomics and macroeconomics, (2) measures of income and output, and (3) the limitations of Gross National Product (GNP) as a measure of change (or of progress).

Key Words

National income accounting	Double counting
Gross National Product (GNP)	Intermediate products
Aggregate demand	Final product
Aggregate supply	Price indexes: Consumer Price Index
Consumption	(CPI), Producer Price Index (PPI),
Investment	implicit price deflator
Government purchases of	Base year
goods and services	Real changes
Net exports	Real per capita GNP
Disposable Personal Income (DPI)	Real per capita DPI
Saving v. savings	Measure of Economic Welfare (MEW)

The Link Between Microeconomics and Macroeconomics

In Chapters 3 to 9, you saw how many individual, microeconomic markets operated. Some of these markets were for goods (Dazzle toothpaste) or services (window washing) and some were for resources (labor markets). We must now change camera lenses to get the overall macroeconomic picture.

Let us first illustrate this macro view with a very simple model. Suppose there are only two products, Dazzle toothpaste and Velvetex paint. Dazzle sells 1,000 tubes a month at $1 each ($1,000). Velvetex sells 500 gallons of paint per month at $5 each ($2,500). The result is shown in the upper loop in Figure 11-1. The business firms making Dazzle and Velvetex are receiving $3,500 per month ($1,000 + $2,500) as long as there are no changes in demand or supply.

Notice also in the lower loop that the $3,500 received by Dazzle and Velvetex is used to pay the factors of production—land, labor, capital, and entrepreneurship. This flow of dollars is in the form of the four factor payments—rent, wages, interest, and profit.

Thus, individual demand and supply decisions make up larger flows. Households demand products supplied by firms. Dollars flow to the firms. Products flow to the households. *Firms* demand land, labor, capital, and entrepreneurship supplied by households. Dollars flow to the households. The factors of production flow to the business firms.

Add all these dollar flows together and we move from microeconomics to macroeconomics. The *micro* view shows what is happening inside each individual market, like the market for Dazzle or for Velvetex. When we put *all* business firms together and add up *all* the income, we arrive at the *macro* view of the economy.

Figure 11-1. How individual micro markets contribute to the macro total.

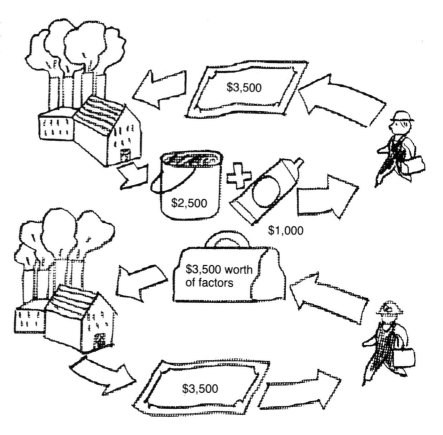

The link between micro- and macroeconomics is the fact that each individual micromarket is a piece of the national macro-pie. Individual buying and selling decisions determine the *size* of the pie. And the size of the pie determines the level of employment and also influences the price level.

The macro model   The macro economy can be visualized by a circular flow diagram (Figure 11-2), just like the one in Chapter 2. The markets for goods and services are in the upper flow. The markets for resources (factors of production) are in the lower flow. Dollars (the dotted line) flow from households to business firms; this flow is called *dollar "votes"* because the household's demands are, in effect, votes that express likes or dislikes for the goods and services that the firms supply. In response to the dollar votes, the business firms try to supply the goods and services the households want (the solid line).

In the lower loop, dollars (again the dotted line) flow from the business firms to the households as the firms bid for (demand) resources owned by the households. This dollar flow is in the form of the four factor payments—

Figure 11-2. A circular flow diagram of the market-price system.

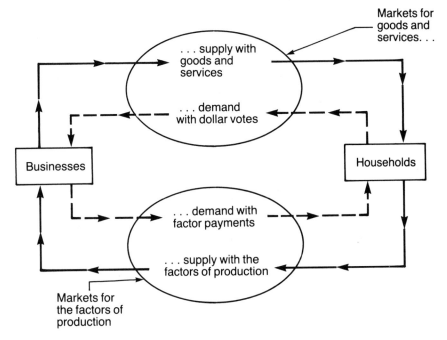

rent for land, wages for labor, interest for capital, and profits for entrepreneurs. If the households find these payment offers satisfactory, the four factors of production flow to the firms (the solid line).

Refining the macro model

Our circular flow model now needs some additions and corrections.

First of all, something large is missing: the government. We have to visualize many dollars flow between the public and some agency of government and between business firms and the government. Taxes flow to the government, and the government buys (demands) goods and services from firms and labor and land from households. The government also receives some of people's savings when people buy government bonds, and the government pays them interest on these bonds. Moreover, the government makes some payments to firms and individuals even when no purchase occurs, such as transfer payments to people on welfare or to those receiving social security checks or unemployment insurance payments.

Second, our dollar flow ignores *saving*. Saving can be done by households and by business firms. People save when they put a portion of their income in banks, buy stocks and bonds, put money into pension funds, or accumulate equities in homes or life insurance policies. Business firms save by retaining some of their profits for future requirements and by setting aside other monies in the form of depreciation allowances. An important question arises: What happens to all this saving?

Many kinds of financial institutions, such as banks, insurance companies, and stockbrokers—often called *financial intermediaries*—handle it and use it for loans or other financial investments. Consequently, there is another loop, not shown in our model, of the unspent portion of incomes going to financial intermediaries who use it for financial investments.

Third, businesses buy from one another. Products such as Dazzle toothpaste go to the public, but businesses also produce parts, supplies, buildings, and machinery that are sold to other businesses. So there are flows of income and goods and services back and forth between business firms. This is the *investment* flow. It also includes unsold goods that remain in inventories.

Fourth, there are many flows (transactions) between members of the public—items in garage sales, used cars, old houses, and so on.

These add up to a lot of omissions from our model. We should not overlook the fact that these other flows are also part of the macro-pie and help to determine its size and, therefore, the level of employment. But the central point is that in all of these flows, the laws of demand and supply determine price and therefore the volume of goods and services and resources that changes hands.

Now we are ready to see how income and output are measured in the United States.

Measures of Income and Output

Most nations of the word keep track of their macroeconomic affairs—total output and income, levels of employment and unemployment, changes in the price level, rates of economic growth, and so forth. They need to know how things are going in order to determine whether or not government policies are helping the economy. The measuring system that has evolved is known as **national income accounting** (sometimes called *social accounting*). The system, in various forms, is now used widely by nations throughout the world.

Some of the major objectives of the system in the U.S. are as follows:*

1. To chart the progress (or lack of it) in the nation's output and income from one year to the next.

2. To keep track of prices and unemployment.

3. To report changes in the supply of money and credit.

4. To report government spending, taxes, and changes in the national debt.

5. To inform us where we stand internationally in relation to exports, imports, and the balance of payments.

---

*One of the best sources of this information is the annual Economic Report of the President, which is usually made available to the public each year in January or February. The report covers the previous year. It is divided into three parts: a report by the President, a report by his Council of Economic Advisers, and statistical tables covering the kinds of measures mentioned in the very brief list above of the objectives of national income accounting.

There are five measures of the nation's output and income. The first three—*Gross National Product (GNP)*, *Net National Product (NNP)*, and *National Income (NI)*—deal with total output and total income. The last two—*Personal Income (PI)* and *Disposable Personal Income (DPI)*—deal with take-home pay, the money consumers have to spend or save. We will consider only the first measure (GNP) and the last (DPI).*

Gross National Product (GNP)

The **Gross National Product** is the largest and most inclusive of the five measures. It is an estimate of the dollar value of the goods and services produced in one year. Changes in income resulting from activities unconnected with production—for example, gains or losses in the stock market, income from crime, and income received in the form of transfer payments[†]—are excluded.

The money total that people spend during a year for newly produced goods and services (that is, produced during the year we are measuring) is called **aggregate demand.** By the same token, the money total of everything business firms supply in the year we are measuring is called **aggregate supply,** and the grand total of everything supplied (produced) is our GNP.

Economists usually take the view that aggregate demand determines aggregate supply because business firms make their supply decisions based on what they expect demand to be. Following this line of argument, then, aggregate demand determines GNP. (There is a school of thought that holds that supply can determine demand; we'll discuss this idea in Chapter 17.)

The total of everything produced, our GNP, can be measured, either (1) by assigning a dollar value to all of the products or services produced, or (2) by totaling the income everyone receives. The first approach is called the "expenditures" approach because it looks at patterns of *spending*. The second approach is called the "income" approach. The totals of spending and income have to match because all the money spent has to wind up somewhere.

The expenditures approach to measuring GNP

Economists put everything everyone buys into four categories: *consumption, investment, government purchases of goods and services*, and *net exports*. Aggregate demand is the sum of these four kinds of spending, and because aggregate demand determines GNP, GNP is also the sum of these four kinds of spending. Let us consider these categories.

---

*NNP is GNP less all depreciation allowances. NI is NNP less indirect business taxes (sales and property taxes paid by businesses). PI is NI plus transfer payments, then minus corporate retained earnings, social security taxes, and corporate profits taxes.

[†]At the end of 1979, transfer payments were running about $252 billion annually, of which about $53 billion were interest payments to owners of government securities. Transfer payments are not included in GNP because they are considered exchanges of money between taxpayers and recipients which have no effect on the "national product" or level of employment until the recipient decides to spend (or save) the money.

1. **Consumption.**   This represents the purchases consumers make in a given year for newly produced products (except for brand-new houses), plus purchases for services from people like doctors and plumbers.

2. **Investment.**   This consists of the purchases of new houses by consumers and purchases of capital goods by business firms including buildings, machinery, vehicles, filing cabinets and other equipment, plus inventories. Production in process and finished goods that have not been sold are included in inventories. They are put in the investment category. Because each year usually begins with inventories representing production in the previous year, and because the measurement of GNP includes only the production of goods and services in the current year, we determine current investment in inventory by subtracting the inventory at the end of last year from the inventory at the end of the present year. Only the net change in inventories is actually reported in the investment figure. Inventory changes can therefore be either positive or negative.

When a soup company manufactures canned soup, the soup first becomes part of the company's inventory and then part of a grocery store's inventory. During this time in inventory, the soup is counted as an *investment*. When someone finally buys the soup, it is subtracted from investment and added to consumption. The experts watch such inventory changes in their attempts to program future production or to forecast changes in business activity and the level of employment.

The investment category also includes depreciation allowances (also called capital consumption allowances). Depreciation allowances are an income-tax-deductible expense for the wearing out of capital goods. For example, if a business buys a machine for $10,000, the business tax accountant can estimate the machine's "life" at, say, ten years. Having done so, she will label as depreciation one-tenth of the cost of the machine per year ($1,000). This is a legitimate business expense. Thus, the investment category includes the creation of new capital goods and an allowance for the replacement of those that have worn out.

To sum up, the term investment means the creation of capital goods and inventories. It does not mean the purchase of a stock or bond. Such purchases are acts of saving, and we'll use the term *financial investment* for them.

3. **Government Purchases of Goods and Services.**   While this term includes all spending at every level of government, ranging from spending for local fire departments to spending for space projects, it does *not* include transfer payments.

4. **Net Exports.**   These are purchases by other countries of our products and services (like air travel) *minus* our purchases of theirs.

The income approach to measuring GNP
All of the money spent on consumption, investment, government purchases, and net exports winds up in someone's pocket. Who gets it?

TABLE 11-1 Simplified GNP, 1979 (in billions)

Income approach		Expenditures approach	
Wages (including payroll taxes and fringe benefits)	$1,459	Consumption	$1,510
Interest	130	Investment	386
Rent	27	Government purchases	476
Profit	319	Net exports	− 4
Depreciation allowances	243		
Indirect business taxes	190		
	$2,368		$2,368

Source: *Economic Report of the President*, 1980.

The answer is fairly simple. All the money goes to pay the four factors of production: wages for labor, rent for land, interest for capital, with any remainder left over going to business owners (entrepreneurs) in the form of profit.

There are, however, two complications: (1) Part of every firm's profit is set aside to take care of "depreciation allowances." National income accountants do not consider depreciation as part of the compensation for any of the factors of production. (2) When we pay sales taxes at retail stores, the stores receiving that money have to forward it on to the government. These "indirect business taxes" are not included in wages, rent, interest, or profit. Because of these two complications, all income generated in producing the nation's GNP is put into *six* "pockets"—the four factor payments plus depreciation allowances and indirect business taxes.

A simplified GNP account for the year 1979 is shown in Table 11-1. The table indicates that we produced $2,368 billion dollars worth of goods and services in 1979, an enormous quantity, probably double that of the Soviet Union, which has the world's next largest GNP. Keep in mind that the $476 billion spent by all levels of government does not include $252 billion worth of transfer payments also spent in 1979. Notice also that net exports were negative, meaning that we imported more than we exported. More about this in Chapter 18.

Disposable Personal Income (DPI)

We have skipped over three measures of income (NNP, NI, and PI) to get to the one that matters most to consumers: **Disposable Personal Income.** To get to DPI from GNP we first subtract from GNP all taxes and monies corporations keep in the form of retained earnings and depreciation allowances. We then add transfer payments—payments such as veterans' benefits, welfare or unemployment insurance payments, social security payments, or interest income on government securities. The idea is to calculate *take-home pay* by subtracting from GNP monies people never see and the money they pay in taxes, but then to add the $252 billion worth of transfer payments that

TABLE 11-2 DPI, 1979 (in billions)

Calculation of DPI	
GNP	$2,368
Minus all taxes and minus monies corporations kept	− 997
Plus transfer payments	+ 252
Total DPI	= $1,623
How DPI was disposed of	
Consumption spending	$1,510
Personal saving	+ 113
	= $1,623

are so important to many Americans. Because transfer payments are included in DPI, economists usually say that DPI is a measure of *income received*, rather than a measure of *income earned*.

One note about taxes. DPI is what is left after *all taxes have been removed*. This includes *personal taxes*, that is, income taxes, personal property taxes, inheritance taxes, and user taxes on vehicles (license plates and registration fees).

Now that we have DPI, what does the consumer do with it? The consumer either spends it on consumption goods or saves it. (Remember that saving might be in the form of financial investments, but these do not constitute investment as economists use the term.)

What was DPI in 1979 and how did consumers divide it between consumption and saving? Table 11-2 summarizes what happened. The table expresses an important fact. In 1979 consumers spent 93 percent ($1,510 billion) of their DPIs and saved 7 percent ($113 billion). Since the end of World War II, this relationship has remained fairly stable, varying from about 92 to 95 percent for consumption and from 5 to 8 percent for personal saving. (Note that DPI = consumption + saving. Therefore, saving = DPI − consumption. This is a way of saying that **saving** is the unconsumed portion of income. Thus any income not spent—that is, put in the bank, stock market, or bonds—is saving. The term **savings** represents one's accumulation of saving from all past years to the present.)

Economists pay considerable attention to these apparently small changes for two reasons: (1) A change from 5 to 8 percent is a 60 percent increase in saving. Such a change nationwide means an important change in consumer attitudes about spending. (2) Despite the significance of these small changes, the fact that consumption spending varies around 93 percent (plus or minus 1 to 2 percent) and saving varies around 7 percent (plus or minus 1 to 2 percent) means that fairly accurate forecasts can be made as to how people will spend and save when DPI changes. If DPI increases by $10 billion because of some new government project, we can forecast that people will increase their spending by about $9.3 billion (93 percent of $10 billion) and their saving by about $700 million.

Limitations of GNP as a Measure of Change

We now want to discuss the problems in using GNP as a measure of change. The fact that it is used to tell us whether we are better or worse off from one year to the next *and* is used in comparisons between ourselves and other countries makes it important to know of some of the difficulties in using GNP in these ways.

Collecting the data for measuring the nation's output is extraordinarily difficult. The Bureau of Economic Analysis of the Department of Commerce does most of this work. It must obtain its information from about 12 million business enterprises and many agencies of government. The results are statistical *estimates* and should not be interpreted as being exact. A famous mathematician, Oskar Morgenstern, once argued that the GNP estimate might be off by as much as 10 percent in either direction. Let us see why the GNP is subject to inaccuracies.

The problem of double counting

Suppose that you, our honest, trustworthy, national income accountant, are busy one day trying to estimate consumption spending. You note the sales of $8,000 cars, but, as you prepare to include such sales in the consumption category, you wonder if you should add to the $8,000 figure the cost of all the materials in the car, perhaps another $4,000, making the consumption-spending figure $12,000 per car instead of $8,000. Obviously, if you do, you'll be demoted to janitor the next day. The mistake involves what is called **double counting** because the $8,000 price necessarily includes the $4,000 worth of materials.

Materials used up in the production of any good are called **intermediate products.** The product that is produced is called the **final product.** Clearly, we want to avoid counting intermediate products and count only final products. Consequently, we try hard to estimate the value of all *final* products (and services) produced—excluding intermediate products—to arrive at GNP.

The problem of price inflation

The term *inflation* means a period of generally rising prices, and, with the exception of the year 1949, average prices have risen every year since 1940. Consequently, when GNP goes up, some, or all, of the increase is the result of higher prices for the *same* quantities. Somehow, we have to take the effect of higher prices out of GNP to determine actual changes in the quantities of goods and services produced.

The process by which we take the effect of higher prices out of GNP is called *deflating the GNP.* Average prices are computed each year by a number of procedures and are published in the form of **price indexes.** There are

The implicit price deflator is an attempt to measure average price changes for the entire economy.

three price indexes: (1) The **Consumer Price Index (CPI)** of the average prices of some 400 retail products and services, (2) the **Producer Price Index (PPI)** for product prices at the wholesale level, and (3) the so-called **implicit price deflator** for the Gross National Product. The implicit price deflator, a combination of both indexes, is an attempt to measure average price changes for the entire economy.

Because price indexes measure average price changes, there must be a starting point so that price changes can be measured relative to some particular year—called the **base year.** In the case of the implicit price deflator, the *base year* against which all others are compared is 1972.* A figure (price index) of 100 is arbitrarily assigned to the average price level for that year. If the implicit price deflator rose to 166 in 1979, you can conclude that prices rose 66 percent in those seven years. You can also say that what cost $1 in 1972 cost $1.66 in 1979.

Now let us use the index to tell us what happened after 1972. In 1972, GNP was $1,171 billion. In 1979, it was $2,368 billion. This makes an apparent difference of $1,197 billion. But in 1979, the implicit price deflator was 166, indicating, as we have noted, price increases of 66 percent. To put it another way, if the price of one pound of hamburger was $1 in 1972 and

The base year for the Consumer Price Index and the Producer Price Index is 1967.

rose to $1.66 in 1979, $1 in 1979 could buy only 0.60 (1.00 ÷ 1.66) pounds in 1979. The loss of about four-tenths of a pound of hamburger is indicated by the 40 percent (1.00 − 0.60) drop in the purchasing power of the dollar.

If each dollar in 1979 bought only 60 percent as much as it did in 1972, then the 1979 GNP was 40 percent too high. If we can find out how much the 1979 GNP bought at 1972 prices, then we can determine how much the country's total output increased (or decreased) in *physical quantities* of goods and services—not just in higher prices for the *same* quantities. The formula for "deflating" the 1979 GNP to find its 1972 purchasing power is as follows:

$$\frac{\text{Base year implicit price deflator}}{\text{1979 implicit price deflator}} \times \text{1979 GNP} = \text{1979 GNP in 1972 prices}$$

Thus,

$$\frac{100}{166} = .60 \times \$2{,}368 \text{ billion} = \$1{,}421 \text{ billion}$$

What does the $1,421 billion mean? It is the 1979 GNP expressed in dollars having the same purchasing power they had in 1972. Economists may simply say, "We have expressed the 1979 GNP in 1972 dollars." Or they may say that the 1979 GNP is now expressed in *constant dollars* and that the change from the $1,171 billion GNP in 1972 to the $1,421 billion GNP is a **real change.** The word "real" means that the income figures being used have been corrected for price changes.

Using constant 1972 dollars as the measuring stick, the real change from $1,171 billion in 1972 to $1,421 billion in 1979 is $250 billion ($1,421 billion − $1,171 billion). We can see now that practically all the apparent $1,197 billion difference is in the form of higher prices for the *same quantities.* Only $250 billion of the increase was *real.**

When we use GNP dollars that are *un*corrected for price changes, like the $2,368 billion figure for 1979, economists say we are using *money GNP, current dollar GNP,* or *nominal GNP.*

What about population changes? Up to the present, as GNP rose, so did the number of people. More and more people have shared in the GNP pie. To uncover the effects of population changes on incomes, economists first change GNP into real terms, as we have done above, and then divide real GNP by population. The result is called **real per capita GNP.**

Let us compare 1972 with 1979. In Table 11-3 the figures in column 3 result from dividing column 1 by column 2. Column 3 indicates that each

---

GNP, DPI, price changes, and population changes are shown in Tables A, B, C, and D at the back of the book.

TABLE 11-3 Real per Capita GNP, 1972 and 1979 (GNP in billions of 1972 dollars, population in millions)

	Real GNP (1)	Population (2)	Real per capita GNP (3)
1972	$1,171	209	$5,603
1979	1,421	221	6,430

person's share of GNP, corrected ("deflated") for inflation, increased by $827 over the seven-year period, or about $118 per person per year.

An even more precise measure is to consider changes in **real per capita DPI.** Remember that, while DPI includes transfer payments, it is the consumer's net income after all taxes have been paid. It is our best measure of take-home pay and represents the money consumers have available for spending or saving. In 1972, real per capita DPI was $3,837, while in 1979 it was $4,509, an increase in real income of $672 over the seven-year period. Real per capita DPI is a better measure of our economic status than real per capita GNP because the former includes the effects of taxes and transfer payments on our incomes. The latter does not. Real per capita DPI is probably our best measure of *economic growth* or lack of it.

The problem of income distribution

Our difficulties are not over. Note that real per capita DPI or GNP figures are *averages*, obtained by dividing real income by population. Averages have a major failing: they conceal the way numbers are distributed.

Suppose there are two countries, X and Y, and that each has a GNP of $1,000 and a population of 10 people. Average per capita income is then $100 per person per year ($1,000 ÷ 10 people) in both countries. Now suppose that the $1,000 is fairly evenly divided in country X but that there is a king in country Y whose annual income is $900. The other nine people in country Y divide up the remaining $100, an average of about $11 per person. In country Y, one person is rich while the others may be starving; nevertheless, country Y's per capita income is still the same $100. The problem of income distribution is important whether we are comparing change in a given country from one year to the next or are making comparisons between countries.

Comparing how GNP is spent

Two examples will illustrate this additional problem. In 1944 and again in 1957, real per capita GNP was coincidentally about $2,600. But in 1944, we were engaged in all-out war, while 1957 was relatively peaceful. In 1944, spending for military services was about $75 billion, or 36 percent of GNP for that year ($75 billion ÷ $210 billion). In 1957, however, military spending was $39 billion, only 9 percent of GNP for that year ($39 ÷ $441 billion). Even though the real per capita GNP for the two years appears to be the same, the people in 1944 were giving up a much larger share of their incomes for fighting the war and receiving necessarily much less for the civilian pleasures of peacetime existence. When comparing per capita incomes in different years or making comparisons of different countries, the composition of GNP is important.

The same problem involves differences in climate. Suppose a cold country like Greenland has the same real per capita GNP as Samoa. Which country is better off? In Greenland, much of the GNP is spent fighting for survival, while in Samoa more of it can be spent on pleasure.

This last point raises an interesting question. Does the fact that we have the largest GNP in the world really make us the richest country? Perhaps not. What does GNP really measure? It measures our desire and effort to obtain goods and services. It may also measure our preoccupation with acquiring income and wealth or the pervasiveness of the "Protestant ethic" in our society. In any case, the GNP is a relatively poor measure of the quality of individual citizens' lives.

The failure to take external costs into account	Our comments so far about GNP were not intended to be criticisms of the concept. Rather, they were intended to show the limitations of the GNP estimate as a measure of change, and particularly as a measure of change in the standard of living of consumers. Recently, however, there has been a growing chorus of criticism of the way GNP is figured—directed mainly at the failure of GNP to take external costs into account.

For example, we count the sale of automobiles as a plus and add it to consumption. We also count the treatment of lung disease, which may have been caused by the exhaust from automobiles, as a plus and also add it to consumption (the purchase of medical services). Some economists now argue that, if the automobile causes damage, or if approach and landing patterns around airfields depress property values, or if a factory pollutes a stream, we should deduct the costs of correcting these problems from GNP rather than add them.

As well-known economist Robert Lekachman put it:

> It follows that national income accounting errs when it stretches the market activity rubric to cover both the pluses of personal gratification and the financial burdens of their continued indulgence. Pluses and minuses are lumped together whenever the totals register both the value of cigarette output and the costs of treating associated cases of lung cancer and coronary occulsion. It is no less misguided to total up auto output and the sums spent to defend individuals against the noxious side effects. Nor does it make sense to sum up liquor sales and the medical expense entailed by alcoholism—and so on.
>
> My prejudices assure me that in relation to the pluses, the minuses are proliferating. . . . Until the estimators redo their sums, we are likely as a nation to continue measuring ourselves rich and feeling ourselves poor.[1]

Other than deducting minuses we should also add pluses for external benefits not reflected in product or service prices. We could also add a plus for leisure time, a point to remember because the time spent working is getting shorter. It has also been suggested that we should deduct an allowance for the depletion of the earth's resources. Efforts are now under way to give us a revised GNP that will take these difficult but important considerations into account.

In one attempt to reckon external costs and benefits that has gained considerable notice, GNP is changed to MEW—**"Measure of Economic Welfare."** The MEW concept subtracts from GNP not only pollution-related activities but also some government expenditures considered "regrettable," such as national defense, police forces, and fire departments. The MEW measure also subtracts a "disaminity premium" for the dissatisfaction one feels from living in crowded cities. On the other hand, the MEW measure includes large "pluses" for leisure time and work done in the home.* The result is an MEW that is more than double the GNP as it is currently measured.[2]

Summary

This chapter has shown how the economy's total output and income are measured. The most inclusive measure is the Gross National Product (GNP). It is determined by everyone's total demand for goods and services—called aggregate demand. The idea is that, after correcting for mistakes in judgment, producers will gear their production to meet this demand. Total production is called aggregate supply.

Disposable personal income (DPI) is the best measure of a person's take-home pay, particularly after it is adjusted for inflation. Changes in "real" DPI are the best measure of economic growth.

There are many pitfalls in using these measures to assess change in human welfare. Among the pitfalls are the problems of double counting, price and population changes, GNP composition and income distribution, and external costs—the problem of treating the costs of economic activity (such as pollution) as if they were pluses.

Discussion Questions

1. If per capita GNP were $100 in Ethiopia and $5,000 in the United States, would you say that Americans were 50 times better off than Ethiopians? Why or why not? Discuss.

2. Assume that your DPI in year X is $7,000 and that year X is the base year. In year Y, your DPI is $10,000, but in year Y the implicit price deflator is 130. How much has your real DPI changed?

3. If a rate of increase changes from 4 percent to 5 percent, how much has the rate changed?

*The MEW concept has been criticized on the grounds that decisions as to what expenditures and activities are "good" and "bad" would require the value judgments of a "philosopher king." (Arthur M. Okun, "Should GNP Measure Social Welfare?" Brookings Bulletin, *Summer 1971.*)

4. If the rate of inflation is 10 percent, how long will it take to reduce the value of a dollar to 50 cents? (Hint: Use the "rule of 72" in Chapter 1.)

5. What are the four kinds of spending that make up aggregate demand?

6. Why are aggregate supply and aggregate demand apt to be equal?

7. Why does aggregate demand determine GNP?

8. Why do we have recessions?

References   1. Robert Lekachman, "Humanizing GNP," *Social Policy*, September/October 1971, pp. 35–39.

2. Kenneth Stewart, "National Income Accounting and Economic Welfare: The Concepts of GNP and MEW," *Review*, Federal Reserve Bank of St. Louis, April 1974, pp. 18–24. The article is a summary of work done by William Nordhaus and James Tobin.

12 The Government's Role as Economic Manager

Owen Franken/Stock, Boston

In Chapter 10 we said that one of the purposes of government is to provide stable prices, enough jobs, and sufficient economic growth to satisfy an increasing number of people who want continual improvements in their standards of living. This chapter, and the following five chapters, describe this function. Although many state and local agencies often affect prices and the number of available jobs, we will limit our remarks to the federal government in its role as manager of macroeconomic affairs.

This chapter is divided into three sections: In the first, we want to examine the record to see how the economy has performed in the past and in recent years. This section sets the stage for a debate that divides the economics profession today and will probably continue to divide it for decades to come; that is, the debate between those who favor letting the economy take care of itself and those who favor governmental care of our economic

Key Words	
Exogenous causes	Theory of gluts
Endogenous causes	Keynesian revolution
Classical economists (classical school)	Deficit spending
Say's Law	Budget surplus
Wage-price flexibility	Employment Act of 1946

health. The second section therefore describes the economic school that says, "Do as little as possible," while the third is devoted to the views of those who want the federal government to be an active manager.

A Brief History of U.S. Economic Performance

We are going to look at our economic record with three measures in mind: changes in business activity, changes in prices, and changes in unemployment.

The record to 1930

The history of the United States, especially from the beginning of rapid industrial growth in the mid-nineteenth century, has been characterized by a number of ups and downs. In the years between 1854 and 1930 there were nineteen so-called "business cycles" during which industrial production expanded and then declined. The periods of expansion averaged about two and one-half years; the periods of contraction averaged about one and two-thirds years. During the expansion periods, production increased an average of 24 percent; coincidentally, during periods of contraction, production declined about the same amount.

During most of these years prices were either stable or actually fell. Amazingly, the consumer price index in 1929 was about what it was in 1800. There were, however, short periods of inflation associated with wartime shortages. During the Civil War, prices doubled; during World War I, prices almost tripled. Sustained, accelerating inflation is a relatively recent problem.

The unemployment record has been uneven. During the years between 1890 and 1929, the average worker went through several periods of hardship. If we divide the 39-year span into periods of minimal unemployment (0–4.0 percent), moderate unemployment (4.1–7.0 percent), and severe unemployment (7.1 percent and over), we find that he would have spent

☐ 14 years with minimal unemployment

☐ 15 years with moderate unemployment

☐ 10 years with severe unemployment

Then came the crash.

The Great Depression

The crash of the stock market in the fall of 1929 signalled the worst economic disaster the world had ever known. Most industrial countries suffered as much as did the United States. A few statistics will help dramatize what happened in the United States:

☐ By July 1932, some $74 billion, five-sixths of the September 1929 total of common stock values, had vanished into thin air.

☐ The nation's money supply contracted by one-third in the first three years of the Depression as 5,000 banks failed.

☐ Total investment spending by businesses dropped from $16.2 billion in 1929 to *$1.4 billion* in 1933.

☐ GNP fell from $103.4 billion in 1929 to $55.8 billion in 1933.

☐ Unemployment rose from 1.6 million workers in 1929 to 12.8 million workers in 1933 (25 percent of the labor force). The unemployment rate remained at more than 14 percent until 1941.

Space does not permit us to examine the causes of the Depression in any detail.* However, they can be briefly described under four headings:

1. A decline in industrial production and housing construction following a post-World War I boom in the early 1920s.

2. An increase in consumer debt (occasioned by postwar buying on credit) that inhibited consumers from continuing to buy new houses and appliances.

3. Common stocks priced far beyond their real worth after a decade of speculation.

4. The inability of the Federal Reserve System to prevent the collapse of the banking system after the collapse of the stock market.

After the Depression

Recall that changes in GNP can occur simply when prices change. "Money" ("current dollar") GNP may increase with no change, or even a decrease, in the quantities of goods and services produced. Thus, *money* GNP is a poor measure of the quantities of goods and services produced and also of the level of employment. It is *real* (deflated) GNP that matters.

The uneven growth of GNP

There is no question about the fact that real GNP has grown since 1929. In 1972 ("constant") dollars, real GNP quadrupled during the period 1929–1978 from $315 billion to $1,391 billion. (Money GNP in 1978 was $2,107 billion.)

Interested students should consult John Kenneth Galbraith's The Great Crash 1929 *(Boston: Houghton Mifflin Company, 1961).*

Figure 12-1. Year-to-year Percentage Changes in Real GNP (selected years).

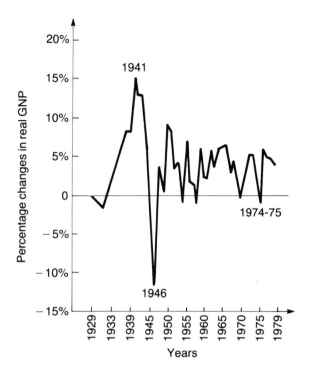

Source: *Economic Report of the President, 1979.*

However, this growth has been very uneven. Figure 12-1 shows the percentage changes in real GNP from one year to the next. In some years—1946, 1974, and 1975—the percentage increase in real GNP actually *declined* from the previous year. Also notable is the large increase from 1933 to 1941. This increase is usually attributed to the heating up of the economy that occurred at the beginning of World War II. However, one can see that there was steady improvement during this period.

The gyrations in real GNP shown in Figure 12-1 represent very large changes. A 5 percent change in a $2,000 billion GNP is $100 billion; that is, *$100,000,000,000*—enough to hire five million people at $20,000 a year each. Clearly, whatever can be done to prevent declines of this magnitude is worthwhile.

Another way to visualize the performance of GNP is to compare what actually happened *(actual GNP)* with what the economy was capable of producing *(potential GNP)*. Potential GNP, which has been calculated in recent years by the Council of Economic Advisors (CEA), is the amount that could have been produced each year with an annual increase in real GNP of about 4 percent per year.

Business Cycle Theory: Trying to Forecast Ups and Downs

Economists have been trying to predict changes in GNP for roughly 100 years . . .

The zig-zag picture of real GNP shown in Figure 12-1 raises a fascinating question: Is there a pattern? Witch doctors, soothsayers, advisors to kings, and, yes, economists have tried for generations to discover such patterns in physical events (such as weather) and human behavior. If only one could know the pattern of, let us say, the stock market, one could buy low and sell high—and so presumably live happily ever after.

Economists have been trying to predict changes in GNP for roughly 100 years by applying *business cycle theory*. The idea is that real GNP and levels of employment and prices go up and down in a wavelike or cyclical motion and that there is a regular and uniform time period between each peak and trough. But no one

In Figure 12-2 (page 248), the upper line represents the real GNPs the economy could have produced, given steady growth rates of 3 to 4 percent per year. The lower line shows what actually happened. The shaded area represents the dollar value of lost production and income.

In the ten-year period 1970–1979, the differences between potential and actual (real) GNP add up to $561 billion worth of lost production and income.

is sure about the existence of a cycle. We continue to live economic lives of uncertainty, lives during which predictions about the stock market, or any form of economic activity, continue to be full of risk. There are no sure things.

The problem is that what appear to be patterns are suddenly disrupted by unforeseen events like hurricanes, droughts, or wars. Such events are called **exogenous causes.** On the other hand, events that occur logically within the framework of a model are called **endogenous.** For example, when we spend more money because our incomes go up, the increase in spending is endogenously related to the change in income. But, *why* did our income change in the first place? It could have changed because of an unforeseen, exogenous event such as the arrival of a large new factory in our town. An exogenous event has caused an endogenous event to occur.

Psychological feelings of optimism or pessimism are also important in influencing events. If we are pessimistic about the future, we will spend less and try to save more. Aggregate demand will fall and so will the level of employment. In fact, our feelings of pessimism help to bring GNP down. This phenomenon of "believing makes it so" is what social scientists call a *self-fulfilling prophecy.* The prophecy works both ways. If we are optimistic, we say to ourselves, "Don't worry about that bank account, the old job is secure, live it up." Spending, GNP, and the level of employment will rise if enough people are optimistic. Believing that the future is rosy makes it rosy.

The point is that these feelings may be exogenously or endogenously caused. To whatever extent our feelings are exogenously caused, they are unpredictable, and attempts to base business cycle theory on them are hopeless.

Despite these difficulties, it is of crucial importance to estimate as intelligently as we can what the future will bring and to plan for it.

The methods of economic forecasting are many. Records are kept of the number and age of automobiles and appliances that we own for the purpose of estimating when we might want a new model. Opinion polls are taken of "consumer sentiment" which estimate feelings of pessimism or optimism and the readiness of consumers to buy. Computerized models of the macroeconomy exist that help us to visualize what may happen. Some of these models involve what are called economic indicators.

Economic indicators are series of data that economists believe are particularly helpful in estimating what is going to happen. There are three types: (1) *Leading indicators* show what is apt to happen several months in advance. Examples are average weekly overtime hours, capital spending for machines, and changes in inventories. (2) *Lagging indicators* represent what has happened in the recent past and help to confirm or deny an upward or downward trend. Examples are the unemployment rate, labor costs per unit of output, and consumer installment debt. (3) *Coincident indicators* show current changes. Some examples are current dollar GNP, retail sales, and help-wanted advertisements.

But, sad to say, even these indicators may send out conflicting signals. Then the experts have to make judgments about which indicators have the greatest value.

It is hard to appreciate how gigantic these numbers are. With that money, we could have built over 5.61 million $100,000 houses! The point is that this production did not take place. It is permanently lost, as are the productive hours of people not hired who could have been.

Figure 12-2 contains a noteworthy bit of history. It marks the worst recession since World War II. (A recession is usually defined as a fall in real

Figure 12-2. Potential versus actual GNP, 1935–1979 (in billions of constant 1972 dollars).

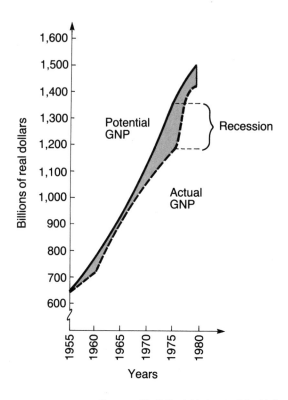

Source: *Statistical Abstract of the United States, 1980.*

GNP over two or more three-month quarters.) Table 12-1 traces GNP history from 1968 through 1979. Any decrease in real GNP is unusual. Decreases have occurred only five times since the 1930s. But in one case—the recession of 1974–1975—real GNP dropped two years in a row.

The unemployment picture in recent years

The cost of the 1975 recession in terms of human welfare was large. Almost eight million workers were unemployed in 1975, an increase of three million over 1974. By 1978, the number of unemployed declined to a still unacceptable six million people, about 6 percent of the labor force.*

We should spend a moment thinking about the cost of unemployment. One measure is, of course, the cost of lost production (all those houses we could have had). But we should remember the human cost as well. An unemployed person's skills deteriorate. Fear, frustration, and perhaps despair

---

The unemployment rate is a percentage derived by dividing the number of people unemployed (a figure determined by the Bureau of the Census through interviewing a large sample of people each month) by the number of people in the civilian labor force. The civilian labor force is the sum of those employed (excluding members of the armed forces) plus those counted as unemployed.

TABLE 12-1 Real GNP Changes, 1968–1979 (in billions of 1972 dollars)

Year	Real GNP	
1968	$1,052	
1969	1,079	
1970	1,075 ◄——— GNP drops	
1971	1,108	
1972	1,171 ◄——► then increases	
1973	1,235	
1974	1,219 ◄——► then drops twice	
1975	1,202	
1976	1,271	
1977	1,333 ◄——► then increases	
1978	1,385	
1979	1,421	

take over. We are all bits of human capital that can deteriorate just as a machine that isn't kept in shape rusts away. Unemployment can be self-

Figure 12-3 shows unemployment rates during the years 1951 through 1978. At first glance, the heavy line showing total unemployment looks as if it is made up of three zig-zags. However, one can discern a pattern of four recessions—in 1954, 1958, 1961, and the bad one in 1975. Note also the drop in unemployment from 1951 to 1953 and from 1961 through 1969, first during the Korean War and then during the war in Vietnam.[†]

Figure 12-3 is a vivid reminder of how the costs and hardships of unemployment fall unevenly upon workers of different groups. It is clear that, at any moment in time, unemployment rates for minority workers are double the overall average, that the rates for teenagers are triple the overall average. Finally, when we draw a trend line through the zig-zags, the slope seems to be up toward increasing unemployment.

Now we'll finish up this discussion of the "record" with a review of our other, most difficult, problem.

In the 1975 recession, 15.2 percent of the eight million unemployed were unemployed for more than 26 weeks. The average duration was about 14 weeks.

†*War affects employment directly by swelling the ranks of the armed services and by increasing the number of jobs in the industries that supply the armed services with food, clothing, shelter, and weaponry. And when these employees spend their increased incomes, many other industries will also hire more people. The initial stimulus of government spending for war becomes multiplied. More on this multiplier effect in Chapter 13.*

Figure 12-3. Unemployment Rates, 1951–1978.

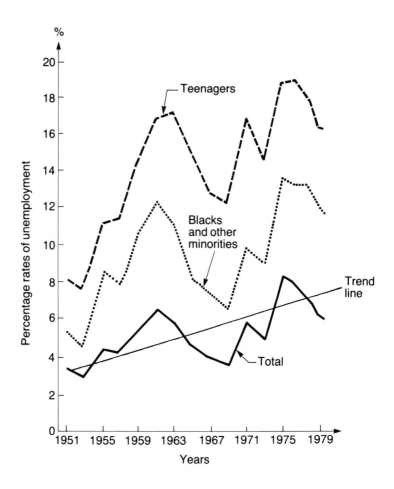

Source: *Economic Report of the President, 1979.*

Inflation: who wins and who loses?

As we noted earlier, sustained, even accelerating, inflation did not become a problem for most Americans until the end of World War II. In this section we will show the recent record of inflation and discuss its effects on various groups of people. (Suggestions for *curing* inflation and unemployment will have to wait until the last macro chapter, Chapter 17.)

Figure 12-4 shows how consumer prices have risen since 1933, the bottom of the Depression. Beginning in about 1965 (when the Vietnam war began to heat up), the rise in prices became much steeper.

Note that the base year of the Consumer Price Index (CPI) is 1967 when CPI equals 100 and that CPI in 1979 was 217.4; in those thirteen years consumer prices increased 117.4 percent, an average of 9 percent (117.4 ÷ 13) per year.

Figure 12-4. The Consumer Price Index, 1929–1979 (1967 = 100).

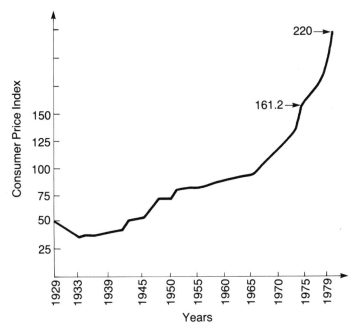

Source: *Economic Report of the President, 1980.*

Now, recall the Rule of 72 from Chapter 1. The rule tells us that in 8 years (72 ÷ 9) consumer prices will double if the inflation rate continues at that pace. This means that in 8 years the purchasing power of your dollar will be cut in half. And, it also means that, unless your savings account is earning at least 9 percent per year *after income taxes, you're losing.*

Politicians like to say that inflation is a "tax" on everyone because rising prices cut everyone's purchasing power. But this is obviously not the case. When you buy something from a store at a higher price, your purchasing power may have been cut, but the store's income has gone up. Rising prices mean higher incomes for somebody. Consequently, the main effect of inflation is to *redistribute* real income and wealth rather than making everyone worse off. We will look briefly at six groups of people to see who wins or loses from inflation.

1. Savers.   We have already suggested that savers lose unless their interest income, after taxes, keeps up with inflation. If the interest income on your savings account is 6 percent, and your marginal tax bracket is 30 percent, you will have to pay 1.8 percent of your interest income (30 percent of 6 percent) to the government in taxes. Your net income on the savings account is now 6.0 − 1.8 = 4.2 percent. If the rate of inflation is, say, 10 percent, your savings account is losing 5.8 percent (10.0 − 4.2) per year. In about 12.4 years (72 ÷ 5.8) your savings account will be worth half of what it is today. The bank and the government win, you lose.

2. Taxpayers.   If you receive a cost-of-living increase in your paycheck, you automatically pay a larger income tax to your state and to the federal government. (We discussed this problem when we analyzed the progressive income tax in Chapter 10.) Winners are the government and wealthy people who can take advantage of more tax loopholes. Losers are taxpayers whose incomes are mostly in the form of wages and salaries. Various plans to index the income tax have been proposed to alleviate this problem.

3. Union versus nonunion employees.   Many union contracts have so-called *escalator clauses*—also called "COLA" (Cost of Living Adjustment) clauses— that provide the workers with automatic pay increases when the Consumer Price Index rises by an agreed-upon amount. The pay adjustments can occur every few months. Workers under such a contract win. The company may or may not lose, depending on its ability (its market power) to pass along the cost of such wage increases to the public in the form of higher prices. In general, workers belonging to strong unions win; those belonging to weak unions or to no union lose.

4. Creditors versus debtors.   Inflation may cause creditors to lose and debtors to win. The debtor wins because each loan payment is worth less in *real* terms. The payments the creditor receives have successively less purchasing power. If, however, the creditor can anticipate the future course of inflation and charge an interest rate that covers it, then the creditor-debtor positions are reversed. We will take up this point again when we look at the sixth group.

5. Those receiving fixed incomes versus those whose incomes vary.   Here we are thinking about people living on relatively fixed incomes, such as pensions or life-insurance payments, versus the wage earner whose income will change. The fixed-income person loses as, each month, the pension check buys fewer groceries, less heating, and so on. To overcome this problem, one should, if possible, have a pension plan with automatic cost-of-living adjustments, like the escalator clauses in some union contracts.

6. Those who anticipate versus those who do not (or cannot).   If you can anticipate inflation, you will win. If you don't or can't, you will lose. This holds for all groups. Corporations with the market power to do so can beat the gun by raising prices before costs go up. Unions can beat the gun, too, and so can creditors. But, according to the record, creditors have not done so well. One estimate is that the redistributional effects of inflation in favor of debtors have probably totalled at least $500 billion since World War II.[1]

Of course, knowing that inflation is coming and doing something about it are two different matters. The small-business entrepreneur may know it is coming but cannot raise prices because competition is too tough. The nonunion or weak union worker may realize that living costs are going up but not have the market power to get a pay raise. Old people may know living costs are going up, but their incomes are too inflexible and too taken up with spending on "inflatable" goods (or increased rents or property taxes) to permit them to take any effective action.

It is odd but true that if people are successful in anticipating inflation and doing something about it, we will certainly have inflation. If we could get everyone to agree that there will not be any inflation, there will not be. This is another example of a self-fulfilling prophecy. If we all believe prices are going up, we will all try to buy before they go up. Then demand curves will shift to the right—forcing prices up. Business managers and unions will raise prices and wages, and inflation will result.

And so we are beginning to realize that long periods of inflation usually penalize those people least able to afford high prices and, further, that inflation feeds on itself. Once we begin to accept inflation, the probability of continued, accelerating inflation increases.

Now we are ready to take up the debate mentioned at the beginning of the chapter. Is it better to leave the economy alone? Or should the federal government manage the economy for purposes of controlling prices, reducing unemployment, and ensuring sustained increases in real GNP? The following section on classical theory explains the first point of view; the section on the Keynesian revolution explains the latter.

Classical Theory: Leave the Economy Alone

Before the Great Depression of the 1930s, most economists accepted the view that a market-price system like ours could solve its own problems without government interference. Those who hold this view are called the **classical economists** or the **classical school.** The founder of classical theory was Adam Smith. Its other early supporters were David Ricardo and Jean Baptiste Say. The classical economists believed not only that the economic system could take care of itself if left alone, but that there were automatic control devices in it, acting like thermostats, which would continuously move the economic system toward full employment without inflation.

The classical school's belief that a market-price system would always tend toward a condition of full employment is best explained by looking at the ideas of Jean Baptiste Say (1767–1832).

Say's Law: "supply creates its own demand"

Say's major work, the *Treatise on Political Economy* (1803), contains a series of propositions that economists have called Say's Law of Markets or, more simply, **Say's Law.**

Say's Law is often reduced to a slogan: "Supply creates its own demand." The slogan means that the act of producing something immediately creates income (the factory payments of wages, rent, interest, and profit, which are paid in the course of production), and that this income creates demand for something equal to the value of what was produced *because income is earned to be spent.*

The act of producing something immediately creates income.

To put it another way, in the course of producing a tube of Dazzle toothpaste to sell for $1, we will immediately create wages, rent, interest, and profit equal to $1 because this is the sum of the factor payments that went into its production.

The most important assumption in Say's line of reasoning was *that income is earned only to be spent.* Thus, in his thinking, if the $1 of income created in the course of producing the tube of toothpaste is earned only to be spent, it constitutes *demand* for something worth $1. If we now consider the total production of *all* things, we can see that the total production of everything creates the income and demand necessary to buy everything. Thus the act of production (supply) creates equivalent income (demand).

Now the crucial point. Producers (suppliers) do not have to worry about demand, because everything they decide to produce will always be sold. If they are good Adam Smithians, motivated by self-interest to make as much money as possible, they will want to produce as much as possible. Consequently, they will offer jobs to all who want to work. There will be *no* unemployment. Note, furthermore, that aggregate supply will be at maximum output (at *potential GNP*), but no one need be concerned: sufficient aggregate demand will be there to buy it.

The classical theorists led by Say answered every possible objection. If people did not want to spend their money on Dazzle toothpaste, for example, they would spent it on something else. Though Dazzle might lose sales and people would be laid off, these workers, it was argued, would soon find jobs elsewhere.

The wage-price flexibility argument

A loss enterprise like Dazzle would tend to recover even if resources did not shift from one industry to another. The reason is central to classical theory.

Figure 12-5. Operation of the economy in classical theory.

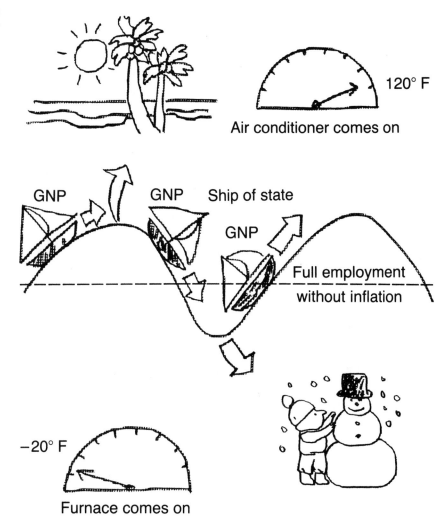

Air conditioner comes on

Furnace comes on

Classical theory is based on the assumption of **wage-price flexibility.** Prices and wages are flexible enough, the classical economists believed, that in bad times they would fall. At lower prices and wages, buying and hiring would both pick up. Recovery from a recession would be automatic.

The classical theorists believed that flexible wages and prices acted like a thermostat that would automatically keep GNP at a full-employment level without inflation. Think of a thermostat that automatically turns on the air conditioner during times of inflation to cool off the economy. (Rising prices discourage buying.) And when sales are sluggish (when the economy is too cold), the thermostat will turn on the furnace. (Falling prices encourage buying.) There may be fluctuations, but GNP always returns to full-employment without inflation, as shown in Figure 12-5.

The saving–investment argument

Even if people decided to save some of their income instead of spending all of it, flexible prices would take care of the problem. If people saved more, the banks would have more money to lend, the interest rate would fall, and when it did, borrowing by business managers for investment would increase. In fact, the interest rate at any given moment would arrive at an *equilibrium price* that would make the quantity of money saved equal to the quantity of money borrowed for investment. Thus, *all* income earned, or saved, would be spent, either by the people for consumption or by business managers for investment.

The essence of the classical argument, then, is that whereas industries may decline or blossom, the overall size of the industrial pie will always be sufficient to provide everyone with a job who wants one. There may be shifting around from one industry to another, but except for these temporary periods of adjustment, there will always be full employment. Anyone unemployed for any long period of time would be *voluntarily* unemployed.

Malthus's objection to classical theory

Malthus, a contemporary of the classical economists, is perhaps the first to have detected a difficulty. In addition to his theory of population (which you will remember from page 8), Malthus is known for his **theory of gluts.** According to Malthus, if a $1 tube of toothpaste were produced and sold, workers would receive something *less* than $1 per tube because the entrepreneur would not hire them unless they produced a product worth *more* than the wage he or she paid them. Total wages paid all workers are therefore something less than the amount necessary to buy all the tubes of toothpaste and *all other* products produced.

All would be well *if* the consumption spending by those Malthus called "unproductive laborers" (service workers like school teachers) plus capital spending by entrepreneurs made up the difference between workers' income and the value of their production. But Malthus further believed that the capitalist-entrepreneur's desire to make ever more money by enlarging his or her enterprise would periodically cause an overproduction of goods—a glut on the market. Because the demand by workers was never sufficient to buy everything produced, there would be periods of slowdowns, unemployment, and general depression. Here we have the first objection to Say's law. Malthus recognized that $1 of supply does not necessarily mean $1 of demand.

Malthus's objection was buried by those who believed in the sanctity of classical theory. The idea that government interference might be necessary—or that uncontrolled capitalism might not work—found little support. Then came the stock market crash of 1929 heralding a depression that engulfed the country.

Its severity and length helped to convince scholars and politicians that something was wrong with classical economic theory. The time was ripe for a new approach to macroeconomic problems.

The Keynesian Revolution: The Economy Needs to Be Managed

The new approach appeared in 1936. In that year, a book was published by an English economist named John Maynard Keynes (pronounced "canes"). The book was called *The General Theory of Employment, Interest, and Money.* Among economists, Keynes's book had such an explosive effect that its influence has been called the **Keynesian revolution.**

Keynes was strongly influenced by Malthus's idea that total demand might not be enough to provide full employment. He argued that the economy could get stuck at any level of unemployment and that there were no automatic forces that would help the economy recover from depressions or excessive inflation. Keynes's views inevitably led to the conclusion that the economy *could not* take care of itself. He believed it was the government's job to pull the economy out of a depression.

The frequent failure of aggregate demand to provide for full employment is at the center of Keynesian theory. If aggregate demand is high enough, the country will have full employment; if it is too low, we will have recessions and unemployment. Keynes's disagreement with classical theory can be summarized as follows:

Objections to the wage-price flexiblity argument

Keynes had two major objections to the classical theory of wage-price flexibility:

First, demand may be inelastic, and a decrease in price may not be offset by a proportionate increase in sales. Further, the classical argument assumes that demand does not change. In reality, if people get tired of a product, demand for it may decrease—may shift to the left—and if this happens, sales may not increase *at all* even when the price falls.

Second, if total wages fall, aggregate demand may decline. As Keynes noted, after a drop in wages the *total* wage of *all* workers hired—even if there are more workers—may be smaller than before. Aggregate demand can, therefore, get stuck at any level of employment.

Objections to the saving-investment argument

There are also three objections to the classical school's saving-investment argument with its interest-rate "thermostat."

First, do entrepreneurs really invest more by borrowing savings because the interest rate falls? Keynes's answer was partly "yes" but mostly "no." The interest rate is certainly an important cost of investment in a capital good or in any new venture, but the entrepreneur must believe that the new capital good will be profitable before borrowing the money at any interest rate. The *expectation of profit* is therefore the major determinant of investment, not the interest rate.

Second, when people decide to save more, does the interest rate fall and are business firms apt to invest more? To this idea, Keynesian theory says, "Nonsense!" If people decide to save more out of the same income, it must mean that they are spending less. If, out of your $100 a week take-home pay, you decide to save $10 instead of $5, your consumption spending must

John Maynard Keynes

The Bettmann Archive.

Englishman John Maynard Keynes (1883–1946—he liked to be called Maynard) was the son of two Cambridge University professors. At the age of four, he was figuring out the economic theory of interest; at fourteen, he had a scholarship to Eton; at seventeen, he was a success at Kings College at Cambridge. After graduation, he came in second on the nationwide Civil Service Ex-amination. (He would have placed first had his testers given him a better grade in economics, about which he knew more than they did.)

By the time he was twenty-nine, he had become the editor of the *Economic Journal,* a post he was to hold (among others) for thirty-three years. He was also a member of the social elite. Professionals in every field, such as George Bernard Shaw and Bertrand Russell, were accustomed to receiving and taking his advice. When World War I broke out, he was called to work for the Treasury and was soon a key figure there.

Following World War I, Keynes was one of the advisors who went to the Treaty of Versailles conference. Although he went to Paris as a representative of the Treasury, he was still only a member of the second echelon and could not engage in the peace negotiations himself. This was one of the most frustrating times of his life. Unable to influence the outcome in any way, he was only able to stand by and watch helplessly as President Wilson was outmaneuvered by Clemenceau, who moved to break up Germany and exact a harsh penalty. Realizing that the signing of the Treaty of Versailles was inevitable, he resigned from the Treasury.

necessarily drop from $95 to $90. If everyone saves more, total spending must fall. Business firms will see sales slackening, and, if anything, they will *reduce* investment spending, regardless of changes in the interest rate.

Finally, are all wages and prices flexible enough in the downward direction to encourage buying in bad times? Keynes believed that there was one price that would not fall far enough to help—the price of borrowed money; that is, interest rates. The interest rates we pay involve a combination of many considerations by the lender: (1) the fact that the lender deserves some reward for giving up the use of his or her money for a period of time; (2) the risk of nonrepayment; (3) the administrative costs of processing the loan plus a normal profit; (4) the lender's expectations about the change in the value of the money (inflation or deflation) when it is repaid. Keynes's reasoning was that some of these elements in interest rates tend to be rigid

Three days before the treaty was signed, he started work on his book, *The Economic Consequences of the Peace.* It was an attack on the treaty and the ineffectiveness, inadequacies, and inequities of the meeting. The book was an instant success, and his reputation as an economic prophet was secured.

Turning his back on government, Keynes returned to Cambridge and teaching but also found time to be chairman of the National Mutual Life Assurance Society, editor of the *Economic Journal,* chairman of the *New Statesman and Nation,* and a director of the Bank of England. He also organized London's Camargo Ballet and Cambridge's Arts Theater, assembled the world's finest collection of Isaac Newton's manuscripts, wrote for the *Manchester Guardian,* and married Lydia Lopokova, a ballerina of the Diaghilev Russian ballet and a celebrity of the period.

By 1935, Keynes was known as one of the most brilliant economists and writers of modern times. He was so prolific that a list of his books, tracts, and essays fills twenty-two pages. Of main interest are his books on mathematical probability (1921), the gold standard and monetary reform (1923), the causes of business cycles

(1930), and his book, *The General Theory of Employment, Interest, and Money* (1936), which consolidated all of the theories of his previous books. *Time* magazine, which made Keynes the cover story of its December 31, 1965, issue, stated of *The General Theory:* "It is an uneven and ill-organized book, as difficult as *Deuteronomy* and open to almost as many interpretations. Yet for all its faults, it had more influence in a shorter time than any other book ever written in economics, including Smith's *The Wealth of Nations* and Marx's *Das Kapital.*"

Keynes's ideas, which encompassed all aspects of economics, were the forerunners of macroeconomics as it is known today. Although other economists of Keynes's time had also called for government spending in times of depression, Keynes was the only one with enough influence to be listened to.

His theories were not adopted overnight (Franklin Roosevelt, in 1934, was not the least bit impressed by Keynes's White House Lectures), but by 1946, Congress had adopted the Keynesian course of action with the passage of the Employment Act of 1946.

and that interest rates will not fall far enough to encourage business borrowing for investment even if the banks have more money to lend.

Keynesian Theory: "demand creates supply"

Keynes's contribution to economic theory was the idea that aggregate demand—the grand total of all intentions to buy something—might *not* be sufficient to provide a job for everyone who wanted one. He argued that *demand created supply,* not the reverse, in the sense that entrepreneurs produce only because they expect that demand for their goods and services exists. If these total intentions to buy were not enough to buy all of the goods and services produced, then enterprises would lay people off, aggregate demand would decline because of the decline in total income, and a recession or depression would result.

When aggregate demand lagged, Keynes argued, it should be given artificial stimulation through fiscal policy—tax cuts or increases in government spending. Keynes also recognized that aggregate demand could be changed by monetary policy—by controlling interest rates charged on loans and the total volume of loans. Low interest rates and a large volume of loans would increase aggregate demand. High interest rates and a small volume of loans would lower aggregate demand.

According to Keynesian theory, government spending should be increased enough to make up for any failure of consumption spending or investment spending to provide full employment. Keynes argued that, in times of unemployment, government spending should increase even if the government had to spend more than it was taking in through taxes.

Deficit spending: when government spends more than it receives

When the government spends more money than it receives, it is engaged in **deficit spending.** Where does the government get the money to spend? It borrows the money by selling government securities for the total of the deficit. The sale of government securities to cover deficit spending is called *deficit financing.* The securities are sold to individuals, businesses, and even government agencies, and the proceeds are spent on dams and highways; or on missiles, bombers, and submarines; or may even be given away in the form of transfer payments (welfare, social security, and the like). As the money is spent on goods and services produced by the private sector, employment rises and the economy gradually recovers.

In most of the years since 1933, the federal government has spent more than it has received from taxes. For example, in 1978, its total income was $402 billion, but it spent $451 billion. The $49 billion difference was deficit spending. This deficit was then financed by the sale of government securities. Each year that a deficit occurs, the *national (or public) debt* goes up by that amount. (The national or "public" debt is simply the grand total of all government securities in existence at any point in time. The public debt is discussed in detail in Chapter 14.)

The idea that the cure for unemployment is deficit spending was extremely controversial in the 1930s. Its logic is that when people buy government securities, they are transforming private savings in bank accounts or other financial investments into government securities. When the government spends the money it receives from securities sales, it spends money that would have been saved. In essence, the government converts inactive (savings) money to active spending. In theory, such spending adds to aggregate demand, causing GNP and therefore employment to rise.*

---

*Deficit spending adds to aggregate demand as long as it doesn't compete with private spending. We'll look at this point in Chapters 13 and 16.

The Employment Act of 1946

Beginning in 1931, the federal government *did* run relatively small deficits, averaging $2 to $3 billion per year, not explicitly to bolster aggregate demand but to provide jobs in such programs as the Works Progress Administration (WPA) and the Civilian Conservation Corps (CCC). During World War II, federal deficit spending increased more than tenfold to pay for the war. With their savings, people bought *$210 billion* worth of government securities, permitting an equal amount of deficit spending. This enormous addition to aggregate demand caused *real* GNP to jump 10 to 15 percent *per year* during the war years. There was a corresponding drop in the unemployment rate to less than 2 percent in 1943, 1944, and 1945. For this reason, many economists believe that the deficit spending during World War II brought the country out of the Depression and showed that Keynesian theory actually worked.

But when World War II was over, people began to wonder if the drop in government spending would plunge the country back into a depression. Unemployment more than doubled in the years 1945–1946 (from 1,070,000 to 2,270,000). Furthermore, federal government spending dropped by more than half (from $84.6 billion to $35.6 billion). In 1945, the last year of the war, the deficit had been $42.1 billion. In 1946, fifteen years of deficit spending stopped. Federal tax receipts in 1946 were $39.1 billion while expenditures were only $35.6 billion. The government actually ran a surplus of $3.5 billion.

A **budget surplus** occurs whenever the government's tax receipts exceed government expenditures. If, for example, the government collects $600 billion in taxes but spends "only" $595 billion of it, there is a $5 billion surplus. A surplus is a withdrawal of money from the dollar flow. This withdrawal has the same effect on the economy that increased saving by consumers or businesses has because the money ($5 billion in our example) is not spent and does not find its way back to business firms in the form of purchases of consumer goods or capital goods.

A government surplus may, therefore, be interpreted as having a depressing effect on business activity and employment. It is just the opposite of a deficit, which adds to aggregate demand and helps the economy expand. The surplus in 1946, added to the tremendous reduction in government spending and the increase in unemployment, gave many people real cause for concern.

In 1946, many people were also worried about whether or not the peacetime economy would grow fast enough to absorb the millions of returning veterans. We should remember that aggregate demand is the sum of the four categories of spending—by consumers, by businesses for capital goods, by the government, and by net exports. When one of them drops— in this case the severe drop in government purchases—aggregate demand is more likely to fall than to rise, causing unemployment to increase still further.

Accordingly, Congress was motivated to pass the **Employment Act of 1946,** which states in part:

The Congress hereby declares that it is the continuing policy and *responsibility* [emphasis added] of the Federal Government . . . to foster and promote . . . conditions under which there will be afforded useful employment opportunities, including self-employment, for those able, willing, and seeking work and to promote maximum employment, production, and purchasing power.

The Act established a three-person Council of Economic Advisors (CEA), with an additional staff of professional economists, to advise the President, mainly about the changes in taxes and government spending that might be necessary to carry out the intent of the act. The Act also established the Joint Economic Committee (JEC) of both houses of Congress to investigate a wide range of economic problems.

The Act is of paramount importance in our discussion of classical versus Keynesian theory. The Act says, in effect, that the market-price system cannot take care of itself and that the federal government will henceforth be responsible for managing the economy in such a way as to provide full employment.

The Employment Act of 1946 paved the way for almost total acceptance of Keynesian theory. *Time* magazine put Keynes on its December 31, 1965, cover and commented that economic policies in Washington were determined by followers of Keynesian theory. President Nixon said later, during his administration, "We are all Keynesians now." By the mid-1970s, however, Keynesian theory came under increasingly severe attack as it became apparent that the theory could not deal effectively with inflation (see Chapter 17). But there are still many elements of Keynesian theory that deserve our attention. For these elements let's now turn to Chapter 13.

Summary

When we look at historical changes in real GNP, unemployment rates, and prices, we find that (1) changes in the rates of growth of real GNP show a zig-zag pattern, (2) unemployment rates appear to show an upward trend, and that (3) prices have risen continuously since the Depression.

Despite the ups and downs of GNP, the classical economists like Adam Smith and Jean Baptiste Say believed that the free-enterprise economy had its own stabilizing mechanisms that made government macroeconomic policies unnecessary. Say's Law of Markets held that supply creates its own demand; that if consumers save more and buy less, entrepreneurs will invest more in capital goods; that when people save more, interest rates will decline, causing entrepreneurs to borrow more for investment (expansion), eventually restoring full employment. These automatic adjustments are based on the assumptions that the income from production in the form of workers' wages, profits, and so on, would be spent on consumer goods or invested in capital goods; that resources, including labor, would be free to move; and that wages, prices, and interest rates would be flexible. But workers try to save more when they expect hard times to come, while entrepreneurs also are often more influenced by their expectations for the future than by interest rates. As a result, attempted increases in saving may not be matched by increases in investment.

Modern economists led by John Maynard Keynes believe that the economy will not automatically take care of itself, that when consumer spending decreases, or saving increases, interest rates may not fall and investment spending may well decrease if increased saving results in reduced consumer spending. Aggregate spending (total spending by consumers, investors, government, and net exports) will then decline, causing unemployment. The Keynesian fiscal cure for inadequate aggregate demand is deficit spending— government spending that exceeds the money it receives from taxes.

Fears after World War II that the country would plunge back into the Depression of the 1930s led to the passage of the Employment Act of 1946, which charges the federal government with the responsibility for promoting full employment. Because it puts the federal government into a position of manipulating the economy, the law is a rejection of the classical belief that the economy can take care of itself.

Discussion Questions

1. What is Say's Law?

2. Why does Say's Law suggest automatic tendencies toward full employment in a market-price system?

3. "If product prices and wages fall far enough, unemployment can be avoided." Critically evaluate this statement.

4. Why does deficit spending increase aggregate demand?

Reference

1. G. L. Bach, "Inflation: Who Gains and Who Loses?" *Challenge* July/August 1974, pp. 48–55.

13 Fiscal Policy: The Keynesian Model

David Powers/Stock, Boston

This chapter continues our discussion of the federal government as an economic manager by reviewing the principal elements of Keynesian theory.* We have seen that Keynes's central point was that total spending (aggregate demand) might not be sufficient to buy everything produced (aggregate supply). When this happened, business firms would have to cut production and unemployment would rise. The Keynesian remedy for unemployment is an increase in government spending or a reduction in taxes even when such changes meant deficits. These changes in government spending or taxes are called **fiscal policy.**

This chapter is divided into five sections: (1) the distinction between automatic and discretionary fiscal policy; (2) the concept of equilibrium

---

Keynesian theory is presented in graphical form in Chapter 13A.

Key Words

Fiscal policy	Unintended disinvestment
Built-in stabilizers (automatic stabilizers)	Intended vs. actual investment
Discretionary fiscal policy	Unintended investment
Equilibrium income (equilibrium GNP)	Paradox of thrift
Income stream	Spending multiplier
Leakages and additions	Crowding-out

---

income, which helps to explain how GNP rises and falls if nothing is done; (3) the multiplier effects of government spending or tax changes on aggregate demand; (4) the pros and cons of using changes in government spending or tax changes to change aggregate demand; and (5) a review of fiscal policy problems.

Automatic Versus Discretionary Fiscal Policy

Fiscal policy—changes in government spending or taxing—is of two types. As the terms above suggest, some changes in spending or taxes occur automatically, while some require deliberate action by the President or by Congress.

Automatic fiscal policy

Automatic changes in government spending and taxing are called **built-in stablizers** (or sometimes **automatic stabilizers**) because they help to smooth the waves of recession and inflation.

The important built-in stabilizers are (1) automatic changes in tax receipts and (2) automatic changes in unemployment compensation and other welfare transfer payments. A word on each.

Tax receipts

As GNP falls, the federal government's tax receipts decline even faster as individual's pay lower income taxes. Not only is there less income to tax, but the tax rates are lower. This phenomenon means that, in times of falling GNP, disposable personal income (DPI) will not fall so far, and therefore consumption spending (usually about 90 percent of DPI) will help to sustain aggregate demand in times of recession. The reverse is true in times of inflation. Rising incomes resulting in higher income tax rates will tend to slow the increase in DPI and also help to slow down the rise in prices.

Unemployment compensation and welfare payments

In times of recession, welfare payments and payments to unemployed workers automatically rise, again helping to sustain DPI. In prosperous times, these payments fall automatically, cooling the economy.

Economists believe the built-in stabilizers are extremely important and will probably become more so if the federal government's influence on aggregate demand should grow. Economists are also agreed, however, that the built-in stabilizers cannot do the whole job of maintaining full employment at stable prices and that other forms of deliberate, rather than automatic, policy measures may be necessary. Moreover, the built-in stabilizers act in response to changes in GNP when such changes might not be desirable. For example, the built-in stabilizers would slow down a period of recovery by increasing everyone's taxes.

Discretionary fiscal policy

When Congress or the President undertakes a deliberate fiscal policy change through new legislation, the subsequent change in fiscal policy is called **discretionary fiscal policy** because the action occurs at the discretion of the Congress or the President. The action is no longer automatic. From now on, we will confine ourselves to discretionary fiscal policy rather than to the automatic fiscal changes that occur as a result of the built-in stabilizers.

To help you understand how discretionary fiscal policy works—and hereafter we'll drop the word "discretionary"—we must first discuss how economists estimate what is likely to happen to GNP if nothing is done.

The Concept of Equilibrium Income (Equilibrium GNP)

The most important concept underlying the assumption of governmental responsibility for managing the economy is the concept of **equilibrium income** or **equilibrium GNP** (the terms are interchangeable).

In Chapter 3, you were introduced to the idea of an equilibrium price at which the quantities demanded and supplied are equal, and also to the theory that an automatic mechanism causes market prices for products or services to move toward such an equilibrium price. (If the market price is above equilibrium, there is a surplus and the price will tend to fall. If the market price is below equilibrium, there is a shortage and the market price will tend to rise.)

This same concept applies to GNP. When *aggregate demand equals aggregate supply* (the sum total of all products and services produced), GNP is at an *equilibrium*, because everything that is produced will be sold.

Now an important point. Although there will always be some price level or level of employment associated with any given equilibrium, the mere fact of equilibrium *does not* guarantee full employment or noninflationary prices. Aggregate demand and supply may be equal in the bottom of a depression or at the height of inflation.

However, the idea of an equilibrium income suggests that there is always some level of GNP toward which the economy tends to move. If aggregate demand exceeds aggregate supply, GNP and aggregate supply will increase. If aggregate demand is less than aggregate supply, GNP and aggregate supply will decrease because people will be laid off as entrepreneurs cut production. Equilibrium exists only when aggregate demand and supply are equal. If we can estimate what this equilibrium level is, we can estimate resulting levels of employment and prices—and then decide whether corrective (fiscal or monetary) measures are necessary.

Now the question arises: If changes in aggregate demand cause changes in aggregate supply, what determines the level of aggregate demand in the first place? Let's examine this question and then pursue the idea of equilibrium.

What determines aggregate demand?

In Chapter 11, you saw that GNP is determined by the four kinds of spending that make up aggregate demand: (1) consumption spending by consumers, (2) investment spending by business firms (purchases from one another for capital goods or inventories), (3) government purchases of goods and services, and (4) net exports (the difference between exports and imports).

So what determines demand in a market-price system on a national, aggregate scale? To put it another way, what determines the four kinds of spending that make up the GNP?

Consumption spending

Consumption spending usually accounts for about 65 percent of aggregate demand. Economists are agreed that consumption spending depends on a lot of things: the cost of borrowing, the price level, expectations of future price changes, the condition and quantity of durable goods (such as cars and washing machines) owned by the public. Most importantly, it depends on the size of present and expected paychecks—that is, present and expected DPI. After all, what determines more than anything else your decision to buy? The answer is your present income and your expectations about its regular arrival in the future.

Investment spending by business firms

This is usually around 15 percent of aggregate demand. It is determined partly by the cost of borrowing (the interest rate), but more than anything by the entrepreneur's expectation of future profit. The entrepreneur must believe in rising sales and profits before he or she will buy a new machine, a building, or increase the size of inventories.

Economists believe that *investment* in capital goods is related to GNP just as the accelerator on a car is related to the speed of the car. Changes in investment spending have the greatest effect of all kinds of spending on changes in GNP—greater than changes in consumption, government purchases, or net exports. Consequently, federal policies to stimulate the economy are often aimed at encouraging business managers to spend for new factories, machines, or larger inventories. Such spending adds to the number of job positions available in the economy and increases the demand for labor.

Government purchases of goods and services

Remember that government purchases *exclude* transfer payments but *include* purchases by all levels of government—federal, state, and local. All levels are important "demanders" of goods and services. Government purchases (*ex-*

cluding transfer payments) average around 20 percent of aggregate demand.* However, the contribution of government purchases to aggregate demand is so much a matter of politics that we will not attempt to discuss it here (or in the following equilibrium model).

Net exports

Net exports are important because export industries employ 3 to 4 million people, but net exports are often close to *zero* percent of aggregate demand. (In 1979, exports were 10.9 percent; imports were 11.0 percent. The net difference was a *minus* 0.1 percent.) Because net exports are also involved with the complications of international exchange rates, we are going to overlook them in this discussion.

The importance of expectations

Note in our description of the four kinds of spending that consumption and investment make up 80 percent of total spending. These two kinds of spending control the size and composition of private (rather than governmental) spending in a market-price system.

But now we are up against a puzzle. Consumption spending depends on present and expected income. Investment spending depends on present and future profit—another way of saying income.

If both depend on income, what determines income? Economists admit that the problem is circular. Income determines demand (consumption plus investment) and demand determines income. The answer to the puzzle is that *consumption and investment spending depend on expectations about the future* that may or may not be favorable. If they are unfavorable, consumers will try to save more and spend less, and business managers will reduce all forms of investment. If the future looks bright, everyone will spend more, and as people spend more, incomes will rise and lead to further increases in spending.

The essence of Keynesian theory is that expectations determine spending, and expectations may or may not be optimistic enough to generate sufficient demand to give everyone a job who wants one. And if private expectations don't motivate people to spend enough, the theory holds, then the government must step in to bolster demand.

Now we'll continue the discussion of equilibrium and observe how GNP rises and falls.

Equilibrium income models

Economists often think of the flow of money from households to business firms (for goods and services) and then from business firms to households (in the form of the four factors payments) as if these flows were like water in a pipe. In fact, the circuit of money flowing around and around is called the **income stream.** When households are taxed or when money is saved,

---

The 20 percent figure here differs considerably from the 32.6 percent figure in Table 10-2, because transfer payments were included in that figure.

Figure 13-1. The income stream with a $1,000 billion GNP.

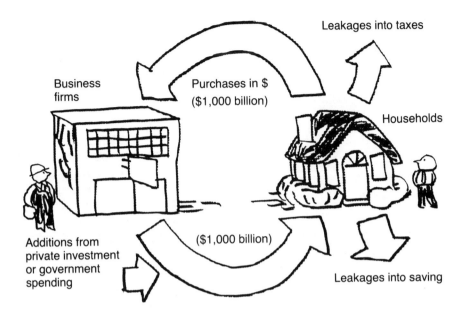

Leakages into taxes

Business firms

Purchases in $ ($1,000 billion)

Households

Additions from private investment or government spending

($1,000 billion)

Leakages into saving

these diversions from the stream are called **leakages.** On the other hand, government spending and investment spending are called **additions** to the stream.

The income stream

Figure 13-1 shows an income stream with a $1,000 billion GNP. As long as the money circulates, producers will be able to employ the people necessary to produce $1,000 billion worth of goods and services for consumers. But if consumers decide to save, or if they are taxed, they will have less money to spend; a leak has developed in the pipe as a result of the saving and taxes. Water is added to the pipe by business investments or by government spending.

We know now that expectations of profit determine investment—an addition to the income stream. We also know that if people save (leak) more out of any given income, they must be spending less. Less spending means that business firms will have lower expectations of profit and that they will invest less. Consequently, at any time, the level of saving (a leakage) can exceed additions to the income stream in the form of investment. When leakages exceed additions in the private economy, GNP is apt to fall and people will lose their jobs. If, on the other hand, additions exceed leakages, GNP will rise and more people will be hired.

The bathtub model

Now let us imagine another economy with a GNP of $1,000 (or $1,000 billion—it doesn't matter) with no government and no foreign trade (and where business firms spend their entire income on production for consumption or

Figure 13-2. The bathtub model: the economy in equilibrium.

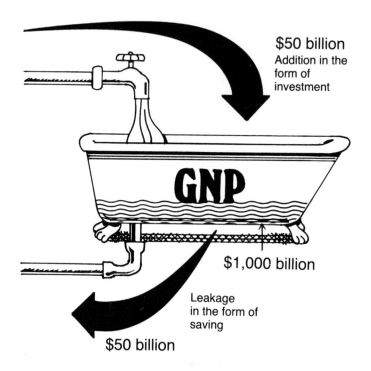

$50 billion
Addition in the form of investment

GNP

$1,000 billion

Leakage in the form of saving

$50 billion

for investment). Assume that the people want to buy $950 worth of consumer goods and business firms want to spend $50 for investment. Therefore, in this model with no government and no foreign trade, aggregate demand is consumption spending plus investment:* $950 billion + $50 billion = $1,000 billion. This spending will cause business firms to produce $1,000 billion worth of goods and services (aggregate supply). Consequently, the total value of what is produced—our aggregate supply—is our GNP. Further, as we saw in Chapter 11, GNP can be measured either as the sum of all spending (the "expenditures" method) or as the sum of all income (the "income" method).

Now, notice that, with GNP and total income at $1,000, and consumer demand at $950, the people must want to save $50. And also notice that *additions* to the income stream in the form of investment spending are equal to the *leakages* from the income stream in the form of saving.

We can illustrate this situation with a *bathtub model* (see Figure 13-2). The faucets that let water into the bathtub provide additions in the form of investment (or government spending). The drain represents leakages in the form of saving (or taxes). The water in the tub represents total production of consumption and investment goods; that is, GNP. And because GNP also equals total income, the water in the tub represents total income.

In this particular situation, the quantity of water coming into the bathtub ($50 worth of investment) just equals the amount draining out ($50

An important point is that business firms produce (supply) all investment goods (capital goods and inventories) but they are also the demanders of such goods.

Figure 13-3. Aggregate demand equals aggregate supply: a picture of equilibrium.

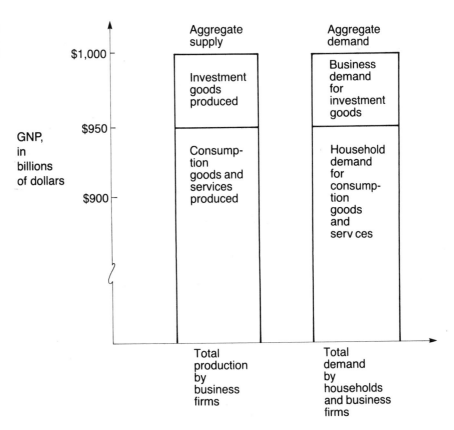

worth of saving). The quantity of water in the tub, $1,000 worth, will remain unchanged. This is another view of equilibrium.

Notice also that the decision to save, to withhold some money from consumption, is matched by producers' decisions to withhold some production from consumption in the form of investment. As long as these sets of decisions match, the economy is in a state of equilibrium. What does this mean? It means that the people will continue to produce $1,000 worth of products and that their GNP will remain at $1,000.

Another way of looking at the bathtub economy is in terms of aggregate demand and supply. Aggregate demand consists of the $950 worth of products demanded by consumers and the $50 worth that producers demand for investment purposes. Aggregate demand, then, consists of the demands of consumers ($950) plus the demands of producers for investment goods ($50), which equal $1,000. Aggregate supply consists of everything actually produced—in this case, $950 worth of consumer goods and $50 worth of investment goods, which equal $1,000. When the economy is in an equilibrium condition, aggregate demand equals aggregate supply. Figure 13-3 shows this equality of aggregate demand and supply.

Figure 13-4. A bank re-cycles the water.

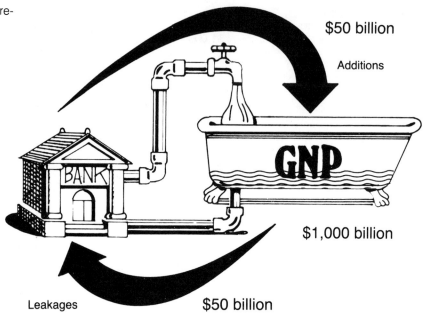

$50 billion

Additions

GNP

$1,000 billion

Leakages $50 billion

**Two important
questions about
equilibrium**

First, does everyone in this economy who wants a job have a job? Not nec-essarily. Equilibrium income can exist at *any* level of employment. The equilibrium condition merely means that GNP will tend to remain at $1,000 as long as the intentions of producers and consumers to divide up production and income remain the same. The $1,000 GNP could involve either depression or prosperity levels of employment.

Second, how is investment spending financed? Business sales for con-sumption are only $950. Where do business firms who want to invest in larger factories or inventories get the other $50? Answer: They get it by *borrowing* the $50 saved by the people. This means we have to add something to the bathtub picture—a connection between the drain and the faucets, because the money drained out is recycled back in. What makes the connection? You guessed it—a financial institution like a bank. Figure 13-4 shows the con-nection.

We need to stress the last point. Remember that saving is the *uncon-sumed* portion of income. The fact that the people do not consume all of their income enables business firms to produce for investment as well as for consumption. Thus, *investment* also represents the *unconsumed* portion of income. Finally, the people's savings provide the funds that finance invest-ment spending. (Because firms might also obtain funds by selling new issues of stocks or bonds to the public or by borrowing from a government agency. To keep it simple, we'll assume businesses obtain all investment monies from banks.)

Figure 13-5. The bath-tub fills: more goes in than comes out.

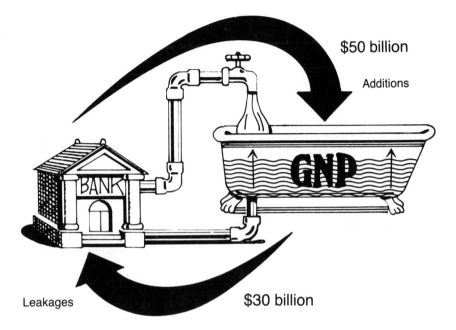

$50 billion

Additions

GNP

Leakages $30 billion

How equilibrium changes

In order to explore increases or decreases in equilibrium GNP, we will make two assumptions: (1) that the people decide to save only $30 instead of $50 out of their total income of $1,000; (2) that all production for investment goes into business firms' inventories and that investment (inventory) spending remains at $50. Additions to the tub now exceed leakages by $20. More water comes in than drains out (Figure 13-5).

Now let us see what happens. If the people want to save only $30, it must mean they plan to spend the remaining $970 for consumer goods. Business firms will now find that some of their investments in inventories have to be used to satisfy the increase in demand. Because production for consumption is set at $950 worth, an additional $20 worth must be taken from inventory. Stores will notice that some varieties of products have disappeared. In an attempt to keep inventories at the intended value of $50 worth, the business firms will have to work longer hours and hire more people. The GNP is now in *disequilibrium*, in a state of change, because GNP will start to rise as production and incomes rise.

Intended and unintended investment

Let's pause for a moment to examine some details of this situation. Aggregate demand is always the sum of everyone's intentions to buy; that is, the goods and services households intend to consume *plus* the amounts business firms intend to invest in inventories. *These intentions may not always be realized.*

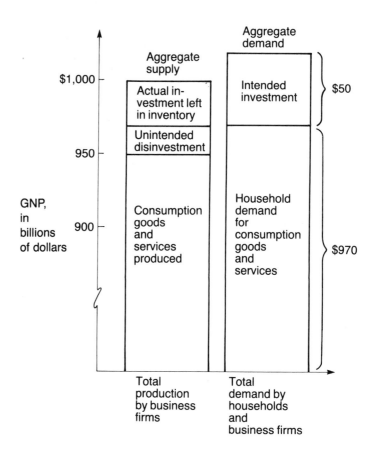

Figure 13-6. Intended, unintended and actual investment.

If households want to buy more than is being produced for them, business firms will see their inventories dropping below the levels they intend. In the preceding example, business firms intend to have $50 billion in inventories, but consumer buying causes inventories to drop $20 billion below that figure to $30 billion—exactly as if a shoe store had begun to run out of several sizes and styles. The unforeseen (or unintended) $20 billion drop in inventories has a name. It is called **unintended disinvestment.** (The prefix *dis* means "to reverse direction" as in *dis*own.)

After the $20 billion worth of unintended disinvestment comes out of the $50 billion in inventory, $30 billion worth of goods are left. Economists speak of this remainder as **actual investment** in contrast to the $50 billion of **intended investment** business firms wanted to have. Figure 13-6 summarizes this situation.

Figure 13-6 is extremely important because it helps to clear up some confusion about the causes of recession or prosperity. We often hear that people aren't buying enough or are buying too much or that businesses have overinvested or underinvested in plant and equipment. Not true. Figure 13-6 shows that the amount households want to buy ($970 billion) is matched by production for consumption ($950 billion) plus the amounts taken from inventories ($20 billion). Therefore, the desire of people to consume $970 billion worth of goods and services was matched by actual production. Furthermore, the $30 billion households want to save is matched by the $30 billion actually invested (left) in inventories. (This statement doesn't hold if households want to buy more than can be produced by business firms operating at full capacity. In that case, output can't increase but prices rise owing to what is called *demand-pull* inflation.)

The key to understanding why GNP goes up or down lies (as Keynes pointed out) in comparing the sets of *intentions* by households to consume and save with the intentions of business firms to produce for consumption or for investment. Clearly, if the sets of intentions do not match, something will have to change.

Equilibrium GNP rises

GNP will rise when aggregate demand ($1,020 billion in Figure 13-6) exceeds aggregate supply ($1,000 billion). And when "unintended disinvestment" occurs, business firms will hasten to increase their orders from suppliers to build inventories back up to intended levels. More people will be hired, and total income will increase.

How large will the increase be? GNP will continue to rise until the intentions by households to spend and save coincide with the intentions of business firms to produce for consumption or for investment.

Two points have to be noted now:

First, if the people become fully employed, it will become harder and harder to increase production. Prices will start to rise if aggregate demand exceeds aggregate supply at or near full employment.

Second, notice that GNP started to rise because the people decided to save less and buy more consumer goods than were being produced for them. The people's saving will now go through an interesting change. As production and incomes rise, they will be able to spend more *and save more*. If GNP reached $1,100, they might very well decide to spend $1,000 instead of the original $950 and save $100 instead of the original $50. The decision to save less leads eventually to the ability to save more.

If, at this new level of $1,100, producers decide to produce $1,000 for consumption and $100 for inventory, a new equilibrium will be reached (Figure 13-7). The decisions of producers and consumers to divide total income coincide. When these two sets of intentions coincide, GNP will stop changing.

Equilibrium GNP falls

As you might guess, equilibrium GNP falls if the people should decide to increase their saving and spend less. Let us go back to the $1,000 GNP. Suppose they decide to save $70 and spend only $930 out of their $1,000 income.

Figure 13-7. A higher
equilibrium.

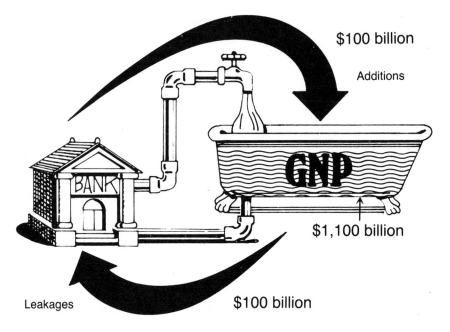

$100 billion

Additions

$1,100 billion

Leakages $100 billion

Production for consumption had been set at $950, with $50 going into inventory. Now business firms are producing $20 too much. This extra $20 worth will be unsold and left on the shelves in the form of extra inventory. Inventories will rise from $50 worth to $70. The extra $20 billion in inventory is called **unintended investment.** (No "dis-" this time because inventories are going up, not down.)

Production will be cut back. People will be laid off and total income will start to fall below $1,000. Again, this is disequilibrium.

GNP starts to move down as a result of the decision to save more and spend less. Leakages now exceed additions. More water goes out than comes in (Figure 13-8).

Aggregate demand is now less than aggregate supply. Aggregate demand is $930 (the people's desire to consume) plus $50 (production for intended inventories), and $930 + $50 = $980. Aggregate supply is still $1,000; that is, $950 intended for consumption plus $50 produced for inventory. Figure 13-9, page 278, summarizes this, (compare with figure 13-6.)

As people are laid off and total income (GNP) falls, we have to ask again: Where will the new equilibrium be? In bathtub terms, we can visualize the water level going down and down. Where will it stop? The answer is that the new equilibrium level of income (water level) will occur only when the people's desire to spend or save coincides with producers' desire to produce for consumption or investment. Table 13-1 shows how the lower equilibrium might look.

Figure 13-8. The bath-tub empties: more goes out than comes in.

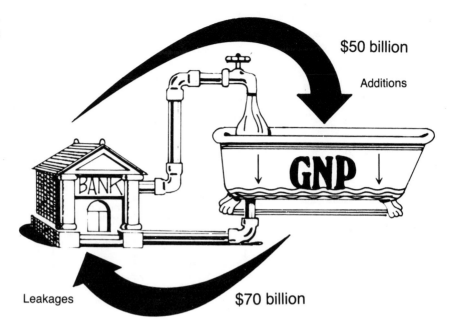

$50 billion

Additions

GNP

Leakages

$70 billion

In terms of the bathtub, the water level drops from $1,000 down to $920. At $920, the amount of water coming in ($20 worth of investment) just equals the amount of water draining out ($20 worth of saving).

Again, two points should be noted:

First, the decision to save *more* led actually to a *lower* level of saving. As incomes fall, we may want to save more to prepare for a period of unemployment, but we are unable to. We have to spend a larger proportion of our reduced incomes in order to sustain ourselves. Thus the decision to save money may lead to less saving. This phenomenon is called the **paradox of thrift.** We saw another version of it when GNP rose. There the decision to save less led to the ability to save more.

Second, an equilibrium can exist at any level of employment or un-employment. With a GNP at $920, many people may be unemployed. They

TABLE 13-1 A New, Lower Equilibrium

Business firms		Households	
Production for consumption	$900	Desired consumption spending by people	$900
Intended investment in inventory	+ 20	Desired saving by the people	+ 20
Total production (GNP)	$920	Total income (GNP)	$920

Figure 13-9. Aggregate demand fails to buy aggregate supply.

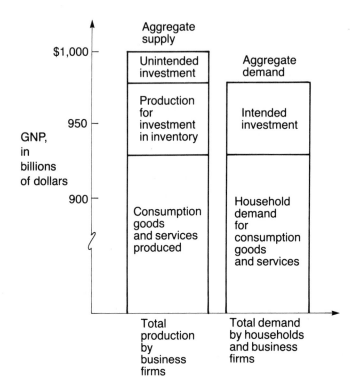

may want a job but be unable to find one. They may face poverty and even hunger. The real point is that GNP may remain at $920 as long as the intentions of consumers and producers to divide income remain the same.

Something must be done at this point to upset this equilibrium and cause GNP to rise. What can be done? This is the question that Keynes answered. As you already know, his answer was: Increase aggregate demand through deficit spending.

Deficit spending

Let us use Figure 13-8 once again to illustrate the problem. The people want to save $70, but business firms want to invest only $50. There will be a net leakage of $20 a year.

The government can then sell securities to savers in the amount of $20 and add that amount to the economy by spending for new post offices, freeways, or nuclear submarines. Figure 13-10 shows what will happen.

Leakages are now $70, but so are additions, with $50 worth of intended investment and $20 worth of government deficit spending. Aggregate demand is $930 for consumption spending plus $50 for investment spending plus $20 for government spending. The bathtub will have $1,000 worth of water (GNP) in it.

But suppose the $1,000 GNP is not enough to provide full employment? Suppose full employment is at some figure higher than $1,000. Now the

Figure 13-10. The government takes care of the leak.

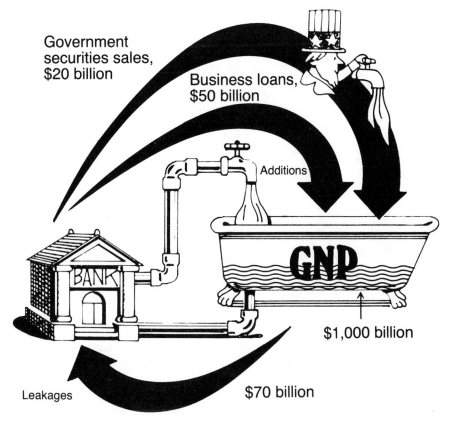

Government securities sales, $20 billion

Business loans, $50 billion

Additions

GNP

BANK

$1,000 billion

Leakages

$70 billion

government must borrow and spend more than $20. Where will the additional money come from? Answer: Because the $20 saving figure represents saving for only one year, the government will borrow and spend from savings accumulated in past years (probably by successful corporations and people with higher incomes).

The government's fiscal alternative is to lower taxes. When taxes are lowered, business firms will enjoy greater profits and households will have greater disposable personal income.

Either way, spending (aggregate demand) will probably go up and GNP will reach a new equilibrium. But, amazingly, GNP will rise by *more* than the change in spending. The next section explains this phenomenon.

The Spending Multiplier

Economists, and Keynes, refer to the phenomenon whereby GNP rises more than the change in spending as "the multiplier." We are going to call it the "spending multiplier" to distinguish it from another multiplier that appears in monetary policy. The **spending multiplier** is defined as the multiple

For the Want of a Horseshoe Nail

The following was written by Art Buchwald during the 1974–1975 recession.

WASHINGTON—The recession hit so fast that nobody knows exactly how it happened. One day we were the land of milk and honey, and the next day we were the land of sour cream and food stamps.

This is one explanation.

Hofberger, the Chevy salesman in Tomcat, Va., a suburb of Washington, called up Littleton, of Littleton Menswear & Haberdashery, and said, "Good news, the '75 Impalas have just come in and I've put one aside for you and your wife."

Littleton said, "I can't, Hofberger. My wife and I are getting a divorce."

Hofberger said, "That's too bad. Then take the car for yourself. I'll give you $100 extra on a trade-in because of the divorce."

"I'm sorry," Littleton said, "but I can't afford

by which total income (GNP) increases as a result of an initial change in spending.

Economists have estimated that the real-world multiplier is about 2. That is, a change in government (or any) spending of, say, $20 billion will change GNP by $40 billion.

The reason for the multiple change in GNP lies in the fact that any change in spending—by the government, households, or business firms—creates a *chain reaction* of further spending. Jackie Vanderbilt buys a new Cadillac from the local Cadillac dealer who buys his wife a new ring from a new car this year. After I settle with my wife, I'll be lucky to buy a bicycle."

Hofberger hung up. His phone rang a few minutes later.

"This is Bedcheck the painter," the voice on the other end said. "When do you want us to start painting your house?"

"I changed my mind," said Hofberger. "I'm not going to paint the house."

"But I ordered the paint," Bedcheck said. "Why did you change your mind?"

"Because Littleton is getting a divorce and he can't afford a new car."

That evening when Bedcheck came home his wife said, "The new color television set arrived from Gladstone's TV Shop."

"Take it back," Bedcheck told his wife.

"Why?" she demanded.

"Because Hofberger isn't going to have his house painted now that the Littletons are getting a divorce."

The next day Mrs. Bedcheck dragged the TV set in its carton back to Gladstone. "We don't want it."

Gladstone's face dropped. He immediately called his travel agent, Sandstorm. "You know that trip you had scheduled for me to the Virgin Islands?"

"Right, the tickets are all written up."

"Cancel it. I can't go. Bedcheck just sent back the color TV set because Hofberger didn't sell a car to Littleton because they're going to get a divorce and she wants all his money."

Sandstorm tore up the airline tickets and went to see his banker, Gripsholm. Sandstorm told Gripsholm, "I can't pay back the loan this month because Gladstone isn't going to the Virgin Islands."

Gripsholm was furious. When Rudemaker came in to borrow money for a new kitchen he needed for his restaurant, Gripsholm turned him down cold. "How can I loan you money when Sandstorm hasn't repaid the money he borrowed?" Rudemaker called up the contractor, Eagleton, and said he couldn't put in a new kitchen. Eagleton laid off eight men.

Meanwhile, General Motors announced it was giving a rebate on its '75 models. Hofberger called up Littleton immediately. "Good news," he said, "even if you are getting a divorce, you can afford a new car."

"I'm not getting a divorce," Littleton said. "It was all a misunderstanding; we've made up."

"That's great," Hofberger said. "Now you can buy the Impala."

"No way," said Littleton. "My business has been so lousy I don't know why I keep the doors open." "I didn't know that," Hofberger said.

"Do you realize I haven't seen Bedcheck, Gladstone, Sandstorm, Gripsholm, Rudemaker or Eagleton for more than a month? How can I stay in business if they don't patronize my store?"

*Reprinted by permission of Art Buchwald from *Los Angeles Times,* 20 February 1975, pt. iv, p. 2.

the local jeweler who decides to take that trip to Hawaii she has been thinking about for years. The jeweler's trip to Hawaii adds to the profit of the airline, which then decides to hire more people and to give Sue Trueheart, one of its passenger agents, a raise. Sue then decides to add a room on her house . . . and so on.

In this example, the chain of spending is in a positive direction. GNP goes up. But the chain reaction can also go into reverse; that is, a reduction in someone's spending can cause total income to decline by a multiple of the initial decrease in spending. Art Buchwald's essay offers an amusing example.

One might jump to the conclusion that the spending multiplier is very large, much more than 2. After all, it would seem the spending chain could affect thousands of people. However, the reason the multiplier is so low is that when spending and incomes start to increase, the *built-in stabilizers* slow down the increases. Income taxes start to take bigger bites. Transfer payments such as unemployment insurance payments drop. What starts out to be a tidal wave ends up as a ripple.

Changing Government Spending Versus Changing Taxes to Increase or Decrease GNP

When private spending fails to maintain aggregate demand at full employment, the government can increase its own spending or reduce taxes. If the President's Council of Economic Advisors is worried about inflation, its members will suggest to the President that government spending be reduced and/ or that taxes be increased in order to reduce private spending.

In the following discussion, we shall make two assumptions: (1) that if discretionary changes in government spending occur—*ceteris paribus*, everything else in the economy (such as taxes) remains the same—and (2) that if we decide to change taxes, government spending and all other components of aggregate demand remain the same. The primary reason for these assumptions is that the effectiveness of deliberate changes in government spending to speed up or slow down the economy will be diminished if taxes are deliberately changed in the same direction. For example, if Congress insists on keeping the budget balanced and matches any increase in government spending with increases in taxes, aggregate demand is increased by the increase in government spending but decreased by the increase in taxes. The effect on aggregate demand will be much stronger if we hold taxes constant and change government spending or hold government spending constant and change taxes.

Another word of explanation. If government spending and taxes start off equal, let us say at $700 billion each, and government spending increases to $710 billion with no change in taxes, there is deficit spending of $10 billion (and an increase in the public debt of that much). If government spending and taxes are both at $600 billion and government spending drops to $590 billion, then the Treasury runs a surplus of $10 billion. The deficit adds to aggregate demand. A surplus reduces it, just as if businesses or households decided to increase saving and reduce spending. Consequently, the relationship of government spending and taxes has an important bearing on equilibrium GNP.

Let us consider changing government spending first and then taxes.

Changes in government spending

Suppose that there is considerable unemployment and that the Council of Economic Advisors (CEA) estimates that equilibrium GNP must grow by $100 billion to provide full employment. How much deficit spending should there be? It all depends on the multiplier. If the multiplier is 2, deficit spending will have to be $50 billion.

Another problem. Suppose equilibrium GNP is *beyond* full employment. This sounds improbable but it is not. Total spending by households, business firms, and the government can exceed the quantities—at current prices—we are capable of producing at full employment. How? By borrowing. In this way total spending can exceed total, current income—even at full employment.

Let's assume that full-employment GNP is at $2,400 billion but that total intentions to spend are $2,600. The CEA will now recommend that spending be reduced to avoid inflation. How much must spending be reduced to bring about a full-employment equilibrium at $2,400 billion? Again, it depends on the multiplier. Assume that the multiplier is 2.

To reduce aggregate demand by $200 billion, we must reduce government spending by $100 billion (200 ÷ 2).

There is always a question of what kinds of government spending should be increased in slow times or decreased in times of inflation. There are two overall categories of government spending—*government purchases of goods and services* and *transfer payments.* Changes in the former are considered to have a stronger effect on the economy than changes in the latter. When the government purchases a new highway, rocket, or dam, real output and employment are directly affected. If the project costs $10 billion, the entire $10 billion is spent and the effect on equilibrium will be the multiplier times $10 billion. If, on the other hand, there is a $10 billion increase in welfare payments, there is no guarantee that the entire $10 billion will directly affect output and employment.

Changes in taxes

We can also change equilibrium by reducing taxes to give households more money to spend or by increasing taxes to reduce household spending.

Tax changes do not affect GNP as strongly as do changes in government spending. A look at income taxes will explain the point.

Remember that disposable personal income (DPI) is divided into consumption spending plus personal saving. When income taxes go up, our take-home pay (DPI) goes down by that amount. But our spending may not drop by the amount of the tax because we can pay part of the tax by taking the money out of saving.

For example, suppose income taxes go up by $10 billion as part of a government program to curb spending and inflation. Also assume that people will change their consumption spending by 80 percent of any change in DPI, and change their saving by 20 percent of any change in DPI. The $10 billion tax could be paid by a reduction of $8 billion in spending plus a $2 billion reduction in saving. The transaction looks like this:

$-$10B	$=$	$-$8B	$+$	($-$2B)
DPI	$=$	consumption spending	$+$	personal saving

As far as aggregate demand is concerned, spending has changed by $8 billion, although the tax change was $10 billion. The multiplier effect will start with an $8 billion change in spending—not a $10 billion change.

A tax reduction works the same way. When income taxes are reduced, DPI will increase, but some people will put part of the increase in income into some form of saving. Spending will not increase by the amount of the tax reduction.

Which method is best?

We can see that a desired change in aggregate demand can be achieved by changing either government spending or taxes. But which method should we choose? We know that government spending changes are more potent than tax changes, because tax changes usually involve changes in saving.

But tax changes have an important feature: Once the law has been passed, the effect is quick. Everybody's DPI instantly changes (assuming that personal taxes are changed), because paychecks will go up when taxes withheld go down.

If the tax change is a tax reduction, who decides how the money will be spent? You do. On the other hand, when there is a change in government spending rather than a change in taxes, our political representatives decide where and how the money will be spent. This is not to suggest that your spending will be any wiser or more foolish than the government's, but it is a fact to consider. Some economists also believe that when the government spends the money the spending is always larger than it needs to be because of political log-rolling. The senator who initiates a bill for federal programs in his state may have to agree to include projects in other states to obtain the votes of his colleagues.

Fiscal Policy Problems

Time lags

One complication is the lag of a year or two between the time a new fiscal policy is launched and the time its effects take hold in the private economy. When the effects take hold, the problem may be over, or worse, the policy may be wrong for the period in which the effects materialize.

Conflicting state and local policies

State and local fiscal policy may or may not coincide with federal policy. During the year of the 1964 income-tax cut, federal tax receipts rose only $500 million from the previous year, while state and local tax receipts rose $6.1 billion. State and local governments may find it irresistible to offset expansionary fiscal policy. When a state governor knows that the federal government is going to increase everyone's income by reducing federal taxes or by deficit spending, he or she might think, "Ah, the people have more money. Now is the time to increase state taxes." Thus, state and local fiscal policy may nullify or diminish the efforts of the federal government to accomplish its goal.

Tax cuts to reduce unemployment

Tax cuts to give the economy a boost are often given to corporations. These tax cuts are usually designed to give corporations incentives to buy new machinery (in the form of extra depreciation allowances). The theory is that (1) the increase in investment spending will spur an increase in GNP and employment and (2) the new machines will produce greater quantities of goods, and these larger quantities will tend to reduce or, at least, slow down inflation. There are two problems:

First, such a tax cut will stimulate investment spending only if businesses expect sufficiently large increases in demand to buy the extra production the new machines will produce. The tax cut will not help if such an optimistic expectation is not present.

Second, the creation of new machines, if it *does* take place, will create jobs for the highly specialized technicians who build the machines. But when the machines begin to produce, they may replace workers. Over the life of the machines, the net, long-term effect may be to increase unemployment.

Crowding-out

Government spending may **crowd out** or substitute for private spending. If the federal government wants to give the economy a boost, it must be careful to find ways to deficit spend that will not conflict with private industry. If government spending conflicts with private investment spending, then aggregate demand may not change as much as the President's Council of Economic Advisors (CEA) would like. One example: government construction of a hydroelectric dam that private industry could have built.

Crowding-out can also occur if deficit spending causes interest rates to rise. When the Treasury offers securities for sale, it will have to offer interest rates that are attractive enough to persuade buyers to put their savings into government securities instead of into financial institutions (savings and loan banks or commercial banks). These institutions will then have to compete for your savings by offering higher interest rates. We can visualize another demand/supply diagram in which the government's demand for funds shifts the demand for loans to the right and raises the price (the interest rate).

As the interest rate rises, business firms will find that borrowing is more expensive. Individuals will find mortgage rates for home purchases and finance charges on installment contracts rising. Private spending will then drop. Government spending has, to some extent, crowded out private spending.

The measure and extent of crowding-out is still another subject of professional argument among economists.[1] The difficulty is that, during a recession, a low level of investment spending occurs, not because of high interest rates, but because of lack of optimism about future profits. But if the economy starts to recover and business managers want to borrow, crowding-out may occur and slow down progress toward recovery.

Inflation and politics

The realization that Keynesian theory is one-sided or "asymmetrical" emerged in the mid-1970s.[2] Few economists will argue that Keynesian theory is not helpful in a depression. But many now argue that the theory is not helpful in times of inflation.

It is easy to get people to vote on expansionary fiscal policy—increases in spending or tax cuts—but tough to get them to do the reverse, to cut spending and raise taxes. Consequently, the reality of politics suggests that fiscal policy may be easy to apply in times of depression when the economy needs a boost, but very difficult to apply when the economy needs to slow down in times of inflation. These political realities and the crowding-out problem have forced a rethinking of Keynesian theory, which we will discuss in Chapter 17.

Summary

Fiscal policy refers to changes in government spending or taxes that change GNP. These changes may occur as a result of changes in taxes or transfer payments that occur automatically when GNP and total income change. Such changes are also called the built-in or automatic stabilizers because they help to level out the swings in GNP.

Deliberate actions by the President or Congress to change government spending or taxes for the purpose of changing GNP are called discretionary fiscal policy.

Fiscal policy and monetary policy are both based on the concept of equilibrium income. Equilibrium income exists when aggregate demand and aggregate supply are equal.

Equilibrium income (GNP) may occur at any level of employment. To change an unsatisfactory equilibrium, the government can change aggregate demand by changing taxes or spending. To increase aggregate demand and equilibrium GNP, the government can reduce taxes and/or increase deficit spending. To reduce GNP (or slow its growth) the government can do the reverse.

Because of the fact that any change in spending starts a chain reaction of further spending, a spending multiplier exists. Changes in GNP that follow changes in spending are multiples of those changes in spending.

Changes in government spending have a more potent effect on GNP than do taxes, but tax changes affect the economy more quickly than do changes in goverment spending.

Discussion Questions

1. Explain the statement "We have a fiscal policy whether we like it or not and whether Congress does anything or not."

2. Why are aggregate supply and GNP the same?

3. Why are expectations so important in Keynesian theory?

4. How do the built-in stabilizers affect the multiplier?

5. Why does Congress tend to increase aggregate demand more often than it decreases it?

6. Why might one prefer a tax reduction to an increase in government spending as a cure for unemployment?

References   1. Keith M. Carlson and Roger W. Spencer, "Crowding Out and Its Critics," *Review*, Federal Reserve Bank of St. Louis, December 1975.

2. John Kenneth Galbraith, *The Age of Uncertainty* (Boston: Houghton Mifflin Co., 1977), p. 225.

13A The Keynesian Cross

Frank Siteman/Stock, Boston

There are many ways to illustrate the concepts of equilibrium GNP, aggregate demand, and aggregate supply. You have seen two of them: the income stream and the bathtub model. There is also a third way, popular with many economists, called the Keynesian Cross. A brief explanation of it is presented here so that it may be helpful to you when you take other courses in economics.

The Keynesian Cross is simply another demand-supply diagram, but with a difference. All of the demand-supply diagrams shown so far have price on the vertical axis and quantity (in physical units) on the horizontal axis. We could do this with GNP too, but, as we have seen, the price level distorts GNP by concealing *real* GNP. Keynes bypassed the problem of price movements and concentrated on the relationship between demand and income.

Key Words

Negative saving (dis-saving)   Aggregate supply = GNP = total income

Income = spending line   Keynesian Cross

Patterns of Spending and Saving

Keynes realized that, as income increases, so does spending, but *not as fast* as income. Imagine a worker who starts with a disposable personal income (DPI) of $100 per week and then, because of extraordinarily good luck, gets a series of $50 raises. Table 13A-1 shows how he or she divides each DPI into consumption spending (C) and personal saving (S).

The table shows that when our worker received $100, he or she spent $120. How can this be? By borrowing, using credit cards, automatic overdraft checking accounts, charge accounts, and so on. Most of us know it is easy to spend more than we make. When we do, we engage in what economists call **negative saving** or **dis-saving.** Now we are in a position to display this information in a graph similar to a demand-supply diagram (Figure 13A-1). On the horizontal axis we will put DPI, our individual's take-home pay. On the vertical axis we will measure the worker's consumption spending at each level of her or his DPI.

Now let us draw a diagonal line halfway between the income axis and the spending axis, so that at all points on this line income and spending are equal. If an individual (or country) is not on the line, income and spending must not be equal. We will call the diagonal line the **income = spending line.**

Notice that the diagonal line bisects the right angle formed by the two axes. Consequently, the diagonal line makes a 45-degree angle with either axis. If we draw a perpendicular from any point on the income = spending line over to each axis, a square will be formed. In other words, every point on the income = spending line is equidistant from each axis. This is just another way of showing that income and spending must be equal at every point on the income = spending line. In terms of the income stream or the bathtub model, there are no leakages or additions if you (or a country) are on the income = spending line.

TABLE 13A-1 DPI, Consumption, and Saving

DPI per week	C	S	
$100	120	−20	Dis-saving
150	150	0	Breakeven
200	180	+20	Positive saving
250	210	+40	
300	240	+60	

Figure 13A-1. Spending (C) does not increase as fast as income (DPI).

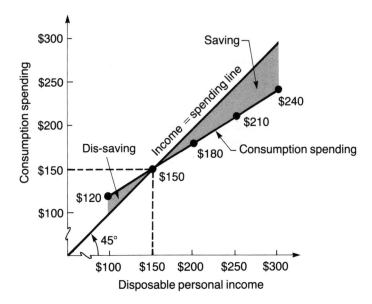

Dis-saving is shown in Figure 13A-1 in the shaded area between the income = spending line and the consumption-spending line at incomes below $150 a week. At $150, our worker breaks even: consumption-spending = DPI and S = 0. Above $150, our worker saves. Now the income = spending line is above the consumption-spending line.

One more point. All this happens because our worker starts by spending $120 at an income of $100. Thereafter, spending increases by $30 with each $50 increase in income, while saving increases by $20 with each change in income.

Now we can use the same ideas as a basis for a diagram that describes the whole economy.

The Keynesian Demand-Supply Diagram

Everything about Figure 13A-2 is essentially the same as Figure 13A-1. On the vertical axis we measure all four forms of spending added together: consumption, investment, government purchases, and net exports. The total of all this spending at each level of GNP is shown by the aggregate-demand line. The aggregate-demand line does not increase as fast as income because most of it (65 percent) is consumption spending, and we know that consumption spending in the real world does not increase as fast as income. The aggregate-demand line has the same relationship to the income = spending line that the consumption-spending line had in Figure 13A-1.

Notice that, up to the $2,000 billion GNP, aggregate demand is above the income = spending line; that is, aggregate demand is greater than income. (More is being added to the income stream or to the bathtub than is being taken out.) It is exactly like the dis-saving area in Figure 13A-1. It may

Figure 13A-2. GNP using the Keynesian model (slope of the aggregate demand line and full employment level of GNP are assumed).

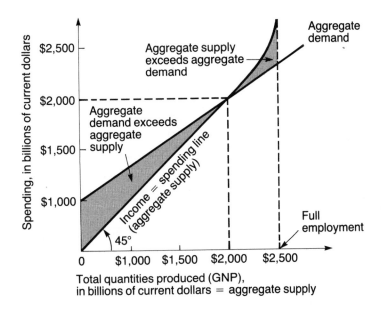

strike you as odd that "dis-saving" could add to the income stream or to the water in the bathtub. Just remember that if there is dis-saving *nationally*, the people as a whole must be borrowing more than all the money saved. Borrowing, presumably for spending, more than makes up for the leakages in the form of saving.

Above $2,000 billion, aggregate demand is below the income = spending line. It is less than income. (Leaks—saving or taxes—must be occurring.)

Finally, note that the income = spending line and the aggregate-demand line form a long, diagonal cross—somewhat on its side. This is the **Keynesian Cross.**

On the horizontal axis and on the income = spending line we measure GNP or aggregate supply. The fact that the horizontal axis and the income = spending line both measure GNP and aggregate supply may not be clear. First of all, GNP represents all the income paid out in the course of producing or supplying everything. Thus, **GNP** and **aggregate supply** are simply different terms that both mean **total income.**

The horizontal axis and the income = spending line are also the same in the sense that the distance *up to the line* is the same as the distance out the horizontal axis. Figure 13A-3 illustrates this.

Now let us return to Figure 13A-2. The income = spending line in Figure 13A-2 becomes vertical at our assumed $2,500 billion, full employment GNP. Production of more than $2,500 billion worth of goods and services regardless of increases in aggregate demand is impossible, or at least extremely difficult.

Equilibrium income in Figure 13A-2 occurs where aggregate supply and aggregate demand are equal at the GNP of $2,000 billion. If GNP is less than $2,000 billion, aggregate demand exceeds aggregate supply. (The people

Figure 13A-3. The income = spending line and the horizontal axis are both measures of GNP, aggregate supply, and total income.

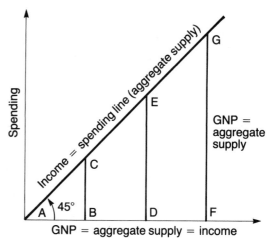

GNP = aggregate supply = income

Distance A B = B C; distance A D = D E; distance A F = F G

must be dis-saving.) GNP will have to increase. If GNP is more than $2,000 billion, aggregate supply exceeds aggregate demand. There will be a surplus of unsold goods, employers will lay workers off, and GNP will slip back to the $2,000 billion equilibrium.

The difficulty with the $2,000 billion equilibrium is that it is $500 billion short of full employment. Unemployment rates will be unacceptably high. To get some or all of these unemployed workers hired, we must increase aggregate demand and create a new equilibrium GNP.

The Keynesian Cross and the Spending Multiplier

The Keynesian Cross is also useful in illustrating the changes in GNP that occur following a change in spending. Figure 13A-4 shows an increase in aggregate demand of $100 billion.

Notice that the aggregate-demand line shifts upward in the amount of $100 billion at every level of income. (Most unlikely in the real world, but our intent is only to show how the "Cross" works.) The change in aggregate demand could be the result of deficit spending, of tax cuts, or the result of a wave of optimism that persuades consumers or business managers to spend more and save less. The change in aggregate demand could also be the result of monetary operations (but we will have to wait until Chapter 16 for that explanation.)

As the increase in spending ripples through the economy, the spending multiplier goes into action. Assuming again a spending multiplier of 2, the increase in equilibrium GNP will be double the change in spending. Figure 13A-4 shows this $200 billion increase in equilibrium GNP with the establishment of a new equilibrium at $2,200 billion. Now many more people will have jobs but still not enough to provide full employment if we assume that that goal is not reached until we reach the $2,500 billion GNP.

Figure 13A-4. An increase in aggregate demand (based on Figure 13A-2).

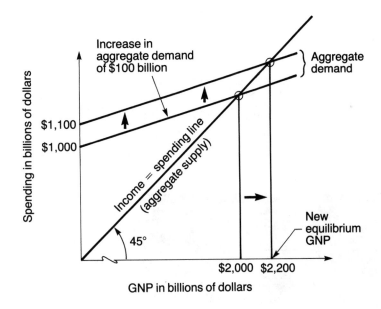

14 The Public Debt: Are We Spending Ourselves into Bankruptcy?

David Krathwohl/Stock, Boston

You will remember that the excess of spending over tax revenues is called deficit spending. The United States Treasury raises this money by printing government securities and selling them to whomever will buy. The securities are promises by the Treasury to pay the owner of those securities some amount of money on some date in the future. The grand sum total of all of these promises to pay is the **public** (sometimes called national) **debt.**

Two preliminary points need to be made about the debt: (1) The public debt described in this chapter refers only to the issuance of government securities by the *federal government, not* by the states or local governments for such things as water or sewage systems. Consequently, think of the public debt as a *federal debt.* (2) Remember that the federal government sends a

---

Key Words

Public debt	Annually balanced budget
Government securities	Countercyclical budget
Net public debt	Functional finance
Internal debt	High-employment budget
External debt	approach

---

great deal of money each year ("federal revenue sharing") back to the states and local governments—in fact, about 18 percent of their total income. Therefore, to some extent, the spending habits of the states and local governments, in fact of all of us, are partly responsible for the federal government's need to raise money by selling government securities.

In this chapter, we will explain the arguments for and against the public debt. Often these arguments are filled with fear and emotion. You hear some people say, "We are spending ourselves into bankruptcy," or "Sooner or later there will be a day of judgment," and so on. It is very important for all of us to understand what this is all about, since the public debt is debated more, by more uninformed people, than is any other topic in economics.

The chapter is divided into four sections: (1) emotional arguments, (2) the size and ownership of the debt, (3) the four budget philosophies, and (4) some hard questions about the debt.

Emotional Arguments: "Heading for Bankruptcy"

Critics of the public debt have plenty of fuel for their anxiety. Annual deficits incurred by the federal government are the rule rather than the exception. In the fifty-two years from 1929 to 1980, the federal government had deficits in all but eight years. Since 1961, there has been only one year without a deficit (1969). The deficits in recent years have been particularly large—averaging around $40 billion per year. The fact that there were only two years between 1946 and 1971 when the deficits were more than $10 billion helps to give these numbers some perspective.

Many intelligent Americans are horrified at this spendthrift behavior. The people in charge in Washington are accused of fiscal irresponsibility and of driving us into bankruptcy. Although Figure 14-1 appeared as part of a full-page magazine advertisement back in 1964, the argument it illustrates is still going on.

There are undoubtedly millions of Americans who share the concern expressed in this ad, including prominent figures in the federal government. Senator John L. McClellan (D-Ark.) once complained that those who control the economy are "callously and mercilessly burdening the livelihood and earnings of the generations that will follow us with a tremendous oppressive national debt." President Eisenhower worried that "We are stealing from our children in order to satisfy our desires of today."

Figure 14-1.

"Dead End"

When you let your expenses go up and up, and instead of paying your bills you let your debts go up, too—*you're heading straight for bankruptcy.* Since time began, debtors have tried to outsmart that fact, and not one ever succeeded, because you can't fool arithmetic:

Fiscal year	U.S. federal expenditures (in billions)	U.S. public debt at fiscal year end (in billions)
1934	$ 6.3	$ 27.0
1939	8.7	40.4
1944	94.9	201.0
1949	39.4	252.7
1954	67.5	271.2
1955	64.3	280.8
1956	66.2	272.7
1957	68.9	270.5
1958	71.3	276.3
1959	80.3	284.7
1960	76.5	290.2
1961	81.5	288.9
1962	87.7	298.2
1963	92.6	305.8
1964 (est.)	98.4	311.8

There comes a time when the money runs out, and you *have* to tighten your belt, and do without the luxuries. Isn't it wiser to restrict the luxuries *yourself*, before you lose the necessities, too?

Size and Ownership of the Debt

Now let's see how bad the problem really is. We'll look at the size of the debt and to whom the debt is owed and use this information to answer the emotional arguments about the "merciless burden" and bankruptcy.

How large is the debt?   Table 14-1 shows how the debt has grown without interruption from a modest $16 billion in 1930 to over $800 billion at the end of 1979, a fifty-fold increase!

TABLE 14-1 GNP and the Federal Public Debt in Selected Years, 1930–1979

Year	(1) GNP[a]	(2) Federal debt[a]	(3) Debt ÷ GNP (in percent)
1930	$ 90	$ 16	17.8%
1940	100	43	43.0
1945	210	259	123.0
1950	285	257	90.0
1955	398	281	71.0
1960	504	290	57.5
1965	685	321	46.8
1970	974	389	39.9
1971	1,047	424	40.6
1972	1,152	449	38.8
1973	1,288	470	36.4
1974	1,407	475	33.8
1975	1,516	544	35.9
1976	1,693	632	37.3
1977	1,900	699	36.8
1978	2,128	772	36.3
1979	2,369	834	35.2

Sources: *Economic Report of the President, 1980,* and *Statistical Abstract of the United States, 1979.*

[a]Figures are in billions of current dollars.

The debt as a percentage of GNP

Economists are more interested in the debt as a percentage of GNP than in its absolute size. For example, in 1930, when the debt was $16 billion, the GNP was $90 billion, and the debt as a percentage of GNP was therefore $16 billion ÷ $90 billion = 17.8 percent. During World War II, the percentage rose to 123, but, by 1979, it had dropped to 35.2.

The rationale for this way of looking at the debt is that it allows us to measure the benefits of the debt. Oftentimes business firms go into debt to build new factories or stores. The success of the new venture measures the wisdom of going into debt. If the extra sales and profits generated by the expansion more than make up for the debt, and help to pay it off, then going into debt was worth it.

If our GNP grows faster than the debt, the debt as a percentage of GNP must fall. The falling percentage shows that the debt has helped our GNP to grow, just as rising sales and profits validate a business firm's debt. This viewpoint suggests one answer to the emotional argument that we are creating a merciless burden for future generations.

The "merciless burden"

Economists dispose of the merciless-burden argument by pointing out that, although the next generation inherits the debt along with its obligation to pay interest to the owners of government securities, it also inherits the assets the securities represent. The debt and its interest cost are minuses, but the securities holders' assets in the form of the securities and interest income from the securities are offsetting pluses.

The merciless-burden argument was probably the result of the tremendous increase in the public debt during World War II. At the beginning of the war, the debt was $16 billion. In 1945, when the war ended, the debt was $259 billion.

Are we now bearing the burden of that war because it was financed by deficit spending rather than by wartime taxes? The answer is partly yes and partly no.

We have to consider this question from two points of view: (1) that of people living during the war and (2) that of people living in future generations. From the point of view of the people living as consumers in the 1941–1945 period, they bore the real burden of the war. During 1942–1944, the most intense period of our involvement, consumption spending as a percentage of disposable personal income fell from the usual 92 to 95 percent to an average of 75 percent. Personal saving rose to a corresponding 25 percent of DPI. These percentages indicate that the people went without innumerable consumption goods—automobiles, appliances, nylon stockings, gasoline—so that resources could be released for war materials. A revealing statistic is that in the year 1940, before involvement in the war, we produced and sold 1 million passenger cars. During the three-year period 1942–1944, we produced only 25,000 passenger cars per year.

But people in future generations may also bear the burden of a war. In 1944, *half* of our GNP went to the war effort. Members of future generations will *forever* bear the opportunity cost of the war in the form of the rapid-transit systems, solar energy projects, hydroelectric dams, or capital improvements in public health and education that could have been created with the resources and talent that were burned up in the war.

The difficulty with this point of view is that if the debt had not been used to fight the war, could we have won it? The war and the debt transferred a burden (lost production and resources) to future generations but also a benefit (freedom from totalitarian rule).

Nevertheless, this discussion indicates that future generations *may* bear a burden from the debt. If the debt finances a use of resources (such as the Vietnam war) that, it can be argued, holds no benefit for future generations, then the future generations do bear a burden with no offsetting benefit. If the debt finances the development of projects such as solar energy, future generations will bear the opportunity cost of using resources in that particular way, but they will also have the benefit of the solar energy. The question of burden or benefit depends on one's value judgments about how the funds obtained from the sale of government securities are spent.

To whom is the debt owed?

The public debt is owed to the owners of all outstanding **government securities.** Consequently, those who own the securities that make up the debt are the creditors. The U.S. Treasury is the debtor.

(Most people are used to the term government "bonds" rather than "securities." The term "securities" is used to describe all of the government's IOUs, regardless of the amount of time that passes before the Treasury (the debtor) must repay the buyer (the creditor). Securities that mature in one year or less are called *Treasury bills*; securities that mature within a one- to five-year time span are called *Treasury notes*. Finally, *Treasury bonds* are long-term IOUs that take more than five years to mature.)

Interest on the debt

The Treasury must pay the owners of the debt interest on the securities. This interest, estimated at more than $57 billion in 1980 (preliminary estimate), must be obtained from taxpayers or from the sale of more securities (which will further increase the interest cost of the debt). Consequently, the interest cost of the debt must be included in every federal budget. On the other hand, when the securities become due, the Treasury can simply print up new securities and sell them to people to obtain the money to pay off the old ones. This is one reason the debt rarely, if ever, goes down.

The enormous interest cost of the debt that must be paid to the holders of government securities creates more fuel for worry about the debt. Consequently, economists also compare the interest cost of the debt with GNP. In 1978, the interest cost of the debt ($44 billion) was 2.1 percent of the $2,107 billion in GNP in that year. This percentage has remained almost constant since 1970.

When we pay taxes to give the debt-owners their interest, a very large redistribution of income takes place. This shift of income from taxpayers to debt-owners raises a difficult question about whether or not the debt makes the rich richer and the poor poorer. We will reserve this question for the last section of this chapter.

Private and public ownership of the debt

But now let's see who the creditors of the $834 billion public debt were in 1979 (Table 14-2). Several items in the table deserve mention. Note that much of the public debt is not owned by private individuals and partnerships. Amazingly, the federal government buys some of its own government securities (line 7). The federal government accumulates money in the social security fund and the highway trust fund prior to spending the money for social security benefits and new highways. These funds may legally purchase government securities as a way to help the Treasury and earn interest, but they cannot be used for investment in the private sector.

TABLE 14-2 Ownership of the Federal Debt, November 1979

	Securities holdings (in billions)	Percentage of total
1. Individuals (including partnerships)	$113.7	13.6
2. Commercial banks	95.0	11.4
3. Insurance companies	18.8	2.3
4. Other corporations	24.0	2.9
5. State and local governments	68.2	8.2
6. Federal Reserve District banks and their branches	118.1	14.2
7. U.S. government accounts	187.1	22.2
8. Foreign and international owners and miscellaneous[a]	208.9	25.2
	833.8	100.0%

[a]"Miscellaneous" includes savings banks, nonprofit institutions, corporate pension funds, and securities brokers.
Source: *Economic Report of the President, 1980.*

Because government agencies own so much of the federal debt, some experts argue that we should separate the amount of the debt owed to the public from the portions of the debt owed to government agencies. In the government agency category we could lump the U.S. securities owned by state and local governments (line 5) and those owned by the Federal Reserve District Banks (line 6) with those that U.S. government agencies own (line 7) and call this total a portion of the debt that is not owed to the public. The three lines total $373.4 billion. Subtract that figure from the $833.8 billion total and we have left $460.4 billion owed to the public. This last figure is sometimes called the **net public debt.**

Are we spending ourselves into bankruptcy?

Now that you know to whom we owe the debt, you will find it easier to understand why ultimate bankruptcy is extremely improbable. The bankruptcy argument involves a misunderstanding. The existence of the debt does not make the country any richer or poorer. The wealth (or poorness) of the country is measured in terms of such resources as factories, houses, appliances, and vehicles, plus our human capital. The $833.8 billion debt does not change the quantity or quality of resources in the country one bit.

We have seen that the lenders (creditors) are the people who own the securities and that the borrower (debtor) is the Treasury. But because the Treasury, like any government agency, is supported by taxpayers, taxpayers are the real borrowers (debtors). Consequently, one portion of the nation (taxpayers) owes the debt to another (the owners of government securities), who are *also* taxpayers. No matter how large the debt becomes, the indebtedness it represents for all taxpayers is offset by the assets (the securities) held by some taxpayers.

Thus, the public debt is a debt *owed to ourselves.* It is as if one member of a family were indebted to another member of the same family. The family's total wealth is unaffected by the intrafamily debt. Economists refer to this largest part of the public debt as **internal debt.**

Because most of the public debt is internally held, its existence will not lead to bankruptcy. Why, then is this argument so popular? Undoubtedly, because we worry, with good reason, about debts *outside* the family.

Buried in Table 14-1 (line 8) is an important exception to the idea that the public debt is *internal.* About 9.6 percent of the public debt is held by non-U.S. owners.* This indebtedness is **external.** When the foreign-held securities become due, we will be taxed the amount necessary by the federal government to send resources to the creditor countries. An external debt, therefore, reduces the real wealth of the debtor in favor of the creditor. Also external are most of the debts we worry about as consumers—private debts in the form of charge accounts, appliance or car loans, and mortgages.

To judge any debt as "bad" or "good" presents a problem. To the extent we can persuade oil-rich countries to send us their oil in exchange for government securities, we can enjoy the benefits of having warm homes, plentiful electrical power, ration-free supplies of gasoline, and so forth. Our present standard of living rises when our suppliers give us credit. If it were not for mortgages, car loans, and other installment types of loans, most of us would be unable to afford many important and necessary purchases until late in life. As always, there is a benefit side and a cost side in any decision to go into debt.

Because the internal public debt is so much maligned, a look at total private (external) debt makes an interesting comparison. Table 14-3 reveals that our 1976 private debt totaled $2,522 billion. That is about *4 times larger* than the public debt of $632 billion of the same year.

Private debt has also grown faster than public debt during the 1940–1976 period—19.6 times for private debt versus about 15 times for the public debt. During this same period, GNP has grown over 17 times. (All of these figures and comparisons are expressed in current dollars, not in real dollars.)

We must keep in mind that public indebtedness is accomplished by borrowing individual or corporate savings. When the borrowed money is spent, it is put into the income stream for consumption or investment spending. Borrowing helps aggregate demand grow, which helps incomes grow,

---

In 1978, $75 billion of our $772 billion public debt—9.7 percent—was held by "official institutions" and "other foreigners" outside the United States. Some (about $8 billion) of these U.S. government securities were in the hands of lending agencies such as the International Bank for Reconstruction and Development, the Inter-American Development Bank, and the Asian Development Bank. Unidentified amounts were held by the Bank for International Settlements and the European Fund. See Statistical Appendix to Annual Report of the Secretary of the Treasury on the State of the Finances (1978), table 94, p. 378.

TABLE 14-3 Private Debt in the United States in Selected Years, 1940–1976 (in billions)

Year	Individual and noncorporate debt	Corporate debt	Total private debt
1940	$ 53	$ 76	$ 129
1950	104	142	246
1955	180	212	392
1960	263	303	566
1965	416	454	870
1970	584	774	1,357
1974	880	1,254	2,134
1975	950	1,306	2,256
1976	1,107	1,415	2,522

Source: *Statistical Abstracts of the United States, 1978.*

which helps people save, which provides funds for loans which in turn helps aggregate demand, and so on.

Consumer indebtedness, particularly from installment buying, is one of the *indicators* (see page 247) that economists use to forecast what is happening or going to happen to GNP. If consumer indebtedness rises, then consumers must be increasing their consumption spending. But if consumer debt rises less rapidly in any month than it did the month before, economists worry that spending may be slackening. Even "worse," if Americans start to pay off old debts faster than they take on new ones, retail stores find their unsold inventories piling up. A business slowdown and rising unemployment are sure to follow, and that is what happened during the 1974–1975 recession.

At this point you must be wondering, "How can the politicians in Washington almost always spend more than tax receipts and get away with it?" Good question. Let's see how the philosophy of government spending has changed over the years.

Four Federal Budget Philosophies

There are four different philosophies of government finance pertaining to the public debt: (1) the annually balanced budget, (2) the countercyclical budget, (3) functional finance, and (4) the federal high-employment budget approach. Let us discuss each in turn.

The annually balanced budget

The philosophy of the **annually balanced budget** says simply that taxes should always equal government spending; a debt should never arise. Prior to the general acceptance of Keynesian theory in the 1960s, any presidential candidate who did not promise to keep the budget in balance was beaten before he started. Americans often equate indebtedness with sin.

Many economists now believe, however, that a budget that always balances spending with taxes is the worst possible course of action for the health of the economy. It will contribute to inflation in times of prosperity and will deepen and prolong recessions. The key to this argument lies with the built-in or automatic stabilizers. In times of growing prosperity, the federal government's tax revenues automatically rise because of increases in income tax collections. If, then, the federal government pursues the annually balanced budget philosophy, it will use this opportunity to increase government spending. The increase in government spending will add to an already increasing aggregate demand and contribute to inflation.

When the economy starts slipping downhill into a period of poor sales for business and increasing unemployment, tax collections automatically fall. If, then, the federal government is forced to reduce spending to keep the budget in balance, the reduction in spending will subtract from aggregate demand and make matters worse.

The countercyclical budget

You are probably already saying to yourself that the federal government should reduce spending in times of inflation and should run a deficit by increasing spending without increasing taxes in times of recession. If so, you are advocating a countercyclical policy. A **countercyclical budget** means that the federal budget should counteract the swings in aggregate demand by reducing spending in times of inflation and increasing it in times of recession or depression.

Remember from our discussion of business cycles in Chapter 12 that no one is very sure whether there is a *regular* cycle or not. Nor does the term "countercyclical" imply that there is a regular cycle. Rather, the term suggests that there are economic policies that can counteract either periods of inflationary booms or periods of high-unemployment busts.

We can visualize the federal government's role in countercyclical activities in Figure 14-2. The solid line shows the ups and downs of an uncontrolled GNP. The dotted line shows GNP after the federal government's attempts to dampen the cycle. The theory is that we can level out the cycle.

Unfortunately, there are two reasons why this beautiful idea will not work. First, the swings in aggregate demand are apt to be uneven; the ups do not necessarily match the downs, either in height or in duration. There is no way of knowing whether the surpluses accumulated during periods of prosperity will match the increases in the debt incurred during periods of depression or recession. Second, the countercyclical philosophy has no provision for helping our GNP grow enough to provide jobs for a growing labor force.

Functional finance

The **functional finance** philosophy stresses the federal government's obligation to achieve the goals stated in the Employment Act of 1946. It views deficit spending and a growing debt as matters that are of secondary importance to the primary functions of government—providing for full em-

Figure 14-2. Counter-cyclical spending and taxing policies.

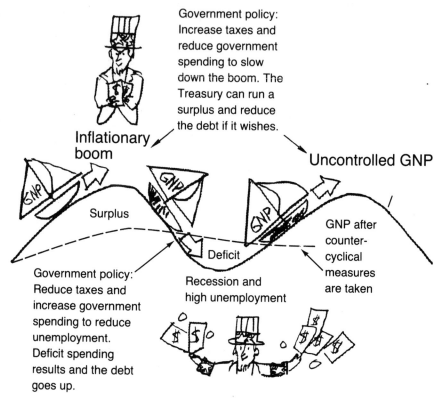

Government policy: Increase taxes and reduce government spending to slow down the boom. The Treasury can run a surplus and reduce the debt if it wishes.

Inflationary boom

Uncontrolled GNP

Surplus

Deficit

GNP after counter-cyclical measures are taken

Government policy: Reduce taxes and increase government spending to reduce unemployment. Deficit spending results and the debt goes up.

Recession and high unemployment

ployment, maintaining stable prices, and helping to solve many domestic social and economic problems. Thus, this philosophy emphasizes the functions of government rather than the deficits or surpluses a noninflationary, full-employment policy might produce. It also takes note of particular problems that need solving whether deficits are incurred or not—problems such as poverty, housing, pollution, and rapid transit.

Furthermore, the functional finance philosophy recognizes the needs of a population that increases by about 2 million people per year. In such an economy, a countercyclical philosophy is inadequate. The government cannot limit itself to leveling out the waves of inflation and recession. There must be some provision for expanding the opportunities of those in and those entering the labor force. Consequently, the functional finance philosophy says that, if we have to run a deficit *every* year to solve social and economic problems, we should do so. This philosophy therefore endorses the idea of an evergrowing debt.

The high-employment budget approach

This fourth and last budget philosophy used to be called the *"full"* employment budget approach. We used to define full employment as 4 percent *un*employment. But as more women and teenagers with high unemployment rates entered the labor force, the 4 percent unemployment figure has seemed

The problem with any federal budget is that it may operate to prevent the economy from reaching full employment.

harder to attain. We currently accept a 5.5 percent rate of unemployment as a reasonable indication of full employment. But because of this changing definition, the Council of Economic Advisors labels this last approach as the "high," rather than "full," employment approach.

Estimating the budget at full or high employment

The problem with any federal budget is that it may operate to prevent the economy from reaching full employment. A simple example will help. Assume a small English-speaking state named Belgravia which has an unemployment rate of 10 percent.

The Minister of Finance, a dignified gentleman named Marshall Thistlewaite, calculates that annual government spending is 100 pips (or dollars, francs, marks, or whatever) and that taxes annually bring in 80. He says to himself, "Ah, good, spending exceeds taxes by 20. Surely, such a deficit will reduce unemployment."

Over cocktails that evening, Marshall happens to mention his finding to his lovely wife, Prunella. Prunella is not only lovely. She has a Ph.D. in economics from Belgravia's major (and only) university, Stanhard.

Prunella quietly informs Marshall that, while his estimates are interesting, he has missed the point. "Dear," she begins, "you should estimate spending and taxes at full employment. Suppose," she explains very patiently, "that at full employment, spending is 100 but at higher incomes, taxes are 110. Our government will be taking 10 more from the people than it gives them. Full employment will be temporary at best. Probably the increased taxes will prevent us," she continues, her voice rising, "from reaching full employment at all!"

Prunella knew her stuff. Economists now are more interested in estimating the impact of the federal budget at full employment than worrying about deficits which occur when the unemployment rate is higher than, say, 5.5 percent. And many economists have accepted the high-employment budget approach; that is, before deciding whether to increase spending or taxes, an estimate should be made of the government's income and expenditures at high employment. If that estimate reveals that a budget surplus would occur at high employment, then, according to this approach, taxes should be cut even if such a tax cut means that a *present deficit will become even bigger.*

Clearly, such a policy supports deficit spending and corresponding increases in the public debt. But, the increases in the public debt may not be as large as they first appear. If the deficit causes GNP to grow, the deficit will tend to disappear. As incomes increase, so will taxes; and, given any level of government spending, the increase in taxes will gradually approach the level of spending—thus erasing all of, or part of, the deficit. The following story illustrates this idea.

The income tax cut of 1964

The income tax cut of 1964 provides a famous example of how the high-employment budget idea operates. The story is also an example of the kind of argument economists get into.

Keynesian theorists often point to the tax cut as real-world proof of the mechanics of Keynesian theory. When President Kennedy took office in 1961, the economy was sluggish and unemployment rates were relatively high.* After two years of urging, the President and Walter Heller, Chairman of the Council of Economic Advisors, persuaded Congress to pass an income tax cut, even though this meant increasing the government deficit. The tax cut that finally took effect in April 1964 amounted to $11 billion. It has been estimated that the increase in consumption and investment spending attributable to the tax cut totaled $30 billion by the end of 1965. As incomes grew, the government's tax receipts increased, even at lower tax rates. Thus, even though there was a deficit in 1965 of $1.6 billion, it was less than half the size of the federal government's deficit for each of the preceding four years.

Actually, the unemployment rate was only 5.5 percent, but in those days such a rate was considered unacceptable.

TABLE 14-4 Civilian Unemployment, 1960–1966

Year	Unemployment rates as a percentage of the civilian labor force
1960	5.5
1961	6.7
1962	5.5
1963	5.7
1964 year of the tax cut	5.2
1965	4.5
1966	3.8

Source: *Economic Report of the President, 1972*, table B-63, p. 269.

The 1964 income tax cut provides apparent proof of Keynesian theory and the high-employment budget approach because it led to an almost-balanced budget and a drop in unemployment rates after 1964, as Table 14-4 shows. But, as always, there is a counterargument. There are two large categories of policies used to change GNP—fiscal and monetary. These two sets of policies also divide economists into *neo-Keynesians*, who favor fiscal measures, and *monetarists*, who believe that the activities of the Federal Reserve System have a more important effect on aggregate demand than does fiscal policy. The monetarists argue that it was the Federal Reserve System's actions, not the income tax cut, that helped the economy in 1964. The evidence is conflicting and complicated, and we cannot hope to decide who is right. (The mechanics and theory of monetary policy will be discussed in Chapters 15 and 16).

How well has the high-employment budget idea worked since 1964? Table 14-5 compares the actual budget deficits that occurred with the deficits or surpluses that *would* have occurred at levels of high employment during the 1970–1979 years.

We draw two conclusions from Table 14-5: (1) the high-employment surplus in 1974 may have contributed to the recession of 1974–1975 and the high unemployment rates that followed; and (2) the large actual and high-employment deficits in the following years may have helped to reduce unemployment. Estimated unemployment for 1979 was 5.8 percent, a healthy decrease from 8.5 percent in 1975. On the other hand, the high-employment budget surplus in 1979 may have helped set the stage for a recession which began in the spring of 1980. By June 1980 the unemployment rate was back up to 7.8 percent.

The great benefit of the high-employment budget concept is that it enables economists to forecast the effect of the federal budget on the economy's ability to achieve full employment and to plan changes in the federal budget over a period of several years. Economists are especially wary of the

TABLE 14-5 Actual and High-Employment Deficits and Surpluses in the Federal Budget, 1970–1979, and the Unemployment Rate (Deficits and Surpluses in Billions of Current Dollars)

Calendar year	Actual surplus (+) or deficit (−)	High-employment surplus (+) or deficit (−)	Unemployment rate (in %)
1973	− 6.7	− 9.8	4.9
1974	− 10.7	+ 9.3	5.6
1975	− 70.6	− 18.2	8.5
1976	− 53.6	− 13.4	7.7
1977	− 46.3	− 18.6	7.0
1978	− 27.7	− 1.6	6.0
1979	− 9.7 (est.)	+ 9.8	5.8 (est.)

Source: *Economic Report of the President, 1974* and *1980.*

surpluses that might occur at or near full employment. The fear is always that the federal government will act as a drag on the economy.

The last two philosophies provide some logic for an ever-growing debt, but, as you well know by now, every decision has its cost; there is no such thing as a "free lunch." Let's see what some of the real costs of the debt are.

Some Hard Questions About the Debt

So far, the arguments about the debt make a growing debt seem painless, even necessary, with the possible exception of the 9.6 percent held externally. The remainder of this chapter is devoted to four problems with which the professionals have difficulty.

Redistribution of income

The debt may cause a redistribution of income away from low-income people to high-income people. The reason is that the owners of government securities probably have higher-than-average income. (One clue: The richest *one* percent of the people owned *60* percent of all bonds, including corporate bonds, in 1972.) Consequently, when all taxpayers have to pay the $60 billion or so in interest income to the owners of government securities, a large redistribution of income undoubtedly takes place.

We should be reminded, however, that this argument pertains only to the tax side of the question. When the money is spent, people in lower income groups may benefit, for example, from such projects as rapid transit or federally subsidized housing.

The debt and inflation

The second argument about the debt concerns its effect on inflation. There is no doubt that deficit spending and a rising debt mean that the government can put more into the income stream than it takes out. The government spending component of aggregate demand can grow without any offsetting decrease in consumption, investment, or net exports. Resulting increases in aggregate demand will tend to raise prices.

Inflation caused by increases in aggregate demand resulting from deficit spending is particularly aggravating if the economy is at or near full employment. Remember that *any* spending by the government means that the government is buying goods and services in private markets. If suppliers are already producing as much as they can, the demand for goods and services by government agencies will cause suppliers to raise prices on the same quantities of goods and services. No one except the suppliers wins in this game.

If, on the other hand, there is high unemployment, increased government spending will cause suppliers to increase production and hire more people. For a time, while the economy gathers steam, prices may remain at their previous levels. This scenario was the one Keynes foresaw as the way out of the Depression.

Deficit spending can also cause inflation in more subtle ways. If the deficit is on the order of, say, $50 billion, the Treasury will have to sell almost *$942 million* worth of government securities *every week* to finance the deficit. To persuade people to buy these securities instead of doing other things with their money, the Treasury will have to offer interest rates that are at least as attractive as those offered by the banks and, allowing for risk, the rates of return offered by the stock market. In short, the Treasury has to compete for your money.

To prevent an outflow of funds to the Treasury, the banks will have to offer higher interest rates. When they do, the cost of borrowing rises, and the cost of doing business rises. Business managers will be forced to cover the highest cost of borrowing by raising prices. Thus, rising interest rates, resulting from deficit spending, contribute to inflation.

Crowding-out

Closely related to the inflation argument is this third argument (mentioned in Chapter 13) that deficit spending may "crowd out" private spending. We have to keep in mind that, as government securities mature, the Treasury often sells new ones to replace the old ones. Frequently, the Treasury will have to sweeten the new offering with higher interest rates. And when the Treasury offers higher interest rates, corporations have a more difficult time selling securities to the public to finance *private* investment. Then business managers may decide to postpone investment spending until borrowing becomes cheaper. The government spending component increases, but at the expense of a drop in investment spending. Aggregate demand and the level of employment may not change at all.

The crowding-out argument assumes that the Board of Governors of the Federal Reserve System is sitting idly by doing nothing. The Board can, if it wishes, counteract the crowding-out effect by increasing the amount of money the banks have to lend, which will in turn result in a lowering of interest rates. We will come back to this point after explaining the mechanics of monetary policy in Chapter 16.

The big government argument

Simply stated, this last argument says that continued acceptance of deficit spending means that there will be no limit on the amounts the government can spend, or on the numbers of agencies it creates, or on the number of people it employs. In this situation, government control of our lives increases and individual liberty decreases.

There is no doubt that these fears are real. Spending at all levels of government has come under attack in the form of "tax revolts" and proposals for constitutional limitations on federal and even state budgets. However, it is not yet clear how much or what services people are willing to forego in order to achieve "smaller" government (less spending and reduced taxes).

Summary

The federal government has spent more than it has taken in in taxes in most years since 1929, with a resultant increase in the public debt to over $800 billion in 1979. Some people believe the debt is leading the country into bankruptcy or causing a "merciless burden" to fall on future generations. However, unlike most private debts, the public debt is largely internal; that is, it is owed by all taxpayers to some of their number (securities holders who are also taxpayers). Only about 9.6 percent of the total debt is owed to foreign investors.

Some people argue that the government should always operate on a balanced budget, but such a policy would exaggerate the ups and downs of the business cycle. Some economists say that federal budgets should be planned to counteract the business cycle by increasing spending above tax revenues in times of recession and increasing taxes above spending in times of inflation. Other economists argue that governmental financial policies should be used to attack social problems such as unemployment, poverty, urban renewal, and pollution; the resulting changes in the public debt should be of secondary concern. This policy is called functional finance.

Finally, some economists believe that deficit spending is valid, because it helps GNP move toward high employment. And if GNP is at or near high employment, the automatic increases in tax collections that come from an expanding economy will erase the deficit and may even produce a surplus.

There are serious arguments against the debt: (1) it contributes to the unequal distribution of income; (2) it contributes to inflation; (3) it may crowd out private spending; and (4) it contributes to an ever-bigger federal government.

Discussion Questions

1. Evaluate the following statement: An individual who is steadily accumulating debt is probably in trouble, but a country that is in debt is probably in good economic health.

2. Why is an annually balanced budget apt to aggravate the ups and downs of inflation and unemployment?

3. What would happen to the economy if we instituted a tax program to pay off the entire debt?

4. Is the sale of $500 million worth of bonds by the American Telephone and Telegraph Company to build new exchanges an internal or external debt? How would you judge whether or not this indebtedness is economically worthwhile?

5. How big can the public debt become? If the debt continues to get bigger, are we in danger of going bankrupt? Discuss.

15

Monetary Policy I: How the Banks Create Money

Tom Tracy

In Chapters 12 through 14 we looked at fiscal policy—the theory and mechanics of changing aggregate demand through changes in government spending or taxes. In this chapter and the chapter that follows we shall explore the other major method of raising or lowering aggregate demand to combat recession or inflation—monetary policy. **Monetary policy** is the manipulation of the money supply for the purpose of changing aggregate demand. In the United States, monetary policy is formulated and carried out by the Board of Governors of the **Federal Reserve System (the Fed).**

It will help to keep in mind two central and easy-to-understand theories upon which monetary policy is based: (1) If borrowing is made easy, total spending (aggregate demand) should increase. (2) If borrowing is made difficult, then spending should stop rising and may even fall.

Key Words

Monetary policy	Member banks
The Federal Reserve System	Federal Reserve Act of 1913
(the Fed)	Legal reserve
Gold Reserve Act of 1934	Required reserve
M_1	Excess reserves
Credit	Federal Reserve District Bank
Commercial bank	Deposit multiplier

Of the two sets of policies to change aggregate demand—fiscal and monetary—the public is generally more aware of changes in discretionary fiscal policy because changes in government spending and taxes are often on the front pages of newspapers and may directly affect us as taxpayers or members of the business community.

The methods of monetary policy are complex. They are employed by the Board of Governors of the Federal Reserve System, a group of seven people who do not have to go to voters or congressmen or to the President to get permission for what they do. When their activities do occasionally reach the front pages, there is little public understanding of what they mean, even though they probably affect us as much, if not more than, discretionary fiscal policy does. Changes in monetary policy also occur more frequently than do changes in discretionary fiscal policy—as often as once a week.

In order to understand how monetary policy works, we must dispose of some important preliminaries. (1) We need to understand what money *is*, and what it is that makes those pieces of paper, those dollar bills, money. (2) Then we need to define the term "money supply" as it is used in monetary policy, because the purpose of monetary policy is to change aggregate demand through changes in the money supply. (3) We need to explain how the banks, where we have our checking accounts, can actually create money. These three topics are the subject of this chapter. We will move on to a discussion of how monetary policy works in Chapter 16.

What Makes Money, Money?

The answer is not as easy as it seems. All kinds of commodities have been used as money in different countries at different times—salt and grain in ancient times, gold and silver, hard candy (by the Eskimos), tea and cheese (China), fish hooks (Alaska), elephant tail bristles (Portuguese West Africa), cocoa beans (Mexico), and even cigarettes (in World War I and II prison camps).

All of these examples hint at the real answer to the question: Money is whatever people decide to use to buy goods and services and to pay off debts. In more formal terms, money is whatever is *generally accepted* as a medium of exchange among the members of a tribe or nation or among nations.

All kinds of commodities have been used as money in different countries at different times.

Many of us are inclined to believe that money, to have worth, must consist of some valuable commodity such as gold or silver. Or, if our money is made of paper, many people believe that it is valuable only because it can be exchanged for precious metals such as gold or silver. Or they believe that if it cannot be exchanged for gold or silver, at least it is backed by some quantity of gold or silver.

The fact is that in the United States our paper money and coins are no longer backed by gold or silver. Our paper money was exchangeable for gold or silver until 1934.* During the early years of the Depression, Americans exchanged large quantities of paper money for gold. When the stock of gold held by the Treasury sank to disturbingly low levels, Congress passed in 1934 the **Gold Reserve Act.** The Act stopped the redemption of paper money (five-dollar bills and up) for gold. Later, in 1963, Congress halted the redemption of one-dollar bills for silver. And in the late 1960s, the silver content of coins was removed and replaced with copper and nickel.

After the 1934 Gold Reserve Act, the following phrase was inscribed on our paper money: THIS NOTE IS LEGAL TENDER FOR ALL DEBTS, PUBLIC AND PRIVATE,

---

*During this time the government could not print money beyond the ratio of the gold and silver in the Teasury to the amount of currency in circulation, thus setting a limit on the expansion of the money supply.

What gives money its value?

AND IS REDEEMABLE IN LAWFUL MONEY AT THE U.S. TREASURY OR AT ANY FEDERAL RESERVE BANK. In 1947, a Mr. A. F. Davis from Cleveland wrote the Treasury enclosing a $10 bill and asked that it be redeemed in "lawful money." After some hesitation, the Treasury sent him two $5 bills. Mr. Davis persisted. He returned one of the $5 bills to the Treasury and insisted on $5 worth of "lawful money." Eventually, the Treasury returned the $5 bill and explained that the term "lawful money" had never been legally defined. A few years later, the reference to redemption in lawful money was removed from our paper money. (There are still a few bills in circulation with the redemption phrase. If you come across one, you might try Mr. Davis's ploy.)

So, if our money is backed neither by gold nor silver (nor "lawful money"), what *does* back it? Despite the changes since 1934, we continue to spend or save our money as always. The question of backing has had no effect on us at all.

Thus, we finally come to the question, what gives money its value? The answer is that money is valuable because we all *believe* it has purchasing power and accept it as a medium of exchange. The value of money is therefore determined entirely by the quantity and quality of the goods and services we can obtain with money, not by its backing.

The purchasing power of money is determined by its scarcity relative to the supply of goods and services it can buy. As money becomes more plentiful relative to supplies of goods and services, prices are apt to rise and money tends to lose its value (inflation). As money becomes less plentiful relative to available supplies of goods and services, it becomes more valuable.

Because the relative scarcity of money is important to its value, and because the quantity of money in circulation is no longer limited by supplies of gold or silver, what or who controls the quantity of money in circulation? Answer: the Board of Governors of the Federal Reserve System. Now perhaps you can appreciate the enormous power the Board has. (There is much debate about limiting this power, a point we shall discuss in the following chapter.)

Although we have been discussing the role of paper money in our society, monetary policy, which concerns the manipulation of the money supply to influence aggregate demand, is concerned with many forms of money in addition to paper money. Therefore, in order to understand monetary policy we must now consider the different forms of money that make up the money supply.

What Is the "Money Supply"?

The theory that GNP rises more quickly or slowly according to increases or decreases in the money supply involves one of the great problems of monetary policy—deciding which ingredients in the money supply have the greatest effect on aggregate demand. The problem is a typical one in the social sciences. When we find that more educated people have higher incomes than less educated people, is it because of their education, intelligence, or hard work, or is it because their parents were rich, their father was president of the company, or the family was especially attuned to the Protestant ethic of work? Which variable is the most important determinant of income?

In the same way, research economists try to sift out the particular ingredients in the money supply that are most closely linked to changes in aggregate demand. And there are lots of ingredients to choose from: money in banks, money in circulation, checking accounts, credit cards, money in credit unions, charge accounts, savings accounts, equities in life insurance policies, government securities that can be easily cashed in, and so forth. There are at least seven different ways to describe the money supply, and there is much debate about which one has the greatest effect on aggregate demand. However, the first and most common definition of the money supply is called M_1.

The M_1 formula

M_1 is defined as currency in circulation plus checking accounts. *Currency in circulation* includes all of the coins and paper money not sitting in some bank but in the possession of the public, whether it is in a wallet, cash register, cookie jar, or in the mattress.

Even though the currency in banks seems easy to obtain by withdrawing it from some account, it is not counted as in circulation. Furthermore, counting the currency in commercial banks and checking accounts would involve double counting. When you obtain $100 in cash by cashing a $100 check, the checking account portion of M_1 goes down by $100 and currency in circulation goes up by $100. M_1 does not change. If, prior to your writing the check, M_1

were to include both the $100 in the bank and the $100 in your checking account, M_1 would be $100 too high. We cannot have it both ways.

Checking accounts require no explanation except that they are called *demand deposits* by the banks, an indication that the banks must deliver a depositor's checking account to the depositor instantly upon the depositor's demand. (Savings accounts, which are not included in M_1, are usually called savings deposits when held by individuals and, sometimes, "time deposits" when held by businesses, because the banks can take time, if they wish, to fulfill the depositor's request for the business firm's money.)

Near money The intent of the definition of M_1 is to describe the purchasing power that is instantly available to the public without borrowing (without using credit cards, charge accounts, overdrawn checking accounts, and the like) and without having to convert time deposits or other financial assets (stocks, securities, insurance policies, and so forth) into cash. Savings accounts and government securities held by the public are called *near money* because they must first be converted to cash before they can be spent.

Table 15-1 illustrates some of the complications involved in deciding what the money supply is. It also reveals the enormous quantity of near money. The large quantity of near money, which is not under the direct control of the Federal Reserve System, raises one of the many difficult questions of monetary policy: If we look only at M_1, can we really tell what is going on?

TABLE 15-1 Currency in Circulation and Near Money, December 1978 (in billions)

M_1	
Coins in circulation (approx.)	$ 10.0
Paper money (Federal Reserve Notes) in circulation	87.5
Total currency in circulation	97.5
Demand deposits (checking accounts)	263.6
Total M_1	$ 361.1
Near money	
Savings accounts in commercial banks (banks that hold checking accounts)	607.8
Deposits in savings and loan and mutual savings banks	626.5
Government securities in the hands of the public (net public debt)	433.0
Total near money	1,667.3
Total M_1 and near money	$2,028.4

Sources: *Economic Report of the President, 1979,* and *Statistical Abstract of the United States, 1978.*

The distinction between M_1 and these other forms of money has been blurred in recent years by various plans offered by the banks to enable depositors to switch money back and forth between checking and savings accounts, in some cases simply by making a phone call. In New England, savings banks offer savers "Negotiable Orders of Withdrawal" ("NOW" accounts) that allow savers to write withdrawal orders, which are essentially checks, on their savings accounts. And by mid-summer 1979, many commercial banks offered to pay interest on demand deposits provided the account balance is kept over some minimum like $2,000. This blending of demand deposits with savings accounts has caused many experts to believe that the M_1 definition of the money supply is too narrow.* Despite this difficulty, we will confine our discussion of monetary policy to the M_1 definition. (But we will return to this problem again on page 344.)

Table 15-1 illustrates another point to keep in mind: the importance of demand deposits in our society and in M_1. As of December 1978, demand deposits were 73 percent of M_1, with currency in circulation making up the other 27 percent. For our purposes, it is sufficient to remember that currency in circulation is about one-quarter of M_1, while demand deposits constitute the other three-quarters.

The fact that demand deposits comprise three-quarters of M_1 is especially important. The Federal Reserve System has little direct control over the amount of currency in circulation, but it can change at will the three-quarters of the money supply that constitute demand deposits. Consequently, our discussion of monetary policy will emphasize changes in the demand-deposit component of M_1.

Credit

Before we continue, we must point out a distinction between money, as we have defined the term, and credit. The term **credit** (which means "I trust" in Latin) refers to a creditor's belief that a borrower will repay a loan. Consequently, credit appears on the scene anytime anyone is given an obligation to repay a loan, credit-card balance, or charge account, by someone else, the creditor.

In Chapter 14 you saw the gigantic extent of public and private debt in the United States. This indebtedness is a mountain of credit, involving someone's belief that someone else will pay. Government securities owners believe the government (the taxpayers) will pay. Private lenders to corporations and individuals believe their loans will be repaid.

When a bank lends money it usually gives the borrower a demand deposit in the amount of the loan. Infrequently, the loan is in the form of currency. Thus the creation of credit—specifically, the lending of money by the banks—causes M_1 to grow.

---

*Hence the recent redefinition of M_1. M_1 is now called M-1A. M-1B is M-1A plus NOW accounts plus interest-earning "share draft" accounts in credit unions on which one can write checks.

How Do the Banks Create Money?

We have said that the banks create money by extending credit, but we need to provide a few more details.

As you know, there are two main kinds of banks—banks that hold demand deposits and banks such as savings and loan banks that hold only time deposits. We will limit our discussion to banks that hold demand deposits, because our objective is to discuss monetary policy as it relates to M_1. Demand deposits are part of M_1; time deposits are not.

So our discussion is pointed at banks that hold demand deposits. Such banks are called **commercial banks.** Finally, our discussion is further limited because we are going to consider only those commercial banks (called **member banks**) that belong to the Federal Reserve System (less than half of all commercial banks).

Commercial banks and a money-creation model

The key to creation of money by the banks is that they can lend out some of the money that is deposited in them.

Let us assume that you deposit $1,000 in a commercial bank and ask for a demand deposit in that amount. The bank gives you a checkbook showing that you have $1,000 in a demand-deposit account and puts the money in what is called its *reserve account.*

As long as the money sits in the reserve account, it earns no interest for the bank. But banks are privately owned corporations that are in business to make money. The bank is immediately anxious to put as much money as it can into some form of financial investment that earns interest. In modern economies, banks operate under what is called a *fractional reserve system.* They have to keep only a fraction of their reserves. The **Federal Reserve Act of 1913,** which describes and limits the activities of the Federal Reserve System, specifies the various fractions of reserves that member banks must keep, depending on their size and location.

The Federal Reserve Act requires the largest member banks to keep a minimum of from 10 to 22 percent of their demand deposits in their reserve accounts. These minima are called the **legal reserve.** The Board of Governors has the authority to vary the exact percentage minimum within this legal reserve range.

Required reserves

While the 10 to 22 percent minima are called legal reserves, the specific percentage selected by the Board within those limits is called the **required reserve.** In recent years the Board has kept the required reserve near, but slightly below, 20 percent for large member banks. To make our arithmetic a lot easier, we shall assume from now on that the required reserve is 20 percent. This means that, whether demand deposits go up or down, the bank must keep a minimum of 20 percent of demand deposits in reserves. But it can lend money out (create credit) or buy stocks or bonds with the other 80 percent and thereby earn interest income.

Amazingly enough, a commercial bank creates money out of thin air when it makes a loan.

Excess reserves

Let us assume that Hugh, the window-washer, wants to borrow some money from the bank where you deposited the $1,000. We will call your bank Bank A.

How much can your bank lend? With a deposit of $1,000, it must keep $200 (20 percent) in reserves, but it can lend out the other $800. The amount that the bank can lend over and above its required reserve is called **excess reserves.**

The banks lend money

Now let us assume that Bank A wants to lend its excess reserves of $800 and that Hugh qualifies for a loan of this amount for the purchase of a used car. (In the real world, however, the bank would rarely lend out all of its excess reserves.)

We shall now assume that Hugh wishes to have the loan in the form of a demand deposit (checking account). Bank A is happy to oblige.

Now the point. When Hugh receives his $800 loan in the form of a demand deposit, demand deposits increase by $800 and the money supply also increases by $800. M_1 has increased by $800 because your $1,000 demand deposit is still there. Amazingly enough, a commercial bank *creates money out of thin air* when it makes a loan.

What happens when Hugh buys the used car with the $800? We shall assume that he pays Honest John Car Dealer with a check for $800. Honest

John deposits the check, we shall assume, in a bank other than Bank A, called Bank B.

Now what happens? Bank B sends the check to the nearest **Federal Reserve District Bank.** The District Bank keeps an accounting of all reserves held by member banks in its district. Accordingly, the District Bank will add $800 to Bank B's reserves and subtract $800 from Bank A's reserves.

After the District Bank completes its calculation of each member bank's reserves, the canceled check is returned to Bank A and eventually finds its way back to Hugh in his bank statement. The processing of the check by the Federal Reserve System is called *check clearing*. Whenever a check is cleared, the bank against which it is drawn loses reserves; the bank in which it is deposited gains reserves.

What has happened to the money supply? It has still increased by $800. The $800 is no longer in Bank A but now exists in Bank B.

Now let us repeat the process. How much can Bank B lend out of the $800? It must keep 20 percent of the $800 in reserves, or $160. It therefore has excess reserves of $640 ($800 minus $160) that it can lend out. We shall pretend that it lends $640 to a Mrs. Stevens.

When Bank B lends the $640 to Mrs. Stevens, the money supply (M_1) increases by another $640. Note that Honest John still has Hugh's $800 to spend. And in addition to the $800 available to Honest John, Mrs. Stevens can spend $640.

Keep in mind that M_1 equals the currency in circulation plus demand deposits. The demand-deposit portion of M_1 has increased by $800 + $640, or $1,440. It all happened because Banks A and B could create credit.

Now let us assume that Mrs. Stevens uses her $640 loan to buy a boat and the boat dealer has an account with still another bank, Bank C. When the boat dealer deposits Mrs. Stevens' check for $640 in Bank C, the process can be repeated again. Bank C has to keep 20 percent of the $640 or $128 (20 percent of $640), but the remaining $512 ($640 − $128) are excess reserves. Bank C can lend out the $512. If it does, M_1 goes up by $512.

The deposit multiplier

You can see that your original $1,000 can result in at least three loans—$800 to Hugh, $640 to Mrs. Stevens, and $512, assuming Bank C decides to lend it. We have a chain reaction going, just like Art Buchwald's spending chain back in Chapter 13. The only difference is that this time it is a lending chain. In short, we have another multiplier.

We called Buchwald's multiplier the spending multiplier. It showed how GNP could increase or decrease by a multiple of a change in spending. This time we are involved with a change in M_1. M_1 can change by a multiple of an initial change in deposits.

We call this multiplier the **deposit multiplier.** The deposit multiplier has been estimated in the real world to be about 5; consequently, M_1 will

TABLE 15-2 The Deposit Multiplier in Operation

Bank	Demand deposit portion of M_1	Loans	Reserves
A	$1,000	$ 800	$ 200
B	800	640	160
C	640	512	128
Subtotal	$2,440	$1,952	$ 488
All other banks	$2,560	$2,048	$ 512
Final totals	$5,000	$4,000	$1,000

rise by five times the first deposit.* Table 15-2 shows the final totals, assuming that all banks act the way Banks A, B, and C did. When you deposited your $1,000 in Bank A, the net effect on M_1 was zero, because the increase in Bank A's deposits was cancelled out by the withdrawal of $1,000 from currency in circulation. Thus, we cannot count the deposit of $1,000 in Bank A as part of the $5,000 increase. The net increase is actually $4,000, all of it the result of bank loans.

If, however, the $1,000 had been deposited in Bank A in some manner that *did not subtract from the existing money supply*, then we could call the entire $5,000 a net increase in M_1.

As we shall see, the Board of Governors of the Federal Reserve System has a way of doing just that. The new deposit does not involve a check drawn on any bank, nor does it involve the deposit of currency.

Notice that each final total is fives time the first amount in each column. The increase in M_1 is shown in the demand deposit column. But this increase in M_1 is deceptive. We assumed that the first deposit (yours) of $1,000 was made in the form of cash. Remember that M_1 is currency in circulation plus demand deposits. Consequently, when the first deposit was made, currency in circulation decreased by $1,000 while demand deposits increased by $1,000. No change in M_1 occurred at that point.

Contracting the money supply   The money supply can also contract by a multiple of a withdrawal. Suppose Bank A has made its $800 loan to Hugh. Having done so, Bank A has no

---

The deposit multiplier varies inversely with the required reserve percentage. If the required reserve is 20 percent, the deposit multiplier is 5, but if the required reserve is 10 percent, the deposit multiplier will be much higher, actually 10—each bank in the chain would then be able to lend 90 percent of its demand deposits instead of 80 percent. The formula for the deposit multiplier is 1 ÷ the required reserve expressed as a decimal. Thus, if the required reserve is 20 percent, the formula reads 1 ÷ .2, and the answer is 5. Over the past seven years (1972–1979) the required reserve percentage for the largest banks has fluctuated between 16 and 18 percent. That is why we have picked 20 percent as a convenient figure.

more money to lend. Its excess reserves are gone. Its reserves are down to the minimum the Board of Governors allows. Bankers would say, Bank A is "loaned up." Now suppose someone comes along and insists on withdrawing any amount of money.

The only currency (cash) Bank A has is in its reserve account. All other monies are out on loan. If Bank A hands over *any* money, its reserves will be below the required minimum.

Consequently, Bank A will have to sell some of its assets (for example, some stocks and bonds), or it will have to allow some loans to mature without relending the money.

Suppose now that the people who buy these assets or repay loans write checks on other banks to pay Bank A. Then these other banks will lose demand deposits, and when the checks are cleared the other banks will lose reserves in those amounts, too.

The first withdrawal can start a chain of withdrawals from demand-deposit accounts resulting in a chain of losses from bank reserves. If the first withdrawal happens to be $1,000, all of the numbers in Table 15-2 become negative. The final changes are $-\$5,000$ in demand deposits, $-\$4,000$ in loans, and $-\$1,000$ in reserves.

As you might guess, the Board of Governors of the Federal Reserve System has a way of starting the withdrawal process. The Board has a way of taking money out of the banks in such a way that the money is *not deposited in any bank.* Consequently, such withdrawals have the effect of letting some of the M_1 evaporate into "thin air." M_1 will collapse by a multiple of the Board's withdrawal. In conclusion, any action the Board takes to expand or contract M_1 will be multiplied by the deposit multiplier. We will examine these actions of the Board in the next chapter. (It's almost as if you're being let in on a secret because the Board's activities *are* often kept secret. The Board's decisions usually appear only in the back pages of most newspapers at least a month after they are made.)

Summary

Monetary policy is the manipulation of the nation's money supply to influence aggregate demand. Money can be any generally accepted medium of exchange. There are several definitions for the money supply, but the most commonly used one is M_1, the total of all coins and paper money (Federal Reserve Notes) in circulation plus checking accounts. Checking accounts, called demand deposits, constitute three-quarters of M_1. Economists call savings deposits and government securities near money because they can be readily converted into currency.

Monetary policy is carried out through the activities of commercial banks, that is, banks that hold checking accounts and particularly those that are members of the Federal Reserve System.

Commercial banks are permitted to have fractional reserves, which means they can lend out a large fraction of the money deposited with them. In the process of lending, new checking accounts are created. The creation of deposits through loans adds to M_1. All banks together can increase M_1 by a multiple of any deposit that is not withdrawn from some other bank. This multiple, or deposit multiplier, is estimated to be about 5. If money is withdrawn, M_1 will collapse by a multiple of the withdrawal.

Discussion Questions

1. How do commercial banks create money? If the legal reserve requirement were 100 percent, could the commercial banks create money? Can they create more money if the reserve requirement is 15 percent than if it is 20 percent? Why or why not?

2. Assume that a commercial bank has $1 million in demand deposits, that the reserve requirement is 20 percent, and that the bank actually has $350,000 in reserves. How much can the bank lend?

3. What happens to XYZ Bank's reserves, if a depositor writes a $100 check and the check is deposited in QRS Bank? What happens to QRS's reserves?

4. How can banks pay off depositors in a fractional reserve banking system? (Answer in terms of the safety of deposits.)

16

Monetary Policy II: How the Board Changes the Money Supply to Change Aggregate Demand

© Rose Skytta/Jeroboam, Inc.

At the end of Chapter 15, we saw how a chain reaction can occur among commercial banks leading to an expansion or contraction of M_1. Now we need to find out how the Board is able to start these chain reactions; that is, what it actually does to change M_1. This discussion is divided into five sections: (1) an overview of monetary theory, (2) how the Fed is organized, (3) what the Board does to change M_1, (4) the monetarists' case, and (5) can monetary policy work?

Key Words

Board of Governors   Discount rate

Federal Open Market Committee   Prime rate

Federal Reserve Notes (paper money)   Hyperinflation

Federal Deposit Insurance Corporation (FDIC)   Monetarists

Open market operations

How Monetary Policy Works: An Overview of Monetary Theory

The theory of monetary policy is easy to understand, but, as we shall see, there is much debate about all aspects of it. You will recall that monetary policy is the manipulation of the nation's money supply for the purpose of influencing aggregate demand. Monetary policy is based on the theory that GNP rises and falls with changes in the money supply.

The idea is that, if we increase the money supply, the banks will have more money to lend, interest rates will fall (assuming no change in demand for loans), and, at lower interest rates, consumers and business managers will borrow more and increase consumption spending and investment spending. When these two important components of aggregate demand increase, the *spending multiplier* will cause equilibrium GNP to rise by some multiple of the change in spending.

A quick summary is in order. (1) An increase in M_1 leads to (2) a decrease in interest rates, which (3) leads to an increase in investment spending, which (4) leads to an increase in GNP that is a multiple of the increase in spending because of the spending multiplier.

If we want to slow the economy down in times of inflation, we will decrease (or slow down increases in) the money supply. The banks will have less money to lend and, again assuming no change in demand, interest rates will rise. With less money available for borrowing and higher interest rates, business managers and consumers will be reluctant to borrow. Consumption spending and investment spending will fall. The spending multiplier will cause GNP to fall by some multiple of the decrease in spending.

When the Board sets a chain of events in motion for the purpose of increasing aggregate demand, it is pursuing an *expansionary* or *easy-money policy*. If the Board wants to slow down an increase in aggregate demand by reducing M_1 and raising interest rates to reduce spending, it is pursuing a *contractionary* or *tight-money policy*.

A caution is needed here. This brief version of monetary policy emphasizes changes in interest rates that occur because of increases (shifts) in the supply of money. Interest rates are simply another price, a price people pay for borrowed funds. Like any price, interest rates are determined by the supply of and the demand for funds that can be borrowed. Consequently, our brief statement of monetary policy ignores changes in demand. When the country becomes more prosperous, the demand for money also increases. As GNP grows our incomes grow, and with higher incomes, most of us want to buy more goods and services. We need money for these purchases. Thus, increases in income cause increases in the demand for money.

Consequently, lower interest may encourage increases in borrowing and spending—causing GNP to rise—but, as it does, the demand for money will probably increase. Then, unless the money supply increases faster than the increases in demand, interest rates will rise. Interest rate changes thus help to cause changes in GNP, but GNP changes can cause changes in interest rates.

How the Fed Is Organized

Now we need to see how the Fed is organized, so that then we can see what the Board does to change M_1. Most industrial countries have a so-called *central bank:* the Bank of England, Bank of France, Deutsche Bundesbank of Germany, the Gosbank in the Soviet Union, the Nippon Ginko in Japan. These banks perform a variety of functions, such as issuing paper money, clearing checks, handling their government's checking account, assisting with international balance-of-payments problems, and supervising the operations of banks in their respective countries. In the United States, the Federal Reserve System District Banks are our central bank.

District Banks

The Federal Reserve Act of 1913 was adopted primarily with the support of the Progressive Party, which did not want control of our central bank to be subject to the influence of the financial giants of New York City or any eastern industrial city. Thus, they decided to divide the country into 12 Federal Reserve Districts, with a central bank in each one.

As the country grew in commercial complexity, the 12 District Banks found they needed help in other major cities within their districts and gradually they acquired a total of 24 branches. Consequently, our central bank is now divided up into 36 parts sprinkled across the country. The map in Figure 16-1 shows the 12 districts, the 12 cities in which the main District Banks are located, and the cities where the branch banks are located.

The District Banks in the Federal Reserve System are known as "bankers' banks." Individuals cannot borrow money there or open a checking account, but the District Banks perform many services (see next section) for the commercial banks in their districts.

The System operates like a set of 12 clubs, in the sense that they are district associations to which member banks belong, but the District Banks also supervise the conduct of their members through bank examiners.

Membership in the System

The Federal Reserve System is organized in such a way that it has been called a quasi-public agency. Like any corporation, a commercial bank is owned by stockholders. Upon joining the System, the member commercial banks are required to buy stock in their respective district banks equal to 3 percent of their demand deposits. Another 3 percent is subject to call (a possible disadvantage of joining). However, member banks receive dividends from the profits of the System, up to a maximum of 6 percent of their invested capital. Profits earned by the System in excess of 6 percent are turned over to the U.S. Treasury.

Figure 16-1. The Federal Reserve System: boundaries of Federal Reserve Districts and their branch territories. (Alaska and Hawaii are in District 12.)

Source: *Federal Reserve Bulletin.*

The Federal Reserve System therefore rests on a foundation of private ownership, with private stockholders owning stock in member banks and member banks owning stock in the District Banks. To supervise the system, however, there is a seven-member Board of Governors appointed by the U.S. President. Thus, the System is both public and private in character.

Because the Federal Reserve Act is federal legislation, it could and did require that all commercial banks chartered by the federal government join the System. Any commercial bank with the word "national" in its name is such a bank. However, the banks chartered by the states have the option of joining or not joining, as they please.

Prior to March 31, 1980, there was a major disadvantage to membership. The main reason that banks did not want to join was that the reserve requirements for member banks were generally higher than for nonmember banks. From Chapter 15 you will recall that required reserves for the largest member banks must be between 10 and 22 percent of demand deposits and are usually nearer the higher figure. But prior to March 31, 1980, nonmember banks in some states were permitted required reserves against demand deposits of as little as 6 percent. Such banks had much greater opportunities for profit because they could invest as much as 94 percent of their depositors' money. Although these banks are extreme examples, the required reserves of nonmember banks were, on the average, 2 or 3 percent less than for member banks—an important advantage in finding extra profit.*

When Chicago's Oak Park Trust and Savings Bank withdrew its $9 million reserves from the System in May 1979, its earnings rose in 1979 by $300,000. See Time, 9 January 1980, p. 90.

At the end of 1979 there were 14,700 commercial banks in the United States, of which 5,450 belonged to the Fed. It would appear that the Federal reserve club was of no great consequence because member banks accounted for only 37 percent of the total number of banks. However, the banks that did belong are evidently relatively large banks, inasmuch as 70 percent of all demand deposits in the United States were deposited with them.

But the Fed was worried. Back in 1950, there were 6,873 members, and each year more banks left the System. Chairman of the Board Paul A. Volcker told the Senate Banking Committee on 4 February 1980 that 69 banks had left the system during 1979 with total deposits of $7 billion. He expressed concern that the System's membership might decline to the point where monetary management is "seriously disrupted." Finally, on March 31, 1980, Congress solved the Fed's problem by passing the Depository Institutions Deregulation and Monetary Control Act of 1980. The new law gave the Board more control over the nation's money supply by establishing the same reserve requirements for all commercial banks—whether members of the System or not. Henceforth, there would be no reason to leave the System.

And there were still good reasons for joining: (1) the appearance of extra safety member banks can present to the public, (2) the privilege of borrowing from a District Bank, and (3) the low cost to members of the Fed's check-clearing service.

The Board of Governors

The **Board of Governors** consists of seven people whose backgrounds may be in finance, industry, commerce, or agriculture, but, in practice, they are usually drawn from some area of finance. (See box essay.) They are usually appointed by the President of the United States for a fourteen-year term. Consequently, several Board members may represent the political views of a previous President and another political party than that of the current President. The fourteen-year terms are staggered so that every two years a Board member retires and a new one is appointed.

Coordinate bodies of the Board

To help the Board carry out its policies, it is assisted by the Federal Advisory Council and the **Federal Open Market Committee.** The Council, which consists of twelve members, one from each district, helps to provide the Board of Governors with data to guide is decision making.

The Open Market Committee is composed of the seven members of the Board of Governors and five presidents of District Banks. The president of the New York City District Bank is a permanent member. The other four presidents serve annually and are elected by presidents of the other 11 District Banks in such a way that different areas of the country are represented. The committee's power is thus divided between the Board of Governors and the presidents of the District Banks, but the seven-member Board constitutes a majority of the twelve-member Committee. As we shall see later in the chapter, the activities of the Open Market Committee are the Board's most important weapon for changing M_1.

Figure 16-2. Organization of the Federal Reserve System.

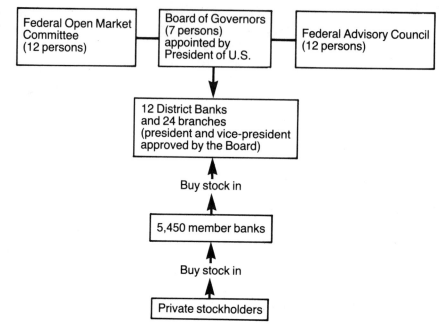

The Board has a close relationship with each of the 12 District Banks. The president and vice-president of each District Bank are appointed subject to approval by the Board of Governors. Approval of these appointments enhances the overall power of the Board and helps to improve the channels of communication with each of the Districts. Figure 16-2 illustrates the organization of the system.

Functions of the Fed   Aside from the methods the Board uses to control M_1, the System issues our paper money, called **Federal Reserve Notes.** It handles the check-clearing mechanism* not only within each district but across the country through what is known as the *Interdistrict Settlement Fund.* In so doing, the Fed not only handles the bookkeeping involved in adding to and subtracting from reserves as checks are cleared, but keeps most member banks' reserves in its possession. We do so much of our business by check that the commercial banks need keep only about 2 percent of their demand deposits on their premises in the form of cash (called *vault cash* or *till money*). The rest is kept by the Fed. This procedure helps the Fed keep track of reserves, provides much more physical safety for the money, and enables the Fed to sort the money continuously for counterfeit or worn-out bills.

Whether a bank's reserves are on their own premises in the form of till money or on deposit with the Fed, they belong to the member bank and

---

Nonmember banks may purchase check-clearing services from the Fed or from private companies.

Presenting—the Board

Because the seven Board members have such immense power and independence, we thought you'd like to meet them. As of October 1979, the seven members of the Board of Governors included three men and one woman nominated by President Carter and three men nominated by President Ford. All but Henry C. Wallich, the member with the longest service, were nominated to fill unexpired terms. Thus, in practice, the current members were not appointed every two years over a fourteen-year period as provided by law. The Chairman, Paul A. Volcker, a 1979 appointee, is from New York, and the Vice-Chairman, Frederick H. Schultz, also appointed in 1979, is from Florida. The two other Carter appointees, Nancy Hays Teeters and Emmett J. Rice, are from Washington, D.C., and Mr. Wallich, Philip E. Coldwell, and Charles J. Partee, are from New York, Missouri, and Texas, respectively. States west of the Continental Divide are not currently represented on the Board.

The youngest member of the Board, Mrs. Teeters, was born in July 1930, and the oldest,

Mr. Wallich, in June 1914. As to education, two members have Ph.D.s in economics (Mr. Wallich and Mr. Coldwell), two have master's degrees in business administration (Mr. Partee and Mr. Rice), two have M.A.s (Mr. Volcker in political economy and government and Mrs. Teeters in economics), and one has a B.A. and two years of law school (Mr. Schultz). All except Mr. Schultz have had experience either with one of the Federal Reserve Banks (Mr. Volcker, Mr. Wallich, and Mr. Rice in New York, Mr. Partee in Chicago, and Mr. Coldwell in Dallas) or on the staff of the Board itself (Mr. Partee and Mrs. Teeters). At the time of his appointment, Mr. Schultz was Chairman of the Board of Barrett Investment Services, Inc., in Florida and had been active in public service throughout his career.

Thus, although there are no occupational or educational requirements for membership on the Board, all current members have had education beyond the bachelor's degree and all of them have had experience in banking, investment, or finance.

jointly serve to determine the bank's reserve position relative to the required minimum.

The System acts as an agent for the federal government by handling (1) the sales of *new* government securities issued by the Treasury (for the purpose of deficit financing), (2) issuing currency, and (3) holding some of the Treasury's deposits.

All members of the System are required to buy insurance from the **Federal Deposit Insurance Corporation (FDIC),** which insures each demand deposit and time deposit in commercial banks up to $100,000.* The banks pay an insurance premium equal to one-twelfth of 1 percent on their deposits for this insurance. Nonmember banks also buy this insurance. Because FDIC insurance now covers almost 99 percent of all deposits in commercial banks, a bank panic or a run on a bank of the kind that was so common during the Depression is now considered completely unnecessary

---

*If your demand deposit or savings accounts total more than $100,000, you can set up other accounts in your spouse's name or jointly with your spouse or a relative and so cover all of your deposits with insurance.

and improbable. Savings and loan institutions also insure deposits up to $100,000 per depositor with the *Federal Savings and Loan Insurance Corporation.*

The FDIC also supervises the operation of banks. Consequently, member banks undergo bank examination by two agencies: the Federal Reserve System and the FDIC.

How the Board of Governors Changes M_1

If the Board wants to give the economy a boost, it will increase M_1 on the theory that such an increase will lower interest rates, which will stimulate more spending by consumers and business firms because of the lower cost of borrowing. If the Board wants to cool the economy in times of inflation, it will reduce M_1, leading to higher interest rates and less spending because loans will be more expensive.

The Board has three methods, called *quantitative controls*, at its disposal for lowering or raising M_1: (1) through its participation in the decisions of the Open Market Committee, called **open market operations,** and through direct control of (2) the discount rate, and (3) the required reserve. These measures are called quantitative controls because they all act on the total quantity of M_1.

The Board can also exercise three so-called *selective* or *qualitative* controls. It can determine down payments (called *margin requirements*) that we must make when we buy stock in the stock market. It can set maximum interest rates member banks can pay on time deposits—called *Regulation Q.* And, it can exert informal pressure on bankers through what is called *"moral suasion."* Moral suasion can also refer to the powerful effects speeches by Board members (usually the Chairman of the Board) have on public attitudes. When a Board chairman says "tight money" is coming, business executives listen and react accordingly.

Open market operations

By far the most important and frequent method of changing M_1 is open market operations—the buying and selling of government securities in the open market by the Board's Open Market Committee.* Government securities in the *open market* are securities that have already been sold by the U.S. Treasury to individuals, corporations, banks, or insurance companies and are owned by someone in the private economy. They are to be distinguished from new government securities purchased from the Treasury. Thus, open market operations are the buying and selling of government securities held by people or institutions in the private economy. Once in the private economy, many of these so-called "marketable" government securities change hands. They are bought and sold at prices that fluctuate around the face value of the security, depending on the forces of demand and supply.

We are deliberately overlooking an organizational detail. The actual buying and selling is done by the "Trading Desk" of the New York District Bank. The Open Market Committee sets the policy.

Figure 16-3. How the Federal Reserve Creates Money.

Step 1

Step 2

Step 3

Step 4

Step 5

Step 6

Increasing M₁

If the Open Market Committee decides that it wants to give the economy a boost through open market operations, the committee will buy government securities in the open market, often in quantities of a billion dollars. Let us suppose the committee decides to buy $1 billion worth of $10,000 government securities on the open market (Figure 16-3, step 1). It looks at the fluctuating market price of these securities (step 2), which might be $9,500 each,* and offers to buy $1 billion worth at a price of $9,600 each. It makes the offer to a select group of stock and bond brokers who specialize in very large transactions. If the brokers are not successful in getting owners of securities to sell to the Fed, the committee would offer a price higher than $9,600, but we shall assume that the brokers do find sellers.

We are using short-term Treasury bills here as an example. The Treasury promises to pay the owner the full $10,000 at time of maturity, but the bill is sold at a discount. The difference between the discounted price and the bill's face value determines the bill's interest rate (which can fluctuate).

TABLE 16-1 Multiplier Effect of Fed's Purchase of $1 Billion in Open Market Treasury Bills (in Millions)

Banks	Demand deposits	Loans	Reserves
As (first round)	$1,000	$ 800	$ 200
Bs (second round)	800	640	160
Cs (third round)	640	512	128
Subtotals	$2,440	$1,952	$ 488
All other banks	2,560	2,048	512
Totals	$5,000	$4,000	$1,000

Where does the Fed get the money for this purchase? The fascinating answer is that the Fed does not get it from *anywhere*. It simply writes checks amounting to $1 billion on itself (step 3). These checks are not written on any checking account. (It is just as if you wrote a check with no money in the bank.) When the checks are received by the sellers of those securities, the sellers deposit them in their commercial banks (step 4). The sellers' banks send the checks to their Fed banks for "clearance" (step 5). The Fed banks honor the checks by adding the amount of the checks to each commercial bank's reserves (step 6). (Why shouldn't the Fed honor the checks? It wrote them in the first place!) Consequently, the initial effect of a $1 billion open market purchase of securities is an increase in commercial bank reserves of $1 billion.

Because everyone, including the commercial banks in which the $1 billion worth of checks are deposited, believes the checks are money, they *are* money. Thus, the Open Market Committee adds $1 billion to M_1. But the story is not over. The deposit multiplier goes to work exactly as in Table 15-2. The commercial banks that initially receive the $1 billion are all first-round banks like the Bank A in Table 15-2 because they receive the first deposit of the money. Then the money gets lent and relent. Table 16-1 illustrates the process (it assumes a 20 percent required reserve).

In Table 15-2, the cash deposited in the Bank A's caused no immediate change in M_1 because the cash was traded for a demand deposit. But in Table 16-1, in the case of open market purchases, the $1 billion deposited in the Bank A's a net addition to M_1 of $1 billion. After the banks lend and relend these new deposits, M_1 will increase by the full $5 billion.

Note in Table 16-1 that member bank reserves go up by $1 billion. Consequently, economists often say that the Treasury Bills were paid for by increasing member bank reserves.

In whatever way you think about it, remember that the securities were paid for *without drawing a check* on any bank account. When the Open Market Committee's checks arrived, they were new additions to M_1.

What happens to interest rates? Assuming that the demand for loans

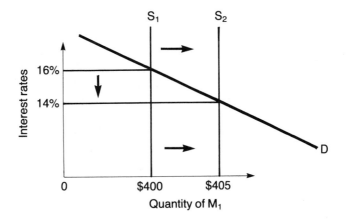

Figure 16-4. Effect of increase of M_1 on interest rates.

does not change, interest rates should fall, because the banks now have excess reserves to lend. (The Bank As had $800 million more to lend after the arrival of the $1 billion.) In Figure 16-4 the supply curves represent the supply of M_1 before and after the securities purchase; D represents the demand for loans and/or money.* The supply curves of money are usually shown as fixed because they are in the control of the Fed. The increase in M_1 shifts supply to the right by $5 billion from a hypothetical supply of $400 billion to $405 billion. Given no change in demand, interest rates will fall from, we will assume, 16 percent to 14 percent. The fall in interest rates will presumably stimulate borowing and spending. If spending *does* increase, GNP will rise by a multiple of the change in spending, owing to the spending multiplier.

Reducing M_1

Now let us assume the Open Market Committee wants to reduce M_1. It can manage this quite easily by selling government securities in the open market. How will it get people to buy? It will sell a $10,000 security at an attractive price, say, $9,300. When the Open Market Committee sells, some of M_1 will vanish into thin air because demand deposits go down when the buyers of the securities write checks to pay the Fed and the Fed reduces member bank reserves as the checks are cleared.

As bank reserves decline, the member banks have to sell assets and reduce loans in order to maintain required reserves, and M_1 declines by a multiple of the securities sale by the Open Market Committee. If the Open Market committee sells $1 billion in securities, member bank reserves and the Fed's holding of government securities will both drop by $1 billion, but M_1 will drop $5 billion, assuming a deposit multiplier of 5.

---

*The demand curve expresses not only the demand for loans but also the demand for M_1. It's the old opportunity-cost problem again. As the interest rate falls, we will prefer to hold money in the form of currency or checking accounts rather than in the form of some interest-earning asset. At high interest rates we will prefer to have more money in savings accounts, less in cash or checking accounts.

Thereafter, interest rates will rise because the banks have less money to lend. The check writing by securities buyers causes reserves to drop, and particularly excess reserves to drop. The money supply curve shifts to the left. Assuming no change in demand, interest rates will rise. The banks will become more choosy about those to whom they lend money. The rise in interest rates will slow down spending (consumption and investment spending) by making loans more expensive, and the economy will become less subject to inflation.* If the Open Market Committee overreacts, aggregate demand may decline too much, and unemployment may rise.

Because the Open Market Committee is free to buy and sell as it chooses, and because its transactions are so frequent, its decisions must be delicate ones. Overreactions in either direction may have serious consequences.

Changing the discount rate

The second, and much less important, way of influencing M_1 is by changing the discount rate—the rate of interest paid by member banks to the Fed when they borrow money.

When a member bank has loaned all of its excess reserves, and it wishes to increase its interest income, it can present evidence of its ownership of loans, stocks or bonds, or other assets as security for a loan from the Fed. Provided that the Fed agrees to the loan, the member bank can lend out still more money with the money obtained from the loan.

Let us assume that the Fed decides to lend $1,000 to the member bank. The Fed may now engage in a common practice in lending—one that could happen to you. If you borrow $1,000 from your bank for one year at 15 percent interest, the bank may subtract (or discount) the 15 percent ($150) from your loan so that you receive only $850, but you must pay back $1,000. The actual interest you pay is 17.6 percent because you are paying $150 for the use of $850. This practice is called *discounting*, and the rate of interest actually charged (the 17.6 percent) is called the **discount rate.**

The Board of Governors has the authority to determine the discount rate on the Fed's loans to member banks. By raising or lowering the discount rate, the Board can encourage or discourage borrowing by the member banks. .

The puzzling fact about the discount rate is that member bank loans are small compared with the money supply. At any time, the Fed's loans to member banks amount to about $1 billion. In a money supply of about $400 billion, such loans only amount to one-quarter of 1 percent of the money supply. However, the discount rate receives a great deal of publicity and does have some effect on the member banks' ability to extend loans to the public. To whatever extent changes in the discount rate affect excess reserves and the volume of loans, the deposit multiplier will again cause a change in M_1 that is a multiple of the initial change in borrowing by the banks.

---

*The experts argue over this point. Less borrowing (because of high interest rates) presumably tends to reduce prices, but, high interest rates increase business costs which tend to push prices up.

You will also see many references to the **prime rate** in the newspapers. The prime rate is the interest rate that commercial banks charge their biggest and best borrowers—large corporations. If the prime rate is 12 percent, the chances are that you or any individual will have to pay at least 18 percent for a loan. The prime rate is determined by the demand for and the supply of money in the banks for large loans.

Changing the required reserve

Within the legal range, the Board of Governors is also free to choose the required minimum that member banks must keep in reserves. Changes in the required reserve within the legal range of 10 to 22 percent are considered very strong medicine and occur very infrequently. It was once estimated that a one-half of 1 percent increase in required reserves meant that banks had to withdraw $500 million from circulation, resulting in a $2.5 billion (5 × $500 million) reduction in M_1. Between November 1972 and April 1978, the required reserves were increased only five times, each time by less than 1 percent.

To sum up: If the Board of Governors wants to increase GNP, it will buy securities, and/or lower the discount rate, and/or lower the required reserve. If the Board wants to slow the economy down—to reduce inflation—it will sell securities, and/or raise the discount rate, and/or raise the required reserve.

What limits the money supply?

The ability of the Open Market Committee to create new money through open market purchases raises a fascinating and important question. Now that the committee no longer has to pay any attention to the gold supply backing for the dollar, what prevents it from expanding M_1 by *any* amount? Instead of $1 or $2 billion, why not add $10 billion or a $100 billion? If the Open Market Committee wanted to, it could do just that, and we would soon be so flooded with new money that our money would become almost worthless, like German money after World War I and Hungarian money after World War II. A condition called **hyperinflation** (skyrocketing prices) would occur.

There is no *legal* limitation on the Board's freedom to expand the money supply by any amount. When asked what did limit the Board's open market purchases, the manager of a District Bank once told the author, "Only the integrity of the people on the Board." Their integrity prevents us from having hyperinflation.

The independence of the Board

The Board can, therefore, if it wants to, increase the money supply by any amount. The Board can also reduce the money supply by any amount, and if it wanted to, it could create a severe recession.

There is no doubt that the Board has enormous power. Once in office, Board members are as immune from the influence of the President and his

(continued on page 340)

The Role of the U.S. Treasury

What does the Treasury do?

What does the Treasury do? Where does the money come from in the first place?

Functions of the Treasury.   The Treasury has five basic functions: (1) It recommends fiscal policy changes to the President (along with the President's Council of Economic Advisors). (2) It serves as the financial agent of the government, collecting taxes and paying the government's expenses. (3) It aids law enforcement (Customs; Secret Service; Bureau of Alcohol, Tobacco, and Firearms). (4) It manufactures coins and Federal Reserve Notes. (5) It plays a role in monetary policy. If we examine (4), we can explain where the money comes from, and thereby understand (5).

Where the money comes from.   The Treasury manufactures all of the coins and paper money. Following manufacture, the money is shipped to the 12 Federal Reserve Districts in quantities re-quested by each District. (To the left of George Washington's picture on a $1 bill, you will see a circle giving the name of the Federal Reserve Bank that issued the bill. A number and letter also identify the Federal Reserve District.) The money becomes the responsibility of someone in each district called the Federal Reserve Agent, usually the president of the District Bank. After the quantities are verified, the money is placed in the District Bank vault.

Member banks obtain the money by paying for it with their reserves. If, for example, a member bank wants $1 million in cash, it can obtain it only by having its *reserve account* reduced by that much. Thus the arrival of new money is entirely controlled by the size of member bank reserves. If nonmember banks need cash, they must obtain it through the services of a member bank.

The cash then flows through the commercial bank to the public in accordance with the public's

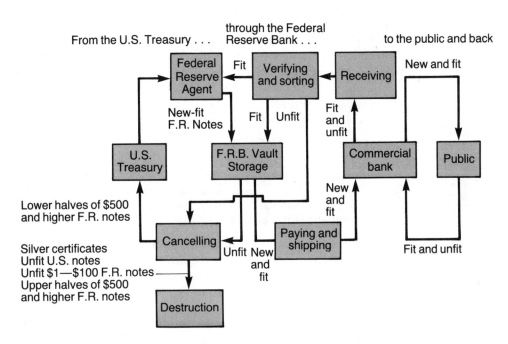

From the U.S. Treasury . . .   through the Federal Reserve Bank . . .   to the public and back

Flow of currency.

Source: *Fundamental Facts About U.S. Money,* Federal Reserve Bank of Atlanta, pamphlet, p. 9.

demand for it and ability to pay for it. The public's ability to pay will be controlled by the size of the public's bank deposits or its ability to obtain credit.

The money flows back to the Fed as the commercial banks deposit unneeded reserves with it, and the money is carefully counted and sorted to identify counterfeit bills and "unfit" ones. Such bills are destroyed and replaced by new bills from the Treasury.

The flow of coins and paper money from the Treasury through the banks to the public and back again is shown in the chart above.

The Treasury's role in monetary policy. The Treasury definitely has an effect on M_1 that is quite separate from the activities of the Board of Governors. The Treasury continuously receives money from tax collections and/or from the sale of government securities. These monies are kept in Treasury deposits (called Treasury Tax and Loan Accounts) either in commercial banks or in the Federal Reserve District Banks. The Treasury then issues checks drawn on these deposits to meet the expenses of government.

The location of these deposits has a direct bearing on M_1. If the deposits are in commercial banks, the commercial banks can count the deposits as part of their reserves and extend that much more credit to borrowers. But the Treasury may decide that these additional loans are contributing to inflation. If so, the Treasury withdraws the money from the commercial banks and deposits it instead in one or more of the District Banks. Such withdrawals reduce commercial banks' reserves, reduce their ability to lend, and, inevitably, reduce borrowing and spending. By adding to or subtracting from deposits kept in the commercial banks, the Treasury can play an important role in the level of spending.

cabinet as are the Supreme Court justices. Only an Act of Congress can change the independence of the Board. And such independence was undoubtedly the intent of members of the Progressive Party who supported the Federal Reserve Act. They wanted to put the Board into a kind of political vacuum apart from the interests of bankers in the 12 districts and independent of political storms in Washington, D.C. Nevertheless, there is an occasional attempt by members of Congress to change the law and put control of the Board in the executive branch of government.

Former Chairman of the Board Arthur Burns, whose term of office was 1970–1978, gave this strong answer to those who wish to make such a change:

> I doubt that the American people would want to see the power to create money lodged in the Presidency—which may mean that it would in fact be exercised by political aides in the White House. Such a step would create a potential for political mischief or abuse on a larger scale than we have yet seen.[1]

But making the Fed more subservient to the wishes of the Presidency, or the Congress, is not easy for the Fed's enemies, because the Fed doesn't depend on Congress for appropriations. Income from its own operations more than supports the system. In fact, the Fed annually turns over to the Treasury $5 to $7 billion in surplus funds. On the other hand, the Board is required, since 1978, to report semiannually to the Congress its targets for changes in the money supply. And the Open Market Committee makes public at each monthly meeting its operations for the previous thirty days.

Nevertheless, these gestures fail to satisfy some of the Fed's most influential critics. Led by Professor Milton Friedman of the University of Chicago, a group of economists called **monetarists** believe that changes in the money supply are *the* most important determinant of change in GNP and the level of employment—more important even than fiscal policy changes. *No one* should have the power to tinker with the money supply, they believe. And moreover, they say, the Board of Governors has usually done the wrong thing at the wrong time.

The Monetarists' Case

Professor Friedman and the monetarists believe that changes in the money supply are considerably more important than changes in fiscal policy in changing GNP and aggregate demand. They also argue that the basic source of inflation is the faster growth in the quantity of money than in output. Let's now present the monetarist "case." What is the evidence? Table 16-2 tends to show they are right.

The table clearly shows that, while real GNP grew 29 percent from 1970 through 1979, M_1 grew more than twice as fast. Inflation had to result.

The equation of exchange

Many economists believe that increases in supplies of money and near money that are available to the public for spending are responsible for inflation. After all, if your supply of money is down, you'll spend less. If it goes up, you'll spend more.

TABLE 16-2 Real GNP, M_1, and Consumer Prices (real GNP and M_1 in billions)

Year	Real GNP (1972 dollars)	M_1	Consumer Price Index
1970	$1,075	$220	116.3
1979	1,431	380	217.4
Percent change 1970–1979	+29%	+73%	+87%

Source: *Economic Report of the President, 1980.*

In macroeconomic terms, if M_1 is $400 billion and GNP is $2,000 billion, M_1 has to be respent five times to buy the $2,000 billion worth of goods and services that GNP represents. The number of times M_1 turns over to equal GNP is called the *income velocity* of money. It is abbreviated V. Thus,

$$M_1 \times V = GNP$$

GNP is also the sum of all prices times quantities. If we abbreviate the prices of everything as P and the quantities of everything as Q, then $GNP = PQ$. And, because GNP also equals M_1V, then $M_1V = PQ$.

After all, if your supply of money is down, you'll spend less.

$$GNP = M, V \qquad GNP = PQ \qquad \boxed{M, V = PQ}$$

This equation is called the *equation of exchange* and is sometimes helpful in explaining inflation. Over the last twenty-five years, V has shown a tendency to increase from about 4 to 5. This means that people are willing to spend their money faster. An income velocity of 4 means that people will turn M_1 over four times a year, or every three months. If V is 5, M_1 turns over every 2.4 (12 ÷ 5) months.

On the average, the quantity of goods and services produced (Q) changes slowly—about 3 percent per year in real terms. Therefore, a double cause of inflation could exist: Prices will certainly increase if the money supply (M_1) *and* income velocity (V) increase faster than increases in the quantity of goods and services (Q) produced. When this combination of events occurs, economists say, "There is too much money chasing too few goods." Inflation is bound to occur.

Inflation, the money supply, and the deficit

The monetarists also argue that gigantic deficit spending by the federal government is inevitably linked to the money supply and therefore to inflation. They point to the fact that deficit spending in the 1965–1979 period totaled almost $350 billion. This argument is important because it reminds us that fiscal policy (in this case, deficit spending) does *not* operate in a vacuum, independent of monetary policy.

When the U.S. Treasury has to sell securities to finance a deficit, an M_1 of sufficient size to buy them has to be present. The Fed's Board can guarantee that M_1 will be of sufficient size by engaging in open market purchases. You will recall that the Open Market Committee simply "writes a check" for these securities. The check is not written on any bank account. The Fed records the amount of the purchase as an increase in member bank reserves. The member banks then have more money to lend out.

Some writers refer to the effect of this practice as "printing money." The Board can guarantee a market for any U.S. Treasury sales of securities that are necessary to finance a deficit through open market purchases, and those purchases will expand M_1 just as if the Fed had printed the money.

Crowding out—once more

The Board's ability to facilitate deficit spending reminds us of the "crowding out" argument mentioned on page 309. Remember that deficit spending tends to raise interest rates, thus raising the cost of private borrowing and spending. When interest rates start to climb as a result of deficit spending, the Board may engage in open market operations to expand M_1 to keep interest rates low, offsetting the crowding-out effect of deficit spending. But if the Board follows this line of action, the effect of deficit spending will be doubly inflationary: (1) from increases in aggregate demand caused by increases in government spending and (2) from increases in the money supply designed to maintain private spending.

The monetarists' prescription

If you get the feeling that the monetarists have had little faith in the Board, you're right. Here is what the monetarists prescribe: Let the Board take whatever quantitative measures are necessary to increase the money supply at a steady rate of 4 percent per year, in good times and bad—no deviations. The 4 percent increase is based on the assumption that this is the increase in *real* GNP necessary to provide enough jobs for the new people entering the labor force plus those displaced by machines. Thus, the monetarist position says, "Let the Board continue in its present role, but limit it to a goal that never changes."

Supporters of the monetarist view hold that the steady 4 percent growth in the money supply would act like a countercyclical governor on an engine—acting constantly to prevent it from slowing down too much (recession) or speeding up too much (inflation). Opponents of the monetarist view argue that depriving the Board of its power in this manner would prevent the Board from acting quickly during times of urgent need. The winter of 1976–1977 is a good example. Snowstorms in the Midwest and Northeast forced plants to close and increased unemployment. The same winter brought drought and threatened economic disaster to the West. During such times, the opponents would argue, the Board must be free to expand the money supply quickly via open market purchases or reductions in required reserves.

The Board changes course

On October 6, 1979, the Board Chairman, Paul Volcker, announced a change in strategy called by "many analysts . . . one of the most significant shifts of government economic policy in modern U.S. history—with profound implications for the jobs and incomes of Americans . . . for years to come."[2] The Board's shift in policy will probably bring its direction closer to that of the monetarist prescription.

First, some background explanation. As Figure 16-3 (page 335) indicated, interest rates are determined by the demand for and supply of money. Given any demand curve for money, the Board can change interest rates by increasing or decreasing the supply of money. An increase in supply would lower interest rates and encourage borrowing and spending. A decrease would promote the reverse (to control inflation).

On October 6, 1979, the Board recognized the fact that it can control the supply of money but *not the demand for it*; that, in effect, it cannot control interest rates. This recognition was also an admission that previous attempts to control interest rates through changes in M_1 had been doomed to failure, a fact long noted by Professor Friedman.

As Professor Friedman once put it, "the Fed (had) given its heart not to controlling the quantity of money but to controlling interest rates, something it does not have the power to do. The result has been a failure on both fronts: wide swings in both money and interest rates."[3] In other words, if the Board changes the supply of money every time changes in demand (over which the Board has no control) cause changes in interest rates, the result will be wide swings in the money supply.

For example, from October 1977 to September 1978, M_1 grew at an annual rate of 8.1 percent per year. During the following six months, the annual growth rate was a *minus* 0.9 percent. And in the six months after that, ending in June 1979, the annual growth rate was a *plus* 11.6 percent.

Friedman's comment: "Unstable and rising monetary growth has been the major reason for the correspondingly unstable and even more rapidly rising inflation."

And so on October 6, 1979, the Board announced a new policy. Henceforth its policy would be governed, not by interest rates, but by the size of commercial bank reserves.

Why is this change so important? The size of bank reserves is much more important than the size of the money supply (by any definition), because, for the *whole banking system*, every dollar in reserves supports about $5 in demand deposits (assuming required reserves are 20 percent). Thus, small changes in reserves can lead to much larger changes in M_1.

The Board will raise and lower the economy's temperature by its usual methods of open market operations, changes in discount rates, and changes in required reserves, but will use a different thermostat to measure the heat in the furnace. This new direction is much to the monetarists' liking, because in its first four months of operation, the new policy produced a slow, steady increase in M_1 projected to average about 5 percent per year. But the new policy's effect on inflation is still an unknown. Professor Friedman once estimated that there is a twenty-month lag between a change in M_1 and a measurable effect on prices.

Can Monetary Policy Work?

First, we should note that it is too early to tell. Perhaps by 1982 we will know if the Board's new policy has succeeded in controlling inflation. Second, we should remember that no one set of policies designed to influence aggregate demand can do the job. Those who design discretionary fiscal policy (changes in government spending and taxes) must cooperate with the Board (and vice versa) to achieve any degree of effectiveness.

One general observation about monetary policy is that it appears to be a more powerful weapon for *reducing* aggregate demand than for increasing it. Economists sometimes use the old saying, "you can lead a horse to water, but you can't make him drink," to describe this difficulty. By that, they mean that a strong tight-money policy designed to raise interest rates (open market sales of government securities, increased legal reserve requirements, and increased discount rates) will reduce member bank reserves and M_1 and will slow down the economy. But, if the Board wants to give the economy a boost with an *easy-money* policy (open market purchases, lower reserve requirements, and lower discount rates), it can increase bank reserves, but it cannot *force* the banks to lend the money. Particularly in a time of depression, the banks may want to be very conservative about lending money. Thus, monetary policy may be more effective as a contractionary than as an expansionary weapon.

But even when we consider the Board's effectiveness in slowing the economy, we have to remember the presence of $1,667 billion worth of near money shown in Table 15-1. This reservoir of funds enables business firms and individuals to convert their near money to M_1 and continue spending.

This immunity from a tight-money policy is especially true of large corporations, which typically hold the largest quantities of near money and are also more likely to be able to pass on to buyers the burden of higher interest costs in the form of higher product prices. Smaller businesses will tend to suffer more than larger ones in periods of tight money.

Economists recognize that a tight-money policy may affect the economy unevenly, that it discriminates against particular industries such as the construction industry and especially against home building and buying. A tract developer typically operates on borrowed money, and the home buyer typically finances his or her purchase with a mortgage. Both the selling and buying ends of the business depend on borrowed money, and the interest rate becomes an important cost in the transaction.

Where does all this leave us? One might conclude that both fiscal policy and monetary policy are doomed to failure, or at least that the real world is too complicated to be manipulated successfully. Our answer is that we must continue to refine our monetary and fiscal tools. Not to do so would be to admit that the problems are hopeless. Moreover, virtually all economists agree that we already know enough about fiscal and monetary policy to prevent a recurrence of the Great Depression of the 1930s.

Summary

Only 37 percent of all commercial banks are members of the Federal Reserve System, but these banks hold 70 percent of all demand deposits. The Federal Reserve System issues paper money, carries the federal government's checking accounts, handles the sale of government securities for the Treasury, supervises member banks, and clears their checks. The Federal Reserve System's Board of Governors, a seven-member board appointed by the President, runs the system.

The Board uses three quantitative methods to change M_1—open-market operations, changes in the discount rate, and changes in the required reserve. If the Board wants to control inflation, it may sell government securities in the open market and/or raise the discount rate and the required reserve. These measures are called tight-money policies. If the Board wants to give the economy a boost, it pursues easy-money policies by buying government bonds in the open market and/or lowering the discount rate and required reserve.

The Board's power is primarily controlled by its own integrity and by the Congressional perorgative to review Board policies every six months. Nevertheless, there have been many attempts to put the Board under the control of the executive branch, a move Arthur Burns believed to be in contradiction with the intent of the Federal Reserve Act of 1913, the Act that created the system.

On October 6, 1979, Board Chairman Paul Volcker announced a new policy whereby the Board would watch changes in commercial bank reserves rather than interest-rate changes in formulating its policies to change the money supply.

Monetary policies may be more effective in reducing aggregate demand than in expanding it, and certain industries like housing may suffer more than others during periods of tight money.

Discussion Questions

1. Where does the Fed get the money to make open market purchases?

2. What effect does the U.S. Treasury have on monetary policy?

3. Why is the 6 October 1979 policy change important?

4. List all of the measures you would propose as a member of the Board of Governors in times of inflation. Explain why your proposals might or might not work.

5. Why might the policies of the Board of Governors be more effective when they are contractionary than when they are expansionary? Explain.

References

1. Arthur F. Burns, "The Independence of the Federal Reserve System," *Challenge*, July–August 1976, p. 23.

2. "Fed Taking Major Gamble to Halt Inflation," *Los Angeles Times*, 21 October 1979, pt. i, p. 1.

3. *Newsweek*, 20 August 1979. See also *Newsweek*, 14 June 1976, 30 October 1978, and 19 February 1979.

17 Is "Fine Tuning" Possible?

© Rose Skytta/ Jeroboam, Inc.

This chapter—the last of the chapters about macroeconomic theories and problems—concerns our most perplexing problem: how to have relatively full employment without inflation. Keynesian theory showed us how to climb out of depressions, and for a while, until the mid-1970s, economists believed they had found the keys to everlasting prosperity. But since the mid-1970s, the persistent presence of inflation and unemployment has sent the experts back to their drawing boards. Many of the experts agree that Keynesian theory can start the engine in a depression, but that we don't know how to "fine-tune" the engine, we don't know how to keep the economy purring along efficiently at a reasonable speed without a good deal of coughing and sputtering. The purpose of this chapter is to show why "fine tuning" is extremely difficult and to present some new ideas about how it might be accomplished.

Key Words	Structural unemployment
Stagflation	Full employment
Demand-pull inflation	The new unemployment
Cost-push inflation	Job participation rate
Profit-push inflation	Phillips Curve
Frictional unemployment	Rational expectations
Cyclical unemployment	Supply-side fiscalism

The combination of high prices and high rates of unemployment that has characterized our economy in recent years is called **stagflation** (from "stagnation"—recession and unemployment—and "inflation"). Our discussion of stagflation is divided into four parts: (1) the causes of inflation, (2) unemployment in theory and practice, (3) stagflation: the nature of the disease, and (4) some ideas about what might be done.

The Causes of Inflation

Remember that inflation is a rise in average prices and that the consumer price index has more than doubled since its base year, 1967. Moreover, as we saw in Figure 12-4, the rate of inflation is accelerating.

There are three major causes of inflation. We have already examined one of them in some detail in Chapter 16—deficit spending and increases in the money supply that exceed the growth in real GNP. That cause was simply "too much money chasing too few goods" so that prices have to rise. We'll call this cause the "money-supply theory."

Demand-pull inflation

Closely associated with the money-supply theory is the idea that if increases in aggregate demand occur when the economy is at full (or high) employment, prices will be pulled up by demand. This type of inflation is often called "classical" inflation because the classical economists assumed we would always have full employment, and **demand-pull inflation** occurs with full employment.

Figure 17-1 is a Keynesian picture of demand-pull inflation. Increases in government spending help to shift demand from D_1 to D_2. No price changes will result if GNP is far below full employment. The increases in government spending help to move the economy toward full employment without inflationary side effects.

But as the economy approaches full employment, aggregate supply curves upward to indicate that producers will have a tougher and tougher time increasing the quantity supplied despite increases in market prices. If demand increases at these near-full-employment levels of output, prices will be pulled up (from P_2 to P_3).

What to do? Keynesian theory had the answer. We control demand-pull inflation by lowering aggregate demand. Tighter money, higher taxes, and less government spending should do the trick.

Figure 17-1. Demand-pull inflation.

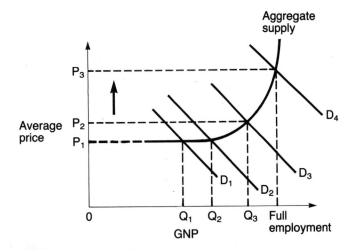

Cost-push or profit-push inflation

Enter the villain. The theory that there will be no overall increase in the price level until demand exceeds supply at full employment was generally accepted until a recession occurred in 1957–1958. During this period, the unemployment rate rose from 4.1 percent in 1956 to 4.3 percent in 1957 and 6.8 percent in 1958. At the same time, industrial production fell 6.5 percent. On

Tighter money, higher taxes, and less government spending should lower aggregate demand.

the other hand, prices, which had been almost stable during the preceding five years, rose 3.6 percent from 1956 to 1957 and 2.7 percent from 1957 to 1958.

Economists began to suspect that something was wrong with the demand-pull theory. Inflation was occurring during periods of rising unemployment and poor business. Their suspicion was confirmed by another business slowdown in 1969–1970, when industrial production fell 3.5 percent, unemployment rose from 3.5 percent to 4.9 percent, but prices increased almost 6 percent in spite of the business decline. Again in 1974 and 1975, prices rose an average of 10 percent, while unemployment averaged 7 percent during the two-year period. And in 1979, prices rose 13 percent, while the unemployment rate was stuck at 6 percent.

Something other than demand-pull was clearly responsible for rising prices during periods of high unemployment. The new theory was called **cost-push inflation.** The term "cost-push" implies that strong unions can force large corporations to grant higher wages, and these higher wages force employers to raise prices even during periods of business slowdown and rising unemployment. So inflation, the theory goes, is caused by the power of the unions.

The unions' retort is that large corporations have so much oligopoly or monopoly power that they can raise prices regardless of increases or decreases in cost, resulting in **profit-push inflation.**

Economists often describe cost-push or profit-push inflation as the effect of *administered prices*. To economists, the term means that corporate executives are able to make administrative decisions about prices that are independent of demand conditions in the economy. This idea leaves open the question of whether the executives' price policy was imposed by rising labor costs or by an urge for larger profits. Nonetheless, it *does* indicate that the corporation's price policy was made possible only because it had sufficient market power to be immune to overall economic conditions.[1]

Any analysis of profit-push or cost-push inflation is complicated by the fact that events external to an industry can start an inflationary spiral. The best examples are, of course, an interruption in the flow of oil imports or a new round of price increases imposed by the OPEC countries.* Resulting shortages send shock-waves of higher costs and prices throughout the economy.

Often cost- and profit-push and demand-pull inflation are involved in this kind of event. Consider, for example, the retail prices of diesel fuel which rose from around 55 cents per gallon in August 1978 to $1 a year later. As

---

*Inflation is often related to international events. The international causes of inflation include higher prices of major imports like oil, but inflation in, say, the United States is inevitably tied to inflation in other countries and also to the value of U.S. currency in relation to the currency of other countries. If the international exchange value of the dollar falls because we have been buying too much oil, the OPEC countries will want to raise their dollar prices still further, requiring us to offer still more dollars for oil, which further weakens the dollar, which then calls for another OPEC price hike, and on and on. We will discuss this further in Part 5.

Figure 17-2. Cost- or profit-push inflation.

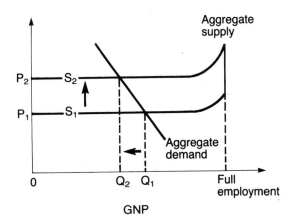

oil prices began to rise, there was a corresponding rise in the prices of gasoline and diesel fuel because of OPEC-created cost-push reasons. At the same time, the demand for diesel cars began to rise faster than for gasoline-using cars, as people discovered that diesel fuel was cheaper than gasoline and provided more miles per gallon.

The prices of diesel fuel and diesel cars were pulled up by demand. And as the number of diesel cars increased, gas stations offering diesel fuel engaged in profit-push price increases to the point where diesel prices in late 1979 were about the same as gasoline prices (even though diesel fuel costs less than gasoline to refine).

Figure 17-2 helps to explain cost or profit-push inflation. Assume the economy is operating at Q_1 GNP, a level far below full employment—perhaps during a recession with high unemployment rates of 7 to 8 percent. Nevertheless, large corporations, for cost-push or profit-push reasons, raise prices from P_1 to P_2. How can they get away with this during a recession? You know the answer. A producer can raise prices any time consumers can't find competitors who offer lower prices. Note also that at the higher P_2 price, the quantity demanded will drop. Those same producers may have to lay off workers as a result of the price increase. Now we can begin to get a picture of the disease of the '70s: rising prices *and* rising unemployment.

Do the producers—for example, the oil companies—mind reduced sales? Probably not. If demand is *inelastic*, total revenue will rise with the price increase even though the quantity sold has fallen. (See page 91 for review of elasticity.) Consequently, it is theoretically possible for some large corporation or large union to walk through the cost-push inflationary fires unscathed.

Large unions may be able to walk through the fires relatively unscathed for two reasons: (1) the labor-management contract will usually provide for raises in hourly wages every six months, and (2) because COLA (cost-of-living-adjustment) clauses automatically increase hourly wages with each percentage point change in the consumer price index. By themselves, COLA clauses only partially handle inflation, but in combination with (1) above, a strong-union, labor-management contract can provide increases which approximate the rate of inflation. Between 1967 and 1978, the consumer price index rose 95.4 percent; meanwhile, average hourly earnings increased 164 percent for steelworkers, 140 percent for autoworkers, and 140 percent for the Teamsters.[2]

Now you can see why it is so important to identify the cause of inflation. If inflation is money related or caused by demand-pull, the tools of fiscal and monetary policy can slow down aggregate demand. But if the cause is cost- or profit-push in nature, we are faced with two grave difficulties: (1) Any attempts to slow inflation down with Keynesian fiscal weapons (increased taxes and reduced government spending) or monetary policy (tight money) may not help. Fiscal-monetary changes will have little effect on the ability of powerful corporations and unions to raise prices and wages. (2) Fiscal or monetary policies designed to reduce inflation will also reduce aggregate demand. Economic activity will slow down and unemployment rates, which may already be unacceptably high, will rise still further. Small firms, small unions, and, in general, people without market power will bear the brunt of these types of antiinflationary policies.

Unemployment in Theory and Practice

In this section, we will first describe three theories of unemployment, then discuss the meaning of full employment, the "new unemployment" created by unemployment compensation programs, and the need for new jobs.

Theories of unemployment

In their efforts to explain why unemployment exists, economists have identified three very broad categories of unemployment: *frictional*, *cyclical*, and *structural*. As we examine each one, ask yourself, "What cure would I recommend? Would my cure be inflationary?"

Frictional unemployment

Frictional unemployment occurs when workers are temporarily unemployed because (1) they are looking for a better job, (2) they are looking for a first job, or (3) they are temporarily laid off because of bad weather (in the construction industry), model changeovers (in the automobile industry), or because the demand for their services is seasonal (migrant farmers, retail clerks).

This type of unemployment is often considered desirable because frictionally unemployed workers may be trying to better themselves voluntarily or employers may be seeking ways to satisfy changes in consumer demand.

Frictional unemployment can often be lessened by matching job seekers with appropriate jobs. One way to accomplish this is to give workers better information about what jobs are available. Research has shown that workers may remain voluntarily unemployed during at least part of their job-changing time. It is generally not in a worker's interest to take the first offer. The continuing job search can be thought of as an *investment* by workers in obtaining more information about the job market. In theory we can reduce this kind of unemployment by lowering costs borne by job hunters in obtaining information about jobs, by providing training, and by subsidizing relocation.

Cyclical unemployment

Unemployment caused by generally poor business conditions is sometimes called **cyclical unemployment** because it is associated with the "trough" of a business cycle. Monetary and fiscal policy can help by lifting aggregate demand. The Fed could encourage spending by increasing the money supply and lowering interest rates; Congress could increase government spending or lower taxes.

Structural unemployment

More serious is **structural unemployment.** The term "structural" means here that a particular industry is having difficulty or that a particular group of people cannot find jobs. Structural unemployment can occur because some products are replaced by new ones (for example, the replacement of adding machines and slide rules by hand calculators). Or environmentalists may cause the closing of a pollution-creating factory. Or machines may replace labor (called *technological unemployment*). *Hard-core unemployment* is another form of structural unemployment. It refers to those who are unemployed because of the unwillingness of employers to hire minority workers, uneducated people, people without skills, or people with special handicaps.

Improved information about available jobs does little to help the situation of unskilled workers who cannot get jobs even when they *know* of the vacancies that exist. The inability of these workers to find jobs is not the result of high information costs but of insufficient investment in their own education and training (human capital). This hypothesis suggests that the appropriate policy to reduce the unemployment of disadvantaged workers is extensive training and skill upgrading. The box essay "Solving a Strange Labor Problem" describes one effort to make sure that the job training offered *really* will help people get a job.

Now that we know something about the causes, and a few of the possible cures, of unemployment, a question remains: What level of unemployment should we try to achieve? What level of unemployment should we call full employment?

Unemployment: Is it under- or overstated?

The experts all agree that **full employment** does not mean zero unemployment. Frictional unemployment and even some forms of structural unemployment are viewed as healthy signs of a growing economy. As you saw in Chapter 14, full employment has in the past been defined as an unemployment rate of about 5.5 percent.

Solving a Strange Labor Problem*

The state of California is trying a new approach to an increasingly common perversity in the labor market, in which young people are unable to find work in a city where employers cannot find workers.

Some California industries—notably electronics, banking, and health care—are forced to recruit workers from other states because they cannot find people here with the skills that they need.

There are a number of reasons for the paradox, but the most important is that there is a very loose connection between the skills being taught in technical schools and the skills being sought in the private sector.

That results in many cases from the fact that school budgets simply cannot cover the expensive new teaching equipment and the refresher courses for teachers that are often required to keep pace with rapid changes in technology and in the skills that the new technology requires.

During the closing days of the recent session, the California Legislature passed a bill, SB 132, sponsored by Sen. Bill Greene (D-Los Angeles), that sets up a new program to match up the skills of the unemployed with the skills that industry needs.

The concept is embarrassingly simple. Instead of putting young people through technical schools and sending them out to look for work, the state will reverse the process.

The Employment Development Department, which functions as a state employment agency in one of its roles, will ask employers what kinds of workers they are looking for, and then train people on their rosters to fill those jobs. . . .

The new program, the California Worksite Education and Training Act, is not yet in full operation. It is more a hope so far than a promise, but the concept is sound, and we have a good feeling about it.

*_Los Angeles Times,_ 10 October 1979, pt. ii, p. 6. Copyright 1979, Los Angeles Times. Reprinted by permission.

There are arguments to the effect that any reported unemployment rate understates the true rate: the rate doesn't show the number of part-time workers who really want to work full time or the number of people who dropped out of the labor force because they became too discouraged to look for a job.

On the other hand, some experts believe that the reported unemployment rate _overstates_ the true rate. They point out that unemployment compensation is making unemployment an attractive alternative to work. Some writers call the unemployment that is induced or prolonged by unemployment compensation **the new unemployment.**[3]

The experience in Massachusetts helps to illustrate the point. With _no change_ in the number of jobs people held in that state, the unemployment rate went from 7.5 percent in October 1974 to 11.1 percent in October 1975, then back down to 7.1 percent in October 1976.[4]

How could the unemployment rates change so much when the number of people employed stayed the same? The increase in 1975 is attributed entirely to an increase in unemployment benefits that became effective January 1975. The number of people claiming unemployment benefits rose by 100,000. Then, in 1976, the governor and the state legislature tightened the

"This is where we register for the postgraduate economics course."

Copyright 1975 by Herblock in *The Washington Post*.

state's unemployment compensation requirements, making it impossible for people who quit their jobs voluntarily to collect benefits. The result? The Massachusetts labor force declined by 120,000 people. The number of people at work increased by 19,000, and the unemployment rate plummeted. National data indicate that our present unemployment policies add between 1 and 2 percent to the unemployment rate.[5]

The problem is that unemployment compensation is often so good that the unemployed worker has little incentive to work. Let's look at one example involving a working couple with two children. The husband makes $6,000 a year, or $500 per month. Out of that, he pays $134 a month in income tax and social security taxes, leaving a net income of $366 per month. But if he is unemployed for a month, he will receive $302 in unemployment compensation that is *tax free*—just $64 less than if he worked. The loss of $64 is 12.8 percent of his gross pay of $500. This means that if the man works, 87.2 percent (100 − 12.8) of the *extra* income he gets from working is lost through taxes. His extra (marginal) income is taxed at a 87.2 percent rate. So why work if one can only become *12.8 percent* better off by working.[6]

Two solutions to the unemployment compensation problem suggest themselves: (1) eliminate o reduce unemployment compensation for those who quit voluntarily; (2) install a nationwide plan that gives workers a chance to keep more than 12.8 percent of the extra income they get if they work.

The need for *new* jobs

Unfortunately, finding jobs for people who want them is not enough. It has been estimated that the U.S. economy must create 72,110 *new* jobs *every week* during the 1980s. That translates into 3.75 million *new* jobs every year for ten years.[7] This is quite a challenge in view of the fact that the number of people actually employed in the civilian labor force grew an average of only 1.25 million per year from 1974 to 1980.

Why do we need so many new jobs? The jobs are needed in three categories: (1) for people seeking work for the first time; (2) for the unemployed, in order to reduce the unemployment rate to 5.5 percent by 1985; and (3) for workers displaced by automation.

And we need more jobs for another special reason. The number of people who *want* to work is increasing. The percentage of men who want to work is dropping, but the addition of increasing numbers of women who want jobs each year more than makes up for the exodus of the men. These data are measured by what are called job participation rates. The **job participation rate** is the percentage of all those over 16 years of age in the labor force as a percentage of the total population over 16 years old. The *labor force* (for purposes of computing the job participation rate) is defined as all those over 16 who are counted as employed (including members of the armed forces) plus those counted as unemployed. Table 17-1 shows the decrease in job participation rates for men, the increases for women, and the net increases overall.

The percentages in Table 17-1 conceal the magnitude of the changes. Women in the labor force will increase in number from 23.2 million in 1960 to 49.3 million in 1990—an increase of about 112 percent! During the same period the number of men in the labor force will increase from 48.9 million to 67.3 million, an increase of only 38 percent. The total labor force will increase from 72.1 million in 1960 to 116.6 million in 1990. If all these people want to work, some means of satisfying them will have to be found.

Now let us take a closer look at the problem of stagflation, the simultaneous presence of inflation *and* unemployment.

TABLE 17-1 The Changing Size and Composition of the Labor Force

	Job participation rates (in percent)	
	1960	1990 (est.)
Men	82.4%	76.7%
Women	37.1	51.4
Both sexes	59.2	73.5

Source: *Statistical Abstract of the United States, 1976*, table 570.

Figure 17-3. An imaginary Phillips Curve.

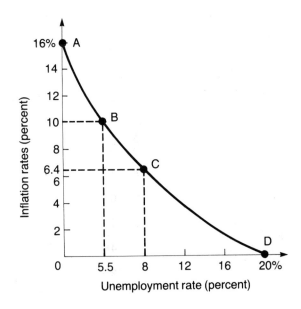

Stagflation: The
Nature of the
Disease

One of the most provocative ideas in economics has been that there was a trade-off between inflation and unemployment. The idea was that we can reduce unemployment by increasing aggregate demand, but that will increase the rate of inflation. Or we can reduce the rate of inflation by reducing aggregate demand, but that will increase unemployment.

The Phillips Curve:
trading inflation for
unemployment—or
the reverse

The trade-off was illustrated by a curve called the **Phillips Curve,** after its inventor, the British economist A. W. Phillips. An imaginary Phillips Curve is shown in Figure 17-3.

Point A on the curve shows that we could have zero unemployment, but the rate of inflation would be a horrendous 16 percent. At the other extreme, point D shows that we could have a zero inflation rate, but the rate of unemployment would be a horrendous 20 percent. Points B and C are intermediate points. At point C, things are better than at point D—in fact about what they were in 1976. The inflation rate is 6.4 percent, but the unemployment rate is 8 percent—considerably above the full-employment rate of 5.5 percent shown at point B. We can get to point B by increased spending, but only at the cost of having the inflation rate rise to 10 percent.

The point of all this is that, if Professor Phillips is right, we *can* reduce inflation or unemployment if we want to. There is a price tag for each action, but at least we know what the price (cost) is.

Now, however, we realize that the choices are not that easy. Changes in aggregate demand, as we have learned, do not change inflation if it is cost-push or profit-push in nature. Nor will changes in aggregate demand reduce unemployment if the cause is structural. In other words, the Phillips Curve assumes that inflation is demand-pull and that unemployment results from inadequate demand.

Figure 17-4. The Phillips Curve in chaos.

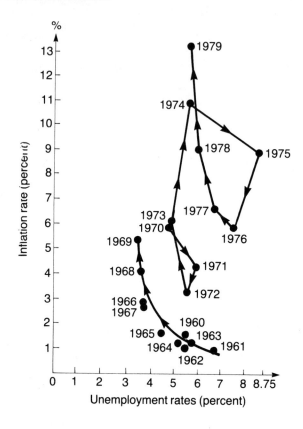

Figure 17-4 shows what has happened to the Phillips Curve in the real world. Note that during the years 1960–1965 there does seem to be a Phillips Curve. Thereafter, however, chaos sets in and the pattern disappears.

What happened after 1965?

Look at the dots for 1966, 1967, 1968, and 1969. If you look only at those years, the Phillips Curve is not a curve at all. It is a straight, vertical line. What does that mean?

Remember that Phillips's idea was that an increase in the rate of inflation would reduce the rate of unemployment, and vice versa. During the late 1960s, the rate of inflation clearly went up, but the drop in unemployment was negligible. A small, black cloud had appeared on the scene. An increase in the inflation rate did *not* reduce the rate of unemployment. At the time, no one worried because the unemployment rates in those particular years were below the 5.5 percent full-employment rate. Demand-pull inflation was undoubtedly the cause.

After 1969, the pattern disappears. The rates of inflation were higher (except for 1971 and 1972) than in the 1960s, and the unemployment rates have usually been higher than 5.5 percent. If we can glean anything from Figure 17-4, it is that the curve (if there is one) seems to be shifting to the right. If this is the case, every inflation rate will either be associated with a higher rate of unemployment, or every unemployment rate will be associated with a higher rate of inflation. A black picture!

A number of explanations have been offered for the surfacing of these symptoms:

1. During the period from 1965 to 1969, while we were fighting the Vietnam war, the Johnson Administration engaged in $42.5 billion worth of deficit spending, not only to fight the war but also to finance a variety of new "Great Society" measures to help the poor. None of this additional spending was offset by tax increases. And the additional spending (adding to the income stream) came during a time when the unemployment rates were *less* than the full-employment rate of 5.5 percent from 1966 through 1969. Prices began to rise. Prior to the 1965–1969 period, the inflation rate was less than 2 percent per year. By 1970 the inflation rate was 5.9 percent.

2. The Nixon Administration's system of price controls, in effect from 1971–1973, collapsed from political pressure, a collapse that resulted in higher-than-before-controls rates of inflation when the lid came off. (The inflation rate was 3.3 percent in 1972, 6.2 percent in 1973, and *11* percent in 1974!)

3. Shipments to the Soviet Union of almost our entire grain reserve in 1972 led to skyrocketing food prices.

4. The doubling and quadrupling of oil prices following the OPEC oil embargo in the winter of 1973-1974 contributed to higher prices for everything.

5. The excessive stimulation of demand during the 1970s by government deficit spending (the $350 billion worth of deficits mentioned on page 342) and "easy" money put still more upward pressure on prices.

These five reasons help to explain the recent surge of prices, but what do they have to do with unemployment?

How inflation can cause unemployment   As we have seen, the Phillips theory holds that inflation and unemployment operate like a seesaw. If inflation goes up, unemployment goes down and vice versa, as follows:

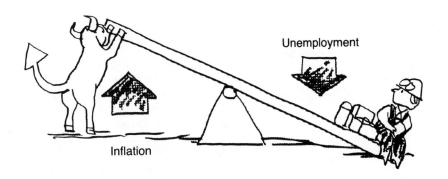

Unemployment

Inflation

Inflation   Unemployment

But recent experience has taught us that inflation and unemployment do *not* necessarily have a trade-off relationship. They can both go up together.

We used to think a little inflation was a good thing. A rise in prices usually meant that business executives were optimistic about the future, that they saw strong demand for their products, and that they were hiring more people. Unconsciously, we believed that inflation was demand-pull; that rising prices signaled either full employment or recovery from a recession.

We did not stop to think about the possibility that everyone would start to accept inflation as a long-term way of life, in good times and bad. And when they did, everyone would try to anticipate further price increases by "beating the gun." Labor unions, anticipating higher prices, will sensibly demand higher wages. Bankers will want higher interest rates on loans. And as people demand more goods before prices rise, prices *will* rise. Because two decades of inflation have so firmly implanted an expectation of continued inflation in our minds, the chances are that each year we will have to trade higher and higher rates of unemployment for each percentage point of reduced inflation.

How does this happen? Sooner or later, inflation leads to reduced spending by those businesses that are forced to buy less out of fixed budgets or those people who are forced to buy less out of fixed incomes. An example brings this point to life. The Chaffey College newspaper once ran an article about the college athletic budget. Some of the reported dialogue with the basketball coach was as follows:

> *Press:* How much is Chaffey College's athletic budget?
> *Coach:* Our budget fluctuates between $50,000 and $60,000. They increase it by a certain percentage as the cost of living goes up. In other words, they give us an 8% increase in budget, but we find out that we're getting pinched, because the cost of the product has gone up 18% in a single year. A basketball that I could buy five years ago for $10 would now cost about $16. The price has gone up, but the increase in our allotment hasn't gone up. So, instead of buying six basketballs, we're only buying four now.[8]

"One of us should be going down."

By permission of Bill Mauldin and Wil-Jo Associates, Inc. Copyright 1979. *Los Angeles Times,* 18 August 1979, pt. II, p. 4.

That is by no means the end of the story. Inflation caused the purchase of basketballs to drop from six to four. The business firm that supplied the basketballs will lose sales. Workers will be laid off. The firm will buy less leather from suppliers. Suppliers will lay people off. The spending multiplier will cause GNP to fall by a multiple of the initial drop in spending. An increase in prices had led to an increase in unemployment. And, obviously, we cannot blame the coach. He did what he had to do.

How inflation can cause more unemployment

Professor Robert Lucas from the University of Chicago is given major credit for a new, **"rational expectations"** explanation of how inflation can cause more unemployment. It works this way:

Workers know that if the rate of inflation exceeds increases in their *money* wages, their *real* wages (in terms of purchasing power) will fall. Older workers especially, who have had long experience with inflation caused by expansionary fiscal and monetary policies, have "rational" (reasonable) expectations of continuing inflation. They react accordingly by trying to find jobs with higher pay (sending up the rate of unemployment), or, at least, higher pay for the jobs they have.

What are the implications of the rational expectations theory? Again, we return to the idea that continuing inflation is the result of a self-fulfilling prophecy; that, somehow, the expectations of continuing inflation have to be reversed. Workers will have to be given convincing evidence that prices will remain stable. Only then will workers believe that their real wages will remain stable and that their present jobs are paying them fairly.

Professor Lucas and others who share his views believe this change in expectations may take years to accomplish. Why? Because (1) one doesn't change expectations based on a decade of experience overnight and (2) because of the time lags involved with fiscal and monetary policies, noted on pages 284 and 344.

Some Ideas About What Might Be Done

The economics profession is sharply divided on the cure for stagflation, because of differing views of the role of government. Consequently, one can separate economists into two groups—those who believe the government should take responsibility for the problem and those who believe the market-price system will take care of the problem—if given some encouragement through relaxation of government controls. As you can see, it's the old argument between the classical economists and the Keynesians.

The active-role-of-government school favors wage and price controls. The promarket-system school favors an approach called "supply-side fiscalism." We'll now summarize the main elements of each argument.

The argument for wage and price controls

Simply stated, this argument holds that the government must set ceilings on prices and wages because nothing else will work. The argument is based on the fact that the American industrial scene is dominated by giant corporations and unions who have so much market power that their prices and wages cannot be controlled in any other way. For example, in 1975, one-tenth of one percent of all corporations owned 65.1 percent of all of the assets of those corporations. Forty-one percent of all union workers belonged to the 8 largest unions in 1976 (out of a total of 176 unions).[9] Wage bargains and pricing policies involving these giant combinations are immune, so the argument goes, to the forces of competition and to general economic conditions affecting the rest of the economy. They can engage in cost- or profit-push inflation almost as easily as OPEC can raise its prices. Economist Robert Lekachman sums up the argument this way:

> The diagnosis implies the therapy. We desperately need permanent statutory authority to establish criteria for wages and prices, and a permanent federal agency to apply and administer these standards. . . .
>
> The sooner we all face the inescapable fact that our more-or-less "free" economy is a melange of forces, some of them exceedingly powerful, the sooner we shall arrive at two necessary conclusions: In a time of dangerous inflation,

Figure 17-5. A picture of a price or wage ceiling.

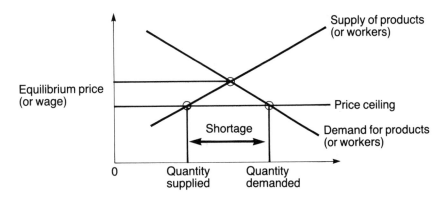

we urgently require mandatory restraints on prices and incomes; and, at all times, government must have in reserve the authority to react quickly to inflationary threats. We shall all be better off for the realization.[10]

The case against controls

The argument against controls reminds us of the effect of any price ceiling (Figure 17-5). Remember that a price ceiling is the *maximum* allowable price. The government initiates the price ceiling because it believes the equilibrium price will be inflationary. The inevitable results: Suppliers will curtail the quantities supplied. (During the Nixon Administration's experiment with price controls, cattle ranchers tried to keep their beef cattle on the hoof rather than sell them. The stores rapidly ran out of beef.) On the other hand, buyers will want to buy more than is being supplied and will end up (1) having to buy something else, or (2) standing in line for what is available (gasoline), or (3) finding a way around the law (black market activities). Economists refer to such consequences as distortions in the allocation of resources.

The opponents of controls cite a long history of their failure, going all the way back to the Roman emperor, Diocletian. In 301 A.D., Diocletian, angry at high prices and the profiteering tactics of merchants, issued an edict setting maximum prices and wages for all important articles and services in the Empire.

"The Edict was until our time the most famous example of an attempt to replace economic laws by governmental decrees. Its failure was rapid and complete. Tradesmen concealed their commodities, scarcities became more acute than before . . . riots occurred, and the Edict had to be relaxed to restore production and distribution. It was finally revoked by Constantine."[11]

Despite this calamity, the urge to control prices and wages, by statutory and other means, has continued. A giant bureaucracy of 60,000 officials supervised controls during World War II. When controls were lifted in 1946, the country suffered the highest annual inflation rate in sixty years (18.2 percent). President John F. Kennedy tried "jawboning" to keep the annual inflation rate under 3.2 percent. This type of effort, continued by President Johnson, dwindled away after a strike in 1966 by aircraft mechanics gave them raises of 5 percent. President Nixon tried controls again between 1971 and 1974. But these gradually were weakened as one business firm or union after another complained that they were being left behind by the firms or unions which had gotten large increases before the controls were instituted. Princeton economists Alan S. Polinder and William J. Newton concluded that by "early 1975 the 1971–74 controls had actually increased inflation by almost one percent over what it would otherwise have been during those years."[12]

In more recent times, President Carter attempted to hold prices and wage increases below 7 pecent, but his guideline was ignored by the Teamsters who won a 9 percent increase in 1979. Thereupon (perhaps to save face), the Carter Administation boosted the guideline to 9.5 percent, only to find that overall price increases in 1979 averaged 13 percent.

The supporters of wage and price controls respond to all this by saying, "Of course, the imposition of controls is going to be tough to enforce, but (1) we need to place controls only on large corporations and unions, and (2) the controls must be left on *indefinitely*, to wipe out any expectation by the participants that they can recover lost wages or profits after the controls are removed."

In the past there was a general understanding that controls were temporary. This understanding encouraged interest groups to exert political pressure on the President to remove controls and led to an explosion of prices and wages when they were lifted.

Supply-side fiscalism: increasing supply to lower prices

The 1970s produced a new line of inquiry into the stagflation problem. Keynesian theory had taken a beating. Demand management via fiscal or monetary policy got a black eye because it was easy for politicians to support expansion (more spending and jobs for everyone) but very difficult to go into reverse to fight inflation. Professor John Galbraith, one of Keynes's greatest admirers, had to admit that "the Keynesian remedy was asymmetrical; it would work against unemployment and depression but not in reverse against inflation. It was a discovery that was only very slowly and reluctantly accepted, and, now, more than thirty years later, there are still some followers of the master who are reluctant to admit the fault."[13]

The new line of inquiry was beautiful in its simplicity. If demand management doesn't work, perhaps we ought to look at *supply*. If we can get supply to increase, given no change in demand, prices will fall. And at lower prices, people will buy more and we will have less unemployment. And even if demand increases, as long as supply increases faster than the increases in demand, prices will still fall.

How do we go about increasing aggregate supply? Several suggestions have been made.

Before we start, let's take one more look at a demand-supply model of the economy. Figure 17-6 repeats the cost/profit-push diagram on page 351.

Figure 17-6. Cost- or profit-push inflation.

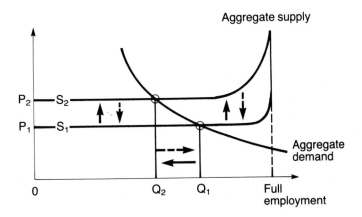

Don't let the arrows pointing upward fool you. They mean that a *decrease* in supply is occurring because suppliers require higher prices for every quantity. The trick is to reverse the arrows—to help suppliers produce every quantity at lower prices (P_1 instead of P_2). At lower prices, the quantities demanded will increase from Q_2 back to Q_1. Business firms will produce more and hire more people. The result will be an ideal combination of lower prices and less unemployment. The dotted arrows in Figure 17-6 show these changes.

How do we produce this desirable situation?

1. Lower business taxes. Give larger tax credits to businesses for investment spending. Reduce or eliminate corporate income taxes.

This idea is based on the fact that productivity in U.S. factories is lagging (a minus 4 percent in the first six months of 1979). We need to modernize our factories and machines to produce more at lower cost. (One caution here: Labor-saving machines may tend to increase unemployment.)

2 Give consumers a reason to save. Why? The idea is simple but extremely important. If we save more we will spend less, putting less pressure on prices. And if we save more, more funds will be available to business firms for investment in capital goods.

The rate of saving in the United States is extremely low—about 4.3 percent of disposable income at the end of 1979. As already noted, we have little incentive to save if inflation and taxes reduce the value of savings. One way to help is to reduce income taxes on interest income. A dramatic example: The Japanese save *20* percent of their disposable income, and they pay no income taxes on interest earned by savings accounts up to $65,000.

3. Reduce the government environmental and safety regulations that cost consumers $100 billion in 1980 (see page 147.) Although we will have to guard against pressures to relax pollution rules, we can certainly dispose of rules which are nonsensical and conflicting. A recent example: a government regulation that says hospital wastebaskets must have plastic liners and another rule that bans the liners because they are fire hazards.

4. Increase price competition among businesses. (Reduce the ability of businesses to engage in profit-push or cost-push price increases.) Reassess government regulatory agencies that reduce competition (like the marketing boards in "A Case of Eggs").

5. Reduce subsidies that keep prices up. Of the $2.2 billion paid to businesses in 1978, one-third was to farmers for not growing anything.

6. Reduce tariffs that protect inefficient business firms. Tariffs cost consumers at least $15 billion a year in higher prices.

7. If necessary, make the government the *employer of last resort*. That is, if the private economy will not provide enough jobs, the government must provide public employment. However, the rate of pay should be below prevailing wages so that people will have no incentive to seek public over private employment.

8. Reduce deficit spending to reduce the government's tendency to increase demand. (This will be difficult because three-quarters of total federal government spending is "uncontrollable"; that is, required by past legislation.)

9. Reduce the zigs and zags of monetary policy so that business executives and the public can plan ahead with some idea of the future availability of credit.

All of the experts interested in these proposals realize that the change from demand to supply management won't be easy. The reductions in government spending resulting from the need to reduce deficits will tend to increase unemployment. Our representatives in Congress will find it hard to vote against federally financed local projects. Public employee unions will fight reductions in public payrolls. "Tighter" money will create additional scarcities of job openings.

With the onset of supply management, there is no guarantee that large corporations will respond to fewer regulations and lower taxes with increased production and lower prices. And we will have to hope that exogenous events like the Russian invasion of Afghanistan don't require increases in government (military) spending that are bound to be inflationary. But whatever happens, the lesson of the 1970s is clear: We will never know whether or not "fine-tuning" works until a consistent, noninflationary policy is left in place over a long period of time.

Summary

Inflation is a period of generally rising prices. From 1967 through 1979, average prices more than doubled. The causes of inflation are increases in the quantity of money, excessive demand at full employment (demand-pull), structural problems in the economy (shortages of important commodities), and pressure from cost-push or profit-push sources.

Unemployment occurs because some work is seasonal and job conditions are in the "down" phase of a cycle (cyclical unemployment); or because of several serious conditions collectively called structural unemployment, especially changes in industrial technology that cause workers to be laid off and the existence of hard-core unemployment of disadvantaged groups. Almost four million new jobs will be needed every year over the next ten years to bring our unemployment rate down to 5.5 percent.

Stagflation is the simultaneous appearance of unemployment and inflation. Stagflation is a relatively recent phenomenon that first appeared in the late 1950s. The elimination of stagflation poses special problems because efforts to reduce inflation may increase unemployment and vice versa.

The Phillips Curve is used to describe the trade-off between inflation and unemployment. In recent years, this trade-off has apparently disappeared because increases in the rate of inflation are not associated with reductions in unemployment. Both inflation and unemployment seem to be rising—an indication of stagflation.

Inflation can reduce spending when people are forced to buy fewer goods and services because of higher prices. When people spend less, the spending multiplier causes a multiple decline in GNP and unemployment rises. However, some unemployment is undoubtedly associated with structural problems, while inflation can be attributed to expansionary fiscal and monetary policies plus cost-push and profit-push pressures.

The late 1970s produced two main approaches to solving stagflation. The first approach emphasizes direct price and wage controls by the government. Although such controls have failed in the past, proponents argue that the controls are the only measures that can affect the wage and price policies of large unions and corporations and that the previous failure of controls occurred because they weren't left in place long enough. The second approach stresses increases in supply (rather than demand) to lower prices and reduce unemployment. This approach recommends lowering business taxes, tariff reduction, tax reduction on savings, reduction of government regulations, and reduction of deficit spending.

Discussion Questions

1. What are the causes of inflation? Why won't a reduction in aggregate demand reduce some types of inflation?

2. What are the causes of unemployment? Why won't increases in aggregate demand reduce some types of unemployment?

3. Outline a plan for "curing" stagflation. Can you devise a plan that will produce full employment without inflation?

4. Do the "new" ideas mean that we can reduce prices without increasing unemployment?

References

1. See Gardiner C. Means, "Simultaneous Inflation and Unemployment: A Challenge to Theory and Policy," *Challenge*, September/October 1975, pp. 6-20.

2. Robert J. Samuelson, "Panic on the Road to Worse Panic," *Los Angeles Times*, 26 February 1980, pt. ii, p. 5.

3. Martin Feldstein, "The Economics of the New Unemployment," *Public Interest*, Fall 1973.

4. Milton Friedman, "Behind the Unemployment Numbers," *Newsweek*, 7 February 1977.

5. Ibid.

6. Feldstein, "The Economics of the New Unemployment."

7. "Challenge to U.S.: 72,000 New Jobs Needed Every Week," *U.S. News & World Report*, 28 June 1976, pp. 20–24.

8. Mike Balchunas and Russell Ingold, "We Can Always Use More Money," *Panther Press*, Chaffey College, Alta Loma, Calif., 17 October 1975.

9. *Statistical Abstract of the U.S., 1978.*

10. Robert Lekachman, "The Desperate Need for Wage-Price Curbs," *Los Angeles Times*, 1 February 1980, pt. ii, p. 5. With permission from Los Angeles Times. See also his book *Inflation* (New York: Vintage Books, 1973).

11. Will Durant, *Caesar and Christ* (New York: Simon and Schuster, 1944), pp. 642–643.

12. "Infatuation with Controls," *Time*, 25 February 1980, p. 77.

13. John Kenneth Galbraith in *The Age of Uncertainty* (Boston: Houghton Mifflin Co., 1977), p. 225.

PART

5

International Economics:
Our Links with Other Countries

We have come full circle. In Chapter 1 we discussed the Malthusian problem of an increasing population demanding increasing quantities of food and other resources. In Chapter 6 we were reminded again that the world's increasing demands for energy must be kept in line with global supplies. Now, we are going to look at the same problems from an international perspective.

Somehow, the world's nations will have to find a way to develop their economies cooperatively and peacefully. No longer can the United States or any country sit back and pretend that the economic problems that threaten to destroy, say, Bangladesh, have no bearing on the welfare of its own citizens.

This last part looks at these problems in three ways: (1) international trade between nations—mainly from the point of view of the United States, (2) socialist development in the Soviet Union and China, and (3) the economic challenges of the eighties.

18 The Economics of International Trade

Peter Menzel

The reasons for trade between nations are the same as those for trade between individuals. Someone once said that we live by "taking in one another's washing." Plumbers hire income tax accountants, and income tax accountants hire plumbers. We depend on what others produce in countless ways. This morning when you got up, you perhaps drank coffee from Brazil with sugar from the Philippines. Your shoes may have come from Korea, your clothes from Taiwan. Your car is probably made with steel from Japan, runs on tires made from Malaysian rubber, and is powered by oil from the Middle East.

If specialization and exchange were unavailable and if each of us had to be self-sufficient, we would be reduced to scratching a living from the earth with the most primitive tools. Imagine trying to be self-sufficient without electrical power, automobiles, housing, and medical care—all provided by the specialized skills of others.

Key Words	Trade deficit
Production possibilities table	Trade surplus
Principle of comparative advantage	International Monetary Fund (IMF)
Tariff	Special drawing rights (SDRs)
Nontariff barriers (NTBs)	Floating exchange rates
"Most-favored-nation" principle	Currency depreciation
General Agreement on Tariffs and Trade (GATT)	"Clean" and "dirty" exchange rates
Trade Expansion Act of 1962	Balance-of-international-payments account
Organization for Economic Cooperation and Development (OECD)	Merchandise trade balance
	Current account balance

This same reasoning applies to trade between nations. The more nations use the specialized skills of others, the wealthier all nations become. The less we depend on the specialized skills of other countries, the more we try to be self-sufficient, the more money we will spend producing goods for which we lack the resources or skills.*

Unfortunately, nations are less apt to accept this harmonious view of living together than are individuals or regions within nations. Differences in wealth (resources), in language, currencies, customs, and religion, as well as differences arising out of past international conflicts over territory, serve to make nations wary of one another and less able to give up the notion of self-sufficiency. Purely from the standpoint of economics, however (overlooking considerations of national defense), we can say that the freer the trade, the better the result is for everyone.

This chapter is divided into six sections: (1) the economic theory of specialization and exchange, (2) obstacles to free international trade, (3) the mechanics of trade, (4) prices and the principle of comparative advantage, (5) the international balance of payments account, and (6) trade, inflation, and jobs.

The Economic Theory of Specialization and Exchange

Adam Smith was one of the first to understand the benefits of specialization and exchange. He realized that it takes time to start a task, stop it, switch to another task, and so on. He realized that people would lose much less start-and-stop time if they had only one job to do and that they would gradually become much more proficient if they could concentrate on that task, rather than try to perform many others as well.

Smith explained this idea in a famous passage about making straight pins for sewing:

We could spend $15 a pound growing coffee in climate-controlled hothouses if we wanted to. But this lavish use of our own resources is unnecessary and foolish if we can buy coffee for $4 a pound from Brazil.

To take an example, therefore, from a trifling manufacture . . . the trade of a pin-maker; a workman not educated to this business . . . could scarce, perhaps, with his utmost industry, make one pin in a day, and certainly could not make twenty. But in the way in which this business is now carried on . . . one man draws out the wire, another straights it, a third cuts it, a fourth points it, a fifth grinds it at the top for receiving the head; to make the head requires two or three distinct operations; to put it on is a peculiar business, to whiten the pins is another; it is even a trade by itself to put them into the paper; and the important business of making a pin is, in this manner, divided into about eighteen distinct operations . . . all performed by distinct hands. . . . I have seen a small manufactory of this kind where ten men only were employed, and where . . . they could make among them . . . upwards of forty-eight thousand pins in a day. Each person, therefore, making a tenth part of forty-eight thousand pins, might be considered as making four thousand eight hundred pins in a day.[1]

But what does this division of labor in a pin factory have to do with international trade? Smith's famous answer to this question is that "the division of labor is limited [only] to the extent of the market."[2] He meant that, if the market is very small, as in a small village, the opportunities for division of labor will be small. There will not be enough demand for shoes to permit someone to do nothing but make shoes or to permit many other specialties to be self-supporting. It is only because the market is big enough to absorb 48,000 pins a day that we can have 10 men doing nothing but making pins, or one man doing nothing but sharpening the wire to a point.

If the market encompasses the whole world, then consumers can enjoy the enormous gains from production divided into the minutest of tasks. Thus, a world market with an international division of labor is at the core of Smith's belief in international free trade.

Just as the pin factory helped Adam Smith to see the benefits of specialization and trade, a model called the *production possibilities table* helps today's economists analyze the benefits of specialization and exchange.

The production possibilities table

Remembering that the reasons for specialization and exchange apply to individuals, cities, states, and regions, as well as to nations, let us assume that there are two people, Tom and Sue, each of whom is skillful at making beds and cooking meals. Should one of them make the beds and the other cook the meals?

We must now make some assumptions about what economists call *production possibilities*. The production possibilities of an individual, state, or nation are the various combinations of products that can be produced, assuming (1) a certain level of technology, (2) a certain quantity of resources, (3) a certain quality of resources, and (4) the full-time occupation (full employment) of the individual, state, or nation in producing its products.

Assuming that these four variables do not change, the problem of opportunity cost arises. Any decision Tom might make to cook another meal will mean that he must give up making some beds. How many beds must he give up? We'll assume that Tom can cook two meals in the time it takes

TABLE 18-1 Tom's Meals-Beds Production Possibilities (per hour)

Possibility	Meals	Beds
A	0	12
B	2	8
C	4	4
D	6	0

him to make four beds; the production of each meal then involves the sacrifice (opportunity cost) of two beds. This constant relationship of one meal for two beds is maintained throughout all of Tom's working hours. The assumption that Tom can always cook another meal at the sacrifice of two beds is called the assumption of constant cost.

Table 18-1 is a **production possibilities table.** It shows four different combinations (possibilities) Tom is capable of producing per hour, using all of his time, resources, and skills. The table has two extremes. Possibility A tells us that if Tom were to spend no time at all cooking meals, he could make twelve beds. The other extreme, possibility D, shows that, if Tom were to spend all of his time cooking meals, he could cook six meals but make no beds. Notice that the relationship of two meals for four beds is maintained with each possibility. Every time Tom decides to cook two more meals, he must sacrifice four beds. Thus, Tom's opportunity cost for cooking each additional meal is always two beds.

Table 18-2 shows similar data for Sue.

TABLE 18-2 Sue's Meals-Beds Production Possibilities (per hour)

Possibilities	Meals	Beds
A	0	9
B	1	6
C	2	3
D	3	0

The principle of comparative advantage

Now the question is, should Tom and Sue live together with one person doing the cooking and the other the bedmaking? The answer isn't easy, because Tom is actually better than Sue at both chores. But we can decide by looking at opportunity cost. We know that every time Tom cooks another meal he must give up 2 beds. What about Sue?

Whenever Sue decides to cook another meal, she must give up (opportunity cost) *3* beds. Thus, the opportunity cost of cooking meals is *less* for Tom.

Does it work the other way? Yes. Whenever Tom decides to make four more beds, we can see that he must sacrifice two meals. His opportunity cost in making each additional bed is the loss of one-half of one meal. Whenever Sue decides to make three more beds, she must sacrifice one meal. The opportunity cost of each additional bed is for Sue one-third of one meal. Because one-third is less than one-half, the opportunity cost for making beds is less for Sue. Clearly, it is cheaper in terms of opportunity cost for Tom to cook the meals and for Sue to make the beds. They have an economic reason for getting together!

When an individual or nation is superior at producing one product, that individual or nation is said to have an *absolute advantage* in the production of that product. In the Tom-Sue example, Tom has the absolute advantage in both tasks. He can make more beds and can cook more meals than Sue can. But identifying who has an absolute advantage does not necessarily tell us who should specialize in which product. For example, a lawyer may be an expert typist, far better than anyone she can hire to do her typing. The lawyer has an absolute advantage in typing. But does that mean the lawyer should do her own typing? Obviously not. The opportunity cost of the lawyer's typing will be much higher than the opportunity cost of typing done by a hired typist. (The lawyer might lose thousands in fees while typing her own briefs. The hired typist's opportunity cost while typing for the lawyer would be measured by the highest hourly wage—perhaps $10 an hour—he might earn while typing for someone else.)

Thus, the answer to the question, "Who should do what?" lies in the opportunity costs of specialization. If one country, or individual, has lower opportunity costs than another in the cooking of meals, for example, then it should cook meals. This conclusion leads us to the **principle of comparative advantage.**

A country, or individual, having lower opportunity costs than others in the production of some product is said to have a comparative advantage in the production of that product. Moreover, if the participants in a *specialization-exchange relationship* permit each party to specialize in making the product in which that country or individual has the comparative advantage, both parties will benefit.

The benefits of specialization and exchange

Suppose that before specialization and exchange, Tom and Sue are both operating at possibility C. Tom cooks four meals and makes four beds; Sue cooks two meals and makes three beds. Therefore, before getting together, their combined production is six meals and seven beds. If they combine their skills, with Tom doing all the cooking (six meals and no bedmaking), while Sue does all the bedmaking (9 beds and no cooking), there is a clear gain of two beds.

The secret of the principle of comparative advantage is that benefits may be obtained by specializing when there is a difference in opportunity costs. In this case, Sue has the comparative advantage in bedmaking, even though Tom can make more beds than she can in the same time (twelve beds versus nine beds). Table 18-3 summarizes the benefit they obtain through specialization and exchange.

TABLE 18-3 The Benefits of Specialization and Exchange

	Meals	Beds
Before specialization at Possibility C		
Tom	4	4
Sue	2	3
Total	6	7
After specialization		
Tom	6	0
Sue	0	9
Total	6	9
Gain		2 beds

The principle of comparative advantage works just as well for nations as it does for individuals. If the Japanese have a comparative advantage in the production of, say, television sets, relative to the United States, the production of television sets in this country will involve a greater sacrifice of the other products we *could* have made (opportunity cost) than for the Japanese. American consumers will benefit by being able to buy lower-priced Japanese TV sets. (Of course, American TV manufacturers will be unhappy, but a decline in their sales will release resources for the production of goods where *we* have a comparative advantage, like farm machinery.

When, however, the complications of transportation costs, differences in quality, and consumer demand are introduced, the basic principle remains the same but specialization may not be complete. The two countries will probably continue to produce some of both products and exchange some of them.

Although specialization and the principle of comparative advantage provide sound reasons for international trade, many nations still seek to benefit their economies by erecting various obstacles to trade. In the last two decades particularly, many efforts have been made to overcome some of these obstacles.

Obstacles to International Trade

There are two kinds of obstacles to trade: tariff barriers and nontariff barriers. Both are important because they interfere with the operation of the principle of comparative advantage.

Tariff barriers

A **tariff** is simply a tax on imported products. The tariff may be a percentage of the product price or it may be a flat fee for a given quantity of the product ($1.25 per twelve-bottle case of French wine). Tariffs fall into two general categories—revenue tariffs and protective tariffs. *Revenue tariffs*, like most taxes, are designed to provide the government with revenue. Typically, they are levied against products the United States does not have, such as tin,

The only ones who will benefit from the tariff are the U.S. shoe manufacturers and their employees.

coffee, and bananas. *Protective tariffs*, on the other hand, are designed to protect a particular American industry from foreign competition by taxing the foreign product so that its price will no longer be so competitive.

Tariffs are not only a barrier to trade; they may also support a less efficient industry at the expense of more efficient ones and cause higher prices for consumers. If, for example, the Italians can produce shoes at a lower opportunity cost than Americans can, and the United States taxes each imported pair of Italian shoes, the tax will cause the American retail price of Italian shoes to rise, making them less competitive with American shoes (the intent of the tariff). Because the taxed Italian shoes now cost more, American shoe buyers will buy more American shoes, causing the shoe factories to hire more people and use larger quantities of all resources. Resources will flow to the protected industry.

But, to the extent that resources flow to that industry, another industry in which Americans are more efficient—perhaps golf ball production—is deprived of these resources. Moreover, consumers will have to pay more for imported shoes because of the tariff *and* for domestic shoes because the tariff protects U.S. shoe manufacturers against foreign competition—and hence price cutting. Golf ball prices will also be higher because golf ball producers will have to pay more for resources. The only ones who will benefit from the tariff are U.S. shoe manufacturers and their employees.

Nontariff barriers   **Nontariff barriers (NTBs)** can be even more crippling to trade than tariff barriers. What if a highly skilled entrepreneur is prevented from producing something that she is particularly good at making because the patent rights to some crucial part are owned by someone else? What if the excellent typist cannot get a job because he or she is black? What if the skilled typesetter cannot get a job because the local typographer's union will not accept new members? These are barriers to entry. Barriers to entry prevent the principle of comparative advantage from working among individuals, industries, and nations.

Nations have created a vast array of rules and regulations that are not tariffs but that accomplish the same purpose. These barriers undoubtedly cause more serious distortions of world trade and the free operation of the principle of comparative advantage than tariffs do. Furthermore, while tariff rates have come down, NTBs seem more meddlesome than ever.

It was once reported that Kentucky-fried chicken could be sold in Japan, but not if the chickens came from Kentucky—or from anywhere except Japan, for that matter. Japanese customs inspectors politely explained that all non-Japanese chickens have skin diseases. There are Kentucky-fried chicken establishments in Japan, but the chickens have to be Japanese.

In France, a tractor can't be sold that runs faster than 17 miles per hour. In Germany it is 13 mph. In the Netherlands it is 10 mph. The point, of course, is that these countries want to develop their own tractor manufacturing industries.

The *Los Angeles Times* once reported that "you can ship fresh fruit from America to the Common Market, but don't be surprised if it never gets unloaded. The customs inspector may be ill or off-duty when the cargo arrives. The fruit spoils on the ship."[3]

But American restrictive practices are also numerous and growing. Dr. C. Fred Bergsten of the Brookings Institution once estimated that U.S. restrictions on imports "cost American consumers at least $10 to $15 billion a year and [that] they cover commodities representing $100 billion of U.S. output or up to 15 percent of all items in the consumer price index.[4]

There are six common kinds of nontariff barriers:

1. *Import quotas* set an absolute limit on the quantity of a product one country allows itelf to buy from another. They are often regarded as even more harmful to American consumers than tariffs, although both import quotas and tariffs can raise prices.

2. *Export subsidies*, either through direct governmental grants to an industry or tax breaks, may enable a domestic producer to export goods at a price his foreign competitor cannot match.

3. *Dumping*—selling a product abroad for less than its price at home—may result from export subsidies.

4. *Buy-at-home policies* may require that products be clearly labeled as to the country of origin, and considerable pressure may be put on consumers to buy domestic products.

5. Rigid health and safety standards may be designed to prove that products from other countries are unhealthy or unsafe.

6. Preferential trading arrangements may favor some countries and discriminate against others. The *Reciprocal Trade Agreements Law of 1934* includes a **"most-favored nation" principle** under which a trade concession granted to one nation will be granted to all other trading partners.

Tariffs and quotas appraised

There are five common arguments for tariffs and import quotas (the most important nontariff barrier), and they have varying degrees of validity.

Tariffs and quotas protect domestic employment

This argument recognizes the importance of net exports in aggregate demand. If imports rise, net exports drop and Americans lose jobs because they no longer produce the products brought in by importers. Therefore, the argument goes, we must use tariffs or quotas to reduce imports.

(For example, the American International Trade Commission voted in March 1977 to raise the tariff rate on imported television sets from 5 to 25 percent to aid the U.S. television industry, which could raise the average price of television sets $56. Similar measures have been proposed for steel products and shoes by labor unions and business executives in the affected industries.)[5]

The position seems logical enough, but it overlooks several facts of life. All nations cannot maintain an export surplus. International trade is a two-way street. One nation's exports are another's imports. If one nation is to have a favorable trade balance, some other nation must have an unfavorable balance, and that nation will experience rising unemployment. A nation in this situation must increase its exports, but if it cannot, because of tariff walls or quotas in other countries, it will very likely try to reduce its own imports with similar restrictions. As countries with unfavorable trade balances retaliate, the exports of all countries will decline and the world will be worse off.

We must also remember that, if a certain country is to buy American farm machinery, it must have acquired a supply of U.S. dollars to pay the machinery manufacturers. How does that country get the dollars? Only by Americans' buying something from it. When Americans buy Japanese cars, the Japanese accumulate dollars because Americans have to buy yen with dollars and the yen are then given to the Japanese manufacturer. The Japanese can then use the dollars to buy American products.

Tariffs help diversify industry

Another argument for tariffs is that we must protect some industries in order to preserve the diversification of industry. This argument holds that we should not allow the principle of comparative advantage to persuade us to put all of our eggs in a few baskets.

There may be some truth to this argument, but it seems hardly relevant in diversified economies like those of the United States or other industrial countries. For countries that are heavily committed to one crop—coffee in

Brazil, cotton in Egypt—the argument assumes greater importance. But the cost of diversifying and protecting new industries with tariffs may be very large. And the consumer always pays that cost.

Tariffs and quotas protect infant industries

This argument calls for the protection of new industries until they become established. Again, the argument makes little sense in the United States. Moreover, a protected infant industry may never grow up. Once it is protected, such an industry frequently puts great political pressure on Congress to continue the protection and may provide extensive financial support for sympathetic congressmen during their election campaigns. However, the infant-industry argument may have relevance for less developed countries, which need to produce a greater variety of their own products.

Tariffs and quotas protect American workers against cheap foreign labor

According to this argument, the more cheap goods we let in, the more American wages will fall in competition with the "cheap foreign labor" of the exporting country. Our standard of living will go down as the wages of others go up, it is said.

Economists reject this argument as completely fallacious. First, the influx of cheap goods helps American consumers, a great many of whom are workers. Low-priced products extend the purchasing power of the dollar; real wages rise as a result.

Second, the cheap-labor argument ignores the fact that labor cost is only one of many costs of production. American labor is highly paid, but American workers use enormously productive machines (capital goods). If a $10-an-hour American laborer produces 1,000 units per hour, the average labor cost per unit is 1 cent. If a laborer earning 50 cents per hour in a poor country produces only 10 units per hour because of the absence of capital goods, the labor cost per unit is 5 cents.

Finally, the American worker earns more than the worker in the poor country because, in addition to having the machine, he or she knows how to use it.

Tariffs and quotas protect defense industries

This argument is a tough one. If America is on the brink of war, it may make sense to protect industries that are closely connected with national defense.

But there are many pitfalls. The benefits of being self-sufficient in defense-connected industries are extremely hard to measure. The trade-off of any such benefit is the immediate loss of goodwill in the countries from which the United States might have bought large quantities of defense-connected supplies. Further, how does one always know whether or not the industry really is a necessary part of national defense? Any industry can claim this role as has the American watch industry, on the theory that the skills of American watchmakers need to be maintained for possible work on military gadgets in time of war.

One possible solution to this argument and several of the others is to give outright subsidies to those industries that voters decide need protection instead of protecting them with tariffs or quotas.

Trade agreements in the last fifty years

Tariff rates have dropped since the 1930s. In the early years of the Depression, Congress passed the *Hawley-Smoot Law*, which raised American tariff rates on imports to 52.8 percent of their value. Countries around the world retaliated, and the result was a breakdown in international trade.

In 1947, in a move to liberalize trade, the United States signed a treaty with 23 other countries called the **General Agreement on Tariffs and Trade (GATT).** GATT, now an organization of 81 nations, has been successful so far in the realm of tariff rates, but has been less successful with nontariff barriers such as import quotas.

The United States supported its commitment to GATT with the **Trade Expansion Act of 1962,** under which the United States and the European Common Market agreed to lower substantially or eliminate entirely tariffs on those products on which they together had 80 percent or more of the world's trade. The Trade Expansion Act has led to many rounds of talks to reduce tariff rates, which in 1979 averaged around 8 percent of the value of imported products. Averages can be misleading, however, because they conceal the effects of high rates relative to low rates. Average tariff rates are calculated only on the basis of the values of goods that actually enter a country. If a product is blocked partially or completely from entering a country because of a high tariff rate, its resulting decline as an import will so reduce the revenues collected on it that the high rate will not noticeably affect the average of all rates.

Although progress has been made in lowering tariff rates, the NTBs have proven much more difficult to eliminate. The United States has been inclined to favor not GATT, but the **Organization for Economic Cooperation and Development (OECD)** formed in 1960 as a more appropriate institution for liberalizing trade.*

Prospects for the future

In the United States, the battle lines are drawn between the advocates of freer trade and advocates for increased protection. On the one hand, firms producing military hardware for export to other countries, firms producing agricultural equipment, and farmers are for free trade because all of them are interested in exporting: They know that, in order to export, the United States must import and maintain friendly trade relations around the world.

The leaders of the protectionists are the industrial unions—steelworkers, glass-bottle blowers, textile workers, machinists, theatrical employees, and merchant seamen. They worry about competition from imports of goods and services (the use of foreign ships in the case of the seamen). The United Automobile Workers (UAW) is in a difficult position because the union rep-

---

OECD members are the United States, the members of the Common Market and EFTA, plus Australia, Canada, New Zealand, Spain, Turkey, and Yugoslavia.

resents some workers who are for and others who are against free trade. (Workers producing weapons and agricultural equipment on the free-trade side face opposition from automobile workers who would like to keep out foreign cars.)

Concern about persistently high unemployment rates is leading to a new wave of protectionism. But we would be foolish to pretend that we can set up trade barriers without retaliation and loss of goodwill around the world. With all the furor over protectionism, we export and import only about 10 percent of our GNP; in a country such as the Netherlands, foreign products account for as much as 45 percent of all goods sold.

The relatively small share of our GNP devoted to international trade tends to conceal the importance of trade to American citizens. *Excluding* oil, we import twelve other materials essential to American industry: asbestos, bauxite (aluminum ore), chrome, cobalt, copper, lead, manganese, nickel, platinum, silver, tin, and titanium. And trade provides jobs. One out of every eight jobs in the U.S. industry and 20 percent of farm income now depends on export sales.

Moreover, as you will see in the next section, international trade requires reciprocity. We *have* to buy from the Japanese. We exchange dollars for yen in order to pay exporters in yen. Those dollars can then be used by the Japanese to pay for American products. If they do not have those dollars, or if dollars become too expensive in terms of yen, purchases from the United States will decline and Americans will lose their jobs.

The Mechanics of Trade

Trade is a two-way street. For the Japanese to buy our products, they must acquire a supply of dollars. As you will see, the Japanese acquire dollars by persuading us to buy their products, for example, Datsuns. By the same token, we can buy Datsuns if we have a supply of yen, and we obtain those yen by selling the Japanese something they need, say, soybeans.

Importing Datsuns, exporting soybeans

The mechanics of buying Datsuns from a Japanese manufacturer are many and varied, but it all comes down to this: the Datsun manufacturer wants to be paid in yen, not dollars. He wants a demand deposit in a Japanese bank in yen so that he can write checks to pay his expenses. Similarly, the American producer exporting soybeans wants dollars to be paid into his demand-deposit account in his local bank.

We can illustrate the process of international buying and selling by showing only the final steps in the transaction. To do this, we will imagine two banks: a U.S. commercial bank, called Mainstreet Bank, and a commercial bank in Japan, called Nippon Bank. The American importers of Datsuns and the American exporters of soybeans have their demand-deposit accounts in Mainstreet Bank. The Japanese exporters of Datsuns and the Japanese importers of soybeans have their demand-deposit accounts in Nippon Bank.

We now want to show one common way of financing the import of a Datsun by an American firm and the export of soybeans by an American company to a Japanese importer.

We will begin with the purchase of one Datsun automobile by the American importer. Keep in mind that the American has dollars to spend, but the Datsun Company wants to be paid in yen. We will assume that the Datsun Company wants 1.2 million yen for one Datsun (excluding all shipping costs and tariffs). How much is that? The exchange rate will tell us. In late 1979, the exchange rate was 240 yen per dollar. The dollar price of the Datsun in Japan is therefore $5,000 (1.2 million ÷ 240).

Step 1.   Our American importer writes a check for $5,000 on his demand-deposit account in Mainstreet Bank.

Step 2.   The check in dollars is now sent to the Datsun Company in Japan.

Step 3.   Of course the Datsun Company wants yen, not dollars. The Datsun Company therefore asks Nippon Bank to credit its demand-deposit account with $5,000 worth of yen (1.2 million yen).

Step 4.   Why should Nippon Bank cash a $5,000 check *drawn on an American bank* and give the Datsun Company 1.2 million yen? This step answers the question. Nippon Bank returns the check to Mainstreet Bank where Mainstreet Bank gives Nippon Bank a demand-deposit account for $5,000.

Step 1   ## Step 2

Step 3   ## Step 4

Note that (1) the demand for the Datsun led to a demand for yen in Japan, and that (2) Nippon Bank was willing to pay 1.2 million yen to the Datsun Company because it was willing to accept in exchange a demand deposit for $5,000 in Mainstreet Bank.

Let us look at the American export of $1,000 worth of soybeans to a Japanese importer (for resale to a Japanese manufacturer of soy sauce). The process goes into reverse. The American firm wants $1,000.

Step 1.   Now, because Nippon Bank has a demand deposit in dollars in Mainstreet Bank, the Japanese importer can buy a $1,000 check from Nippon Bank drawn on Nippon Bank's American account. The check will cost the Japanese importer 240,000 yen ($1,000 × 240), which Nippon Bank will deduct from the importer's account.

Step 2.   The $1,000 check is now sent to the Soybean Company in the United States.

Step 3.   The Soybean Company deposits the check in Mainstreet Bank. The Soybean Company's account goes up by $1,000.

Step 4.   Mainstreet Bank clears the check by deducting $1,000 from Nippon Bank's demand-deposit account.

Step 1   Step 2

Step 3   Step 4

You may have noticed a peculiarity in this example: Nippon Bank has an account in Mainstreet Bank but not vice versa. In the real world this happens because other countries are used to using dollars as an international medium of exchange. However, this condition is not necessary. Mainstreet Bank could have a deposit in yen in Nippon Bank. We have selected an approach that emphasizes the customary use of dollars. Recent indications are that the American dollar is losing its international importance as a medium of exchange, and that other countries will increasingly prefer to deal in their own or other currencies.

This example has been deliberately rigged to illustrate the typical pattern of our trade with Japan. We bought more from the Japanese (the $5,000 Datsun) than they bought from us (the $1,000 worth of soybeans). For the past twenty years our *total* imports from Japan have been greater than our total sales (exports) to Japan.

Why, if the Japanese continue to pile up dollars from their exports to the United States, are they willing to continue to accumulate dollars in their accounts? Our transaction has shown that the Japanese need these dollar accounts for their Japanese customers who may wish to buy in the United States or who may wish to use these dollars for purchases in any country. As the Japanese supply of dollars increases, however, we can visualize that banks such as Nippon Bank will become more and more reluctant to pay out yen to Japanese exporters such as the Datsun Company in exchange for deposits in dollars in the United States.

The excess of purchases from foreign countries over sales to foreign countries is called a **trade deficit.** An excess of sales over purchases is called a **trade surplus.** There is a *trade imbalance* whenever purchases and sales are not equal.

The demise of gold in international trade

Up until 1971, the U.S. trade position seemed secure. We had always managed to have a trade surplus. But in 1971 we had our first trade deficit in ninety-three years. It amounted to $-\$2.3$ billion. (In 1978 it was almost fifteen times larger: $-\$34.1$ billion.)

Until August 15, 1971, gold served as an international medium of exchange, and all currencies were expressed in terms of a quantity of gold. For example, suppose that the U.S. Treasury announces that one dollar is worth 1/40 of an ounce of gold. The official price of gold in the United States is then $40 per ounce. And further suppose that the French announce that one franc is worth 1/200 of an ounce of gold. The official price of gold in France is then 200 francs per ounce.

When all currencies are expressed in terms of gold in this manner, we can determine how valuable they are in terms of each other. In the example above, $40 = 1 ounce of gold in the United States; 200 francs = 1 ounce of gold in France. Therefore, $40 = 200 francs, $1 = 5 francs, and 1 franc = 20 cents (one-fifth of a dollar).

The domestic price of gold in each of the 124 nations belonging to the **International Monetary Fund (IMF)** (see box essay on page 391) determined international exchange rates until 1973. Moreover, until August 15,

TABLE 18-4 Decline in the U.S. Stock of Gold in Selected Years, 1949–1977 (in billions)[a]

Year	U.S. gold stock
1949	$24.6 billion
1953	22.1
1957	22.9
1961	17.0
1965	13.8
1969	11.9
1970	11.1
1971	10.2
1972	10.5[b]
1973	11.7[b]
1974	11.7
1975	11.6
1976	11.6
1977	11.7

[a]In official prices ranging from $35 to $44 per ounce.

[b]These apparent increases occurred because the official U.S. price of gold was increased at the end of 1971 and again in 1972 and 1973.

Source: *Economic Report of the President, 1979.*

1971, the United States agreement with the IMF member nations was that we would give any country that was holding dollars one ounce of gold for every $35 it held. The generally accepted theory was that the agreement to redeem dollars for gold guaranteed the strength of the dollar.

But on August 15, 1971, President Nixon made a speech, during which he announced "Phase One," the government's attempt to halt inflation with direct price and wage controls. In that speech, the President also announced that the United States would no longer redeem dollars held by foreigners with *gold*.

Why did he do it?

President Nixon had a good reason for his action. We were running out of gold as a result of having had to redeem some of the dollars owned by other countries in order to finance our balance-of-payments deficits. Table 18-4 shows what has happened to the U.S. supply of gold since 1949.

Our gold disappeared for one basic reason: Other countries accumulated far more dollars than our accumulations of their currencies. By 1972, 80 billion U.S. dollars were held in foreign accounts. Until President Nixon's action, these dollars could be redeemed for gold—and often were.

There were four main causes of this foreign accumulation of dollars:

1. As our industrial trading partners recovered from World War II, they began to outsell us in international markets. Often they sold more to us than

they bought from us. Other countries accumulated dollars, just as the Japanese did in the Datsun-soybean example.

2. American travel overseas contributed to the outflow of dollars.

3. Private investment overseas by American multinational corporations added to the exit of dollars.

4. And finally, U.S. government spending overseas, particularly for military purposes like the NATO armies and the rental of Air Force and Navy bases, added to foreign holdings of dollars.

Following President Nixon's refusal to exchange dollars for gold, gold gradually began to lose its importance in international trade. There were several significant events along the way:

1. You will remember from Chapter 15 that the United States abandoned the gold standard for its own citizens back in 1934 and also made it illegal for Americans to own gold.

2. The major trading countries decided in 1967 (the Rio de Janeiro agreement) to supplement gold with **special drawing rights (SDRs)** because world supplies of gold were insufficient to support growing world trade.

3. In 1975, the U.S. government reversed its 1934 decision to prohibit the private ownership of gold. Thereafter, the U.S. Treasury began to auction off its gold stocks—typically, 1.5 million ounces at a time—to anyone wanting to buy.

4. In the Jamaica agreement of 1976, the IMF members agreed to abandon gold as a measuring stick and to use SDRs only—the value of SDRs to be determined by a "basket" of sixteen major currencies. Further, the IMF was authorized to auction off one-third of its gold holdings, the original value to be returned to the contributors, but the profits to be given to less-developed countries ("LDCs"). Finally, the Jamaica agreement endorsed **floating exchange rates:** The world's major currencies were allowed to find their value relative to one another without reference to gold—or even to SDRs. Henceforth, the demand and supply for one another's currency determined exchange rates.

And so gold gradually "died," particularly during the 1970s, largely because the wealthiest trading nation of the world refused to exchange its currency for gold. But we should hasten to add that gold is very much alive in private markets. In December 1979 the free-market price of gold reached $800 per ounce. South African one-ounce gold coins called "Krugerrands" became a popular form of saving in anticipation of continuing gold-price increases. And there are many economists who still prefer the stabilizing effects of gold as a measuring stick rather than the floating rates that may change the value of one's currency daily. But now let's examine in more detail how floating exchange rates work.

When exchange rates float

Until the mid-1970s, international exchange rates were covered by a number of complex controls. Suffice it to say that these controls were dropped and that exchange rates are now as free to change as any price is free to change (assuming no government-set price floors or ceilings). For example, if the

U.S. trade deficit persists, the Japanese will not exchange as many yen for each dollar as they did before. If the exchange rate is free to float, it will change. When the American importer of Datsuns decides to buy another Datsun, he may find that Nippon Bank will pay out only 200 yen for each dollar deposited in the United States instead of 240. In international jargon, the yen has "floated upward," the dollar "downward."

Currency depreciation

When the number of yen given by the Japanese for each dollar drops, as in the example above, from 240 to 200, the dollar has *depreciated*. Do not be deceived by the drop in the number of yen per dollar. Before the depreciation of the dollar, the yen was worth $\frac{1}{240}$ of a dollar. After the drop, one yen was worth $\frac{1}{200}$ of a dollar, a *larger* amount. In this example, the dollar has depreciated 40 yen or about 17 percent ($240 - 200 = 40$ and $40 \div 240 = 16.67$ percent).

If there is a 17 percent depreciation of the dollar relative to the yen, what happens to the price of Datsuns? Remember from page 384 that the Datsun company still wants to be paid 1.2 million yen for one Datsun. Before depreciation, $5,000 would buy 1.2 million yen. If the dollar is worth only 200 yen, the new Datsun price to Americans will be $6,000 (1.2 million ÷ 200). Not everyone will be happy. American consumers lose, and the Datsun company may not sell as many Datsuns. But what about the Soybean Company? Before depreciation, the Japanese importers of soybeans had to pay 240,000 yen to obtain the $1,000 for the purchases of soybeans. Now Japanese importers need pay only 200,000 yen to obtain $1,000. The price of soybeans has dropped—not in the United States, but in Japan. The Soybean Company should enjoy an increase in exports to Japan, and Japanese purchasers of soybeans should see a drop in the Japanese retail price of soybeans.

Notice that when the dollar depreciates relative to the yen, Datsuns, Toyotas, and Hondas all become more expensive for American buyers and, consequently, a lesser threat to U.S. car makers. The prices of American cars begin to look relatively more attractive. When the dollar depreciates, American producers, like the Soybean Company, have the chance to increase their exports to other countries as the dollar drops in value relative to other currencies. But as exports continue to increase, the international price of dollars will increase and the whole process will go into reverse.

Thus, depreciation of a country's currency tends to inhibit imports by raising the prices of imported goods and spur exports by making its goods less expensive abroad. Exporters love depreciation of their currencies and deplore appreciation, while importers favor appreciation and oppose depreciation.

"Clean" and "Dirty" Exchange Rates

Let us return to the Japanese example for a moment. When the yen *increases* in value from 240 yen per dollar to 200 yen, and Americans find Datsuns more expensive, American imports of Datsuns will decrease. Moreover, as our example indicated, the Japanese will buy more American soybeans because the dollar is cheaper. The U.S. trade deficit with Japan will tend to disappear; the Japanese trade surplus with the United States will tend to disappear.

Consequently, a freely floating exchange rate *may* automatically tend to erase trade imbalances. The only way a country can get ahead is to make its product better or cheaper, but its advantage will be short-lived. A situation exactly like pure competition exists. A company might earn pure profits temporarily (achieve a trade surplus), but then the profits (the surplus) are wiped out by competitors.

When exchange rates are free to float in this "purely competitive" manner in which the rate is entirely determined by the forces of demand and supply, it is called a **"clean" exchange rate.**

This statement that floating exchange rates tend to erase trade imbalances is the subject of considerable argument. During the 1970s, oil-exporting countries accumulated dollars at the rate of around $50 billion per year as the United States continued to import 50 percent of the oil it consumed. The oil imports invariably led to trade deficits and a weakening of the dollar in international exchange. Theoretically, the weakening dollar should encourage other nations, particularly those with dollar surpluses like the OPEC countries, to increase their purchases from the United States—thus creating a demand for dollars that would tend to restore the dollar to its former value. To some extent this scenario was followed as the OPEC countries bought large quantities of U.S. products—particularly military hardware. But the OPEC countries also began to realize that they were receiving ever-cheaper dollars for their oil, a realization that then prompted them to raise the price of their oil, resulting in a further enlarging of the U.S.'s trade deficit to them. This sequence of events has led some observers to question the self-correcting mechanism that floating rates are supposed to create.

Now suppose that Japan, or any other trade-surplus country, wants to keep its trade surplus in order to maintain its export industries at a high level of employment. Japan might tell its banks, "Don't let the yen go up. Go right on giving the Americans 240 yen per dollar. We don't want the Datsun company to lose any sales." In fact, if the Japanese wanted to increase Datsun's sales still further, Japan might ask its banks to give *more* than 240 yen per dollar.

Interference by a government to fix an artificial exchange rate produces what is called a **"dirty" exchange rate.** But, if other countries realize what is going on, a "price war" could result.

Prices and the Principle of Comparative Advantage

How are decisions made about importing certain quantities of products from abroad and exporting others to foreign countries when prices and exchange rates are taken into account? We used the Tom-Sue example to illustrate the principle of comparative advantage, which encourages countries to specialize in producing certain products and then to exchange them for others.

However, the Tom-Sue illustration was limited to physical units (meals and beds). No prices were used. Nor did we consider what would happen if

(continued on page 392)

The International Monetary Fund: "Fed" to the World

As its name indicates, the IMF is a fund of monies deposited by member nations.

As its names indicates, the International Monetary Fund (IMF) is a fund of monies deposited by member nations, the nations that are not members of the communist bloc. Each country deposits an amount of gold and an amount of its own currency in the Fund. These sums, called *quotas,* are determined by each country's income and wealth. The United States has by far the largest quota—about 25 percent of the total.

Thereafter, the IMF serves the function of a world central bank, like the Fed in the U.S. Its primary function is to lend currencies to member nations who have deficit problems. If a country has used up its supply of German marks, for example, but still wants to buy more German products, it can apply to the IMF for a loan of German marks. Such a loan is usually in the form of a *repurchase agreement,* in which the borrowing country buys the marks with its own currency but agrees to repurchase its currency, with some other currency acceptable to the IMF, at some future date—usually three to five years. The borrowing country must also pay a small interest charge.

Since 1976 and the Jamaica agreement's endorsement of floating exchange rates, in which the world's major currencies were allowed to find their value relative to one another through demand and supply, the function of the IMF has diminished. It exists now mainly as a lending agency for developing countries.

TABLE 18-5 U.S. and France: Production Possibilities in Golf Balls and Wine

Production possibilities	United States		France	
	Golf Balls	Wine	Golf Balls	Wine
A	0	6	0	9
B	3	4	2	6
C	6	2	4	3
D	9	0	6	0

Tom and Sue belonged to different countries and used different currencies. In this section, we will show the connections among production possibilities, the principle of comparative advantage, and trade in different currencies.

In order to show how prices, production possibilities, and the principle of comparative advantage are related, let's design another production possibilities table (Table 18-5). This time, we will replace Tom and Sue with the United States and France. The two products are golf balls and wine instead of meals and beds.

Keep in mind that in any discussion of production possibilities we assume that these are combinations of products that can be produced at full employment. Thus, if either country wants to produce more golf balls, it must take resources away from wine and vice versa.

As Table 18-5 shows, the United States can make nine golf balls if it pours all of its resources into golf ball production, but France can make only six. On the other hand, France can make nine bottles of wine with complete specialization; the United States can make only six. Table 18-6 shows the situation in terms of opportunity cost. Because U.S. specialization in golf balls has a lower opportunity cost (comparative advantage) than in France, the United States should specialize in golf balls. France, on the other hand, has the comparative advantage in wine.

The United States will trade golf balls for wine as long as the French will exchange more than two-thirds of a bottle of wine for each golf ball (the opportunity cost, measured in lost wine, of producing one more golf ball in the United States); France will trade wines for golf balls as long as the United States will exchange at least two-thirds of a golf ball for each bottle of wine (the opportunity cost of each wine measured in lost golf balls in France).

TABLE 18-6 U.S. and France: Opportunity Costs in Golf Balls and Wine

United States	France
9 golf balls = 6 wine bottles	6 golf balls = 9 wine bottles
1 ball = .67 bottles	1 bottle = .67 balls
1 bottle = 1.5 balls	1 ball = 1.5 bottles

The Americans are happy to get one bottle of wine for one golf ball.

The stage is set. Let us now relate the prices of individual golf balls and wine bottles, using the exchange rate of 5 francs per dollar. The price of one golf ball in the United States is $1.20; the price of a bottle of wine in France is 6 francs. When U.S. exporters sell one golf ball to the French, the French pay 6 francs to get the $1.20 golf ball (overlooking shipping costs). The Americans can now use those 6 francs to buy a bottle of wine in France.

Are both countries happy? Yes. The Americans are happy to get one bottle of wine for one golf ball because their opportunity cost of producing each additional bottle of wine is 1.5 golf balls. The French are happy to give up a bottle of wine for a golf ball because their opportunity cost of producing golf balls is 1.5 bottles of wine.

All is well so far. Now suppose that the United States buys more wine (measured in dollars) than the dollar value of French purchases of golf balls. The result is a U.S. trade deficit in which the French accumulate dollars and we lose our supply of francs. From our point of view, the decrease in our supply of francs will cause the price of francs as measured in dollars to rise. From the French point of view, the increase in their supply of dollars will cause the price of dollars as measured in francs to fall. As the French accumulate dollars, they begin to look less and less favorably upon the dollar.

Suppose that because of a persistent trade deficit with France the dollar will buy only 4 French francs instead of 5. Now $1.20 will buy only 4.8 francs. In order to buy the 6 francs a bottle of wine costs, we will have to pay $1.50. If we decide to buy the wine at this price, the French have $1.50 with which to buy our $1.20 golf ball. They can now obtain 1.25 (1¼) golf balls in exchange for one bottle of wine.

Now, the final question arises. Will the Americans be willing to give up 1.25 golf balls (instead of one) to obtain a bottle of French wine? Yes, they will. In the United States, the opportunity cost of producing one bottle of wine is still 1.5 golf balls. Therefore, even at 1.25 golf balls per bottle of wine, it is cheaper for the United States to specialize in golf balls and trade them for French wine.

But when we add the real-world costs of shipping to the increased price of French wine, we may find that the drop in the value of the dollar makes the importation of wine too expensive. The French will probably lose sales, and American consumers will switch to New York or California wines. American wine growers will be happy, but American consumers will undoubtedly have to pay more for American as well as French wine because the American wine producers will not have to compete as hard as before.

The Balance of International Payments Account

Governments try to keep track of all money and credit that flows into or out of their countries so that they can predict what is apt to happen (1) to exchange rates, (2) to their "credit rating" (their ability to borrow) with the IMF, and (3) to their stocks of international reserves. For these purposes, nations keep a **balance of international payments account.**

A nation maintains a balance-of international-payments account to record all transactions with other countries in a given year. In the United States, the account is kept by the Department of Commerce for the three purposes just mentioned. Our balance-of-international-payments account is an attempt to measure not just U.S. exports and imports, but all transactions that lead to a loss of dollars to foreign ownership or to a gain in U.S. ownership of foreign currencies.

The transactions that lead to these outflows or inflows of money are numerous. When General Motors buys control of an Opel factory in Germany, GM must first buy German marks with dollars, leading to an increase in dollar deposits owned by Germans, just as the U.S. purchase of a Datsun leads to an increase in dollar deposits owned by Japanese. On the other hand, if the GM investment in Opel is profitable, the profits return to the United States via the purchase of dollars with marks so that American owners of GM stock can receive dividend payments in dollars.

There are a host of other ways dollars flow into or out of our control. If we fly on a French airline, sail on a Greek cruise ship, catch a train in Spain, buy British insurance, put money into a Swiss bank, or send money to relatives in Israel, we are buying foreign currencies with dollars and causing the dollar holdings of foreigners to increase. And if foreigners use our services or travel in this country, we obtain increased deposits of their currencies.

All of these transactions involve private individuals or enterprises. We must also take into account government spending—rent payments for Air

TABLE 18-7 U.S. Balance of International Payments, 1978 (in billions)

I. Current account transactions resulting in U.S. ownership of foreign currency

(1) Exports	+$141.8
(2) Investment income (net)	+ 19.9
(3) Other services	+ 3.3
(4) Total	+$165.0

II. Current account transactions resulting in foreign ownership of U.S. dollars

(5) Imports	−$176.0
(6) Private gifts and government grants	− 5.1
(7) Total	−$181.1

III. Current account balance	−$16.1
IV. Private capital flows	− 25.7
V. Increase in foreign ownership of U.S. government securities	+ 34.0
VI. Changes in U.S. international reserves	− 3.7
VII. Statistical discrepancy	+ 11.5
VIII. Balance of all the pluses and minuses	$ 0.0

Source: *Statistical Abstract of the United States, 1980.*

Force or Navy bases overseas; grants or loans to other countries; payments to foreign countries for food, utilities, and foreign labor for the servicing and maintenance of our bases and diplomatic embassies or missions. Table 18-7 is a simplified version of all of these dollar flows in 1978.

When you read newspaper references to this summary of international transactions, often there will be a mention of the **"merchandise trade balance,"** in this case, line 1 minus line 5 = +$141.8 billion − $176.0 billion = −$34.2 billion. And you will also see references to the **"current account balance"** (line III). The −$16.1 billion shown here is the sum of lines 1 through 7.

The private capital flows (line IV) were largely bank loans to foreigners in 1978 (made in order to give them a supply of dollars).

Note on line VIII that the account "balances." All of the pluses and minuses add up to zero. This is because in international accounting, there is a plus for every minus. Our export of soybeans to Japan is a plus, but their payment to us is a minus. Thus, it is incorrect to think of any plus or minus as either "bad" or "good." However, look at lines V and VII. The sum of these two lines is a plus $45.5 billion. Line V shows that foreigners purchased $34 billion of government securities, giving us their currencies in exchange. These purchases helped us buy that much of other countries' products, but Line V also shows that foreigners are increasing their holdings of our public debt (see page 301 for what this might mean). Line VII shows that all *known* transactions in 1978 actually added up to a minus $11.5 billion. But because every minus has a plus, this balancing item is included even though we don't know where the $11.5 billion went—(perhaps secretly to a Swiss bank account).

Trade, Inflation, and Jobs

Remember that nothing happens without affecting something else. A recession in Europe hurts U.S. exports. A recession in the United States will seriously injure several economies by damaging *their* exports to the United States.

By the same token, inflation, jobs, and trade are closely intertwined. A trade deficit in the United States tends to promote inflation. The deficit "cheapens" the dollar by causing it to depreciate, to float downward. As the dollar floats downward, we find that more of our dollars are required to buy yen, marks, or, more to the point, Arabian riyals with which to buy more oil. For Americans, oil becomes more costly. As the American price of oil rises, so will many other prices. (The downward float of the dollar will also cause the prices of foreign cars, television sets, and cameras to rise.) Inflation in the United States is worsened. And finally, a downward float of the dollar that causes prices to rise may kick off another round of cost-push price increases (Chapter 17) which in turn may eventually result in lower sales and increases in unemployment.

Summary

Adam Smith argued that free trade permits an international division of labor whereby consumers can enjoy the benefits of products produced more cheaply abroad than at home. According to the principle of comparative advantage, even when a country is superior at producing everything, there are still many products it should buy from other countries. Despite the country's superiority, there may be differences in the opportunity cost of specialization relative to other countries, thus providing a logical basis for specialization and exchange.

Trade restrictions fall into two broad categories—tariffs and nontariff barriers. Since 1934, the United States has passed legislation and participated in treaties that have helped lower tariff rates. The most important pieces of legislation are the Reciprocal Trade Agreements Act of 1934 and the Trade Expansion Act of 1962. Treaties with other countries have led to U.S. participation in the eighty-one-nation General Agreement for Tariffs and Trade (GATT) and the twenty-four-nation Organization for Economic Cooperation and Development (OECD). Although these efforts have helped lower tariff rates, nontariff barriers in the form of import quotas, licenses, "buy-American" campaigns, and so forth are apparently more difficult to deal with. Concern in the United States about high unemployment rates is leading to a new wave of protectionism.

To the extent that trade restrictions interfere with the operation of the principle of comparative advantage, a nation's real wealth and income may suffer. Trade restrictions in the long run lead to retaliatory measures in other countries and thus to a general breakdown in the international division of labor.

When two countries want to trade, they must first buy each other's currency so that they can pay for the product they want in the currency of its producer. When they buy the currency of another country, they give their own currency in exchange.

If country A buys more goods and services from country B than B buys from A, A has a trade deficit with B, and, as a result, A's supply of B's currency will dwindle and B's supply of A's currency will increase. Conversely, if A has a trade surplus with B, A's supply of B's currency will increase and B's supply of A's currency will decrease.

Exchange rates of IMF-member nations float in response to the forces of demand and supply for each other's goods and services. Floating rates serve as an automatic adjustment mechanism to eliminate deficits and surpluses.

Countries may lose or gain supplies of one another's currency by virtue of many kinds of spending—government spending, private investment, and travel. A country's total of all international gains or losses of its currency is shown in its balance-of-international-payments account.

Discussion Questions

1. What is the "wealth of a nation"?

2. If Tom can make two beds in the same time that it takes him to wash and dry twenty dishes, and Sue can make three beds in the same time that it takes her to wash and dry twenty-seven dishes, who has the absolute advantage in what? Who has the comparative advantage in what? How should they divide up the two tasks? Explain.

3. Why do average tariff rates fail to reflect high tariff rates?

4. Why would exporters favor depreciation of their own country's currency?

5. How do floating exchange rates serve as an automatic control mechanism? Is there any evidence that floating rates don't work?

6. What, if any, might be the relationship between a depreciation of the dollar and the level of employment in the United States?

References

1. Adam Smith, *An Inquiry into the Nature and Causes of the Wealth of Nations* (Chicago: Great Books Series, Encyclopedia Britannica, 1952), p. 287.

2. Ibid., p. 3.

3. Sterling F. Green, "Maze of Tariffs, Taxes Trap Free World Trade," *Los Angeles Times*, 3 May 1972.

4. Ibid.

5. See "25% U.S. Tariff on TV Sets Urged—Federal Panel Seeks to Protect Domestic Firms," *Los Angeles Times*, 15 March 1977, pt. i, p. 1.

19 Socialism, the U.S.S.R., and the People's Republic of China

UPI

The term **socialism** means a system in which (1) the people—that is, the government—own and operate the major industries of a country, (2) resource allocation is done by central planning rather than by free markets, and (3) a major goal of the system is to make more equitable the distribution of wealth and income.

It is important for us to understand socialism for at least two reasons: First, Americans often discuss socialism with a good deal of heat. Various administrations are accused of leading the country down a disastrous road toward socialism because of such public works as the Tennessee Valley Authority or welfare-oriented legislation like Medicare. Socialism is depicted as a fate worse than death.

Key Words	
Socialism	Gosplan
Communism	Turnover Tax
Karl Marx	*Nomenklatura*
Proletariat	Mao Tse-tung
The Communist Manifesto	Commune
Alienation	Brigade
	Team

Second, we need to understand socialism because a very large part of our world considers itself to be living in a socialist system. Some fifty-three countries with over 40 percent of the world's population are in this group. In these countries, socialism connotes an idea of a higher order.

Our discussion of socialism is divided into three sections (1) Karl Marx and the genesis of socialism, (2) the Union of Soviet Socialist Republics (the U.S.S.R.), and (3) the People's Republic of China.

Karl Marx and the Genesis of Socialism

We usually think of Marx as the father of communism, not of socialism. But as you will see Marx thought of socialism as a transition stage in society's path toward its true ideal—a communist world. To a Marxist, Communism represents the purest form of socialism. For this reason, many of the world's socialist countries like to believe they are following the Marxian path to communism. (You will find a short biography of Karl Marx on pages 402–403.)

Communism and socialism compared

Communism, like socialism, is also a system in which all of the means of production are owned and operated by the workers. But communists, *in theory,* go considerably farther than socialists in their belief in ownership and control by workers.

Communists believe the institution of private property is the cause of the most important defect of capitalism: unequal distribution of income. As long as entrepreneurs own the means of production and hire others to work for them, the communists say, there will be separate classes of people, and the entrepreneurs and landowners will exploit the industrial workers and agricultural laborers. Because the entrepreneurs own the land and capital, according to communist theory, they can prevent the workers from being anything more than slaves, for the workers cannot earn a living without using tools or land owned by the entrepreneurs.

Socialists generally believe that people should be paid in proportion to their contribution to production: "From each according to his ability, to each according to his *work.*" This form of socialism is viewed by the communists as a transitional step toward an ideal society. A socialist state will have to set up planning agencies to answer the three questions of what, how, and for whom, to produce. But after this work is done, the theory goes, the state and its supervisory agencies are supposed to "wither away," leaving a classless society of workers and peasants all equal with one another and all owning the means of production. When this true communism has arrived, workers will live by a new philosophy: "From each according to his ability, to each according to his *need*."

Because today, of course, true communism has not yet arrived, a communist is a socialist who is, at least in theory, working toward a stateless, classless society. Thus, the two most famous examples of communism—the Soviet Union and the People's Republic of China—are actually socialist countries.

To understand how communism came to be opposed to capitalism, we need to understand how communism originated. No person has contributed more to the spread of the communist ideal than has **Karl Marx,** who predicted the downfall of the entire capitalist system.

Marx's attack on capitalism

Marx believed that labor's contribution to production was the source of all value, but that the wages received by laborers were always far below the value of the products they produced. The reason for this disparity, he thought, was that capitalists "expropriated" this "surplus value"* in the form of profit.

Moreover, the capitalists' desire for more and more profits caused them to pay lower and lower wages so they could extract the maximum possible surplus value from the working people. And the capitalists' desire to grow richer motivated them to invest their profits, wrung from labor in the form of surplus value, in bigger factories and more machinery.

Because of the ever-increasing production that resulted, and constantly depressed wages, Marx thought, sooner or later people would not have enough money to buy the increasing quantities of goods produced. As demands for goods slackened, the working people making them would be laid off, so that there would be fewer people earning wages to buy goods. This would cause a depression to occur (like the Depression in the 1930s in the United States). Depression would follow depression, each worse than the previous one because of the continually lessening demand for the increasing supply of products coming from bigger and bigger factories.

With each depression, he predicted, the plight of the working class—which he called the **proletariat**—would become worse, because of lower wages and higher unemployment, until finally it would become so bad that the working people would overthrow the capitalists and establish a socialist state. Thus, **The Communist Manifesto,** which Marx wrote with his friend Friedrich Engels, ends with these ringing exhortations:

According to Marx, all value is created by labor. The land is worthless until labor is applied. Capital (machines and factories) represents "embodied labor" because people create it. Therefore, the laborer is entitled to the whole product of his labor. But the greedy capitalist pays him only a portion of the value he creates—just enough for his subsistence. The remainder—in the form of profits, interest, or rent (the other three factor payments)—goes to the capitalist. That remainder was called "surplus value" by Marx.

> They [the communists] openly declare that their ends can be attained by the forcible overthrow of all existing social conditions. Let the ruling classes tremble at a communist revolution. The proletarians have nothing to lose but their chains. They have the world to win. Working men of all countries, unite!

Marx's attack on capitalism was particularly directed at the concentration of the ownership of private property in one class, that of the capitalists. He believed the capitalists would accumulate capital (the "means of production") at the expense of a growing number of propertyless proletarians. He also believed that the one way such laboring men could improve their status was to seize the capitalists' wealth and property and control the means of production themselves.

This violent solution need not always happen, however. History has proved Marx wrong by showing that force is not necessary to redivide income and wealth. Through labor unions and social and economic legislation, the lot of working people can be improved, and certainly *has* been improved over the years in the United States. In the years between 1939 and 1979, real spendable weekly earnings (earnings adjusted for inflation and after taxes) doubled.

Still, though Marx might concede that the worker's lot might improve a bit under capitalism, he would insist that capitalism involves a fundamental conflict between the owners (capitalists) and nonowners (proletarians) of the means of production. This conflict, he would say, inevitably produces economic instability in capitalistic countries, as indicated by their periodic recessions, and allows workers to continue to be paid less than the value of their work and deprived of power to make production decisions. These ideas are the essence of Marx's most famous work, *Capital (Das Kapital)*.

Marx might also correctly point out that while average real per-capita income has grown, income and wealth are still not distributed equally. Moreover, to any assertion that the working person's lot has improved, Marx might reply, "For what reason? Because of the market-price system? Or because of labor unions and social welfare legislation?"

Marx was particularly interested in the way industrial capitalism tended to separate workers from the products they created. Today workers in large factories find themselves on an assembly line working on only a small part of the whole—say the door assembly of the automobile they produce. No one worker or group of workers is in a position to enjoy the act of creating the whole automobile. Individual workers lose their pride in creativity, the kind of pride skilled artisans like painters, plumbers, or farmers have when they can see their productive efforts "come to life." Industrial workers, Marx pointed out, begin to feel that their jobs and their own existence are meaningless—and this feeling of meaninglessness is worsened by the fact that a capitalist, not the worker, owns and controls the means of production.

Psychologists now call this sense of meaninglessness and powerlessness **alienation,** and Marx is to be given much credit for identifying the problem.

Karl Heinrich Marx, 1818–1883: The Father of Communism

The Bettman Archive

Karl Marx's father was born Hirschel Levi and was the descendant of a long line of rabbis. However, because of anti-Semitism in the German town of Trier, where he lived, he changed his name to Heinrich Marx and joined the Christian church. His wife, who was also of rabbinical lineage, remained faithful to her religion until 1825 when, after seeing all of her seven children baptized into the Lutheran church, she decided to follow suit. Perhaps because he witnessed the religious dissension between his father and mother, Karl Marx became an enemy of all religious dogma.

Gifted from early childhood, young Karl turned for friendship and intellectual stimulation to his father, who was a successful lawyer and philosopher, and to a family friend, Ludwig von Westphalen, the Royal Prussian Privy Councillor. Although von Westphalen was far removed from the Marx family socially, he was much impressed by the young Karl Marx and so was his daughter, Jenny.

During his early years, Marx dabbled in poetry, and it was reported, Jenny would "burst into tears of joy and melancholy" every time she read one of his new poems. Marx's father worried that Karl and Jenny's infatuation with each other might cause friction with the von Westphalens, so he was happy when his son went away to the University of Bonn in the fall of 1835.

On his own, and away from home, Marx immediately began sowing wild oats, running up debts, and neglecting his studies. He was also arrested for noisiness and drunkenness. His involvement in a duel led to a state investigation, as a result of which Marx left Bonn and returned home. He and Jenny von Westphalen became engaged, which may have been a deciding factor in his later life, for he went to Berlin for another

However, alienation is not just a capitalist problem. The same sense of powerlessness is found in socialist countries among industrial workers under the control of a central authority.

Marx has left a valuable legacy for social scientists by pointing out that (1) the exploitation of any class is dangerous; (2) capitalism has a tendency to breed periods of unemployment and human suffering; and (3) a system based on entrepreneurial self-interest tends to produce ever-larger enterprises that stifle competition and concentrate power in the hands of a relatively small number of people. Marx reminds us also that violent revolution remains a possibility if a large class of people begins to believe it is powerless to achieve the same standard of living enjoyed by many others.

Two Marxist societies born in revolution are the Soviet Union and the People's Republic of China. Let's look at both to see how communist theory has worked in practice.

try at university work and eventually earned a doctorate in philosophy.

The death of his father in 1838 left Marx with no close family ties because his mother refused to support him, and he had never cared for his other relatives. To earn a livelihood, in 1842 he became associated with the *Rhine Gazette,* a left-wing newspaper, and became its editor. Never noted for his tact, Marx soon alienated German government officials with his editorials, and in 1843 the *Gazette* was officially suppressed, leaving Marx a self-styled martyr with an interest in socialism. He was forced to leave Germany for Paris. Against his mother's wishes, he married Jenny von Westphalen and embarked upon a life of poverty.

The year 1844 was a turning point in Marx's life, for it was then he met Friedrich Engels, son of a German cotton manufacturer, who was working in one of his father's factories in England. Engels had had the opportunity (as Marx had not) of observing first hand the plight of industrial workers in England—the fifteen-hour days, starvation wages, and unsafe working conditions.

In 1845, a diplomatic incident occurred in France which caused the expulsion of all foreigners, and Marx and his family moved to Belgium. In Belgium, he founded the first Commu-nist Party, an organization with no membership formalities, no political program, and no members of the proletariat, but still it was a move from theoretical to active socialism. In the following years, Marx was occupied with constant writing and political struggle, culminating in *The Communist Manifesto,* which he and Engels drafted in 1848.

Failing to get communism established on the Continent, Marx moved to London in 1849 to continue studying and writing, and in 1852 he became a political correspondent in England for the *New York Tribune.* Still, he earned very little and was always engaged in a struggle to find means to support himself and his family. Indeed, despite being almost completely dependent upon Engels for support during the last thirty-four years of his life, he was so poor that several of his children died. Despite these difficulties, he completed *Capital,* his most famous work, and it was published in 1867.

Marx continued to work on additional volumes of *Capital,* but was unable to complete them. When his wife died in 1881, he said, "The Moor [as his children called him] is dead, too." He died fifteen months later. Engels edited the rest of the material of *Capital* and brought out the second and third volumes after Marx's death.

The Union of Soviet Socialist Republics

The Soviet Union grew out of a revolution in 1917 against capitalism under the Russian tsars, where the majority of the people were exploited laborers or peasants working on land that did not belong to them. Since the revolution, the U.S.S.R. has been gradually transformed into an economic system in which more than 95 percent of all enterprises are owned by the state, the rest being only a few shops and markets selling produce from private agricultural plots.

Like many socialist states, the Soviet Union operates under a central economic plan. Production goals are given in a five-year plan (planned by a bureaucracy called the **Gosplan**), which is broken down into hundreds of targets or quotas each industry must meet. Three to four million people are involved in the Gosplan planning mechanism, using elaborate inventories to measure the quantities of goods produced and sold and complicated computer operations to decide how to obtain and use resources.

Wages vary from occupation to occupation, although not as much as they do in the United States, and workers are paid a national average of $187 per month. Bonuses, however, may quadruple a worker's income, and they are widely used to push production beyond specified quotas. Piece-rate systems are also used to push workers harder, and there are a variety of extra privileges used as incentives—better housing, access to products in short supply, villas in the country, vacations on the Black Sea, and so forth.[1]

An overriding goal in the Soviet Union has been the creation of heavy machinery and factories to provide the equipment necessary for growth. To achieve this goal, the government has had to direct resources away from consumer products; that is, it has demonstrated that the opportunity cost of capital formation is sacrificed consumption. For a long time, Soviet women could not buy lipstick, and there are frequent shortages of fresh meat, chicken, and fresh vegetables. When products people want suddenly appear—shoes, for example—there are long lines of people waiting to buy.

How do the Russians take resources away from producing the consumer products people want? A heavy sales tax called a **turnover tax** is put on consumer goods, usually at the wholesale level. Sometimes this tax amounts to as much as 44 percent of the retail price of a product. By varying the amount of the tax, Soviet planners can raise or lower the retail price of consumer goods and encourage or discourage their purchase. Discouraging the consumption of, say, automobiles releases resources for building trucks.

There is no question about the material success of socialist planning in the Soviet Union. Economists generally agree that the rate of growth of the Soviet economy has been equal to or greater than that of the United States, particularly during the 1930s, and in recent years Soviet living standards have risen. However, because the U.S. economy produces almost twice as much as the Soviet economy ($2,100 billion versus $1,200 billion in 1978), the smaller U.S. growth rate still provides vastly more goods per year than the larger Soviet rate. A 5 percent growth on $1 is only a nickel, whereas a 5 percent growth on $5 is a quarter.

Despite its gains, socialist planning has its costs. Citizens of a socialist-planning system have little or no political and economic freedom—to choose an occupation, start a business, or vote for opposition candidates. Socialist planning may build in mistakes on a large scale. A Czechoslovakian economist once told the author he was working with a computer operation that attempted to keep track of 1.5 million items! Imagine trying to estimate the quantities, sizes, colors, and so on of just the items people wear and eat. Planning mistakes will produce shortages of desired goods and surpluses of things no one wants. The desire to fill quotas may cause the production of items that cannot be sold. If you are running a nail factory and your quota is expressed in weight, you will probably produce the heaviest nails. You will pay little attention to producing a variety of shapes and sizes. During the Soviet prohibition on lipstick manufacture, some employees falsified their plant's inventories and sent materials to an illegal factory where lipstick could be secretly produced at night. (The lipstick "entrepreneurs" were later caught and jailed.)

Since Stalin's death in 1953, the Soviets have relaxed many of these controls and have tried to improve consumer welfare. In Moscow, the people appear healthy, well-dressed, and happy. Undoubtedly they are far better off then they were under the tsars.

Will the Soviets move along the socialist path toward communism? At present, this seems unlikely. They have apparently adopted a system of wage payments and awards of privileges that has created different classes of people with different standards of living—much like the scheme of things in a capitalist country. Furthermore, Soviet style planning requires totalitarian government and the people who have this power will not want to give it up.

Hedrick Smith, former *New York Times* correspondent in Moscow, states that the Russians have developed a pyramid-shaped society with a small elite class at the top.[2] A secret roster of those who have joined the elite is called the **nomenklatura** (nomenclature). These people and their families enjoy all of the privileges previously reserved for the tsar and his nobles. The *nomenklatura* exists on all levels and at all places, from villages to the Kremlin. According to Smith, it "operates like a self-perpetuating, self-selecting fraternity, a closed corporation."[3] It is this kind of elitism that the Chinese are trying hard to prevent, but in Russia those who run the show, the bureaucrats and experts, reserve for themselves the privileges of chauffeur-driven cars, villas, and deluxe apartments, which are not available to others at *any* price.

Many Russians are cynical about their version of socialism, but they appreciate having complete economic security, which means they do not have to worry about unemployment or income during retirement. One Russian told Smith that the big difference between American capitalism and Russian socialism was that "I don't have to worry about the future, and you do!"[4]

| The People's Republic of China | On October 1, 1949, **Mao Tse-tung*** announced to the Chinese people that Chiang Kai-shek's armies were defeated. The Chinese people call this day a day of liberation, and today when they talk of history they speak of "before liberation" and "after liberation." They have good reason. |

| Before and after liberation | Before liberation people died in the streets on cold nights. An American newspaper in Shanghai ran an article in early 1949 stating that eighty corpses had been found in the morning after a cold wind the night before. Young girls were forced to become prostitutes. Drug addiction from opium was widespread. Rich peasants charged 100 percent interest every six months on loans to tenant farmers. Taxes were repeatedly collected by warlords until |

The spelling of Mao Tse-tung is from the so-called Wade-Giles system. At the start of 1979, the Chinese officially adopted a new system called the "Pinyin" (phonetic) system which more closely approximates Chinese pronunciation. Under the Pinyin system, Mao Tse-tung becomes Mao Zedong; Peking becomes Beijing; Teng Hsiao-ping becomes Deng Xiaoping, and so forth. We will stick with the older, Wade-Giles system on the theory that it is still more familiar to most readers.

the people were paying taxes a year in advance. Large cities like Canton, Nanking, Peking, and Shanghai were divided up into walled concessions owned by foreign companies or governments. In one such concession in Shanghai there was a park with a sign that read NO CHINESE OR DOGS ALLOWED.

People were often treated like beasts of burden, forced to work in the factories and fields from the age of seven. Work was long, averaging twelve hours a day, and wages were barely sufficient to maintain life. Workers and peasants were so poor they could not maintain their families and often sold their babies into slavery for a few pennies. No wonder China went Red.[5]

Today, the Chinese economy is growing rapidly. Despite the fact that there are tremendous masses of people—more than four times the number in the United States in a country only 2.5 percent larger geographically—all receive, at minimum, a subsistence diet, all have a place to live, adequate clothing, medical care, and free education. Illiteracy, starvation, prostitution, venereal disease, and drug addiction have virtually ceased to exist. Cities are clean. Flies, mosquitoes, and other common pests have almost disappeared. A near-miracle seems to have occurred.[6] How has this come about?

Mao fought for control of China for roughly twenty-two years, from 1927 to 1949. During this time he came to realize that the key to his success lay in selling communism not just to the urban workers but to the peasants in the countryside, since the peasants constitute 80 percent of the population. Mao also learned a basic economic fact of life: the rural areas had to be organized to produce a surplus of food before resources—land, labor, capital—could be released to produce other things like factories.

Throughout his struggles with Chiang Kai-shek and the Japanese during World War II, Mao taught his soldiers to be helpful to the peasants. As a result, the peasants often fed him and hid him and his troops from the enemy.

Conversion of the countryside to socialism took about ten years after liberation, and most agricultural land is now organized into **communes** (see Figure 19-1). One example is Ping Chow commune near Canton, which is situated on 50,000 acres of land, of which 12,000 acres are under cultivation, and with 69,000 people living in 16,000 households.

The commune is divided into 20 production **brigades,** each brigade consisting of 14 teams with about 200 members each. The **team** is the basic accounting unit for purposes of measuring production and determining how food, shelter, and pay will be divided among the people. Communes, brigades, and teams are headed by revolutionary committees elected by the people. The election process is done, not by ballot, but by discussion, until consensus is reached.

Mao constantly called for self-reliance, and the communes reflect this principle. Most of them have their own schools, hospitals, power sources, machine shops, and metal works. Except for production of sophisticated machinery, a commune is almost self-sufficient.

The Ping Chow commune's crops are rice, vegetables, fruit, peanuts, and sugar beets. Farm animals are pigs, water buffalo (seen everywhere as draft animals), dairy cows, and poultry. There is a printing plant, a peanut-

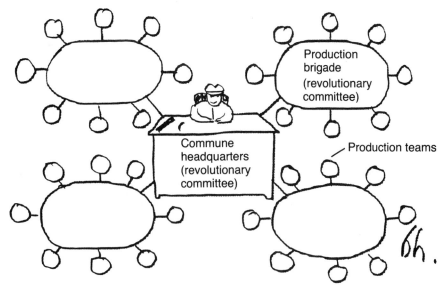

Figure 19-1. How an agricultural commune in China is organized.

Production brigade (revolutionary committee)

Commune headquarters (revolutionary committee)

Production teams

oil refinery, and factories for food processing, production of lime, cement, textiles, and rattan baskets.

The communes are efficient agricultural units in that they permit organization of a large area. In the Ping Chow commune, for instance, 50 miles of flood-control channels and 150 miles of high- and low-voltage transmission lines have been built. The large area permits much specialization and pooling of equipment.

The cities in China are organized much like communes with their brigades and teams. The cities are divided into districts, neighborhood committees, and finally residential committees (See Figure 19-2). Like the team, the residential committee is responsible for about 200 people.

The state owns all enterprises, although the workers often feel that they own a commune or factory collectively. Production from "private" plots in communes still accounts for about 2 percent of total production. Answers to the three basic questions (What? how? for whom?) are determined by an exchange of information between enterprises and ministries located in cities, counties, provinces (states), and the national government in Peking. Enterprises in China seem to have much more say in what and how to produce than they do in the Soviet Union. There is also less pressure to fulfill production targets; consequently, there is less cheating.

The organization of the entire society into these small groups makes it possible for the people to share their feelings about the national tasks that confront them. Through these groups the sense of national purpose is kept high.

The organization of the entire country into groups of about 200 people gives the people a sense of living in a small town despite the enormous population. This sense of community unites the people in their struggle for

Figure 19-2. Political organization of the People's Republic of China.

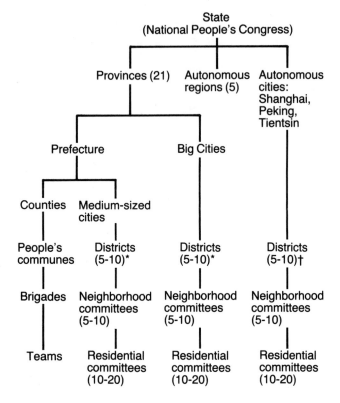

* Do not include surrounding counties

† include surrounding counties

equality and economic improvement. The small-town type of grouping also provides discipline, for everyone knows what everyone else is doing and people who get out of line are soon discovered. Mistakes, crimes, marital or other interpersonal problems, and "capitalist-roader" thinking are ironed out in these small groups by the revolutionary committees responsible for each team or residential area. For this reason, crime and divorce are rare and, despite power struggles in Peking, the people are remarkably united.

Although wages are very low, the people have enough because expenses are minimal. A family can save 25 percent of its income per year for highly prized purchases like a bicycle ($70) or a sewing machine ($70). In a family of four with both husband and wife working, combined income is about $50 per month. Each month they pay about $8 for food, $3 for rent, $2 for heat, $1 for electricity, and 10 cents for water. Medical care runs a few dollars a year. Once or twice a year they spend about $10 for clothing (everyone's outer garments are almost alike). Thus, there is plenty left over for saving, which they may put in a bank where it will earn interest at 2.16 percent per year (immediate withdrawal permitted) or 3.25 percent per year if left in for one year.

(Continued on page 411)

Mao Tse-tung, 1884–1976: "Serve the People"

The Bettman Archive

When Mao Tse-tung died in 1976 at the age of eighty-two, he was already a legend in his own time. Millions of Chinese consulted the little red book, *Quotations from Chairman Mao Tse-tung,* for guidance in all types of situations. His slogans such as "Serve the people," and "Friendship first, competition second," were held up as a model for conduct throughout the country. His portrait was everywhere, in places where groups meet, at national shrines, and in people's homes. During his lifetime, China changed from a country where starvation and disease were commonplace and foreign gunboats patrolled the rivers to one in which people had enough to eat, their health was greatly improved, and their country was no longer subject to foreign control.

The oldest of three children of a hardworking peasant in Shaoshan, Hunan Province, in central China, Mao attended a local primary school for five years, then went to work full time for his father. However, he was an avid reader and dreamer, and so at 16 he ran away from home to continue his education and enrolled at the middle school (high school) in Changsha, the capital of Hunan Province.

In 1911, his education was interrupted by a revolution which brought down the Manchu Empire. Caught up in the radical fervor of the time, Mao joined the revolutionary army as a private. Leaving the army after six months, he tried law school, classes in soap making, and police work before enrolling in a teacher-training school in Changsha.

Although ridiculed by other students and teachers for his peasant ways, he persisted for five years and at age twenty-four finally graduated.

In 1918 he married the daughter of a favorite teacher and made his first trip to Peking. Like most other Chinese, he felt betrayed by the post-World War I Versailles Treaty, which gave former German concessions in China to Japan rather than restoring them to China. More travel, extensive reading, and work as a university library assistant and journalist began to crystallize his radical tendencies, and in 1921 he helped organize the Communist Party of China. He attended the first party meeting in Shanghai and then returned to Changsha to recruit party members, organize labor unions, and further study Marxism.

In 1925 he went among the peasants, calling together fact-finding conferences in villages and county towns. From this experience he was able to describe the classes of Chinese society. The rural masses, he stated, were made up largely of "semi-owner" peasants, who were constantly in debt, and poor peasants, who were little more than slaves. Semi-owner peasants, he said, receive "only half the harvest or even less for their year's toil." The poor peasants "have neither adequate farm implements nor funds nor enough manure, their crops are poor, and with little left after paying rent, they have even greater need to sell part of their labor power. In hard times they piteously beg help from relatives and friends, borrowing . . . grain to last them a few days, and their debts pile up like loads on the backs of oxen.''[7] Mao believed both peasant groups were receptive to revolution.

In his 1926 *Report on an Investigation of the Peasant Movement in Hunan,* Mao wrote that "In a very short time . . . several hundred million peasants will rise like a mighty storm, like a hurricane, a force so swift and violent that no power, however great, will be able to hold it back.''[8] The Communist Party, he felt, had three alternatives: to lead the peasants, to trail behind them, or to oppose them. Mao favored leading the peasants, although for a long time his fellow communists did not agree.

In 1927, the Kuomintang, a nationalist party led by Chiang Kai-shek, broke with the Communists and launched a program of extermination in which many members of the Communist Party were killed, including Mao's wife. Mao and his band were forced to flee to the mountains, where they joined ex-warlord-turned-Communist Chu Teh and his forces and built a small Red Army. Recruits were educated in Marxism and trained to treat the peasants with respect (until then an unheard-of-practice). They were instructed not to take even so much as a single needle or thread, to turn in everything they captured, to be polite, pay fairly for what they bought, and return everything borrowed. Here Mao laid down the principles of guerrilla warfare that proved successful for the Red Army: "The enemy advances, we retreat. The enemy camps, we harass. The enemy tires, we attack. The enemy retreats, we pursue."

The Red Army resisted four attempts by Chiang Kai-shek's forces to surround their mountain headquarters. Finally, in 1934, 100,000 of Mao's troops broke through the Kuomintang lines and started on their famous 7,000-mile Long March, fighting as they went. En route, the Communist Party met in Tsuni, Kweichow Province, and elected Mao chairman. When the Red Army finally reached Yenan in northwest China in late 1935, only one-tenth of its soldiers were left. But in Yenan the army gradually gained recruits and fought successful guerrilla operations directed by Mao from a spartan cave.

When Japan invaded China in 1937, Mao and Chiang Kai-shek joined forces for a united (but uneasy) alliance against Japan, but even then the Red Army continued to grow, and by the end of World War II it numbered 900,000. After the war Mao's army entered into an all-out struggle with Chiang's Kuomintang, which was supplied with arms and equipment by the United States. Finally, in 1949, Chiang's remaining army escaped to Taiwan, and the People's Republic of China was proclaimed.

Mao's land reform policies, begun as areas were liberated in northern China, were now put into effect. Peasants seized control of local administrations and drove out or killed landowners and others accused of exploitation. National campaigns were launched to retrain bureaucrats and scholars, and gradually both landowners and capitalists were eliminated. During the transition an estimated 200,000 to 2,000,000 persons were killed.

During Mao's leadership of the country, Russian aid was secured in 1948 and withdrawn in 1960, the Great Leap Forward campaign in 1957–1959 established rural communes and factories in the fields, and the Great Proletarian Cultural Revolution of 1966–1967 sent young Red Guards throughout the country to root out the tendencies of bureaucrats and party workers to give themselves special privileges. Throughout, Mao's concern was to break down China's ancient ruling-class tradition and Confucian teachings on the natural inequality of status between men and women, elders and youth, rulers and ruled. To him, class struggle—eliminating the differences of status between town and country, worker and peasant, and mental and manual labor—was at least equal in importance to technical advance, even if continuing revolutions were required to break up newly formed elites.

After Mao   Mao's great contribution to China was in giving the peasants a feeling that their status was just as important as a technician's or scientist's. Mao's philosophy was like that of a coach who believes that it's more important for everyone on the team to play—and to have the right spirit—than to win the game.

After Mao's death in September 1976, this point of view changed drastically. Although Mao's protégé, Hua Kuo-feng, became premier, the man responsible for the change was Teng Hsiao-ping, Vice Chairman of the Communist Party and Army Chief of Staff.

Teng initiated a new program called the "Four Modernizations"—of China's agriculture, industry, science and technology, and defense. To accomplish his goals, Teng abandoned Mao's egalitarianism with his let-everyone-play-on-the-team philosophy. Teng decided that winning the game was what counted.

Some examples will help to dramatize the change. Prior to Mao's death, the universities were open to any "worker-peasant-soldier" recommended by his or her team or neighborhood committee. Examinations had been eliminated and students were chosen for ideological (Maoist) purity.

Mao's fear was that the universities had become elitist institutions for the sons and daughters of Party big-wigs. His removal of admission standards was an attempt to destroy the elitist character of higher education. Teng reinstituted a strict examination policy. The universities became reserved for China's most able.

Teng also changed Mao's doctrine of self-reliance. During 1978, 530,000 tourists visited China, including thousands of business executives looking for new markets. Coca-Cola was granted exclusive rights to sell in the People's Republic. And what would have been considered the height of "capitalist-roading" during Mao's regime is now being built near Peking—a golf course!

China has entered into a $20 billion trade agreement (oil for steel) with Japan, a $13.5 billion agreement with France (which includes the construction of two nuclear power plants), and other smaller trade agreements with Denmark, Sweden, and Britain. The United States is involved in several agreements including building a chain of hotels and landing rights at various airports for Pan-Am.

Teng—or his heirs—has a long way to go. In 1978, there were 630,000 students enrolled in China's universities (versus 10 million in the United States). Teng's program for agriculture requires the purchase or building of nearly 5 million pieces of farm machinery; for industry, the replacement of machines often twenty years old; for defense, the modernization of an air force whose most recent bomber was made in 1954.

Table 19-1 shows that by most measures of a modern society China has a long way to go to catch up with the Soviet Union and the United States. The section about agriculture reveals the gravity of China's problem. Chinese production of grain is not much more than that in the United States, but China has more than four times as many people (an estimated 1 billion in 1979). And most of China's people (85 percent) are needed to work in agri-

TABLE 19-1   A Long March (latest comparable data from U.S., Soviet, and Chinese sources)

	U.S.	U.S.S.R.	China
Area	3.6 million square miles	8.6 million square miles	3.7 million square miles
Population	220 million	262 million	1 billion*
GNP	$2.1 trillion	$1.2 trillion*	$444 billion*
Industry			
Steel production	135 million tons	166 million tons	34 million tons
Oil production	474 million tons	629 million tons	110 million tons
Coal production	654 million tons	796 million tons	651 million tons
Auto production	9.2 million	1.3 million	15,000*
Computers in use	340,000	30,000*	2,000*
Agriculture			
Percentage of work force engaged in agriculture	3.3	25	85*
Grain production	294 million tons	259 million tons	325 million tons
Tractors	4.4 million	2.5 million	225,000*
Communications			
Telephones	155 million	22 million	5 million*
Television sets	133 million	60 million	700,000*
Paved roads	3.1 million miles	200,000 miles	161,000 miles
Air-passenger miles	193 billion	84 billion	1 billion
Social indicators			
Average yearly industrial wage	$13,400	$3,000	$360*
Average life expectancy	73 years	69 years	65 years
Residential living space per capita	450 square feet*	133 square feet	30 square feet*
Days' earnings to buy bicycle	1¼	7	67
Percentage of population under 20	35	37	40–45*

*Estimates

Source: Adapted from *Newsweek*, 5 February 1979, p. 43. With permission from Fenga & Freyer, Inc.

culture because the number of tractors is relatively meager. Somehow food production will have to be increased and mechanized to release people for work in other activities. Achieving a food *surplus* is the first, necessary step toward economic growth.

The economics of love and sex

Table 19-1 does not show China's massive efforts to control population growth.

Under Mao, China's preoccupation with controlling population resulted in a rigid code of sexual behavior. Holding hands or other forms of affection between sexes was frowned on. Premarital sex, or even worse, a premarital birth, resulted in extreme public disapproval. Such amenities of American life as coed dorms would have been beyond imagination.

Mao's wife, Chiang Ching, was to a large extent responsible for China's puritanical value system. She became the dictator of China's cultural life—its literature, music, art, ballet, movies. Under her guidance everything cultural had a mission: the support of Mao's revolutionary efforts to root out "capitalist-roading." China's music became militant; western music was banned. The ballets portrayed struggles between landlords and workers—a problem-solving soldier was often in the hero's role. Love and sex in art, literature, or movies disappeared. They were considered too distracting from the main goals of Maoism. Couples married, not for love (ostensibly), but to improve their efforts to "building socialism ever faster and better."

Soon after Mao's death, Chiang Ching was declared a criminal—one of a so-called "Gang of Four" responsible for the revolutionary excesses of the previous decade. Ironically, she was accused mainly of enjoying a high-style of living—with palaces, non-Maoist clothes, chauffered limousines, beach resorts for her exclusive use, and so forth—a "capitalist-roader" of the worst sort.

Her straitjacketing of culture into a revolutionary mold was not appropriate to Teng's four modernizations. And so love and sex are making a slow reappearance in Chinese literature and movies—and in real life. Couples can once again be seen holding hands in public. Whether or not this relaxation will hurt China's massive effort to control population remains to be seen.

In true Malthusian fashion, the Chinese frown on marriage before age twenty-five for women and age twenty-eight for men. After marriage, the couple is strongly encouraged to have no more than two children—one is preferable. Brigade and neighborhood clinics dispense free birth control devices and pills. "Barefoot doctors," as the Chinese call them (paramedics with one or two years of medical training), help to teach the importance of population control. But even with all of this effort, China's population increase is estimated at around 1.5 percent per year (compared with six-tenths of 1 percent in the United States). When the grand total is 1 billion people, 1.5 percent means 15 *million* more people to feed each year. And 1.5 percent (according to the Rule of 72) means a doubling every 48 (72 ÷ 1.5) years.

Let's sum up our impressions of the Soviet Union and China. We cannot make positive measurements about the success of Soviet versus Chinese planning. In both cases the planning mechanism attempts to coordinate production of all major products—grain, oil, steel, electrical power, and so forth. Observers have commented, however, that lines of people trying to buy scarce items are common in the Soviet Union but are not seen in China. Somehow the Chinese have adjusted incomes and prices so that the quantities demanded do not exceed quantities supplied.

Of course the pushing and shoving for scarce goods one sees in the Soviet Union is a measure of the people's ability to buy, whereas the absence of lines in China may be an indication of the people's *inability* to buy. But, although the Chinese are terribly poor by American standards, what there is is divided among the people so that everyone is surviving.

Which state is closer to the communist ideal? There is no doubt that China was, prior to Mao's death, working for a classless society far more diligently than the Soviets. Now, under Teng's Four Modernizations program, the two nations will probably begin to look more alike.

Summary

Socialism is an economic system in which the public, through its government, owns the major enterprises in a state, allocates resources through central planning, and attempts an equitable distribution of wealth and income. Socialist countries in the West are examples of mixed systems—mixtures of capitalism and socialism.

In other socialist countries the term "communism" is used to indicate that the country is following the principles and writings of Karl Marx, one of the earliest leaders of the Communist Party (1847).

Communist theory states that socialism is an interim stage leading eventually to a classless society in which the state has withered away.

Socialism exists in many forms among fifty-three nations, involving more than 40 percent of the world's population. Most socialist countries try to equalize incomes; those countries considered communist also try to do away with private property so that all industry and agriculture are collectively owned by the people.

The Soviet Union and the People's Republic of China are both examples of socialism. In both cases almost all property is owned by the state. The Chinese economy, and its whole social fabric, are undergoing a period of fundamental change from egalitarianism under Mao to emphasis on growth under Teng Hsaio-Ping.

Discussion Questions

1. Why did Karl Marx believe capitalism would destroy itself?

2. What are the distinctions between socialism and communism?

3. How does the People's Republic of China differ from the Soviet Union?

4. In what respects is the Soviet Union "capitalistic"?

5. How are the people motivated to believe in equality in China?

6. What has happened to the goal of equality since Mao's death?

References

1. For many examples, see Hedrick Smith, *The Russians* (New York: Quadrangle/New York Times Book Co., 1976).

2. Smith, *The Russians.*

3. Ibid., p. 29.

4. Ibid., p. 70.

5. See Edgar Snow, "Why China Went Red," *The Other Side of the River* (New York: Random House, 1962).

6. The author was able to observe many of these developments during a visit to China for twenty-two days in April and May of 1976, on a trip arranged by the United States-China Peoples Friendship Association. The trip involved visits to agricultural communes, schools, hospitals, factories, stores, and a bank. Of course, twenty-two days do not an expert make. There are many descriptions of the Chinese economy but little official information. See James Tobin, "The Economy of China: A Tourist's View," *Challenge*, March/April 1973; J. K. Galbraith, *A China Passage* (Boston: Houghton Mifflin Co., 1973); Joseph Kraft, *The Chinese Difference* (New York: Saturday Review Press, 1972); Joan Robinson, *Economic Management in China* (London: Anglo-Chinese Educational Institute, 1973); Thomas G. Rawski, "Chinese Industrial Production 1952 to 1971," *The Review of Economics and Statistics*, May 1973; John W. Gurley, "The New Man in the New China," *The Center Magazine*, May 1970; K. P. Wang, *The People's Republic of China—A New Industrial Power with a Strong Mineral Base* (Washington, D.C.: U.S. Bureau of Mines, 1975); Christopher Howe, *China's Economy* (New York: Basic Books, 1978); Frederic M. Kaplan, Julian M. Sobin, and Stephen Anders, *Encyclopedia of China Today* (New York: Harper & Row, 1979).

7. *Selected Readings from the Works of Mao Tse-tung* (Peking: Foreign Language Press, 1971), p. 16.

8. Ibid., p. 24.

20 Economic Challenges of the Eighties

Ida Kirschenbaum/Stock, Boston

The 1980s will be a crucial decade that may well determine the capability of human beings to survive on this planet. A bewildering number of crises confront us: the ability of our own nation to cure stagflation, the challenges posed by continued rivalry between Marxist societies and mixed systems, the struggle of poor countries to become richer, the effects of dwindling supplies of resources like oil, the falling international value of the dollar, the consequences of increases in pollution or population, the pressure on world food supplies, and the increases in world spending for arms. And more.

From this list of issues, we're going to extract three we think are extremely important because each one involves elements common to all of the above problems. Accordingly, the chapter is divided into three sections: (1) the challenges of poverty in the developing countries, (2) the increases in world spending for arms, and (3) the "Doomsday Model."

Key Words

Physical Quality of Life Index (PQLI)	Intermediate technology
Revolution of rising expectations	Triage
Capital-output ratio	Prisoner's dilemma
Social overhead capital (infrastructure)	Doomsday model
Group of 77	Zero population growth (ZPG)
Official development aid (ODA)	Zero economic growth (ZEG)

Coping with World Poverty: The Developing Countries

This section is about poverty among nations. Poverty is, of course, a relative matter. Whenever there is any inequality in the distribution of income, some people will always be poor *relative* to others. But much of the world is so abjectly poor that some observers speak of *absolute* poverty—"a condition of life so degraded by disease, illiteracy, malnutrition, and squalor as to deny its victims basic human necessities."[1]

Almost one billion people—one-quarter of the world's population—are in this category. One quarter of a million people in Calcutta are homeless. They eat, live, and die in the streets. Three million people in Bolivia out of a total population of 5 million have a life expectancy of thirty years of age. The average Bolivian eats less than one-half of one ounce of meat per year; in effect, the peasant population is too poor to eat any meat at all.[2]

What is a "developing country"?

Several terms are used to describe countries that are poorer than others: "underdeveloped countries," "third world countries," sometimes even "fourth" or "fifth world countries." Economists have no specific dividing lines or explicit definitions of such terms. A nation's position is usually determined by dividing its GNP by population (per capita GNP) so that there is a "ladder" of countries from rich to poor—from $15,480 per person per year in Kuwait to $70 per person per year in Cambodia in 1978.

Usually, all countries are classified as either "developed" or "developing," with about two dozen countries in the first category and all the rest in the second. The dividing line is *approximately* $1,000 per person per year, but such a division is arbitrary and often unrevealing. We know that GNP says little about the quality of life. Moreover, a per capita GNP figure conceals the distribution of income within a nation. For example, per capita GNP in Brazil was $1,140 in 1978, but 30 million of Brazil's 110 million people had average annual incomes of only $77.[3] And so we are left with an imperfect measure as the box essay on the next page indicates.

The placement of countries in the "developed" or "developing" categories is done by the Organization for Economic Cooperation and Development (OECD). Usually, the $1,000 per capita GNP dividing line is observed. But other criteria are also used.

In an attempt to broaden the definition of "developed," economists have made up an index called the **Physical Quality of Life Index (PQLI)**—a

The Trouble with Comparing Per Capita GNPs

When we use per capita GNPs to compare countries we find ourselves trapped by numbers which are of little help in describing real differences in the standards of living between people of different countries. Not only is GNP an imperfect measure of welfare or progress *within* a country, as we saw in Chapter 11, it has even less meaning when used for intercountry comparisons. Two examples will clarify this point.

1. In a poor, less-developed country like Tanzania with a per capita GNP of $180 per year, the $180 figure is imperfect because it is based primarily on cash transactions. But much of such a country's production and consumption will typically involve little or no cash. The people in Tanzania's villages feed themselves out of their own production, just as the people in the Chinese communes do. Therefore, in most cases, per capita GNP figures in poor countries understate their true incomes. Of course, that doesn't mean such people are rich. We could double the numbers, and these people would still be abjectly poor by any standard.

2. In the fall of 1978, the author had the good fortune to spend three months in New Zealand with an opportunity to observe and compare New Zealand life styles with ours. At that time, New Zealand's per capita GNP was about one-half of United States' per capita GNP. But, it would

have been very foolish to conclude that their standard of living was one-half that of the average American. Fresh food prices were generally one-half of U.S. prices, so that with much lower wages, the New Zealanders ate just as well or better than we do. Housing costs (rents and home purchase prices) were also about one-half. Education, medical care, and retirement pensions were all provided from a highly progressive schedule of income taxes. One real-life example: that of a highly-skilled construction worker who retired at age sixty. At the time of retirement, he earned $3.80 per hour, by our standards abysmally low after a lifetime of work. Nevertheless, he owned a home and automobile free and clear, had $50,000 in the bank, and began receiving a pension of 80 percent of his highest earnings. He and his wife were comfortable, content, traveled overseas occasionally, and had no financial worries.

Offsetting these amenities, the prices of manufactured, imported products like automobiles were very high by U.S. standards. But the problem is, how does one evaluate these differences in life styles? Can one say that Americans are better off than New Zealanders or vice versa? The question is impossible to answer. Nevertheless, the GNP per capita method of comparison is the method most commonly used.

composite of a nation's life expectancy, infant mortality, and literacy.[4] The index for Sweden is 97, for the United States, 94, for Bangladesh, 35. The index reveals the weakness of looking only at GNP per capita: GNP per capita in Saudi Arabia is a healthy $4,480 (1978), but its PQLI is only 28. For that reason the OECD classifies Saudi Arabia as a "developing" country.

This section reviews the plight of the developing countries. It describes the distribution of the world's income: discusses the reasons why the developed countries, particularly the United States, should be concerned with world poverty; analyzes the two major problems of population increase and lack of capital, and presents some conclusions.

Distribution of the world's income   Just as income is unevenly distributed in the United States, so is it unequally distributed throughout the world. Figure 20-1 shows that, in 1975, 57.7 percent of the world's population received only 9.7 percent of the world's

57.7% of world population (68 countries) produces 9.7% of world GNP—less than $500 per person

16.7% of world population (30 countries) produces 33.4% of world GNP—$2,000 to $4,999 per person

14.8% of world population (59 countries) produces 9.7% of world GNP—$500 to $1,999 per person

10.8% of world population (25 countries) produces 47.2% of world GNP—$5,000 and over per person

Figure 20-1. Distribution of world income in 1975

GNP, whereas the richest countries with 10.8 percent of the population received 47.2 percent of the world's GNP.

Moreover, the gap is widening, as Figure 20-2 indicates, and may continue to widen. Simple arithmetic shows why. Assume from Figure 20-2 that

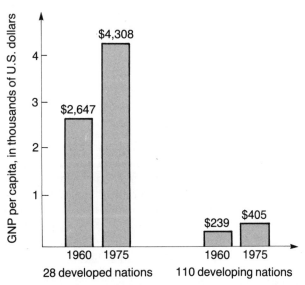

Figure 20-2. The widening gap: GNP per capita in 1960 and 1975.

Source: From *Military Budgets and Social Needs: Setting World Priorities,* by Ruth L. Sivard, Public Affairs Pamphlet No. 551. Used with permission.

average GNP per capita is $4,000 in the 28 developed nations and $400 in the developing nations. Further assume that per capita GNP grows at an annual rate of 3 percent in both groups. At that rate, per capita GNP will double in (72 ÷ 3) 24 years. Then per capita GNPs will be $8,000 and $800, but the difference between the two groups will be $7,200 ($8,000 − $800) instead of the initial difference of $3,600.

Note that in both cases, per capita GNPs in the developed countries are ten times larger than in the developing countries. The *relative* difference is the same, but the *absolute* difference is greater. It all comes down to the fact that 1 percent of $400 is $4; 1 percent of $4,000 is $40.

We have to draw the uncomfortable conclusion that the income gap is almost certain to widen and that the relative unhappiness of people in the developing countries is almost certain to increase—unless the rich countries take strong measures to help.

Why should we be concerned?

Aside from the moral issues involved, self-interest provides several basic arguments for our concern with the problems of developing countries. In one way or another, they are our problems too.

Our need for strategic and other materials

An industrial society like the United States cannot function without certain raw materials. One estimate (already noted in Chapter 18) is that there are thirteen such materials essential to the United States.[5] Some examples are oil, asbestos, bauxite (aluminum ore), chrome, cobalt, copper, lead, manganese, nickel, petroleum, platinum, silver, tin, and titanium. Many of these essentials come from the developing countries, and our dependence on other countries is growing. In 1950 we relied on other countries to provide us with more than half of our needed supply of four of the thirteen materials. By 1985 we will want more than half of this supply of *nine* of the thirteen from other countries.

Many of the developing countries are following the lead of OPEC and forming cartels to control supplies (and prices) of bauxite, tin, coffee, bananas, tea, rubber, and pepper, to name a few. The United States will have to form new relationships with cartel countries to whom it formerly dictated prices.

The need for political stability

It is sometimes said that "only the rich can afford democracy." Consider a nation of starving, uneducated people. It is easy for them to turn to an authoritarian political party or a dictator, whether of the left or the right, who persuades them that he or she can solve their problems. If the dictator becomes the source of international tension, or even war, as in some of the African or Latin American states, the peace of the world may be threatened. No one (rich) nation like the United States can afford to permit a people's suffering to threaten the development of a stable political order throughout the world. Economic assistance to poor nations reduces the risk of internal revolution and military adventurism.

Time is running out

In a world of growing populations and declining food reserves, the time left to solve the world's poverty problems is getting short. The world's population is increasing at the rate of 64 million per year now, rising perhaps to 100 million per year by the year 2000.[6] Roughly 87 percent of these new mouths to feed will be in the developing countries. Some experts believe that, if we don't act *now* to solve the problems of population and environmental pollution, by the mid-twenty-first century the human race will begin to starve and suffocate (see pages 433–36).

The revolution of rising expectations

Some of our responsibility to help less-developed countries stems from the imperialism of the nineteenth century—the empire period of mother countries and colonies. The United States turned Cuba into its supplier of sugar; Brazil, Colombia, and Central America into its suppliers of coffee and bananas; Chile and Venezuela into its suppliers of copper, nitrates, and oil. And of course the United States was not alone in molding other countries and colonies into one-crop, one-resource economies that were dependent on their mother countries for capital goods. In most cases, the capital goods that were supplied by the United States and other mother countries were for the purpose of assisting the production of one crop or resource. Dependency on "mother" was encouraged, diversified development discouraged.

But as time went on, the colonies became aware that there was a double standard of existence. The imperialists who were visible on the scene lived in mansions and treated the people in the colonies like servants. The imperialists brought with them all of the props of development—varied diets, refrigeration, automobiles, country-club enclaves. It was natural for the colonial peoples to demand a new life style.

What has taken centuries of development in the rich countries, from the Renaissance through the Industrial Revolution, the poor countries want *now*. The result has been called a **revolution of rising expectations.** The poor recognize the need for *power*, and we must recognize this need as legitimate.

Problems that must be solved—and some solutions

The developing countries share a number of common problems, any or all of which may be present in any given country. We will take up two of them,* and in each case give some ideas about what might be done. The two problems are (1) increases in population that can wipe out any gains in food production, and (2) the difficulty of obtaining all forms of capital—financial, tangible (machines), and human (skilled workers) and of putting this capital to work.

Population and poverty

We are today proving the population side of Malthus's equation. The world's population was 4.3 billion in 1977, and that figure was about *one billion* more than it was in 1960. This last billion was added in *just 17 years.*

---

*Military spending by developing countries is discussed in a later section of this chapter.

It is absolutely essential that the developing countries slow their rates of population increase.

Many of the developing countries face ruinous rates of population increase, high rates of infant mortality, and relatively poor life expectancy. For example, the average annual growth rate in the United States, 1970–1977, was .8 percent (eight-tenths of one percent) per year. The Rule of 72 tells us that at that rate, the United States population will double in 90 (72 ÷ .8) years. By contrast, the comparable rate in India was 2.1 percent per year during the same period. Consequently, India's population will double in 34.3 years (72 ÷ 2.1) unless the Indians manage to slow the rate down. The average rate for all developing nations was 2.3 percent during the three-year period, 1975–1977.[7]

To persuade people of the developing countries to slow their rates of population increase is essential—and enormously difficult. In most such countries, adults want and often need large families. The children can help perform manual labor in the fields and support their parents as their parents grow old. Children are the "social security" system in poor countries.

But if the result of economic aid is to keep people alive longer (better food, health care, sanitation) so that more people reach reproductive age and produce more offspring, then the benefits of aid will be swept away in the rising tide of population. Consequently, massive programs to educate the people to have smaller families is a prerequisite for development and for aid.

The People's Republic of China has shown that such a massive educational program can work. As we saw in Chapter 19, premarital sex is frowned upon; women are discouraged from marrying until age twenty-five and the men until age twenty-eight. Families are encouraged to limit their children to two. Free birth-control devices, abortions, and vasectomies are easy to obtain. In overcrowded Szechwan province with a population of 90 million, parents are offered extra rice rations and cash bonuses for stopping at one baby. China's new goal is to halve its rate of population increase from 2 to 1 percent per year.[8]

Singapore has also instituted a successful plan by imposing penalties on couples who have more than three children. The working mother forfeits maternity leave; the delivery fee is higher. If the couple has more than four children they get a lower priority for choice of primary school and the lowest priority in obtaining subsidized public housing.

It may also be much cheaper for a rich country to help a poor country develop by subsidizing a population-control program than by paying for a program to increase production. Remember that welfare is usually measured by comparing per capita GNPs, and that a nation's per capita GNP is determined by dividing GNP by population. We can make per capita GNP go up by increasing the country's GNP *or* by reducing its population—or by trying to do some of both. Most economists believe that it is far cheaper to raise a country's per capita GNP by reducing its population—*because the cost of preventing a birth is as little as one dollar per adult per year.*

Dr. Stephen Enke comments, "The moral is clear: if the objective is higher income per head, money spent to reduce births will be as much as 100 times more effective than money invested to raise output."[9] Here is a simple example. Assume GNP is $100,000 and population is 1,000. Per capita GNP is therefore $100,000 ÷ 1,000 = $100. The developing country now receives a grant from rich countries of, say, $500 to build a factory. Because of increased production, GNP increases by $100 to $100,100. Per capita GNP is now $100,100 ÷ 1,000 people = $100.10. The people are 10 center per capita better off than before. Now suppose instead that the $500 is used to reduce population and that population is reduced by 100 people. Per capita GNP is now $100,000 ÷ 900 = $111.11. The people are now $11.11 per capita better off, roughly 100 times better off than they were with their 10 cent increase following the $100 increase in GNP.

Obtaining and using capital

Assuming the developing country tries to increase production (as well as slow its rate of population increase), it can choose any or all of three paths: (1) It can make sure that everyone is working as hard as possible—that there is no "disguised unemployment" doing make-work jobs or working so inefficiently that fewer people could do the same amount of work. (2) It can follow the lessons of Adam Smith's pin factory by reorganizing the work in order to obtain a greater division of labor. (3) It can acquire tangible capital (machines) or human capital (educated know-how) to increase the productivity of its labor force. Let's look at the third option, as economists do.

The capital-output ratio.   Let us assume that a developing country does not want or need massive amounts of capital, but *some* capital in small amounts is necessary. How does a developing country go about getting it? A simple model will help.

Assume that a poor country has a GNP of $100 million, that production of food is $100 million, and that the people eat all of the food they produce. Under these conditions, total income is $100 million and the people spend the entire $100 million. Saving is zero and so is investment, because all production is devoted to consumption, a not unusual situation in a very poor country.

As long as all of the people are busy producing food, none of them can be released to produce capital. There are two exceptions to this line of reasoning: (1) If there is disguised unemployment in the fields, people *can* be released without lowering food production. (2) People might learn how to produce more food by reorganizing the work (through a better division of labor, for example) without having to obtain more capital.

At this point an expert from the United Nations arrives and shows the agricultural workers how they can reorganize their work so that some of their people can be released for investment in capital goods. These released workers now produce $15 million worth of capital goods. GNP is now $100 million plus $15 million or $115 million. Total income must also be $115 million, out of which the people spend $100 million and save $15 million.

Note that (1) we followed the course of one of our exceptions: consumption did not have to be cut because a way was found to reorganize the work, and (2) when income increased to $115 million, the people did not increase their consumption of food. They chose (or were forced) to continue consuming the same $100 million amount and to save $15 million. The $15 million worth of saving made the $15 million worth of investment possible.

Now the question is, what good will the $15 million worth of investment do?

The **capital-output ratio** helps to explain. The capital-output ratio is the ratio (measured in dollars) between the cost of capital and the annual income it produces. In the United States, the capital-output ratio is about 3:1. That is, $3 worth of capital will produce about $1 worth of income per year. In other words, $3 worth of saving will permit investment of $3, which will, in turn, produce $1 worth of income per year. In our simple model of a developing country, $15 worth of investment would produce $5 worth of income annually.

The problem is that, in a developing country, the capital-output ratio is more likely to be 5:1. This means that it takes *$5* worth of capital to produce $1 worth of annual income. Each dollar's worth of capital operates less efficiently in a poor country than in a rich one.If the developing country invests $15, it will get $3 worth of income, not $5. To obtain $5 of extra income, it would have to invest *$25*, not $15. And to invest $25, it would have to *save* $25.

The developing country is therefore in a tough spot. It has to save more than a rich country does to obtain the same extra dollar's worth of income. And saving—refraining from consumption—is far more difficult when one is hungry than when one spends only a modest portion of one's income for food (17 percent in the United States).

A word about why the capital-output ratio is so much higher in a developing country. If the capital-output ratio is 3:1, a capital investment produces enough income to pay for itself in three years, a return of 33⅓ percent. When the ratio is 5:1, the return is considerably less—20 percent. Why so much less? In a developing country, if a capital good, say, an electric generator, breaks down, it may take days to find someone (or find spare parts) to fix it. The efficiency of capital depends on the condition of a country's **social overhead capital** or **infrastructure** (its transportation and communication systems), as well as on the know-how of its workers. All of these forms of human and nonhuman capital are of better quality in rich countries than in poor ones and improve the return on capital investments in the rich countries.

The need to save in order to export.   A developing country also has to save if it wants to buy capital goods from other countries. Let us return to our simple model again. If GNP is $100, and consumption is $100, the country has nothing to export. It is consuming all of its income. As we saw in Chapter 18, this means that a developing country is unable to obtain the Swiss francs, German marks, Japanese yen, or U.S. dollars it will need to buy capital goods from these industrial countries.

Thus, a developing country must export to obtain the international reserves with which it can pay for capital goods from other countries. And to export, it must save. It must refrain from consuming some of its production.

If a developing country is unable to export, it will have to obtain foreign exchange through loans or grants from richer countries. But this approach has its own difficulties. The money has to come from somewhere and lenders usually want to be paid back. The developing countries who do have the means to pay back such loans are in trouble, as the next section indicates.

The financial capital problem.   The financial plight of the non-OPEC developing countries became highly visible following the OPEC oil embargo of 1973. The developing countries' ability to import capital and other necessities worsened badly as (1) they had to pay higher and higher prices for oil and as (2) the international markets for their exports became sluggish as a result of the worldwide recession during 1974–1976.

By 1979, developing countries had borrowed $48 billion from the United States alone.* The bankers aren't worried about middle-income cases like

---

*Total indebtedness of the developing countries in early 1980 was a staggering $348 billion. See "World Bankers Juggle the Huge Oil Debts," Time, 3 March 1980.

the Philippines, Taiwan, Brazil, and Mexico. But the bankers *are* worried about non–oil-producing developing countries like Dahomey, Upper Volta, Turkey, and Zaire. For them, one official noted that their "choice will be either lowering their living standard or cutting their development programs. Neither choice is any good."[10]

In an attempt to solve their financial plight, many of the developing countries have formed alliances such as the **Group of 77.**[11] The Group of 77 has made three kinds of proposals: (1) a general debt moratorium, which would permit them to make *no* debt payments over some period of time; (2) agreements for "indexing" their commodity prices to the prices of the industrial goods they buy,* and (3) the creation of a "common fund" to finance the stockpiling of the commodities they sell.

All three plans have problems. A debt moratorium might bankrupt the banks that loaned the money. An indexing arrangement designed to help all less-developed countries could only by the "sheerest coincidence," as one scholar pointed out, be appropriate for any one country taken singly.[12]

The third plan would establish a common fund that would finance the stockpiling of commodities produced by the developing countries in times of excess supply and replenish the fund by selling the stockpile when the quantities demanded exceeded the quantities being currently produced. Again, there are formidable obstacles—principally, getting all the participants to agree on their initial contributions to the fund and on the quantities they would produce. The "common fund" idea would involve all of the difficulties our egg producers faced back in Chapter 7 (stemming from the urge to undersell or outproduce one another)—with the further difficulty that we are talking now about many different countries with different national aspirations. Still, the "common fund" idea is probably the best chance for the less-developed countries to provide themselves with a steady income.

More aid from the rich?   The United States could probably extend more **official (government) development aid (ODA).** Many governments give larger percentages of their GNPs (though not more money in absolute terms) to the developing countries than does the United States.† Private investment by rich countries in the developing countries can also provide the latter with capital goods and higher wages. But the pattern of private U.S. investment overseas has shifted from development of natural resources in the developing countries to manufacturing in other rich countries. In the 1890s, the bulk of our private overseas investment was in the developing countries. Now only about 25 percent of our overseas investment is, and the percentage appears to be falling.[13] Conscious effort by government agencies to encourage

---

An indexing plan would enable a developing country selling, say, coffee, to raise coffee prices 10 percent if the United States (or any supplier) selling capital goods to it raised its prices 10 percent.

†*In 1977 we gave $4.1 billion, 0.22 percent of our 1977 GNP. Other percentages of aid as a percentage of GNP were were as follows: France, 0.63; West Germany, 0.27; Canada, 0.51, Britain, 0.38; Netherlands, 0.85; Sweden, 0.99; Australia, 0.45.*

U.S. corporations to invest in the poorer countries would help. Needless to say, this is not easy. The developing country may very well treat outside investment as a return to colonialism, and the corporation might easily consider the possibility for foreign takeover too risky.

A comment on human capital.   The developing countries are desperately in need of a literate population for informed decision making and for the know-how to operate and maintain complicated forms of tangible capital. Before people can be trained in, say, soil chemistry, they have to be able to read. If a country's labor force is illiterate, its labor force can perform only the simplest tasks—usually manual labor in the fields.

Let's compare our illiteracy rate with India's. In the United States only 1 percent of the people over age fifteen can neither read nor write in any language. In India, the comparable figure is 66 percent. In 1977, the average illiteracy rate in 100 developing countries was 50 percent.[14]

The apparent solution is for the developed countries to send technicians, teachers, and medical doctors to the developing countries—much like the United States' Peace Corps program. The idea seems attractive on its surface, but there may be an unintended effect. Educational training divides people into classes; some get left behind; income differences grow. In the previous chapter we noted that, under Teng's thrust to modernize China, education at the university level is to be reserved for an elite few. Perhaps the first efforts to help developing countries should be those that disturb the status quo the least.

Intermediate Technology.   The most innovative solution to all of these capital problems comes from a British economist, E. F. Schumacher.[15] Schumacher's solution is to send very modest forms of capital called "intermediate technology" to the developing nations.

The term **"intermediate technology"** means a simple tool, the operation of which can be easily understood by an illiterate peasant in a developing country. Dr. Schumacher's prescription: a tool that enhances a worker's energy by, say, 1 horsepower, rather than 300. Dr. Schumacher and his group of scientists have developed a $16 hand-operated metal-bending machine that Nigerian villagers use to make agricultural tools; the cheapest non–hand-operated machine available to do the same job requires electricity and costs $1,750. Other forms of intermediate technology the group has developed are machines that make egg cartons from recycled paper, old tires adapted for use on oxcarts, a 20,000-gallon water tank that costs Botswanans $40 to build. Use of such tools will not transform a developing nation into a U.S.A. tomorrow, but it will start it on a path of gradual growth.

The use of simple tools has several advantages: (1) simple tools do not require large amounts of human capital (skill or training); (2) simple tools will not displace workers; (3) simple tools will not require large amounts of saving; (4) simple tools will not be hard to manufacture or fix; (5) simple tools will not require large amounts of energy; (6) the purchase of such tools—if the tools have to be purchased—will be less of a financial burden than will the purchase of large machines.

What conclusions can we make?

The first conclusion is that there is *no* general conclusion that will fit all of the developing countries except one: They must all learn how to reduce their population rates of increase. The second conclusion is that economic analysis can only go so far. Many of the poor countries' problems are political, social, and religious. We cannot, for example, tell the Hindus in India to eat their Brahman bulls when the bulls are sacred.

We have ignored the whole area of politics in this discussion. If a country has a dictator or has, at least, an authoritarian bureaucracy (as does the Soviet Union), it can order its people to eat less, have fewer babies, and save more for investment. And at present, authoritarianism *is* attractive to many less-developed countries, which want to get a job done *now* and which believe democracy is too slow. They could be right.* But the cost of such a direction would have to be measured over the long pull in terms of loss of personal freedom and the political instability that can occur when dissenters disagree with the authorities.

There is one particular argument we want to discuss. Some people say, "We can't possibly help them all. Let's try to select the ones who are most likely to make it."

Such a policy is called **triage,** a French noun meaning "choice." The term was used by the French during World War I to describe the need to choose those individuals among the wounded who might profit from the scarce medical resources that were available. The implication is that the rest must be abandoned.

Other variants of this suggestion exist. One writer likens the world to that of a lifeboat containing a few rich people while masses of poor people swim outside the lifeboat in the ocean.[16] Any attempts to help will increase their number and increase the likelihood that they will climb into the lifeboat and sink it.

Other writers don't go to the extent of saying that the poor countries will sink us, but they insist that at least the quantity of aid that will materially help them has got to make us poorer. As Professor Gunnar Myrdal says, "The blunt truth is without rather radical changes in the consumption patterns in the rich countries, any pious talk about a new world economic order is humbug."[17]

Another theory is that Americans just will not give that much anyhow. If, for example, Americans are asked to help, it would require that they go on "producing like Americans" but be content to consume much smaller amounts. But this is impossible, because the act of producing is inextricably involved with the act of consuming. To produce, we consume food, transportation, health services, appliances, houses, take vacations—all activities that replenish us and give us the incentive for further production.[18]

These are tough arguments, but if we agree, we consign millions of people to hunger, misery, and death. Moreover, it is possible that these

---

The remarkable record of the Chinese in feeding, housing, educating, and providing health care for their people is an example of what can be done with a combination of central planning and the common acceptance of an ideology. Moreover, the Chinese experience shows that survival is possible with very little outside help.

statements are guilty of a fallacy. The fallacy is the assumption that the supply of resources, the space in the lifeboat, is *fixed*, that any gift of resources, or of space in the "lifeboat," will subtract from what is left for the occupants. Consequently, we must hope that knowledge will *expand* the quantities of resources and the size of the lifeboat. By so doing, there can be more for everyone.

World Military Spending

Part of the problem in helping the developing countries results from the fact that rich and poor nations alike are caught up in an arms race. The superpowers fear one another; many poor countries fear everyone. Both groups feel that they must have their arsenals of weapons. The result is a catastrophic waste of resources which could otherwise be used to raise everyone's standard of living.

The topic is appropriate for the last chapter of an economics text because military spending has micro, macro, and international implications. Micro effects occur because government purchases of military products distort the prices in all markets where such purchases occur. Furthermore, the prices paid by the government are often higher than those paid in the private economy because of cost overruns or the failure of government agencies to obtain competitive bids. Then, insofar as military spending contributes to aggregate demand, it has macro effects because it contributes to employment. The connection between military spending and employment has caused some critics to wonder if we are beginning to accept military spending as necessary for economic health. Finally, as you will see, military spending creates international rivalry, which tends to be self-perpetuating.

This discussion will be divided into two sections: (1) the size of military spending and (2) the arms race.

The size of military spending

By the end of 1977, world military spending reached $434 billion, about 6 percent of total world GNP of $7.7 trillion.[19] After accounting for inflation, that is, in constant dollar terms, the nations of the world spent 15 percent more for military purposes in 1977 than in 1968. Tragically, the military share of GNP in developing countries (5.9 percent) surpassed that in developed countries in 1977 (5.6 percent).

Figure 20-3 shows military spending and spending for public health and education, relative to GNP, in developed and developing countries in 1977. Total world military expenditures were more than twice those for public health and slightly more than those for public education. For the world as a whole, there was approximately one soldier for every teacher, but eight soldiers for every doctor.

Military spending per soldier in 1977 was far greater in absolute terms in developed than in developing countries: $31,800 and $6,200, respectively. But in *relative* terms, military spending is far more expensive for developing countries. In the developed countries, average GNP per capita in 1977 was $5,380. Thus, to support one soldier, the work of 5.9 ($31,800 ÷ $5,380)

Figure 20-3. Relative spending in developed and developing countries for military, education, health, 1977.

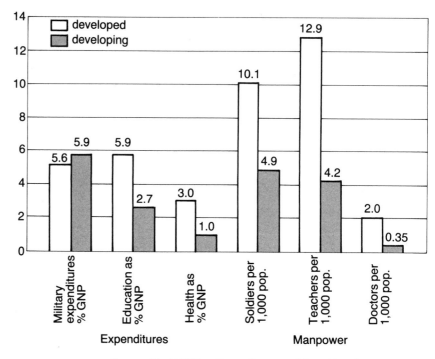

Source: *World Military Expenditures and Arms Transfers, 1968–1977.*

people was necessary. Average GNP per capita in the developing countries was $490 in 1977. To support one soldier in those countries, 12.7 ($6,200 ÷ $490) people were necessary.

The arms race and the "prisoners' dilemma"

The outlook for the future is not especially heartening. There is evidence that world military spending will continue to rise and that distrust among the great powers will result in continued increases in the development and production of nuclear weapons.

The **"prisoners' dilemma"** helps to explain why nations fear one another and why the arms race may well continue—despite continuing efforts like the SALT talks of 1979 to slow the arms race.

Here's the dilemma: Once upon a time a prison governor had two prisoners named Sleazy Sam and Dirty Dan whom he could not hang without a voluntary confession from at least one of them.

Accordingly, he summoned Sam and offered him his freedom and a $1,000 reward if he would confess at least a day before Dan did. Dan would thereupon be hanged.

If Dan should confess at least a day before Sam, however, Sam was told, then Dan would be freed and rewarded with $1,000, and Sam would be hanged. "And what if we both should confess on the same day, your Excellency?" asked Sam. "Then you each will keep your life but will get ten years in prison." "And if neither of us should confess, your Excellency?"

Figure 20-4. The prisoners' dilemma.

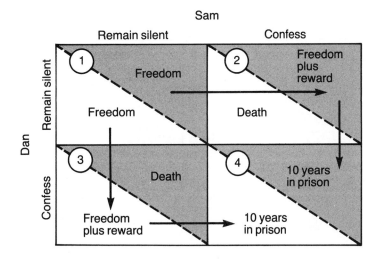

"Then both of you will be set free—without any reward, of course. But will you bet your neck that Dan—that crook—will not hurry to confess and pocket the reward? Now go back to your solitary cell and think about your answer until tomorrow." Dan, in his interview, was told the same, and each man spent the night alone considering his dilemma.[20]

The alternatives available in the prisoner's dilemma are usually displayed in a matrix diagram that looks like Figure 20-4. The diagram indicates that if both prisoners remain silent, they both go free (square 1). But if one

Each man spent the night alone considering his dilemma.

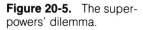

Figure 20-5. The super-powers' dilemma.

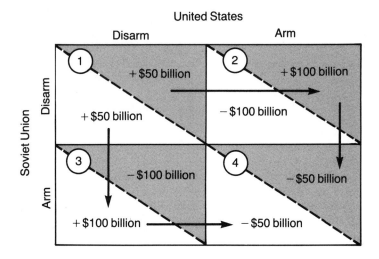

of them confesses before the other, the first to confess goes free and receives a reward and the second one is hanged (squares 2 and 3). Finally, if they confess simultaneously, both will spend 10 years in prison (square 4).

What is the logical decision for them to make? Confess. First, note the arrows. Sam can improve his lot by moving from square 1 to square 2 where, by confession, he will receive his freedom and a reward. Similarly, Dan can improve his lot by confessing (moving from square 1 to square 3). The second point is, of course, that only by confession can each prisoner be sure of keeping his life. The logical decision for both to make is to confess, resulting in ten years in jail (square 4).

The tragic point is that both could go free if they remained silent. But can they afford to? They cannot, unless they have absolute faith that neither one will doublecross the other and confess first. In short, mutual distrust is the nub of the problem.

The prisoners' dilemma has many other applications, but our purpose is to show how it applies to the arms race. Let's pretend that the two countries (instead of two prisoners) involved are the United States and the Soviet Union and that they have a choice between disarming or building rockets at a cost of $50 billion to each country. If one country builds the rockets and the other does not, the country that arms will be in a position to command trade agreements that will give it a $100 billion advantage (and the country that disarms a $100 billion disadvantage). Finally, if both disarm, each will be $50 billion better off (by not having to spend the money on rockets). Figure 20-5 summarizes the situation.

What will they do? If they could trust each other, they would disarm. But again notice the arrows. Each country can improve its situation by moving from disarmament (square 1) to arming (squares 2 and 3). In an atmosphere of distrust, however, neither can afford to be the disarmed country if the other has armed. The unfortunate result—both arm (square 4) and each is $100 billion worse off than in square 1 (−$50 billion versus +$50 billion).

Figure 20-6. World model with "unlimited" resources, pollution controls, and "perfect" birth control.

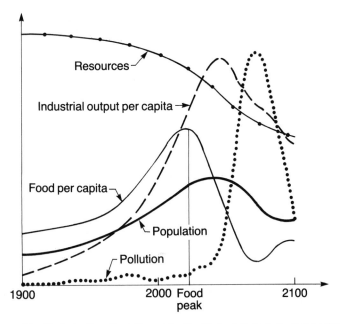

Source: *The Limits to Growth: A Report for the Club of Rome's Project on the Predicament of Mankind,* by Donella H. Meadows, Dennis L. Meadows, Jorgen Randers, William W. Behrens III. A Potomac Associates Book published by Universe Books, New York, 1972, 1974. Graphics by Potomac Associates.

Only by changing the climate of distrust can the major powers break through the dilemma of the two prisoners and agree to live in square 1. But enemies cannot trust each other because each must behave in such a way as to justify the other's distrust. When the United States and the Soviet Union display visible mutual distrust, as in containment policies, expansionist moves, and increasingly sophisticated weaponry (the Trident submarine and the Cruise missile)—the distrust can only reinforce their dilemma and oblige them to move to square 4. Because each nation believes the other is an enemy, the other nation becomes, in reality, an enemy, and each must arm in self-defense.

The Doomsday Model

In the late 1960s and early 1970s, there was a renaissance of Malthusian concerns, very likely generated by the crises of those years involving oil shortages, urban crowding, pollution, the threat of nuclear war, and an almost continuous series of violent incidents in various parts of the world.

These concerns led a group of one-hundred intellectuals, called the Club of Rome, to undertake a serious study of our ability as a species to survive.[21] A computer model—since nicknamed the **"Doomsday model"**—was designed by experts at MIT. The model involved (1) the depletion of scarce resources, (2) population increases, (3) food per capita, (4) industrial output per capita, and (5) pollution. One of the Club's computer models is shown in Figure 20-6.

The computer model assumes a number of favorable conditions, all to begin in 1975: a reduction of pollution by 75 percent (which the authors admitted was highly improbable), a doubling of world food production, and voluntary birth control, which would prevent the births of all unwanted children.

One can see from the model that despite these assumptions, food production peaks early in the twenty-first century. And although industrial output per capita rises sharply, so does pollution, reaching a disastrous peak around 2060. Pollution begins to fall only after industrial output per capita peaks and then falls. Thus, the last half of the twenty-first century is a picture of declining food supplies and pollution, but pollution declines only because industrial production slows down.

The authors of the Doomsday model insist that "none of these computer outputs is a prediction." But they go on to say that "the basic behavior mode of the world system is exponential growth of population and capital [industrial output], followed by collapse."[22] The authors conclude by arguing that we must stop population and industrial growth or face the prospect that growth *will* be stopped by "pressures that are not of human choosing" [famine, war, and disease]. Consequently, the Doomsday model is often associated with those who argue for **zero population growth (ZPG)** and **zero economic growth (ZEG).**

As you can imagine, the Doomsday model created a storm of controversy. Who, after all, wants to be told that the world as we know it is coming to an end?

One of the best known rebuttals came from Robert Solow, also at M.I.T.[23]

Professor Solow's objections

Professor Solow's argument has four main points: (1) we are more likely to be willing to help poor countries if we grow wealthier ourselves; (2) the Doomsday model overlooks the market forces that would ration scarce resources,* (3) the world *may* find solutions to overpopulation and (4) solutions to pollution are available.

1. Solow's first point hardly needs embellishment. If the developed countries are now having difficulty giving sufficient aid to developing countries, the former will find it even less palatable to share their wealth if a ZEG policy is adopted. It's easier to share a banquet than a sandwich. But Solow cautions us that growth doesn't guarantee generosity. We can be generous with or without growth, but we're more apt to be generous *with* growth than without it.

2. Solow's second argument is that a freely operating market system will help us to conserve scarce resources. "Higher and rising prices of exhaustible resources lead competing producers to substitute other materials." We can see this process taking place now as higher and higher oil prices are gradually forcing us to find other sources of energy.

Two years after their first report, the Club of Rome corrected this oversight but still forecast widespread starvation in 2025 unless the developed countries gave massive amounts of aid.

3. No one can say for sure what the population of the earth *should* be. Every society has, at a *point in time*, an "optimum" population. An optimum population means that there are enough people to permit a division of labor that is refined enough to allow the existence of symphony orchestras or neurosurgeons for patients with complex problems. Consequently, as population grows, GNP per capita may very well grow because of these gains from specialization and exchange. Eventually, GNP per capita may turn down with further increases in population—*unless* new technology extends people's capabilities.

In 1979, six years after Solow's article, a massive study called the Fertility Survey concluded that world population growth is beginning to decline.[24] During the 1969–1979 decade, world population growth slowed from 1.9 percent per year to 1.7 percent per year. "New projections indicate that global population may stabilize early in the next century at about 8 billion—double the present number but only *half* the total once predicted." Nonetheless, the director of the study, Phyllis T. Piotrow, warns that as a result of the doubling there will be "a horrifying crest of population-related famines, revolutions, and migrations in the next two decades." (It may be no accident that one of the highest rates of population increase in the world—3 percent—is in Iran where a revolution broke out in the fall of 1979.)

4. Solow's final point is that pollution occurs because of "an important flaw in the price system." Factories, power plants, and car drivers pollute the air and water "because a scarce resource (the waste-disposal capacity of the environment) goes unpriced." To correct this flaw we must tax those who pollute with an "effluent charge."* Effluent charges do three things: "They make pollution-intensive goods expensive and so reduce the consumption of them; they make pollution-intensive methods costly and so promote abatement of pollution by producers; they generate revenue that can, if desired, be used for further purification of air or water or for other environmental improvements."

Are Doomsday models helpful?

Doomsday models are helpful if they call attention to serious problems. But they are not helpful, if as Solow comments, they divert "attention from the really important things that can actually be done, step by step, to make things better."

And doomsday models may make the mistake of assuming human beings cannot change their destiny. A computer model of the future made in 1900 might very well have concluded that we would suffocate from coal dust in the air or drown in horse manure in the streets. Fortunately, times do change.

But what about war?

War is one of those accidents external (exogenous) to models that make prediction of any outcome difficult. Nevertheless, at least one well-known economist, Robert L. Heilbroner, believes that the problem of war is one of our "imminent dangers."[25]

See the discussion of effluent charges on page 111.

Like the Fertility Survey, Heilbroner argues that pressures on the developing countries to feed their people will become explosive—particularly in the next two decades. Out of these pressures will come a period of revolutionary social disorganization—perhaps like that which took place in Iran in late 1979. The outcome of such revolutions will be, according to Heilbroner, a dictatorial government of a "military-socialist cast." Such a government may find a resort to war as the only alternative to starvation.

And the probability of a *successful* war may be great if the developing country can produce a nuclear bomb—not unlikely in Heilbroner's view, as the creation of atomic bombs in China and India have shown. With nuclear capability, a developing country under a dictator's control might find the bomb an attractive "instrument of blackmail to force the developed world to transfer large amounts of wealth to the poverty-stricken world."

Admittedly, these are assertions subject to much debate. But we should not ignore the evidence so far presented—of increasing population and starvation in poor countries and of the mutual distrust and fear on which the arms race is based. We should not assume that everything will automatically work out for the best. Certainly, the 1980s (and 1990s) will be a period of the greatest challenges to face man- and womankind so far.

Summary

The world is divided into two groups of countries—developed and developing. There is no exact definition of a developing country because countries exist at every level of income. In general, by "developing" we mean countries with incomes lower than $1,000 per person per year and particularly those countries with high levels of illiteracy and low life expectancies.

There are several reasons for helping these countries: (1) our dependence on the strategic materials they supply; (2) the need to promote world political stability; and (3) the urgent nature of the developing countries' needs.

Most developing countries have common problems: dependence on one or two crops, lack of machinery, difficulty in obtaining capital, the need to save in order to export (to obtain the foreign exchange needed to buy necessities), population increases that keep per capita incomes low, illiteracy, and excessive financial indebtedness to other countries. Of all of these, the need to reduce the rate of population increase and to obtain capital are the most important.

Some argue that helping the developing countries will destroy us, that too many people will try to climb into the lifeboat. Others argue that the amount of aid necessary to do them any good would require a radically lower level of consumption in the rich countries, and that Americans would not be willing to sacrifice that much anyway. These arguments are fallacious in that they assume the quantities of food and other resources are fixed. If we can expand total supply, there should be more for everyone.

World spending for defense exceeds spending for education or public health. The production of military products and services is apparently the world's largest industry, and it is growing. Defense spending is increasing at a more rapid rate among the low-income (developing) countries than richer (developed) countries. Rivalry and distrust among the major powers seem to be rising, as evidenced by inability to reduce spending on nuclear delivery systems.

The doomsday model developed at MIT tends to show alarming levels of pollution and insufficient food per person at some time before 2100. Many arguments exist about the model, the most important of which is that market prices will force us to conserve scarce resources.

Discussion Questions

1. Imagine that you are with a group of people on an island, cut off from contact with the rest of the world. How would you increase per capita consumption? Could you manage this democratically or would a dictator be necessary?

2. There may be some forms of sophisticated capital a developing country cannot produce by itself (a computer, perhaps). How should it go about obtaining the computer from another country? What options does it have?

3. Why do families in rich countries have fewer children than families in poor countries?

4. Explain Enke's argument.

5. How are the "lifeboat" and "triage" arguments similar?

6. Explain the prisoners' dilemma. How might it apply to the advertising strategies of large companies?

7. Explain Solow's four arguments against the Doomsday model.

8. Will a market-price system necessarily adopt Solow's solution to pollution? Explain.

References

1. Robert S. McNamara, "The Moral Case for Helping the World's Poor," *Los Angeles Times*, 28 September 1973, pt. ii, p. 7.

2. Harvey Morris, "Life of Bolivian Indians Remains Harsh," *Los Angeles Times*, 31 March 1977, pt. i-a, p. 1.

3. *U.S. News & World Report*, 31 July 1978.

4. See *Los Angeles Times*, 4 April 1977, pt. ii, p. 6.

5. Charles W. Maynes, Jr., "Are the World's Poor Undeserving?" *Los Angeles Times*, 8 December 1974, pt. vi, p. 1.

6. See Nathan Keyfitz, "World Resources and the Middle Class," *Scientific American*, July 1976; "Running Out of Food," *Newsweek*, 11 November 1974; Lester R. Brown, "The World Food Prospect," *Science*, 12 December

1975; Thomas Y. Canby, "Can the World Feed Its People?" *National Geographic*, July 1975; and Douglas N. Ross, *Food and Population: The Next Crisis* (New York: The Conference Board, 1974).

7. *Statistical Abstract of the U.S., 1978.*

8. *Los Angeles Times*, 2 April 1979, pt. i, p. 16.

9. See Stephen Enke, "Economic Development through Birth Control," *Challenge*, May/June 1967.

10. See Robert V. Roosa, "The Debts of the Poor: Preventing the Crash," *The New Republic*, 22 January 1977.

11. See Jon McLin, *The Group of 77*, American Universities Field Staff Report, 1976.

12. Roosa, "The Debts of the Poor."

13. *Statistical Abstract of the U.S., 1975*, p. 801.

14. *U.S. News & World Report*, 7 July 1978.

15. See E. F. Schumacher, *Small Is Beautiful* (New York: Harper & Row, 1973).

16. Garret Hardin, "Lifeboat Ethics: The Case Against Helping the Poor," *Psychology Today*, September 1974.

17. Gunnar Myrdal, "The Equality Issue in World Development," *World Issues*, October/November 1976.

18. Keyfitz, "World Resources and the Middle Class."

19. All data are from *World Military Expenditures and Arms Transfers 1968–1977* (Washington, D.C.: U.S. Arms Control and Disarmament Agency), October 1979.

20. See Karl Deutsch, *The Analysis of International Relations* (Englewood Cliffs, N.J.: Prentice-Hall, 1968), p. 120.

21. Donella H. Meadows, et al., *The Limits of Growth* (Washington, D.C.: Potomac Associates, 1972).

22. Ibid.

23. Robert M. Solow, "Is the End of the World at Hand?" *Challenge*, March/April 1973.

24. World Fertility Survey quoted in *U.S. News & World Report*, 6 November 1979.

25. Robert L. Heilbroner, *An Inquiry into the Human Prospect* (New York: W. W. Norton & Co., 1974).

Abbreviations

CEA	Council of Economic Advisors
COLA	Cost of Living Adjustment
CPI	Consumer Price Index
DPI	Disposable personal income
FDIC	Federal Deposit Insurance Corporation
GATT	General Agreement on Tariffs and Trade
GNP	Gross National Product
IMF	International Monetary Fund
JEC	Joint Economic Committee of Congress
LDC	Less-developed country
MEW	Measure of Economic Welfare
MRP	Marginal revenue product
NNP	Net National Product
NTB	Nontariff barrier
OGA	Official government aid
OECD	Organization for Economic Cooperation and Development
PAC	Political action committee(s)
PI	Personal income
PQLI	Physical Quality of Life Index
SDR	Special drawing right(s)
V	Income velocity
ZEG	Zero economic growth
ZPG	Zero population growth

Key Words with Definitions

Chapter numbers are in boldface type, followed by page numbers in lightface.

Ability-to-pay principle   A principle of taxation holding that taxes should be collected from people in accordance with their ability to pay. Best example: the personal income tax. (**10;** 211)

Absolute change   See *Relative and absolute changes.* (**5;** 92)

Additions   Money that is added to the income stream by government spending or business spending for investment. See *Leakages.* (**13;** 269)

Aggregate demand   The total demand to buy all goods and services. In modern theory, aggregate demand is the sum of consumption spending for goods and services, business spending for capital goods (investment) and inventory, government purchases, and net exports (exports minus imports). (**11;** 231)

Aggregate supply   Everything actually produced. (**11;** 231)

Aggregate supply = GNP = total income   Aggregate supply, the total value of everything produced, equals GNP, which in turn equals the total of everyone's income. (**13A;** 291)

Alienation   A feeling by workers that their jobs (and lives) are meaningless and that they are powerless to change their condition. Attributed to Karl Marx's criticism of capitalism. (**19;** 401)

Annually balanced budget   One of four philosophies of government budgets. This one says that a government's budget should always be balanced; that government spending should always be equaled by tax revenues. Under this philosophy, a public debt would never exist. (**14;** 302)

Average tax rate   The income tax rate on one's entire taxable income rather than on the last increment of income. See *Marginal tax rate.* (**10;** 214)

Balance-of-international-payments account   Measures all international inflows and outflows of money. Includes not only spending for imports and exports (the trade balance) but also overseas investments and government spending abroad. (**18;** 394)

440

Barriers to entry   Anything that prevents the free movement of a resource as, for example, labor into a chosen occupation. Typical barriers are franchise agreements, discriminatory hiring policies, patent rights, and capital requirements (necessary to start a factory). (**2;** 26)

Base year   The year against which all other years are compared for changes in the average price level. Base-year-average prices are given an index number of 100. The base year for the implicit price deflator for the GNP is 1972; for the consumer price index the base year is 1967. (**11;** 236)

Benefits principle   A principle of taxation holding that an individual who pays a tax should receive the benefit when the government spends that money. Best example: the gasoline tax used for road building benefits drivers who paid the tax. (**10;** 211)

Board of Governors   Seven-person board that supervises the Federal Reserve System and its member banks. Board members are appointed by the U.S. President for fourteen-year terms. (**16;** 329)

Brigade   See *Commune*. (**19;** 406)

Budget surplus   The reverse of a deficit. A surplus occurs when tax revenues exceed government spending. Results in a net leak in the income stream. (**12;** 261)

Built-in stabilizers   Changes in taxes and government spending that occur automatically to stabilize the ups and downs of economic activity. Also called *Automatic fiscal policy*. (**13;** 265)

Capital-output ratio   The ratio between an amount of capital and the amount of income it produces. If $9 worth of capital produces $3 worth of income, the ratio is 3:1. (**20;** 424)

Capitalism   A system in which most things are privately owned, where people are free to choose their occupation, where the three questions are answered by prices and people searching for a profit, and where there is a substantial amount of competition. (**2;** 23)

Cartel   A group of business firms producing the same product or service who, with or without permission of law, agree on output and price so that they do not have to engage in price competition. Example: U.S. airlines operating under regulation by the Civil Aeronautics Board. (**6;** 117)

Ceteris paribus   A Latin expression meaning "all other things equal." Social scientists use this expression to indicate that all conditions not specifically mentioned in a model remain the same.   See *Model*. (**3;** 40)

Classical economists   Term used for a group of economists, beginning with Adam Smith, who believe that a market-price system would always tend to have full employment provided its government did not interfere. (**12;** 253)

"Clean" and "dirty" exchange rates   "Clean" exchange rates are those freely determined by the forces of demand and supply. "Dirty" rates are exchange rates artificially set by a government usually to make its currency cheaper in terms of other currencies to stimulate exports. (**18;** 390)

Coefficient of elasticity   The number obtained when the percentage change in quantity is divided by the percentage change in prices. If the coefficient is two, it means that the percentage change in quantity is double that of the percentage in price. When the coefficient is greater than one, demand is elastic; less than one, inelastic; just equal to one, unitary elastic. (**5;** 95)

Cogeneration   A process by which the heat that is lost when electricity is generated is used to heat buildings. (**6;** 123)

Commercial bank   A bank that carries demand deposits (checking accounts). (**15;** 319)

Commune   Rural administrative unit in China. May encompass 50,000 acres of land on which 70,000 people live. Further subdivided into brigades and teams. (**19;** 406)

Communism   Often used to refer to the Soviet Union and other totalitarian systems. However, in Marxist theory, the term refers to a system in which there is no command planning, where the working class owns and operates the means of production. (**2;** 23 and **19;** 399)

Communist Manifesto   An appeal written in 1848 by Karl Marx and his friend Friedrich Engels to persuade workers to overthrow the capitalists. (**19;** 400)

Complementary goods   Goods that go together, such as automobiles and tires, phonographs and records, typewriters and typewriter ribbons. (**3;** 48)

Conglomerate   A combination of companies producing a variety of goods and services under one management. (**7;** 144)

Consumer Price Index (CPI)   A method of measuring the average price level of the goods and services typical urban workers buy. The prices of some 400 items are measured in different parts of the country. The average is expressed by an index number; 100 is the index number for the base year, 1967. A new index number is computed monthly. (**11;** 236)

Consumer sovereignty   An economic system that functions for the benefit of consumers—where the consumer is king—in contrast to societies that function for the benefit of a ruling class. (**2;** 26)

Consumer surplus   The surplus of satisfaction consumers receive over and above the amount they pay for a good when they would have been willing to pay a price higher than the equilibrium price. (**8;** 167)

Consumption   One of the four components of aggregate demand. Consists of all services (like doctors and plumbers) and products newly produced, except housing, that consumers buy. (The purchase of new houses is put in the investment category.) (**11;** 232)

Cost-push inflation   Rising prices that occur when firms and unions have sufficient market power to increase prices and wages independent of the forces of demand and supply. Contributes to inflation even in times of recession or rising unemployment. (**17;** 350)

Countercyclical budget   The second philosophy of government budgets. Argues that government spending and taxing should counteract the ups and downs of the economy by engaging in deficit spending in times of unemployment and running a surplus in times of inflation. (**14;** 303)

Credit Refers to the trust extended by lenders to borrowers that a loan will be repaid. (**15**; 318)

Crowding-out The possibility that government borrowing for deficit spending may "crowd out" private spending by driving interest rates up, thereby making private borrowing and spending more expensive. (**13**; 285)

Currency depreciation A fall in the international value of a country's currency as a result of a decline in demand for that country's exports. The equivalent of a currency floating downward. (**18**; 389)

Current account balance Exports of goods and services plus income from overseas investments minus imports of goods and services, minus income from foreign investments in the United States, minus private gifts to foreign individuals, and minus government grants to other countries. See *Balance-of-International-Payments Account.* (**18**; 395)

Cyclical unemployment General unemployment because of poor business throughout the country. Associated with the trough of a business cycle. (**17**; 353)

Deficit spending Government spending that exceeds tax revenues, financed by selling government bonds. Leads to increases in the public debt and an unbalanced budget. (**12**; 260)

Demand The number of units of a good or service a buyer will be willing and able to buy during some period of time at various prices. See *Demand schedule* and *Demand curve.* (**3**; 42)

Demand curve A graph of a demand schedule. The vertical axis always shows the price per unit, and the horizontal axis shows the quantity demanded at each price. See *Demand Schedule.* (**3**; 45)

Demand-pull inflation Price increases that occur as a result of increases in aggregate demand when the country is at full employment. (**17**; 348)

Demand schedule A schedule showing the quantities of a good or service a buyer will buy during some period of time at various prices. (**3**; 43)

Deposit multiplier The amount by which banks cause a multiple expansion of the money supply. (**15**; 321)

Derived demand Refers to the demand for any factor of production like labor. The demand for the factor is "derived" because it is derived from, and depends on, the demand for the good or service the employer is producing. (**9**; 181)

Discount rate The interest Federal Reserve district banks charge on loans to member banks. Has some effect on all interest rates. (**16**; 336)

Discretionary fiscal policy Changes in taxes or government spending undertaken deliberately by the President and Congress to boost or slow down the economy. (**13**; 266)

Discrimination Job discrimination exists when an employer's hiring or promoting decision is based on sex or race. Wage discrimination exists when an employer pays workers differently for doing the same job. Both are hard to prove. (**9**; 187)

Disposable Personal Income (DPI) Personal income minus personal taxes (income taxes, personal property taxes, gift and inheritance taxes). (**11;** 233)

Doomsday model A computer model of the world indicating that by roughly 2100 A.D. the human race will be on its last legs as a result of pollution, starvation, and possible war. (**20;** 433)

Double counting One of the problems involved in estimating GNP. If we counted, for example, the value of steel in a car and the price of the car in GNP, we would be counting the steel twice. (**11;** 235)

Economic profit The amount of profit left over after all explicit and implicit costs have been deducted from total revenue. (**7;** 131)

Economic system A body of laws, habits, ethics, customs that a group of people use to satisfy their material wants. (**2;** 17)

Economics A social science that analyzes the expected effects of private and public decisions on human material welfare. (**1;** 14)

Effluent charges Charges imposed on a producer or user for every pound or gallon of waste he allows to pollute the air or water. (**6;** 111)

Employment Act of 1946 An Act that gave the federal government the responsibility of promoting full employment. The Act's significance is that it rejects the classical idea that the economy can take care of itself. (**12;** 261)

Endogenous Causes Factors within an economic system which cause changes in economic activity. Examples are changes in investment spending following the depreciation of capital goods or changes in consumption spending following changes in income. (**12;** 247)

Equilibrium income (GNP) A level of GNP at which aggregate demand is sufficient to buy everything produced (aggregate supply). Because GNP moves toward equilibrium, experts can forecast if GNP is about to rise or fall. Does not mean full employment. (**13;** 266)

Equilibrium price The price at which the quantity supplied equals the quantity demanded. If the price is above or below equilibrium, automatic forces will usually cause the price to return to equilibrium. (**3;** 60)

Excess reserves Reserves in excess of the legal minimum banks are required to keep. Excess reserves are those reserves a bank is free to lend or use for financial investments. (**15;** 320)

Exclusion principle Recognition of the fact that any price excludes the people who cannot afford to buy or do not want to buy from buying. Also used in connection with situations where people cannot be excluded, like pollution. (**3;** 42)

Exogenous causes Factors external to an economic system, like hurricanes or droughts, which cause changes in economic activity. (**12;** 247)

Explicit costs Costs involving an actual payment of money to someone. See *implicit costs*. (**7;** 129)

Exploitation Exists when workers are paid less than they would be paid in a market where employees bid competitively for their services. (**9;** 186)

External costs (or benefits)   See *External effects*. (**6;** 109)

External debt   An external debt is owed by one economic unit to another; for example, an individual's debt to a store or one nation's debt to another. When such a debt is paid, the debtor becomes poorer, the creditor richer. Most private debts (charge accounts, bank loans) are external debts (**14;** 301)

External effects   Effects on people outside the seller-buyer transaction. External benefits are those that are beneficial to society, such as education; external costs are harmful effects, such as pollution. (**6;** 109)

Factor payments   Economists divide all forms of income into the payments each factor of production receives: rent for land, wages for labor, interest for capital, and profit for entrepreneurship. (**2;** 25)

Factors of production   All resources are divided into four factors of production: land, labor, capital, and entrepreneurship. (**2;** 21)

Federal Deposit Insurance Corporation (FDIC)   An insurance corporation that insures deposits up to $100,000 so that if a bank fails, depositors will not lose their money. Commercial banks belonging to the Federal Reserve System must buy this insurance. (**16;** 330)

Federal Open Market Committee   Twelve people, including the seven board members of the Federal Reserve System and five presidents of district banks, who buy and sell government securities for the purpose of increasing or decreasing the money supply. (**16;** 329)

Federal Reserve Act of 1913   The law that created the Federal Reserve System. (**15;** 319)

Federal Reserve District Bank   The Federal Reserve System is the U.S. central bank. The system includes twelve district banks, and they have a combined total of twenty-four branches. The district banks and their branches are nicknamed the Fed. (**15;** 321)

Federal Reserve Notes (paper money)   U.S. paper money, so-called because they are issued by Federal Reserve district banks even though they are printed by the Treasury. (**16;** 330)

Federal Reserve System (the Fed)   A nationwide network of twelve regional Federal Reserve (district) banks with twenty-four branches, each serving a particular U.S. geographical area. Its policies seek to provide monetary conditions favorable to business and employment, maintain the purchasing power of the dollar, and help the economy grow. (**15;** 312)

Federal revenue sharing   Monies given the states each year by the federal government. (**10;** 210)

Final product   The price paid by the final user of a product. Excludes intermediate products. GNP is an estimate of final products and services produced in one year. (**11;** 235)

Fiscal policy   Changes in taxes and/or government spending which cause changes in total output and spending. Such changes may be automatic or deliberately undertaken by the President and/or Congress. See *Built-in Stabilizers* and *Discretionary Fiscal Policy*. (**13;** 264)

Fixed costs   Costs such as rent, taxes, insurance, or interest on loans that do not change with changes in a factory's output. As in the Velvetex case study, the term also includes overhead costs such as executive and other white-collar salaries. (**8;** 160)

Fixed demand   Occurs when the quantity demanded does not change with price changes. Examples: the demand for very inexpensive items such as matches or paper clips remains about the same over a range of prices; fixed demand may occur if a buyer is hooked on a product like heroin. (**4;** 82)

Fixed supply   Occurs when the quantity supplied does not change with changes in price. Examples of fixed supply are famous paintings or the quantities of anything in existence at a moment in time such as freeway space, parking spaces, hospital beds, houses. (**4;** 78)

Floating exchange rates   International currency exchange rates that are free to change as a result of changes in demand or supply for goods, services, or currencies in international trade. (**18;** 388)

Foregone income   The income one could have earned while going to school. Estimated to be 50 percent of the cost of a college education. (**1;** 13)

Free good   A good that exists in such abundance that greater use of it by one person does not subtract from its availability to everyone else. (**1;** 11)

Frictional unemployment   Unemployment that occurs because workers have difficulty shifting from a declining industry to a rising one. Classical theory admits the problem but argues that unemployment will be only temporary. (**17;** 352)

Full employment   Usually said to exist when 94.5 percent of the people who want jobs have them. Thus, a 5.5 percent unemployment rate is the equivalent of full employment. (**17;** 353)

Functional finance   The third philosophy of government budgets. This theory argues that the need to guarantee jobs for a growing labor force and to finance public works, like rapid transit, in good times or bad, may require deficit financing on a permanent basis. Acceptance of the functional finance philosophy indicates acceptance of a growing public debt. (**14;** 303)

General Agreement on Tariffs and Trade (GATT)   An organization of eighty-one countries to which the United States belongs. Formed in 1947, its purpose is to reduce barriers to trade. (**18;** 382)

Geometric increase   A rising rate of increase caused by multiplying a given number over and over again by some number. For example, if we keep multiplying 3 by 2 we get: 6, 12, 24, 48, 96, and so on. The increase becomes greater and greater (**1;** 8)

Gold Reserve Act of 1934   Act that set the price of gold at $35 per ounce and stopped Americans from exchanging dollars for gold in order to prevent hoarding of gold. (**15;** 314)

Gosplan   Name given to the central economic planning agency in the Soviet Union. (**19;** 403)

Government purchases of goods and services   One of the four components of aggregate demand. Refers to spending by all levels of government—local, state, and federal—but excludes transfer payments. (**11;** 232)

Government securities   Government securities (often called bonds) are of three types: (1) Treasury bills that mature in less than one year, (2) Treasury notes that mature in one to five years, and (3) Treasury bonds that take longer than five years to mature. (**14;** 299)

Gross National Product (GNP)   GNP is the sum of consumption, investment, government purchases of goods and services, and net exports. GNP is determined by aggregate demand. (**11;** 231)

Group of 77   An organization of seventy-seven countries (most of them, but not all, are less-developed countries) to help poorer countries obtain financial aid. (**20;** 426)

High-employment budget approach   The surplus of tax revenues over government spending the federal government would have if the economy were operating at high employment. High employment usually means a 5.5 percent (or less) rate of unemployment. This is the fourth budget philosophy relative to the public debt. (**14;** 304)

Horizontal merger   A merger in which one company acquires another in the same type of business. Example: the merger of two food chains. (**7;** 142)

Hyperinflation   A rate of inflation that accelerates faster and faster, as in Germany after World War I and Hungary after World War II. Occurs when a government must print ever-increasing amounts of money to finance operations because the people are too poor to tax. Result: money becomes worthless. (**16;** 337)

Imperfect markets   Any market that does not satisfy all of the criteria of perfect competition. (**8;** 164)

Implicit costs   The opportunity costs borne by a business firm (or individual) of employing resources in a particular way. Measured by the sacrifice each factor of production makes when it is employed: wages that might have been earned in other jobs (implicit wages), rent that might have been earned for land or buildings (implicit rent), interest that might have been earned on the money tied up in a business or home (implicit interest), and profit that might have been earned in other business ventures (normal profit). See *Explicit costs* and *Economic profit.* (**7;** 129)

Implicit interest   Interest you could have earned on money you have tied up in a business (or home). See *Implicit costs.* (**7;** 130)

Implicit rent   The rent that you could have earned by renting out a building that you own instead of using it yourself. See *Implicit costs.* (**7;** 130)

Implicit Price Deflator   A large price index combining both wholesale and retail prices which is used to correct (deflate) GNP for the effects of inflation. (**11;** 236)

Income effect   The effect a falling or rising price has on our ability to buy more or less with a given income. (**3;** 44)

Income-spending line   A 45-degree angle line that bisects a right angle formed by a spending axis and an income axis. At all points on the line, spending and income are equal. (**13A;** 289)

Income stream   The flow of dollars from the public business firms and government, from the firms to the public and government, and from the government to firms and individuals. For purposes of simplification, the discussion here omits the flow of tax monies to the government and government expenditures, but these elements of the income stream must be considered in analyzing the real world. The concept is useful in describing why market-price systems have inflation and unemployment. (**13;** 268)

Inflation   A general rise in prices. See *Cost-push inflation* and *Demand-pull inflation.* (**1;** 5)

Inflation psychology   A state of mind tending to intensify any existing inflationary conditions. If people believe prices are rising, they will try to buy more before the prices do rise; they will also increase their wage demands to keep up with increases in the cost of living. The increases in demand cause prices to rise even faster, resulting in further increases in demand. Thus, the belief that prices are rising contributes to their increase and constitutes a self-fulfilling prophecy. (**3;** 49)

Information costs   A barrier to entry in the sense that if information about a product, service, or entrepreneurial opportunity is difficult or costly to obtain, resources will be prevented from moving to those activities most desired by society. (**7;** 133)

Infrastructure   See *Social overhead capital.* (**20;** 425)

Intended vs. actual investment   Intended investment means the amounts of money business firms want (intend) to spend for capital goods and inventories. Actual investment may differ from these intentions if slack sales cause inventories to rise above intended levels (unintended investment), or if brisk sales cause inventories to fall below intended levels (unintended dis-investment). (**13;** 274)

Intermediate products   Products used in the production of others; for example, steel in a car. In computing GNP, the value-added method is used to eliminate intermediate products that might otherwise be double-counted. (**11;** 235)

Intermediate technology   Refers to the invention and creation of simple tools and machines that a developing country can make itself and that will not cause technological unemployment. The idea comes from E. F. Schumacher's influential book *Small Is Beautiful.* (**20;** 427)

Internal debt   A debt owed by one member of a family to another member; by one branch of a corporation to another; by some people in a nation to others in the same nation. The existence of such a debt does not change the wealth of the family, corporation, or nation because payment involves a transfer of income within an economic unit. The public debt is mostly internal. (**14;** 301)

International Monetary Fund (IMF)   An international financial institution that provides funds to its member nations as they are needed and attempts to stabilize exchange rates in order to encourage international trade. The IMF was created by the Bretton Woods (New Hampshire) agreement of 1944. (**18;** 386)

Investment   The creation of tangible capital and/or the production of goods for inventory. Not a sum of money. Investment is one of the four categories of aggregate demand. Includes business spending for all capital goods, inventories, and business and personal spending for buildings. (**11;** 232)

Job discrimination   See *Discrimination.* (**9;** 187)

Job participation rate   The number of all those in the labor force who are (or wish to be) employed expressed as a percentage of a nation's total population. (**9;** 191 and **17;** 356)

Keynesian Cross   Cross formed by the crossing of the income-spending line by a line that represents aggregate demand. Purpose is to show that aggregate demand may be greater than, or less than, total income. (**13A;** 291)

Keynesian revolution   The revolution in economic theory following the publication of John Maynard Keynes' book, *The General Theory of Employment, Interest, and Money.* The book was revolutionary because it argued that an economic system could get stuck at any level of unemployment; and that market-price economic systems do not automatically provide everyone who wants to work with a job, as had previously been argued by the Classical economists. See *Classical economists* and *Say's Law.* (**12;** 257)

Landrum-Griffin Act (1958)   Officially known as the Labor-Management Reporting and Disclosure Act. The act was aimed at making the internal operation of unions more democratic and preventing union bosses from using funds to their own advantage. (**9;** 178)

Law of demand   According to the law of demand, as the price falls, the quantities demanded by buyers will increase. Price and quantity are inversely related. (**3;** 44)

Leakages   Money that "leaks" out of the income stream in the form of saving or taxes. *See Additions.* (**13;** 269)

Legal reserve   The minimum reserve a bank must keep as a percentage of its deposits. (**15;** 319)

Long run   A period of time long enough for entrepreneurs to vary all of the costs of production including the costs of acquiring additional stores or factories or cost-reductions from the sale of stores or factories. (**8;** 160)

M_1   One definition of the money supply. The sum of currency (coins and paper money) in circulation plus demand deposits (checking accounts). (**15;** 316)

Macroeconomics   The study of the functions of the whole economy, particularly the whole economy's ability to provide enough jobs, a fair distribution of goods and services, and an average price level that does not rise too fast (inflation). (**1;** 14)

Malthus, Thomas Robert (1766–1834)   English economist, best known for his beliefs that population would increase faster than the food supply and that, consequently, the world would be subjected to periods of disease and famine. Occasionally, war, disease, and famine would interrupt the growth of population, but then it would start again. See *Theory of Gluts*, his idea that a market-price system would have periods of unemployment caused by overproduction and underconsumption. (**1;** 8)

Mao Tse-tung (1884–1976)   Leader of the People's Republic of China. Tried to enforce economic equality for the people. (**19;** 405)

Marginal cost   Technically defined as the change in total cost when one more unit is produced. In the Velvetex case study, the term refers to costs associated only with production, excluding salaries of white-collar employees. (**8;** 162)

Marginal-cost pricing   A pricing policy wherein the business firm charges just enough to cover production costs exclusive of such overhead costs as interest payments, taxes, and executive salaries. Presumably, the firm will engage in this practice only with a portion of its production and will do so to increase sales and minimize losses. Such a firm will try to set prices on the rest of its production that are high enough to cover *all* costs, including overhead (**8:** 171)

Marginal revenue   The addition to total revenue when one more unit is sold. (**8;** 162)

Marginal revenue product (MRP)   The change in total revenue that occurs when the extra production of an additional worker is sold. The assumption is made that all other resources (like capital) do not change when the additional worker's extra production is measured. (**9;** 180)

Marginal tax rate   The percentage income tax rate paid on the last dollar of one's income rather than on one's total income. The last dollar defines one's tax bracket. The marginal tax rate applies only to one's tax bracket. (**10;** 214)

Market   Any place or means by which a buyer can communicate with a seller to negotiate a price. (**2;** 20)

Market period   A period in which all costs are in the past and the product is ready for sale. (**8;** 160)

Market power   The power buyers or sellers can exert over other buyers or sellers to control the market price. (**3;** 62 and **7;** 127)

Marx, Karl (1818–1883)   German political philosopher and socialist who predicted the collapse of capitalism. He believed that greedy capitalists would try to extract more and more profit from workers who were paid as little as possible. Overproduction and subsistence wages would create chronic deficiencies in aggregate demand leading to worse and worse depressions and finally revolution by the working class (the proletariat). Considered the founder of communism. Author of *Das Kapital (Capital)*. (**19;** 400)

Measure of Economic Welfare (MEW)   A new way to measure GNP that would subtract pollution-related activities and "regrettables" such as police forces and national defense but would add an amount to reflect leisure time. (**11;** 240)

Member banks   Privately owned banks that belong to the Federal Reserve System. (**15;** 319)

Merchandise Trade Balance   The difference between exports of merchandise and imports of merchandise. Excludes exports and imports of services. See *Balance-of-international-payments account*. (**18;** 395)

Microeconomics   The study of the functioning of the individual parts of the economy, like individual consumers, business firms, and unions, in contrast to the study of national problems like unemployment and inflation. Microeconomic theory is specially concerned with how prices are determined and how prices determine the production, distribution, and use of goods and services. (**1;** 14)

Mixed capitalism   An economic system predominantly capitalistic but also containing elements of other systems such as socialism. (**2;** 23)

Model   A simplified version of the real world requiring a set of assumptions. Example: a recipe for baking bread. (**3;** 39)

Monetarists   Name given to those economists who believe that monetary policy is more important than fiscal policy in changing the price level or level of employment. (**16;** 340)

Monetary policy   Control of interest rates and borrowing through control of the money supply. Like fiscal policy, monetary policy is employed to increase or decrease aggregate demand. Monetary policy is based on the theory that aggregate demand can be made to rise or fall with changes in the money supply; that changes in the money supply cause changes in interest rates, which make borrowing for spending more or less expensive. (**15;** 312)

Monopolistic competition   An economic system in which entry barriers to an industry are still low, as in pure competition, but in which brand names are now used to convince buyers that the brand-name product is better than products without brand names. Where brand names are used, firms often compete by advertising special ingredients rather than price. (**7;** 135)

Monopoly   Exclusive control of an industry by one firm (seller). Examples: the only movie theater in a small town; a utility with no competitor. (**7;** 139)

Monopsony   Exclusive control of a market of sellers by one buyer. Monopsony exists where a firm or industry sells its entire output to one buyer, the monopsonist. (**8;** 171)

Most-favored-nation principle   Holds that trade concessions granted to one nation will be granted to all other trading partners. The principle was inaugurated by the Reciprocal Trade Agreements Law of 1934 and has been included in all noncommunist trade agreements since then. (**18;** 380)

National income accounting   The accounting system used to measure a nation's total output and income. (Also called social accounting.) (**11;** 230)

Natural monopoly   A business firm that is allowed by a government agency to be a monopoly in a geographical area. Usually a utility. (**7;** 139)

Negative saving (dis-saving)   Results from private spending that exceeds income. If we spend more than we make we have to borrow or take money out of savings. Borrowing or savings reduction is called negative saving or dis-saving. (**13A;** 289)

Net exports   One of the four components of aggregate demand. The difference between exports and imports. If exports exceed imports, the difference adds to aggregate demand, but if imports exceed exports, as they did in 1971 and 1972, the difference subtracts from aggregate demand. (**11;** 232)

Net public debt   The total federal debt minus the amount borrowed by government agencies. (**14;** 300)

New unemployment   Unemployment that is induced or prolonged by unemployment compensation. (**17;** 354)

No-tax threshold   The minimum level of taxable income at which one must pay an income tax. (**10;** 214)

Nomenklatura   A secret roster of the privileged people in the Soviet Union who can obtain groceries, housing, cars, and vacations not available to the ordinary Soviet citizen. (**19;** 405)

Nonprice competition   Competition among competing brands, not in terms of price, but in terms of special ingredients or services. Usually indicates competition in the form of advertising. (**7;** 137)

Nonrenewable resource   A resource that exists in some finite amount, the supply of which cannot be renewed or replenished. Best example: oil. (**6;** 114)

Nontariff barriers (NTBs)   Barriers to trade where no tariff is imposed. Examples: import quotas, import licenses, export subsidies, dumping, buy-at-home policies, health and safety standards, red tape, preferential trading arrangements. (**18;** 379)

Normal profit   See *Implicit costs.* (**7;** 130)

Official development aid (ODA)   Financial aid extended by governments rather than from private sources. (**20;** 426)

Oligopoly   The domination of an industry by three or four very large firms (sellers). Any one of them is large enough to influence the price of the others. (**7;** 138)

Open market operations   The purchase or sale of government bonds on the open market by the Federal Open Market committee. Bonds purchased or sold on the open market are bonds owned by commercial banks, corporations, or the public. (**16;** 332)

Opportunity cost, trade-off   The value of any opportunity or alternative that is sacrificed when a decision to do something is made. Sometimes called alternative cost or trade-off. What do we trade off (lose) in exchange for obtaining something we want? (**1;** 12)

Organization for Economic Cooperation and Development (OECD)   An organization of twenty countries to liberalize trade. (**18;** 382)

Paradox of thrift   The paradox in which a desire by the people to increase their saving and spend less results in reduced savings; their desire to spend more and save less leads to increased saving. (**13;** 277)

Phillips Curve   A curve that describes the inverse relationship (trade-off) between inflation and unemployment. The "dilemma" is that the more we try to reduce prices by reducing aggregate demand, the more unemployment will rise. Also suggests that the price of full employment is a high rate of inflation. (**17;** 357)

Physical Quality of Life Index   A composite of three measures of a nation's life expectancy, infant mortality, and literacy. (**20;** 417)

Poverty   Poverty exists when a nonfarm family's income is less than the cost of a nutritionally balanced diet multiplied by three. The income that just equals that amount is often called the "poverty line." Estimated poverty-line income for a nonfarm family of four in 1981 is $8,000. (**2**; 18)

Price ceiling   A price below equilibrium legislated by the government. Because the law says that the price cannot rise above the ceiling, a shortage results. Examples are wage-price freezes. (**4**; 83)

Price discrimination   The practice whereby a seller sells the same (or almost the same) product or service to different buyers or even the same buyer, at different prices. (**8**; 165)

Price-elastic   Refers to the responsiveness of buyers (demanders) or suppliers to changes in price. If the response is large relative to the price change, the good is said to be price-elastic. If not, it is price-inelastic. (**5**; 91)

Price floor   A price above the equilibrium legislated by the government. Because the law says the price cannot fall below the floor, a surplus results. Examples of price floors are farm-price supports and minimum-wage laws. (**4**; 82)

Price index   Measure of average prices relative to a base year. Base-year-average prices are given an index number of 100. If ten years later average prices have risen 50 percent, the new price level is given an index number of 150. There are three indexes: the consumer price index (retail items), the wholesale price index, and the implicit price deflator for the GNP. The latter index is an all-inclusive composite of retail and wholesale prices. It is used to correct GNP for price changes (deflate the GNP). (**11**; 235)

Price-inelastic   See *Price-elastic*. (**5**; 91)

Primary job market   Jobs requiring skill, investment by employers in training, avenues for promotion, career possibilities for employees, and low turnover. (**1**; 13)

Prime rate   The rate of interest commercial banks charge their biggest and best customers (large corporations). The prime rate is usually the lowest interest rate obtainable on loans. (**16**; 337)

Principle of comparative advantage   According to this principle, an individual or nation should specialize in producing products where the opportunity cost of specialization is lower than that of other countries. (**18**; 376)

Prisoner's dilemma   Refers to the idea that when two people or two companies or two nations do not trust each other, they follow much more costly courses of action than if they cooperate. (**20**; 430)

Private costs   Costs borne by the producer or user in producing, using, or disposing of a product. Term does not include external costs borne by society in connection with pollution. (**6**; 109)

Private good   A good or service that is divisible into units—a pencil or a visit to a doctor. Such goods involve private costs and benefits to buyers and sellers. Those who cannot afford to buy or sell (produce) are excluded from the market. (**10**; 200)

Private labeling   The practice whereby a manufacturer permits a retail store to sell the manufacturer's product under the store's brand name, rather than the manufacturer's. (**8**; 171)

Producer Price Index   A new name for what used to be called the Wholesale Price Index. As the name suggests, it is an index that measures average prices at the producers' or wholesale level. (**11;** 236)

Production possibilities table   A table showing the different combinations of products individuals or countries can produce at full employment (**18;** 375)

Profit-push inflation   Price increases initiated by powerful corporations in search of higher profits. See *Cost-push inflation* and *Administered prices.* (**17;** 350)

Progressive taxes   Taxes in which the assessment as a percentage of income rises as income rises. Best example: personal income taxes. (**10;** 212)

Proletariat   Karl Marx's term for the working class. (**19;** 400)

Proportional taxes   Taxes in which the assessment as a percentage of income remains constant. If everyone paid 10 percent of income, the amount collected would rise as income rose, but the tax rate would remain the same; that is, in proportion to income. (**10;** 212)

Public debt   The total of all government securities (bonds) in existence. The bondholders are the creditors, having lent money to the Treasury when they purchased the bonds. The Treasury (representing the people) is the debtor. (**14;** 294)

Pure competition   An economic situation in which an industry has so many small firms that no one of them can influence the market price. Barriers to entry are so low that any pure profits are squeezed out by incoming firms. (**7;** 132)

Qualitative changes   Changes in the quality of a good or service in contrast to changes in quantity. (**4;** 76)

Quasi-social goods   Goods that are partly private because they are divisible but also social because they confer costs of benefits that are indivisible to those outside the transaction. Examples are education, parks, health care, and antipoverty programs. (**10;** 201)

Rational expectations   A theory that holds that workers quickly realize the effects of present and expected inflation on their real wages; that when this (rational) realization occurs, workers will react by either (1) demanding higher pay for their present jobs or (2) seeking jobs with higher pay. (**17;** 361)

Real changes   Changes that occur in income or GNP after the income or GNP has been deflated (expressed in constant dollars). Thus, a real change denotes that the data have been corrected for inflation. (**11;** 237)

Real per capital DPI   Disposable Personal Income adjusted for inflation and divided population. (**11;** 238)

Real per capital GNP   A deflated GNP divided by population. (**11;** 237)

Real terms   See *Real changes.* (**1;** 12)

Regressive taxes   Taxes in which the assessment as a percentage of income rises as income falls. Best examples are sales taxes, personal property taxes, and social security taxes. (**10;** 213)

Relative and absolute changes   An increase of from 4 to 6 quarts is an absolute change of 2 but a relative change of 50 percent: the change of 2 relative to the starting number 4. Absolute changes do not reflect relative importance; a change from 8 to 10 is also an absolute change of 2, but this time the change is only 2 relative to 8, or 25 percent. (**5;** 92)

Required reserve   The percentage of demand deposits (or savings accounts) the Board of Governors of the Federal Reserve System requires member banks to keep at all times. (**15;** 319)

Reservation price   The minimum price set by the seller in an auction. (**4;** 79)

Revolution of rising expectations   After slumbering for centuries in poverty, the LDCs now see how people in the richer countries live. The people in the LDCs have begun to want and to expect rapid increases in their standards of living. (**20;** 421)

Role differentiation   Term used to describe the conditioning that occurs in childhood causing girls to be less aggressive in seeking better jobs. (**9;** 191)

Rule of 72   A rough guide as to how many years it will take a number to double at some interest rate compounded annually. If the interest rate is 6 percent, divide 72 by 6. The answer is 12, indicating that it will take about 12 years for whatever number you started with to double. (**1;** 9)

Saving   The unconsumed portion of one's income or the portion of a business firm's income it elects to keep. See *Savings*. (**11;** 234)

Savings   The accumulation of past saving. See *Saving*. (**11;** 234)

Say's Law   Expressed as a slogan: "Supply creates its own demand." The idea was that the act of producing something created the income and the demand to buy it. Thus, all goods produced would be sold and there would be no unemployment. (**12;** 253)

Scarcity   "Scarcity" arises because people generally want more than is available at any given time. Because our wants exceed the supply of everything available, we are always faced with having to choose some things at the expense of giving up others. Scarcity gives rise to opportunity cost. The fact of scarcity is the reason economics as a study exists. (**1;** 11)

Secondary job market   Jobs requiring little skill or training. Characterized by low wages, poor working conditions, layoffs, little chance for advancement, and high turnover. See *Primary Job Market*. (**1;** 13)

Self-fulfilling prophecy   Occurs when the belief that something will happen causes it to happen. (**3;** 49)

Short run   A period of time in which entrepreneurs can vary some costs like labor or materials, but not others like taxes or interest payments on bank loans. (**8;** 160)

Social costs   The total burden to society of production, use, and disposal of some good. Social costs are made up of the private costs to sellers and buyers plus the costs of external effects. (**6;** 109)

Social good   A good that is indivisible, like the light from a lighthouse. Such goods cannot be sold unit-by-unit, and nonbuyers cannot be excluded from the market. When the light is turned on, everyone will see it whether they have paid for the lighthouse or not. (**10;** 200)

Social overhead capital   The transportation, power, and communications system a society needs to facilitate production and distribution of goods and services. Also called infrastructure. (**20;** 425)

Socialism   An economic system in which the major industries, like steel, coal, oil, transportation, electricity, telephone, and telegraph are owned and operated by the government. Socialism may involve a democratic or totalitarian political system. (**2;** 22 and **19;** 398)

Special Drawing Rights (SDRs)   Sometimes called paper gold. SDRs are additional funds created by the IMF that can be used to purchase member nations' currencies. (**18;** 388)

Spending multiplier   Any change in spending will cause a chain reaction in spending so that the final increase in total income (GNP) is greater than (a multiple of) the original change in spending. The number of times the change in spending is multiplied is the spending multiplier. Thus, if the multiplier is 2.5 and the change in spending is $10 billion, the change in total income (GNP) is $25 billion (2.5 times $10 billion). (**13;** 279)

Stagflation   The simultaneous presence of recession (stagnation) and inflation. (**17;** 348)

Structural unemployment   Unemployment caused by poor business in a particular industry, such as unemployment in the automobile industry in 1980. (**17;** 353)

Substitute goods   Goods that compete with one another (are good substitutes for each other), like two brands of coffee. (**3;** 47)

Substitution effect   The result of a price reduction on a product. As the price falls, consumers substitute the product for others and find more uses for it. (**3;** 44)

Supply   The number of units a supplier (producer or seller) of a product will offer for sale at various market prices during some period of time. See *Supply schedule* and *Supply curve.* (**3;** 53)

Supply curve   A graph of a supply schedule. The price per unit is on the vertical axis. The quantities supplied are on the horizontal axis. (**3;** 55)

Supply schedule   A schedule of prices and quantities showing the quantities supplied at each price during some period of time. (**3;** 55)

Supply-side fiscalism   A theory that holds that supply should be increased via business tax cuts and reduced government regulation as a cure for stagflation. (**17;** 364).

Taft-Hartley Act (1947)   Declared the closed shop illegal but permitted the union shop. Also gave the states the right to pass "right-to-work" laws banning the union shop. Provided a no-strike eight-day "cooling-off" period for industrial disputes in some industries. (**9;** 177)

Tariff   A tax imposed on imported products by the government of the importing country. (**18;** 377)

Tax incidence   The final resting place of the burden of a tax. Often a taxpayer does not bear the burden of a tax if he can shift the burden (cost) of the tax to someone else. See *Tax shifting.* (**10;** 222)

Tax loopholes   Provisions in tax laws that permit taxpayers to avoid income taxes. Best examples: tax exempt securities, taxes on capital gains, the oil depletion allowance. (**10;** 214)

Tax shifting   The transfer of the burden of a tax to someone other than the taxpayer. Taxes may be shifted backward by retailers to wholesalers (or manufacturers) or forward by retailers to customers. (**10;** 222)

Team   See *Commune.* (**19;** 406)

Theory of gluts   Malthus's idea that we would have periodic recessions because of gluts (supplies of unsold goods) on the market. The gluts would be caused by insufficient aggregate demand, a result of the fact that total wages paid are less than the total value of everything produced. (**12;** 256)

Total revenue   The total amount of money received by a company from the sale of a good or service. Equals price times quantity. (**5;** 91)

Trade deficit   An excess of imports over exports. (**18;** 386)

Trade Expansion Act of 1962   An agreement with the Common Market countries to lower tariffs on products where the Common Market and the United States together had more than 800 percent of the world's trade. (**18;** 382)

Trade surplus   An excess of exports over imports. (**18;** 386)

Traditional, planning, and market-price systems   Traditional systems answer the what, how, and for whom questions by copying the decisions of previous generations. Planning systems answer the questions with a national, centrally made plan. Market systems answer the questions via the forces of demand and supply which determine prices. (**2;** 19, 20)

Transfer payments   Unemployment insurance payments, farm price support payments, social security payments, welfare payments, and interest paid on government bonds. Sometimes thought of as payments by government to recipients who have not rendered any productive service in return. (**10;** 205)

Triage   French term meaning "choice." Refers to the suggestion that we should help the LDCs that can be helped and forget the rest. (**20;** 428)

Turnover tax   A sales tax used by Soviet planners to encourage or discourage consumption of particular items. Has averaged as much as 44 percent of the retail price. (**19;** 404)

Unintended disinvestment   A drop in inventories below desired (intended) levels because of an unanticipated increase in sales. (**13;** 274)

Unintended investment   An increase in inventories above desired (intended) levels because of an unanticipated drop in sales. (**13;** 276)

Variable costs   Costs that change with a firm's output. (**8;** 160)

Variable pricing   Occurs when different prices are charged for each unit of a product or service. (**4;** 81 and **8;** 167)

Variable supply   Occurs when the quantities supplied by sellers can change as a result of price changes. The opposite of *Fixed supply.* (**4;** 78)

Vertical merger   A merger in which one company buys another that supplies or perhaps sells directly to retail customers. Example: an oil refining company buys a service station. (**7;** 142)

Wage discrimination   See *Discrimination*. (**9;** 187)

Wage-price flexibility argument   The classical argument that, if workers are laid off during an economic slowdown, wages and prices will fall. When they do, employers will hire more people. People will buy more products, and full employment will be restored. (**12;** 255)

Wagner Act   Gave the workers the right to form unions. (**9;** 177)

White Market   Term used to describe the sale of gasoline ration coupons by people who do not need them to people who do. The buying and selling of coupons would create a market and a market price for them, a "white" (legal) rather than a "black" market for gasoline. (**6;** 122)

Zero economic growth (ZEG)   The maintenance of a constant, rather than increasing, level of production. Like ZPG, urged by some to conserve resources and control pollution. (**20;** 434)

Zero population growth (ZPG)   The maintenance of a constant, rather than increasing, level of population. Urged by many to conserve resources and to reduce pollution. (**20;** 434)

TABLE A Gross National Product, 1929–79, in Billions of Dollars

Year or quarter	Gross national product	Personal consumption expenditures	Gross private domestic investment	Net exports	Government purchases
1929	103.4	77.3	16.2	1.1	8.8
1933	55.8	45.8	1.4	.4	8.2
1939	90.8	67.0	9.3	1.1	13.5
1940	100.0	71.0	13.1	1.7	14.2
1941	124.9	80.8	17.9	1.3	24.9
1942	158.3	88.6	9.9	.0	59.8
1943	192.0	99.4	5.8	-2.0	88.9
1944	210.5	108.2	7.2	-1.8	97.0
1945	212.3	119.5	10.6	-.6	82.8
1946	209.6	143.8	30.7	7.6	27.5
1947	232.8	161.7	34.0	11.6	25.5
1948	259.1	174.7	45.9	6.5	32.0
1949	258.0	178.1	35.3	6.2	38.4
1950	286.2	192.0	53.8	1.9	38.5
1951	330.2	207.1	59.2	3.8	60.1
1952	347.2	217.1	52.1	2.4	75.6
1953	366.1	229.7	53.3	.6	82.5
1954	366.3	235.8	52.7	2.0	75.8
1955	399.3	253.7	68.4	2.2	75.0
1956	420.7	266.0	71.0	4.3	79.4
1957	442.8	280.4	69.2	6.1	87.1
1958	448.9	289.5	61.9	2.5	95.0
1959	486.5	310.8	77.6	.6	97.6
1960	506.0	324.9	76.4	4.4	100.3
1961	523.3	335.0	74.3	5.8	108.2
1962	563.8	355.2	85.2	5.4	118.0
1963	594.7	374.6	90.2	6.3	123.7
1964	635.7	400.4	96.6	8.9	129.8
1965	688.1	430.2	112.0	7.6	138.4
1966	753.0	464.8	124.5	5.1	158.7
1967	796.3	490.4	120.8	4.9	180.2
1968	868.5	535.9	131.5	2.3	198.7
1969	935.5	579.7	146.2	1.8	207.9
1970	982.4	618.8	140.8	3.9	218.9
1971	1,063.4	668.2	160.0	1.6	233.7
1972	1,171.1	733.0	188.3	-3.3	253.1
1973	1,306.6	809.9	220.0	7.1	269.5
1974	1,412.9	889.6	214.6	6.0	302.7
1975	1,528.8	979.1	190.9	20.4	338.4
1976	1,702.2	1,089.9	243.0	8.0	361.3
1977	1,899.5	1,210.0	303.3	-9.9	396.2
1978	2,127.6	1,350.8	351.5	-10.3	435.6
1979	2,368.5	1,509.8	386.2	-3.5	476.1
1977:					
I	1,820.2	1,169.1	280.4	-9.2	380.0
II	1,876.0	1,190.5	300.0	-6.0	391.6
III	1,930.5	1,220.6	315.7	-6.3	400.5
IV	1,971.3	1,259.7	316.9	-18.1	412.8
1978:					
I	2,011.3	1,287.2	327.0	-22.2	419.4
II	2,104.2	1,331.2	352.3	-7.6	428.3
III	2,159.6	1,369.3	356.2	-6.8	440.9
IV	2,235.2	1,415.4	370.5	-4.5	453.8
1979:					
I	2,292.1	1,454.2	373.8	4.0	460.1
II	2,329.8	1,475.9	395.4	-8.1	466.6
III	2,396.5	1,528.6	392.3	-2.3	477.8
IV	2,455.8	1,580.4	383.3	-7.7	499.8

Source: Department of Commerce, Bureau of Economic Analysis.

TABLE B Gross National Product in 1972 Dollars, 1929–79, in Billions of Dollars

Year or quarter	Gross national product	Personal consumption expenditures	Gross private domestic investment	Net exports	Government purchases
1929	314.6	215.6	55.9	2.2	40.9
1933	222.1	170.7	8.4	.2	42.8
1939	318.8	220.3	33.6	2.0	62.9
1940	343.3	230.4	44.6	3.0	65.2
1941	398.5	244.1	55.8	.8	97.7
1942	460.3	241.7	29.6	-2.5	191.5
1943	530.6	248.7	18.1	-7.3	271.2
1944	568.6	255.7	19.8	-7.2	300.3
1945	560.0	271.4	27.8	-4.5	265.3
1946	476.9	301.4	71.0	11.6	93.0
1947	468.3	306.2	70.1	16.6	75.4
1948	487.7	312.8	82.3	8.5	84.1
1949	490.7	320.0	65.6	8.8	96.2
1950	533.5	338.1	93.7	4.0	97.7
1951	576.5	342.3	94.1	7.4	132.7
1952	598.5	350.9	83.2	4.9	159.5
1953	621.8	364.2	85.6	2.0	170.0
1954	613.7	370.9	83.4	4.5	154.9
1955	654.8	395.1	104.1	4.7	150.9
1956	668.8	406.3	102.9	7.3	152.4
1957	680.9	414.7	97.2	8.9	160.1
1958	679.5	419.0	87.7	3.5	169.3
1959	720.4	441.5	107.4	.9	170.7
1960	736.8	453.0	105.4	5.5	172.9
1961	755.3	462.2	103.6	6.7	182.8
1962	799.1	482.9	117.4	5.8	193.1
1963	830.7	501.4	124.5	7.3	197.6
1964	874.4	528.7	132.1	10.9	202.7
1965	925.9	558.1	150.1	8.2	209.6
1966	981.0	586.1	161.3	4.3	229.3
1967	1,007.7	603.2	152.7	3.5	248.3
1968	1,051.8	633.4	159.5	-.4	259.2
1969	1,078.8	655.4	168.0	-1.3	256.7
1970	1,075.3	668.9	154.7	1.4	250.2
1971	1,107.5	691.9	166.8	-.6	249.4
1972	1,171.1	733.0	188.3	-3.3	253.1
1973	1,235.0	767.7	207.2	7.6	252.5
1974	1,217.8	760.7	183.6	15.9	257.7
1975	1,202.3	774.6	142.6	22.6	262.6
1976	1,273.0	820.6	173.4	15.8	263.3
1977	1,340.5	861.7	200.1	10.3	268.5
1978	1,399.2	900.8	214.3	11.0	273.2
1979	1,431.1	924.5	214.8	17.7	274.1
1977:					
I	1,315.7	849.2	191.0	11.1	264.5
II	1,331.2	853.1	199.6	10.9	267.6
III	1,353.9	863.7	206.7	13.2	270.3
IV	1,361.3	880.9	203.0	5.8	271.5
1978:					
I	1,367.8	882.7	209.0	5.3	270.7
II	1,395.2	894.8	216.8	12.3	271.3
III	1,407.3	905.3	214.0	13.3	274.7
IV	1,426.6	920.3	217.4	12.9	276.0
1979:					
I	1,430.6	921.8	217.2	17.0	274.7
II	1,422.3	915.0	221.7	13.2	272.4
III	1,433.3	925.9	214.2	20.1	273.1
IV	1,438.4	935.2	206.2	20.7	276.3

Source: Department of Commerce, Bureau of Economic Analysis.

TABLE C Total and Per Capita Disposable Personal Income and Personal Consumption Expenditures in Current and 1972 Dollars, 1929–79

Year or quarter	Disposable personal income				Personal consumption expenditures				Popula-tion (thou-sands) [1]
	Total (billions of dollars)		Per capita (dollars)		Total (billions of dollars)		Per capita (dollars)		
	Current dollars	1972 dollars	Current dollars	1972 dollars	Current dollars	1972 dollars	Current dollars	1972 dollars	
1929	82.3	229.8	675	1,886	77.3	215.6	634	1,769	121,875
1933	45.5	169.7	362	1,350	45.8	170.7	364	1,358	125,690
1939	69.9	230.1	534	1,756	67.0	220.3	511	1,681	131,028
1940	75.2	244.3	570	1,849	71.0	230.4	537	1,744	132,122
1941	92.0	278.1	690	2,084	80.8	244.1	605	1,830	133,402
1942	116.5	317.3	863	2,353	88.6	241.7	657	1,792	134,860
1943	132.9	332.2	972	2,429	99.4	248.7	727	1,819	136,739
1944	145.5	343.9	1,051	2,485	108.2	255.7	781	1,847	138,397
1945	149.0	338.6	1,065	2,420	119.5	271.4	854	1,939	139,928
1946	158.6	332.4	1,122	2,351	143.8	301.4	1,017	2,131	141,389
1947	168.4	318.8	1,168	2,212	161.7	306.2	1,122	2,124	144,126
1948	187.4	335.5	1,278	2,288	174.7	312.8	1,192	2,133	146,631
1949	187.1	336.1	1,254	2,253	178.1	320.0	1,194	2,145	149,188
1950	205.5	361.9	1,355	2,386	192.0	338.1	1,266	2,229	151,684
1951	224.8	371.6	1,457	2,408	207.1	342.3	1,342	2,219	154,287
1952	236.4	382.1	1,506	2,434	217.1	350.9	1,383	2,236	156,954
1953	250.7	397.5	1,571	2,491	229.7	364.2	1,439	2,283	159,565
1954	255.7	402.1	1,574	2,476	235.8	370.9	1,452	2,284	162,391
1955	273.4	425.9	1,654	2,577	253.7	395.1	1,535	2,391	165,275
1956	291.3	444.9	1,731	2,643	266.0	406.3	1,581	2,415	168,221
1957	306.9	453.9	1,792	2,650	280.4	414.7	1,637	2,421	171,274
1958	317.1	459.0	1,821	2,636	289.5	419.0	1,662	2,406	174,141
1959	336.1	477.4	1,898	2,696	310.8	441.5	1,755	2,493	177,073
1960	349.4	487.3	1,934	2,697	324.9	453.0	1,798	2,507	180,671
1961	362.9	500.6	1,976	2,725	335.0	462.2	1,824	2,516	183,691
1962	383.9	521.6	2,058	2,796	355.2	482.9	1,904	2,589	186,538
1963	402.8	539.2	2,128	2,849	374.6	501.4	1,979	2,649	189,242
1964	437.0	577.3	2,278	3,009	400.4	528.7	2,087	2,755	191,889
1965	472.2	612.4	2,430	3,152	430.2	558.1	2,214	2,872	194,303
1966	510.4	643.6	2,597	3,274	464.8	586.1	2,365	2,982	196,560
1967	544.5	669.8	2,740	3,371	490.4	603.2	2,468	3,035	198,712
1968	588.1	695.2	2,930	3,464	535.9	633.4	2,670	3,156	200,706
1969	630.4	712.3	3,111	3,515	579.7	655.4	2,860	3,234	202,677
1970	685.9	741.6	3,348	3,619	618.8	668.9	3,020	3,265	204,878
1971	742.8	769.0	3,588	3,714	668.2	691.9	3,227	3,342	207,053
1972	801.3	801.3	3,837	3,837	733.0	733.0	3,510	3,510	208,846
1973	901.7	854.7	4,285	4,062	809.9	767.7	3,849	3,648	210,410
1974	984.6	842.0	4,646	3,973	889.6	760.7	4,197	3,589	211,945
1975	1,086.7	859.7	5,088	4,025	979.1	774.6	4,584	3,627	213,566
1976	1,184.5	891.8	5,504	4,144	1,089.9	820.6	5,064	3,813	215,203
1977	1,305.1	929.5	6,017	4,285	1,210.0	861.7	5,579	3,973	216,898
1978	1,458.4	972.5	6,672	4,449	1,350.8	900.8	6,179	4,121	218,594
1979 *p*	1,623.2	994.1	7,363	4,509	1,509.8	924.5	6,848	4,193	220,466
1977:									
I	1,250.1	908.0	5,781	4,199	1,169.1	849.2	5,406	3,927	216,244
II	1,286.0	921.5	5,936	4,254	1,190.5	853.1	5,495	3,938	216,643
III	1,323.2	936.3	6,094	4,312	1,220.6	863.7	5,622	3,978	217,119
IV	1,361.2	951.8	6,256	4,374	1,259.7	880.9	5,789	4,049	217,586
1978:									
I	1,395.0	956.6	6,401	4,389	1,287.2	882.7	5,906	4,050	217,942
II	1,437.3	966.1	6,583	4,425	1,331.2	894.8	6,097	4,098	218,335
III	1,476.5	976.2	6,748	4,461	1,369.3	905.3	6,258	4,137	218,814
IV	1,524.8	991.5	6,954	4,522	1,415.4	920.3	6,455	4,197	219,286
1979:									
I	1,572.2	996.6	7,157	4,536	1,454.2	921.8	6,619	4,196	219,690
II	1,601.7	993.0	7,275	4,510	1,475.9	915.0	6,704	4,156	220,166
III	1,640.0	993.4	7,430	4,501	1,528.6	925.9	6,926	4,195	220,715
IV *p*	1,678.8	993.4	7,586	4,489	1,580.4	935.2	7,142	4,226	221,291

[1] Population of the United States including Armed Forces overseas; includes Alaska and Hawaii beginning 1960. Annual data are for July 1 through 1973 and are averages of quarterly data beginning 1974. Quarterly data are average for the period.

Source: Department of Commerce (Bureau of Economic Analysis and Bureau of the Census).

TABLE D Population by Age Groups, 1929–79 (thousands of persons)

July 1	Total	Age (years)						
		Under 5	5–15	16–19	20–24	25–44	45–64	65 and over
1929	121,767	11,734	26,800	9,127	10,694	35,862	21,076	6,474
1933	125,579	10,612	26,897	9,302	11,152	37,319	22,933	7,363
1939	130,880	10,418	25,179	9,822	11,519	39,354	25,823	8,764
1940	132,122	10,579	24,811	9,895	11,690	39,868	26,249	9,031
1941	133,402	10,850	24,516	9,840	11,807	40,383	26,718	9,288
1942	134,860	11,301	24,231	9,730	11,955	40,861	27,196	9,584
1943	136,739	12,016	24,093	9,607	12,064	41,420	27,671	9,867
1944	138,397	12,524	23,949	9,561	12,062	42,016	28,138	10,147
1945	139,928	12,979	23,907	9,361	12,036	42,521	28,630	10,494
1946	141,389	13,244	24,103	9,119	12,004	43,027	29,064	10,828
1947	144,126	14,406	24,468	9,097	11,814	43,657	29,498	11,185
1948	146,631	14,919	25,209	8,952	11,794	44,288	29,931	11,538
1949	149,188	15,607	25,852	8,788	11,700	44,916	30,405	11,921
1950	152,271	16,410	26,721	8,542	11,680	45,672	30,849	12,397
1951	154,878	17,333	27,279	8,446	11,552	46,103	31,362	12,803
1952	157,553	17,312	28,894	8,414	11,350	46,495	31,884	13,203
1953	160,184	17,638	30,227	8,460	11,062	46,786	32,394	13,617
1954	163,026	18,057	31,480	8,637	10,832	47,001	32,942	14,076
1955	165,931	18,566	32,682	8,744	10,714	47,194	33,506	14,525
1956	168,903	19,003	33,994	8,916	10,616	47,379	34,057	14,938
1957	171,984	19,494	35,272	9,195	10,603	47,440	34,591	15,388
1958	174,882	19,887	36,445	9,543	10,756	47,337	35,109	15,806
1959	177,830	20,175	37,368	10,215	10,969	47,192	35,663	16,248
1960	180,671	20,341	38,494	10,683	11,134	47,140	36,203	16,675
1961	183,691	20,522	39,765	11,025	11,483	47,084	36,722	17,089
1962	186,538	20,469	41,205	11,180	11,959	47,013	37,255	17,457
1963	189,242	20,342	41,626	12,007	12,714	46,994	37,782	17,778
1964	191,889	20,165	42,297	12,736	13,269	46,958	38,338	18,127
1965	194,303	19,824	42,938	13,516	13,746	46,912	38,916	18,451
1966	196,560	19,208	43,702	14,311	14,050	47,001	39,534	18,755
1967	198,712	18,563	44,244	14,200	15,248	47,194	40,193	19,071
1968	200,706	17,913	44,622	14,452	15,786	47,721	40,846	19,365
1969	202,677	17,376	44,840	14,800	16,480	48,064	41,437	19,680
1970	204,878	17,148	44,774	15,275	17,184	48,435	41,975	20,087
1971	207,053	17,177	44,441	15,635	18,089	48,811	42,413	20,488
1972	208,846	16,990	43,948	15,946	18,032	50,254	42,785	20,892
1973	210,410	16,694	43,227	16,310	18,345	51,411	43,077	21,346
1974	211,901	16,288	42,538	16,590	18,741	52,593	43,319	21,833
1975	213,559	15,879	41,956	16,793	19,229	53,735	43,546	22,420
1976	215,152	15,345	41,459	16,928	19,630	55,129	43,707	22,954
1977	216,880	15,248	40,575	16,966	20,077	56,706	43,795	23,513
1978	218,717	15,378	39,623	16,935	20,461	58,380	43,876	24,064
1979	220 584	15,649	38,643	16,838	20,726	60,161	43,910	24,658

Note.—Includes Armed Forces overseas beginning 1940. Includes Alaska and Hawaii beginning 1950.

Source: Department of Commerce, Bureau of the Census.

Index

Key words are in **boldface** type.

Absolute advantage, 376
Absolute change, 92, 95
Administered prices, 350
AFL-CIO, 178
Aggregate demand, 231, 257,
    259–60, 261, 265, 266, 267–68,
    270, 271, 273, 275, 276, 278, 279,
    290, 291, 292, 313, 316, 326, 380
Aggregate supply, 231, 266, 270,
    271, 275, 276, 292, 364–66
Alienation, 401–2
American Federation of Labor (AFL),
    178
American Federation of State, County,
    and Municipal Employees
    (AFSCME), 179
American Federation of Teachers
    (AFT), 179
American Indian Movement (AIM),
    190
American International Trade
    Commission, 380
American Plan, 176
Antitrust laws, 143
Arab-Israeli war, 113
Arms race, 432–33

**Balance-of-international-payments
    account,** 394
Balance-of-payments deficits, 387
Bangladesh, 418
Baratz, Morton, 141
Barriers to entry, 26, 41, 132–33, 379
Base year, 236

Bathtub model, 270–71
Bergsten, C. Fred, 379
Birth control, 413, 423
Bolivia, 417
Borrowing, 272
Boycott, primary, 177
Boycott, secondary, 177, 179
Brigades, 406
Buchwald, Art, 280–81
Budget philosophies:
    annually balanced, 302–3
    countercyclical, 303–4
    functional finance, 303–4
    **high-employment budget
        approach,** 304–5, 306, 307, 308
Budget surplus, 261
Budgets (government):
    federal, 205–8
    local, 208–10
    state, 208–10
**Built-in stabilizers (automatic
    stabilizers),** 265, 266, 282, 303
Bureau of the Census, 248
Burns, Arthur, 340
Business cycle theory, 246
Buy-at-home policies, 379

California Worksite Education and
    Training Act, 354
Capital, 22, 400
    defined, 22
    goods, 22
    human, 24, 184, 427
    private, 24

    social overhead, 24, 425
Capital consumption allowances. *See*
    Depreciation allowances
Capital (Das Kapital), 401
Capital formation (investment), 24,
    27
Capital-output ratio, 424–25
Capitalism, 23, 400–2
    mixed, 23
Cartel, 117, 152
Celler Anti-Merger Act of 1950, 143
Central bank, 327
Ceteris paribus, 40, 41, 50, 74
Chavez, Cesar, 179
Check clearing, 321
Check-off, 176
Chiang Ching, 413
Chiang Kai-shek, 405, 406, 410
China, People's Republic of, 400,
    405–14, 423
    Four Modernizations, 411, 414
    wages in, 408
Civil Aeronautics Board (CAB), 145
Civilian Conservation Corps (CCC),
    261
Civilian labor force, 248
**Classical Economists (Classical
    School),** 253–56, 257, 362
    saving-investment argument, 256,
    257–59
    wage-price flexibility, 255–57
Clayton Act (1914), 143, 173
Closed shop, 177
Club of Rome, 433, 434